THE CREED OF HALF JAPAN

THE CREED OF HALF JAPAN

HISTORICAL SKETCHES OF JAPANESE BUDDHISM

BY

ARTHUR LLOYD, M.A.

LECTURER IN THE IMPERIAL UNIVERSITY, NAVAL ACADEMY, NAVAL MEDICAL
COLLEGE, AND HIGHER COMMERCIAL SCHOOL, TOKYO ;
SOMETIME FELLOW OF PETERHOUSE, CAMBRIDGE

LONDON
SMITH, ELDER & CO., 15, WATERLOO PLACE

1911

TO THE MEMORY OF

MY DEAR WIFE

MARY

WHOSE LOVING CARE AND CONSTANT
GOOD COMRADESHIP, DURING EIGHTEEN
EVENTFUL YEARS, HELPED ME ALONG
MANY OF THE STONY DEFILES OF HUMAN
LIFE

PREFACE

I CAN only plead for my book that it is the work of a pioneer, and every pioneer knows that his labours must necessarily be crude and imperfect. I foresee all the strictures that criticism will pass upon my labours, and shall be more than content if what I have written stimulates others to further research.

More should have been said about the lives and teachings of Hōnen, Shinran, and other leaders of the Jōdo or Pure Land sects. The omission is due to the fact that I have already dealt with these thinkers in a monograph entitled "Shinran and His Work," which I published in Tokyo last year. Even with these omissions I fear this book will seem rather bulky.

My best thanks are due to the Master of Peterhouse, who has put himself to much trouble on my behalf.

A. LLOYD.

TOKYO,
    June 24, 1911.

CONTENTS

CONTENTS

The ornament on the side of the cover is a facsimile of Shinran's handwriting, representing the character for Buddha.

THE CREED OF HALF JAPAN

CHAPTER I

Mahāyāna

The Mahāyāna is a form of Buddhism. The word means "the Large Vehicle" or "Conveyance," and is used to distinguish the later and amplified Buddhism from the Hīnayāna or Small Vehicle, which contains the doctrines of that form of Buddhism which is purely Indian. The original language of the Hīnayāna Scriptures is Pali, the language of Magadha in S'akyamuni's lifetime; that of the Mahāyāna books is Sanskrit, the literary tongue of the Brahmans, adopted by Greeks, Parthians, and Scythians as a means of theological expression, when they came in turns to be masters of North-West India and the fertile valleys watered by the Indus and its tributaries, in the Punjaub and in Afghanistan, the language of many a controversy about philosophy human and divine, as Brahman and Buddhist strove in the early centuries of our era for the spiritual supremacy of India.

It would be a mistake to suppose that the Greater Vehicle differs from the Lesser only because it contains in it more of subtle dialectic and daring speculation. The case is not so: the Pali books are every whit as deep and every whit as full of speculation as their Sanskrit

B

rivals. The Hīnayāna is the Lesser Vehicle only because it is more limited in its area. It draws its inspiration from India and from India only, and had it been possible to confine Buddhism within the limits of the Magadhan kingdom, or even within the limits of As'oka's actual dominions, we may safely infer that it would have continued to be Hīnayāna only, as has been the case in Ceylon, where it has not been obliged to rub shoulders with deeply modifying or disturbing influences. But when once Buddhism stepped outside the limits of India pure and simple, to seek converts amongst Greeks and Parthians, Bactrians, Medes, Turks, Scythians, Chinese, and all the chaos of nations that has made the history of Central Asia so extremely perplexing to the student, immediately its horizon was enlarged by the inclusion of many outside elements of philosophic thought. It was no longer the comfortable family coach in which India might ride to salvation : it was the roomy omnibus intended to accommodate men of all races and nations and to convey them safely to the Perfection of Enlightened Truth. It is true that it never forgot the rock from whence it had been hewn ; that it always spoke of itself as a religion intended primarily for the world of India. With a touching shamefacedness, it tried to gloss over the inconsistency of its own missionary zeal. The boundaries of India were supposed to enlarge themselves as the missionaries of Buddhism advanced towards the East. The Hindu Kush and the Himalayas ceased to be the boundaries of the sacred land of Jambudvīpa. In process of time Jambudvīpa included Central Asia, China, and even Japan.[1]

---

[1] Nichiren, for instance, constantly speaks of *ichi em bu dai* (which is his way of writing Jambudvīpa) as = India, China, and Japan. It was a protest, by way of adaptation, against the idea that a Buddha could not be born outside of India.

The Mahāyāna was probably a matter of slow and, at first, unobserved growth. Among the numerous sects which divided the Hīnayāna at the commencement of the Christian era, some were probably more comprehensive, more advanced, than others, and there must have been some which had almost reached to the expansive fulness of the Mahāyāna itself. Very little indeed is known of the history of Buddhism between the death of As'oka and the dawn of the Christian era—during the period, that is, when the Mahāyāna was in the state of gestation. What we do know is that about the end of the first century of the Christian era, between five and six hundred years after the death of Buddha, the Mahāyāna comes into existence in Kashmir and North-West India and the valley of the Indus ; that it enjoys the patronage of the Scythian conquerors of those districts, whose conversion to Buddhism may have been due, in the first place, to a politic desire to stand well with their newly acquired Buddhist subjects ; that it was adorned by some great names of saints and doctors ; and that it spread from the land of its birth to the most distant regions of Northern and Eastern Asia.

It is not necessary in this work to write a long and elaborate life of S'akyamuni. That subject has been exhaustively treated of by many great scholars, and Japan has very little of new material to contribute towards it. I shall take up the main thread of my story from the time when the Mahāyāna makes its first distinct appearance on the stage of Eastern religious life, that is, during the first century of the Christian era. In doing so, I shall have to touch on the first beginnings of Christianity also, the contemporary faith which, in those early days, converted the West, while failing, comparatively, to win the East for Christ, just as the Mahāyāna seemed to be hindered from impressing itself on the West, while it has had a free course and a lasting success in the lands of the Far East. In the course of these pages certain considerations will be advanced (with how much of convincing power it must rest with the reader to decide) to show that the two faiths came into actual contact with one another in many points during the first and second centuries of our era, and that each contributed something to the success and failure of the other. It is a most difficult subject to handle, and before setting myself to work at it, I can but pray—a good old-fashioned custom for which I am almost ashamed to feel myself obliged to offer an apology—that nothing I write may offend against that sacred cause of Truth, which should be the only aim of the scientific and Christian scholar.

But, before plunging into my subject proper, it seems but right that I should devote a few short chapters to the consideration of the person of the Founder, and of the extent of As'oka's influence, as shown by the rock inscriptions which that monarch has left behind him. These chapters will enable the reader more accurately to estimate the extent of the acquaintance which we may suppose Europe and India to have had of one another at the time when Christianity and the Mahāyāna sprang simultaneously into life.

CHAPTER II

THE Sūtras which are commonly received as giving an authentic account of the teachings of the S'akyamuni,[1] will also furnish us with certain geographical and other data which are necessary for us if we would form a correct picture of India in the sixth century B.C., the India in which S'akyamuni taught and laboured.[2]

We need not take a very wide geographical survey. What actually concerns us is a small portion of the valley of the Ganges, comprising practically the two districts of Oudh and Behar,[3] stretching to the east as far as Patna, to the west as far as Allahabad. The Himalayas form the northern boundary of S'akyamuni's country, the Ganges is practically its southern limit; the only exception being that Bodhigaya and the district intimately connected with the Enlightenment of the Tathāgata lie to the south of

---

[1] Cf., in Japanese, "Buddha no Juseiron" (by Maeda); in English, "Buddhism in Translation" (Warren), "Gospel of Buddha" (Paul Carus); and in German, "Die Reden des Gotama Buddhas" (Neumann). The first of these is the most useful for the purposes of this book, because it has been compiled from a frankly Mahāyānistic point of view.

[2] The importance of the sixth century B.C., which inaugurated so many movements of a religious and philosophical nature, it is hard to overestimate.

[3] Behar is said to derive its name from *Vihara*, a Buddhist monastery. It was one of the last, as it was also one of the first, strongholds of Buddhism in India.

the sacred river. Later developments of the Buddhist communities may make it necessary for us to enlarge our geographical inquiries, but for the present these boundaries will suffice for our consideration. They will enable us to follow the life of the Great Master in all its principal phases.

The Buddhist Sūtras tell us a good deal about the population of the country in which the Wheel of the Law was set in motion.

The India of S'akyamuni's time was under the domination of an Aryan race, which had conquered the land and brought into it institutions not unlike those which we find in some other Aryan countries, Athens, for instance.[1] They had divided the population into four great castes, of whom the fourth, possibly also the third, may have been mixed with some of the conquered races, whilst the two higher ones certainly belonged to the nobility of the conquest. In S'akyamuni's time the *Sudras*, or low-caste people, and the *Vaisyas*, or merchants and farmers, lived quietly, without any part or lot in the privileges of national life, contented to devote themselves to the pursuit of their several vocations ; the *Kshatriyas* and *Brahmans*, having accomplished the subjugation of the other two castes, were struggling against each other for supremacy in State and Society. Chief among the Kshatriyan tribes which resisted the supremacy claimed by the Brahmans were the clans known collectively as the S'akyans, who were politically supreme in the districts actually affected by S'akyamuni's life. S'akyan was, however, only a collective name : the clans were distinguished

---

[1] In Athens we find, *e.g.*, the population of the autochthons divided into four classes corresponding to the four castes of India. Cf. Grote's "Hist. of Greece," chap. x. For the Aryan races, see Hunter, "Brief History of the Indian people," chap. iv. pp. 52–73.

from one another by tribal names as well, such as Lic-chāvis, Vrijjis, Mallas, Andhas, etc., some of which remain to the present day. The S'akyan nobles,[1] it is said, welcomed the person of S'akyamuni, their kinsman prophet, whose teachings encouraged them in their resist-ance to Brahman usurpations, but they were not always equally willing to adopt his practical teachings. The Brahmans, ultimately victorious in the struggle for political and religious supremacy in India, have had their revenge on these S'akyan tribes by refusing to consider them as families of pure descent. It is hard to determine the point. All Buddhists claim that S'akyamuni's lineage came from *Ikshvaku*,[2] the descendant of Manu, the de-scendant of Brahma. Licchāvis ruled later, by virtue of Kshatriyan descent, in Nepaul, Bhutan, Ladakh, and (through marriage) in Tibet, and the Licchāvi dynasty in Nepaul was succeeded by a line of Malla kings. At the same time it must be admitted that we have from the very earliest times traces of intercourse between Nepaul, Tibet, and China, which should be considered.

China, as shown by the late Prof. Lacouperie and others, *e.g.* Mr. Morse (in his " Trade and Administration of the Chinese Empire "), was occupied, before the advent of the Chinese from Western Asia, by many aboriginal

---

[1] The documents tell us how eagerly the S'akyans of Kapilavastu and Magadha welcomed the teachings of Buddha. The very name S'akya-muni implies that he was officially accepted as the "teacher of the S'akyans," and that his creed became, as it were, the national religion of the district, though Brahmanism still continued to be tolerated. There are, however, *e.g.* in Kern's " History of Buddhism," stories which show that S'akyamuni had to maintain his claim as a religious teacher by demonstrating to the satisfaction of the S'akyan nobles that he was as skilful in the use of arms as they were themselves.

[2] Hewett, "Notes on Early History of India," pt. ii., in *J.R.A.S.*, April, 1889, p. 276, has a note to show that the *Ikshvakus* came from Assyria and the Euphrates valley.

tribes, whom it took the Chinese centuries to absorb successfully into themselves. Many of these original tribes, such as the Lolo, the Mantsze, and the Miao, took leading parts in Chinese history, and many of them would seem to have had dealings with nations beyond the borders of their empire. The earliest traditions of Nepaul ascribe the first draining and development of their land, in pre-Buddhistic times, to the Bodhisattva *Manjusri* (Jap. *Monju*), whose chief temple is at *Wu-tai-chan*, near Pekin, who is the patron deity, *par excellence*, of the western and northern tribes of China, and who is considered to be perpetually reincarnated in the person of the *Manchu* sovereign of China.[1] It seems probable, therefore, that *Manjusri*[2] was originally the deified hero of one of the tribes of Northern China, possibly the *Mantsze*, that he distinguished himself during his lifetime by his successful development and colonization of Nepaul, and that he was

[1] Prof. Pelliot, in " Bulletin de L'École Française de l'Extrême Orient," viii. 3 and 4, has an account of a recent find of manuscripts and books which will do much to settle the question of Manjusri. According to the Tibetan history recently published at Calcutta, with Index and Analysis, by Sarat Chandra Das, the conversion of India must be ascribed to S'akyamuni and his consort Tarā, that of Bactria and Central Asia to the labours of the Bodhisattvas, that of China to Manjusri or Manju-ghosha, and that of Tibet to Avalokitesvara. The mention of Tarā clearly shows the lateness of the tradition, but there is in Mr. Tada Kanae's lectures on the *Shōshinge* (" Shōshinge Kōwa," p. 289) mention of a certain Buddhist patriarch who went from India to China because he heard that Manjusri had been there, as though Manjusri had once been a real person living in China. If Manjusri may be considered as a real person, and if the Bodhisttvas of Central Asia are also historical, it may be possible to assign the place of origin of many of the Mahāyāna Sūtras according to the speakers in them, those of Central Asian origin being mainly spoken by one or other of the Bodhisattvas, and those intended, as it were, for the Chinese market bearing the Manjusri influence, at least in later revisions. But it is impossible to dogmatize with the scanty information at hand.

[2] Sylvain Levi, "Histoire du Nepal," vol. ii. p. 69.

subsequently adopted into the Buddhist pantheon by the all-embracing Mahāyāna. As M. Sylvain Levi has said, it is impossible as yet adequately to define the extent of the influence exerted on Buddhism in remote times by China and neighbouring countries.

Buddhism has always been the religion of merchants. The Sūtras tell us of many wealthy traders who supported the order by their generous donations. There must have been a great volume of trade. The S'akyan nobles, who constantly address S'akyamuni as *gotama*, "herdsman" (apparently a common mode of address), were of the same race as the herdsmen of the Himalayas. There is at least one Sūtra which speaks of the wool merchant from across the mountains, and it is indeed to wandering S'akyan herdsmen that is attributed the opening up of the valley of Lhassa in Thibet. One of S'akyamuni's earliest disciples was a merchant's son from Benares named Yaśas. He has been identified (wrongly, as I think) with S'anavaśas, the third patriarch of the Northern succession. Now, S'anavaśas is described as having been a ship-captain. True, he may only have been the skipper of a Ganges barge; but there are two later patriarchs of whom it is expressly stated that they had penetrated as far as Turkestan in their travels.

To the lowest class, the Sudras, belonged one at least of S'akyamuni's disciples, Upali, the barber. But there are traces of lower strata of society more degraded even than the Sudras. There is a record of a mission,[1] conducted by the master in person, to a tribe of cannibals, whom he

[1] This incident is of importance as showing one of the best features of the creed as taught by S'akyamuni. The Brahman religion frankly left out of consideration all those who were not of the "Twice-born," which was the name given to the privileged castes. The Kshatriyas, or Warriors (amongst whom we must include the S'akyans), whilst eager to assert the privileges of their order as against the sacerdotal caste, were

converted to better ways; and many have seen in the
Nāgas, Gandhāras, Kinnaras, and other half-mythical
companies of beings, the traces of aboriginal tribes of a
low order. This is especially the case with the Nāgas,
who are so constantly appearing in the Sūtras. They
were most probably savages whose name was given to
them from their worship of serpents (still practised in
India). In the Nepaulese legend they appear as the
original inhabitants of the swamps opened up by the
civilizing Manjuśri. Driven out by Manjuśri, they take
refuge in *Nāgaloka*,[1] the world of the Nāgas, or serpents,
which to the Nepaulese is Thibet. Strange to say, the
Thibetan records also speak of Nāgas and Nāgaloka; but
in their case Nāgaloka is China. This seems to me to
be another instance of a very early intercourse between
India and China, or at least with those districts of Central
Asia which had early connections with that empire.

Hindoo philosophy, such as we now understand it,[2]

not perhaps equally eager to have emphasis laid on the universal
character of the new faith. The Buddha was not fighting for the
privileges of any class, but was busied with a salvation which was to be
a blessing to all men alike. His mission to the cannibals must have
been as distasteful to the Kshatriyas as it was to the Brahmans. See
Watanabe's "Story of Kalmasapada," published by Pali Text Society,
1910.

[1] See Sylvain Levi, *l.c.*, and the Analytical Index to the Tibetan
"History of the Rise, Progress, and Downfall of Buddhism in India,"
edited by Sarat Chandra Das (Calcutta, 1908). See also article on
"Serpent Worship in India," by Surgeon-Major Oldham in *J.R.A.S.* for
July, 1891. For us the question of the Nāgas will have special interest,
because the Mahāyāna tradition asserts that it was a Nāga king that
revealed to Nāgārjuna, in the Dragon Palace under the Sea, the holy
text of the Avataṃsaka, or Kegon Scriptures.

[2] I think it may be shown that there was very little philosophy before S'akyamuni's time, nothing like the six definite schools which
appear in later centuries. The philosophy of the Hindoos arose partly
from the need for definite thought brought out by the controversies
between Brahmans, Buddhists, and sectaries, and partly also from

did not exist. That would seem to have been the product
of a later age. The Brahman religion existed, but in its
infancy. The day of the Vedic gods was not yet over;
men still bowed before Indra, Varuna, and the rest of the
ancient deities, and the gods whom Buddhism has adopted
into its pantheon, such as, *e.g.*, the twin deities that guard
the entrance to the temples of the older sects in Japan,
belong exclusively to the early period. The Brahmans
had doubtless begun the formation of the theological
system which was to fetter the intellect as it had fettered
the social liberties of the people; but the system was not
yet completed, and there were many among the Kshatriyas
who openly resisted the pretensions of the sacerdotal
class.[1] It was, also, a period of great religious zeal and
inquiry. Time and again, in reading the biographical
notices connected with the proceedings of S'akyamuni, we
find that his converts were men who had for years been
searchers after truth; in some cases, as, *e.g.*, that of
Uruvilva Kaśyapa, they had themselves been religious
teachers, and drew their own followers after them to swell
the ranks of S'akyamuni's disciples. But it would seem
as though before S'akyamuni's time there was but one
path known for the searcher after truth to follow—the way
of austerities and penance, which brought power and
influence to the sacerdotal Brahmans, without always
leading the searcher to the much-coveted enlightenment
and peace.[2]

contact with extraneous thought, especially Greek. It is interesting to
trace the contemporaneous development of philosophy in India and in
Greece.

[1] The order of the castes in Buddhist authors is (1) Kshatriyas,
(2) Brahmans, (3) Vaiśyas, (4) Sudras. See *J.R.A.S.*, April, 1894,
pp. 341 ff.

[2] And yet S'akyamuni's preaching was nothing new. He was appealing to truths which had been overlaid and forgotten. Nichiren speaks
of a Buddhism before Buddha.

Not all these searchers were convinced by Buddha's methods. S'akyamuni had many rivals, of whom one at least founded a system of belief which has endured to our own time. Mahāvīra, the founder of the Jain sect, was the contemporary of S'akyamuni, and died in the Kosala country, not many miles from the place where S'akyamuni went to his rest, apparently in the same year as his more celebrated rival. Jainism and Buddhism are kindred faiths, and the Jainists and Buddhists seem to have always looked upon one another as brethren, or, at least, as spiritual cousins.[1]

It was in such a country and in such an age that S'akyamuni was born. The son of Suddhodhana, King of Kapilavastu, and of his wife, the Lady Māyā, his birth is said to have been accompanied with marvels which really belong to a later chapter of our book, and his boyhood was marked by a singular precocity of intellect and purity of character. The wise men summoned to the palace at the time of his birth,[2] and especially one of their number, the aged sage Asita, told the happy father that the new-born babe would be either an epoch-making emperor or a world-saving Buddha; and the father, feeling perhaps that charity should begin at home, determined that, if possible, his son should be prepared for the former of the two alternatives. The young Prince Siddhārtha was brought up as became a S'akyan prince of high degree; trained in arms, literature, and science, he was surrounded

---

[1] It is quite in accordance with the proper fitness of things that in *Kim* Rudyard Kipling should make the old Lama seek a home for himself at Benares in a Jain monastery.

[2] A Chinese legend, undoubtedly false, says that Laotze was present on that occasion. It is perhaps also worthy of notice that later Chinese legend credits Laotze with a virgin birth from the side of his mother, which is very much like that ascribed to S'akyamuni in the Buddhist traditions. The same claim was made for Jinghis Khan and Christ.

with nothing but objects pleasant for his eye to rest upon, and the most beautiful person in his harem was his wife, the carefully selected Princess Yasodhārā.[1]

Many incidents, however, show that his mind was not at ease in the midst of all his luxury, and this feeling of dissatisfaction was increased by several sights which brought home to him the inherent misery of the world. A ceremonial ploughing-festival, which, as Crown Prince, it was his duty to attend, revealed to him the strife that there is in Nature, the upturned earth showing the worms cut in two by the ploughshare to become the prey of the birds that followed in the wake of the plough-man. Shortly after, he met, at short intervals, an aged person, a sick man, a corpse, and a holy monk. He learned about the sorrow and pain that there are in the world, he also learned that there was a way by which escape from the "Welt-schmerz" was possible, and he resolved to follow it. He had received his call, and he obeyed the vocation.

It was not mere selfishness that induced him to leave his home to follow after the Truth. When he bent over the sleeping forms of his beloved wife and his new-born son at the moment of his departure, he resolved that, when he had found the Way, he would come back and save his loved ones, and he kept his promise. But the Way was not easy to find, and the search was long and difficult. For six long years, by self-imposed fastings, austerities, and penance, his strained soul, dwelling in an emaciated body, constantly exposed to the temptations of Māra, the Evil One, searched patiently for the Truth, but

---

[1] Out of whom later Buddhist legend has developed the goddess *Tarā*, the spiritual consort of the glorified S'akyamuni, intended, possibly, to offset the claims of the B.V.M. as S'akyamuni in the Mahāyāna was intended to offset those of Christ.

in vain. At last he gave up his fruitless efforts, partook of food after a long abstinence, had one last combat with the Evil One who strove to appeal to his pride and fear, and then sat down " under the fig-tree " at Bodhi-Gaya and awaited enlightenment. Had he been a Christian or a Jew, we might have said that " he listened to what the Lord God should say unto him."

What his soul heard was as follows : " (1) There is Pain in the world, and Pain is universal. (2) All pain is the result of Concupiscence (*Trishna*). (3) Destroy Concupiscence and you free yourself from Pain. (4) There is a path by which you can attain to the Destruction of Concupiscence, and its end is Liberation." The Liberation is what is known as Nirvana, and the " result of Concupiscence," which leads to action, is Karma.

These propositions are known as the Four Great Truths. They contained nothing new, and yet the Light which S'akyamuni threw upon them was a fresh one. *Karma* and *Nirvana* were words well known to India before S'akyamuni's discovery of them ; the things themselves were known in Greece and to the Jewish people.

The great question of the retribution that waits on human actions had been brought solemnly before the Asiatic world by the impressive fall of the Babylonian Empire, before both Asia and Europe, during the lifetime almost of S'akyamuni himself, by the overthrow of Xerxes at Marathon and Salamis. The Greek theologian-poet Æschylus treated of this theme in his " Eumenides," and again in his tragedy of the " Persians." The prophet of the Captivity, Ezekiel, had been proclaiming to his country-men (Ezek. xviii.) a new law of retribution. Each soul, said the prophet, should bear its own burdens ; there should be no more reason to say in Israel, " the fathers had eaten sour grapes, and the children's teeth had been set on edge." We shall also do well to remember that the deutero-Isaiah and Ezekiel had both insisted on the value and benefit of the sabbath day, and that a fresh impetus had been given to the moral law by the labours of Ezra, the reviser of Holy Scripture (Isa. lvi. 6, 7; Ezek. xx. 12, etc., xviii. 2, etc.; Deut. viii. 12; Ps. cxix.).

What S'akyamuni taught was this: the universal existence of Pain (and Pain must be taken in its widest sense); the root of Pain, which is the Lust that is in the human heart; the end to be attained, which is the Destruction of Desire; and the way to obtain it. Desire, Karma, the wheel of Life and Death: the quenching of Desire, the Destruction of Karma, the Peace of Nirvana.[1] Karma is no Nemesis, such as in Æschylus pursues the unjust and the slayer. Nemesis is vengeful, seems to be given to wrath, and to be guided by anger; Nemesis, to men's eyes, is fitful, irregular, and therefore unjust. Karma, as S'akyamuni saw it, is a universal law, working quietly and steadily along a twelve-fold chain of causation, and binding its victim to the ever-revolving wheel of Life and Death. It works unobtrusively, but surely; yet it can be broken. There is what S'akyamuni calls a noble Eight-fold Path, of right views, right aims, right actions, etc., which leads in time to the destruction of evil Karma by the quenching of Desire, and it seems to have been S'akyamuni's life-work to instil into his hearers the way of the Noble Path, which alone can lead to emancipation. Of philosophy he spoke but little;[2] the so-called Philosophy of Buddhism was a later product.

[1] If we remember that most Pali writers speak of the Enlightenment as the *Nibbana* and of the Death as *Parinibbana*, we shall have some light on the word *Nirvana*. S'akyamuni had had a vision of the Truth, and "the Truth had made him free." He had many doubts and troubles after that, but he was at peace (*J.A.S.B.*, Jan. 1908, p. 9, *note*).

[2] Neumann, "Buddha" (Danish edit.).

He did not profess to teach a new doctrine. What he taught was the "Way of the Buddhas."[1] He recognized that there had been Buddhas before him,[2] as there would be Buddhas after him. He was thus enabled freely to adopt many things that seemed good in systems other than his own, and flexibility has always been a mark of his religion. To us it will seem easy to conjecture the quarter from which he got his idea of a weekly *sabbath*,[3] and the fact that the Order of Monks kept their sabbath days for many centuries after the Nirvana will make it easier for us to recognize and admit the doctrine held by a large section of northern Buddhists, that Buddha also taught, personally and during his earthly life, the salvation worked out for many by another Buddha, who is Boundless in Life, Light, and Compassion, and whom Japan knows as Amitābha.[4]

> [1] " Do not commit evil,
> Do all that is good,
> Cleanse your own heart—
> This is the way of the Buddhas."
> "Light of Buddha," p. 37.

[2] There is a list given of these pre-Buddhistic Buddhas, in, *e.g.*, Hardy's " Manual of Buddhism."

[3] *Sabbath*. In the *Proceedings* of the Asiatic Society of Bengal, vol. iv. part 1, Jan. 1908, there is an article by Mr. H. C. Norman, showing that the question of the keeping of the *Uposathas* or sabbath days was one of the causes that led to the convening of As'oka's Council. The sabbath was, however, a Babylonian and Assyrian institution as well as a Jewish one. See Mahler, " Der Sabbat," in *Z.D.M.G.*, vol. lxii. part i. p. 36, etc.

[4] On this point the Japanese Buddhists with few exceptions are very clear. They place the Sūtras in which S'akyamuni spoke of Amitābha in that period of silence towards the end of his ministerial life when we lose our track of him, and can no longer follow him from year to year. The doctrine thus proclaimed was taken with the seceders after the Second Council beyond the Himalayas (some say to south India). It reappears after many years, in the country to which it had been taken, in the lifetime of Nāgarjuna, and when the Kushan conquests

S'akyamuni was no atheist. He did indeed teach that the enlightened Buddha was higher than the gods of the Brahman pantheon, higher than Indra, Varuna, Agni, Emma-San or Kompira Sama, who now fill subordinate places in Buddhist temples. These gods were creatures of fancy, subject, like Venus, Juno, Neptune, to the Law of Change, and liable to that extinction which has befallen the gods of Assyria and Babylon, of Egypt, Greece, and ancient Rome. From the denial of such gods to the denial of all gods is a very long step, and I think it may be shown that S'akyamuni never took it. Rather I would say, and this I hope to make clear as I proceed, that wherever S'akyamuni's own influence reached, it served to give men higher and truer ideas of the Divine Nature, and that his teachings were thus intended to prepare the way for the acceptance of the highest of all truths.

had united North-West India and the Central Asian lands for a short while under one sceptre. The history of the Amitābha doctrine is well worked out in the "Shôshinge Kōwa," to which I have already alluded. Amitābha is the original Buddha, the First Cause, the Father, not exactly the Creator, but the originator of the Law of Cause and Effect through which the universe came into existence. He has revealed himself many times, the long list of previous Buddhas in the *Sukhāvati Vyūha* being recorded to give definiteness to this idea, and S'akyamuni was the latest of these manifestations. The Ophite Gnostics held exactly this idea, making Christ a still later manifestation superseding all that had gone before, just as Amitābha supersedes all other previous Buddhas. In connection with the questions thus raised, a Japanese scholar, much interested in religion, has pointed out to me that in some early forms of the Apostle's Creed there is no clause "Creator of heaven and earth." I shall have to refer to the character used for writing "Buddha" later on. Here I would point out that Buddha to the Shinshu believer is always Amitābha, whose "Divine Name" is pronounced in worship as *Namu Amida Butsu*. This formula is interpreted to mean, "Trust in me, I will save you," which is not a translation of the formula, but is one of the Name of Christ. The Shinshuists call this formula "the Divine Name of the Six Letters," for which see Irenæus, ii. 24.

CHAPTER III

The Buddha and his Greatest Disciple

Thanks to the labours of many students of the Buddhist books, both Pali and Sanskrit, we are able to form a vivid mind's eye picture of the ministerial life of the Founder of Buddhism; indeed, the general indications of time are so wonderfully precise that we can trace his labours year by year for quite one-half of the forty-six years which his ministry occupied. There is a gap of about fifteen years near the end of his career for which we have no precise sequence of events; but even here we are not left entirely in the dark, for there are many indications given of the troublous days through which India in general, and the Buddhist community in particular, was then passing.[1]

[1] Northern Buddhists assign to the closing years of this period of silence the pronouncement of two or three most important Sūtras. The "Saddharmapundarika Sūtra" is said to have taken seven years to deliver in its fulness, and (as we have seen) the three Sūtras relating to the Mercies and Vow of Amitābha are all ascribed to this period. It is hard to believe that they can all have come from the same mouth at about the same time, for in the one set Amitābha is exalted to the highest of all places; in the other, he occupies only a very inferior position. It seems certain that these Sūtras in their present form were not composed until long after S'akyamuni's time. It is possible, however, that in the case of Vaidehi, the Queen of Bimbisara, S'akyamuni may actually have pointed the distressed lady to the Mercies of Amitābha. That amongst the Kshatriyas many monotheistic ideas were afloat about the period of S'akyamuni's activity seems very probable. The worship given by the Bhāgavatis to Krishna Vasudeva, which Dr. Grierson has treated of in *J.R.A.S.*, is very much akin to the cult of

We are shown the successes which attended on S'akya-muni's first preaching. Conversions were numerous and rapid, converts of all ages and both sexes flocked into his community from every class of society, and were welcomed without distinction of caste and rank. Thousands caught the enthusiasm of the Buddha, and left all to follow him, while in the crowds who felt no vocation to the monastic life were kings and merchants, who vied with each other in the generosity of their gifts.

Among all these varied personages S'akyamuni moves like a king among men. Bimbisara recognizes the king-ship that is in him, and offers to make him the Crown Prince of the Magadhan kingdom, S'akyan noblemen herald him as the teacher and saint of their clan; and the universal esteem in which he is held is shown by nothing more strikingly than by the settlement of a dispute about rights of water which is referred to his arbitration by the tribes concerned. Evidently, the historical Tathāgata was a practical person, far removed from the ecstatic dreamer of the Hokekyō.[1]

Religious India had need of a sound mind with a practical bent, for the times were fraught with evil. Wars and rumours of war vexed the minds of the people ; there was civil strife in Magadha, and sounds of more distant thunder came rolling over from Western Asia. All these hindered "the running of the wheel;" so did

Amitābha. Clearly such conceptions as the unity of the Godhead and salvation by faith were known in India at a very early date. The troubles in Magadha, the civil wars which ended in the destruction of Kapilavastu, as well as some of the conspiracies against S'akyamuni's life, all fall into this " period of silence." Beyond the limits of India all Asia was in the excitement of the great preparations for the expedi-tion of Xerxes against Greece. Dr. Maeda, in the appendix to "Bukkyō Seiten," gives a very convenient chronology of S'akyamuni's life, which is probably, however, based on the work of Western scholars.

[1] This is the Japanese name for the " Saddharmapundarika Sūtra."

also the conflicts with heretics, the dissensions among the disciples, and the many breaches of discipline which weakened the strength and vigour of his Buddhist followers.

S'akyamuni was a brave man and strong, but he felt the dissensions among his disciples most keenly, and there were many moments in which he sank into the lowest pit of despondency, and which his biographers have described as conflicts with the Evil One. These conflicts came at many periods in his life; they cannot be said to have shortened his days, for he lived to be over eighty, but they were evidently the result of the sorrows and anxieties which embittered the later years of his life.[1]

The end had probably been drawing on for some time; strange to say, it was hastened by a meal of dried boar's flesh, of which he partook in the house of Chanda, the blacksmith—a proof that abstinence from flesh cannot have been an integral portion of the early rules of Buddhism.[2] His death has been very touchingly described in the "Sūtra of the Great Decease," which gives us also

[1] I have heard a Buddhist preacher draw a contrast between Buddha and Christ. The latter, he said, lived all His life in the midst of enemies who were constantly seeking opportunities to destroy Him. He was therefore perpetually in an atmosphere of suspicion, fear, and danger, and the quiet and repose which are so necessary for the teacher of religion, and which were so conspicuous a feature in the life of S'akyamuni, were lacking in the case of Christ. But a perusal of S'akyamuni's life, as it is given, e.g., in the pages of Kern's scholarly work on Buddhism, tends to show that Buddha was a fighter quite as much as was our Lord or St. Paul, and that there was in his ministerial life just as little of rest and quietude as there was for Christ during His three years of similar activities.

[2] The doctrine of transmigration is given as one of the reasons for abstinence from animal food. If S'akyamuni on this occasion deliberately partook of boar's flesh, it will strengthen the position taken up by many that the Twelvefold Chain of Causation implies, not transmigration or re-birth, but heredity.

his last words to his disciples, as well as the account of his obsequies. The extent of his influence and the high esteem in which he was held throughout Central Asia are shown by the eagerness with which the surrounding tribes craved for a portion of his cremated bones for purposes of reverence and adoration.

The evidence to hand seems to show that it was the strong ruling hand of the master that alone was able to preserve the unity of the large number of his disciples and followers in his later years. The Tathāgata had been attended during his last moments by the well-beloved Ananda, the disciple who had for some time been acting as his private secretary and coadjutor; Kaśyapa, the most weighty of all the *Sthaviras*, or Seniors, did not arrive in time to see his master again in life. When a Council was summoned at Rajagriha soon after the interment, it was Kaśyapa who took the chair, whilst Ananda, in spite of his intimate relations with the master, found himself at first excluded altogether (Kern, "Buddhism," vol. ii. p. 239). There is a northern tradition of a rival Council held outside the Grotto, whilst the official Council within was pursuing its labours.[1] Other traditions (see Kern, *l.c.*)

---

[1] In "Bukkyō Kakushū Kōyō" (vol. i. fol. 1 and 2), a semi-official manual of Buddhism published in Tokyo in the twenty-second year of Meiji (1889), mention is made of three Councils, one within the grotto (洞 中) at Rajagriha, consisting of 500 arhats under the presidency of Kaśyapa, which drew up the Canon of *three* Pitakas; another outside the Grotto (洞 外), at which Bashika (婆 師 伽) and others drew up a Canon of *five* Pitakas; and again a third, a Council of the Mahāyāna, under the presidency of Ananda and Maitreya (not to be confounded with the Buddha of the Future). The two Hīnayāna Councils represent the Sthavira and Mahāsanghika respectively; the third is possibly an invention of later times, fabricated as a means of accounting for the existence of the Northern or Mahāyāna Canon. This account is based on Hiouen Thsang (Kern). The *five* *Pitakas* will be found in Nanjo's catalogue. They comprise nothing but Mahāyāna Sūtras (no Vinaya or Abhidharma), there being in the

make the exclusion of Ananda from the official Council to have been but temporary, but the fact remains that the successions of Patriarchs in north and south were from the very beginning different. Both successions begin with Kaśyapa, but both assign to him only a short tenure of office. He was an old man, older than S'akyamuni, and most probably died soon after his master. After Kaśyapa, we have, in the south, Upali the Barber, who recited the Vinaya-pitakam; then Dâsaka, Sonaka, Siggava, and Chandavajji, and Tishya Maudgalyāyaniputra, who is said to have presided over As'oka's Council. In the north, during the same period, we get Ananda, the coadjutor of Buddha and the reciter of the Sūtra-pitakam ; Madhyantika, the Apostle of Kashmir ; S'ānavaśas, who was present at the Second Council, Upagupta, who acted as guide to As'oka when that monarch, in the interval between his conversion and his ordination to the priesthood, made a tour of the holy places ; [1] and finally Dhītika, who, during the period of missionary fervour which followed the Third Council under As'oka (possibly even independently of that Council's authority), went into Turkestan and there

Chinese Canon a special section for the Hīnayāna Sūtras, and a miscellaneous section for Sūtras of later addition. The five sections are : (i.) Prajnāpāramitā, 22 works ; (ii.) Ratna Kûta, 37 ; (iii.) Mahāsannipāta, 27 ; (iv.) Avatamsaka or Kegon, 35 ; and (v.) Nirvana, 12. It seems probable that these sections represent each the books cultivated by a particular school, sect, or country, and that they have thus been grouped together so as to preserve the characteristic features of the different schools. Thus the Amitābha books fall entirely into the Ratnakūta class, etc. Strange to say, the Saddharmapundarika, which plays so important a part in Japanese Buddhism, is classed among the miscellaneous Sūtras of later addition.

[1] According to the Record of the Transmission of the Dharmapitaka (Nanjo Cat. Trip., No. 1340), both Dhītika and his successor Micchaka laboured in Turkestan, their activities coming somewhat after the times of As'oka.

became a successful apostle of Buddhism.[1] The two lists
have no names in common, except the first, and the
northern histories ignore As'oka's Council. The inference
seems to be a legitimate one, that north and south were
independent of one another.

A second Council (for we must consider the meetings
at Rājagriha to have constituted but one Council) was
held at Vaiśāli just about one hundred years after the
Parinirvana of the Master to settle some questions of
discipline which had arisen within the community of
monks. Was it permissible for the monks to keep a little
salt in a horn, in case the food supplied by the charitable
should contain none ? Was it permissible to dine after
midday, when the sun cast shadows more than two inches
in length ? Was it permissible for brethren belonging to
the same community to keep the sabbaths separately ?
Might the brethren drink palm-wine, sit on elaborate
cushions, handle gold and silver, etc. ?[2] These and
similar questions were brought before the Council of
Vaiśāli by the monks of Vaiśāli, who maintained their
lawfulness. We can see how strong was the current of
party feeling from the question about the sabbath. The
opposing parties could evidently no longer meet together
for the joint celebration of the customary observances, and
the tension between the monks of the east and west was
very great. A leading part in the Synod was taken
(Kern, vol. ii. p. 248) by Yaśas, whose identification with
S'ānavaśas, the Mahāyāna patriarch, would, if accepted,[3]

[1] This tour, according to the Chinese (see Prof. Pelliot in *Bulletin
de l'École Française de l'Extrême Orient*), extended as far as to Wu-tai-
shan in North China, the traditional home of the mythological Manjuśri.

[2] These are technically known as the *Ten Indulgences*.

[3] Whilst some traditions seem to identify the two, the authorities
quoted by Kern treat them as distinct persons, and represent Yaśas as

show that the breach between Hīnayāna and Mahāyāna was not yet definitely recognized. The decision went against the Vaiśāli monks, who seem to have belonged chiefly to the proud Vrijji clan of S'akyans, and from that moment Buddhism began to be hopelessly shattered by ever-increasing schisms and divisions.[1]

Before a third Council was summoned, India had undergone the shock of invasion, and Alexander's victorious arms had penetrated as far as the Punjaub. The immediate effect on Buddhism of the Macedonian invasion was not so great as might be imagined.[2] When the Greek armies came to a check in the Punjaub, there were still several hundreds of unconquered miles between them and the kingdom of Magadha. The strictly Hellenistic influences came later: the immediate effect lay in the shock and terror with which the weak princelets and peoples of India must have viewed the advancing invader, and the despair which must have paralyzed every one. With the sole exception of King Pōrus, there does not

appealing to S'ānavaśas for his advice and assistance. But the accounts are hopelessly inconsistent and confusing. *Kāla As'oka* was the king under whom the Council met.

[1] Murakami, in his "Handbook of Buddhism," gives the 18 Hīnayāna sects immediately after the Second Council. A fuller list will be found in *J.R.A.S.* for January, 1892, p. 5. It is impossible and unadvisable to burden the memory with what are after all mere names, though some of the sects, the Dharmaguptas, for instance, and the Sarvāstivādins, appear frequently in Chinese Buddhism. The followers of the two Vehicles lived side by side for several centuries after Christ: sometimes we have cases of a teacher following the Mahāyāna in his theological speculations, and the Hīnayāna in his tenets on discipline.

[2] It would almost seem as though, in the interval between the Parinirvana of S'akyamuni and the accession of As'oka, Buddhism in India had lost a great deal of ground, and that it was the patronage of As'oka only that saved S'akyamuni from the oblivion which befel his predecessors in the Buddhaship. Megasthenes describes Brahmanic religious rites and life, but is practically silent about Buddhism.

seem to have been a single native prince of any power or weight, and the kingdom of Magadha was especially helpless under the rule of the effeminate Nanda dynasty. A mere adventurer, the son of a barber, who had found his way to Alexander's camp, conceived the bold idea of raising himself to the throne which its feeble occupants left practically unprotected. After trying in vain to engage Alexander in further enterprises, Chandragupta bided his time till the conqueror's death gave him the opportunity for action. Then a successful mutiny made him master of the Punjaub, the possession of which secured for him the command of the necessary sinews of war. A few months later we see him master of Magadha, with a capital at Pataliputra and dominions extending from the mouths of the Ganges to the Indus, from the Himalayas to the Vindhya. Chandragupta was the founder of the so-called Mauryan dynasty; he first defied Seleucus Nicator, and then entered into an alliance with him, compacted by a marriage with the Greek king's daughter. It was to his court that Megasthenes[1] was sent as minister resident of the Seleucid monarch, and it is to Megasthenes that Europe owes its first just notions of India. Chandragupta was not a Buddhist, and he has no importance for the historian of religions. He is, nevertheless, a personage far too weighty to be passed over without mention.

Chandragupta's grandson was the celebrated As'oka, who changed Buddhism from the form of belief adopted by a few unimportant tribes in Central India to a creed of world-wide importance. Chandragupta (B.C. 320–297) was succeeded by his son Bindusara (297–272), a sovereign of whom very little is known beyond the fact that he extended his dominions considerably; that, whilst he was

[1] Megasthenes was the author of a book, still extant, which gives a very detailed account of the life at the court of Chandragupta.

on the throne, the King of Egypt sent an embassy, under a certain Dionysus, to Pataliputra; and that on one occasion he wrote a letter to Antiochus, King of Syria, asking to have a professor of Greek sent to him. Greek writers speak of him as Ἀμιτροχάτης, a name which suggests that he adopted the Sanskrit title *Amitraghāti*, "the slayer of his foes." He was succeeded in B.C. 272 by his son As'oka, one of the greatest of the rulers of India. Of As'oka we know that in his early days he bore anything but a good reputation; indeed, it was said of him that, like a traditional Oriental potentate, he waded to the throne through the blood of his near kinsmen and their friends. His coronation, for some unknown reason, was deferred for some two or three years after his accession, a fact which inclines us to believe that in the early years of his reign he may have met with a good deal of opposition. In B.C. 261 he was engaged in a successful war with the Kalingas in southern India, a war so full of horrors and misery that the contemplation of it filled the conqueror with remorse and pity, and caused his conversion, not necessarily to Buddhism, but at any rate to religion. He soon took political measures for acquainting his subjects with his change of views; and he has left us a series of edicts, inscribed on rocks and pillars in different parts of India, which give us our best insight into the character of his religious aspirations. Whatever his religious views were, he was not ashamed to publish them abroad, for he sent embassies[1] to many of the leading

[1] These embassies must have been sent in the early part of his reign, soon after his conversion to religion. One of the kings thus approached was Magas, King of Cyrene, who died in B.C. 258. One can see a possible reason for the alliance between As'oka and Antiochus Theos in the fact that the year B.C. 256, in which it was concluded, also saw the establishment of the Parthian kingdom of the Arsacides, and the revolt of Bactria under Diodotus. In such a crisis the friendship of As'oka, who was practically sole ruler of Hindustan (as may be gathered from

Hellenic sovereigns of Western Asia, and the treaty of amity which he concluded with Antiochus Theos in B.C. 256 must have given him a much-desired opportunity for impressing his beliefs on the Hellenic mind.

By the year 249 his mind was turning definitely towards the acceptance of the teachings of S'akyamuni in preference to those of any other of the religious teachers who laid claim to the allegiance of religious India. He went on a solemn pilgrimage to the sacred places of India with Upagupta, the patriarch of the Northern School, as his guide, and the sight of the Lumbini grove, where S'akyamuni was born, of Bodhigaya, where he attained to Enlightenment, of Benares, where the Wheel of the Law was set in motion, and of the Sacred Grove, in which he died, moved him apparently to a further step. In 240 he was ordained as a monk, and in the Bhābhrā Edict, dated soon after that, he proclaimed himself definitely as a Buddhist. Between As'oka's ordination and his death (which Vincent Smith assigns to B.C. 231) must be placed his Council, the data for which are so confusing that writers like Kern have come to the conclusion that it never took place at all, but was a mere figment of chronologists and history-writers of the Southern School. Northern Buddhism, it is true, knows nothing of As'oka's Council, but there is nothing in this fact to justify a denial of its having taken place. It is probable that the Council took place, and that it was an effort on As'oka's part to procure reforms of abuses which had crept in during the 230 years which had elapsed since the death of the Founder. It is also reasonable to suppose that he laboured at the Council for the promotion of those views which he had so persistently advocated in the long succession of rock edicts.

the locations of the inscriptions), must have been of paramount importance to the Seleucid government.

CHAPTER IV

The Pre-Christian Expansion of Buddhism

THE great As'oka, king of Maghada, the Constantine of Indian and Ceylonese Buddhism, has no official place, as I have said, in the history of the Mahāyāna, which takes absolutely no notice of the Council that is said to have been held during his reign. The Council naturally concerned only those monks that lived within As'oka's extensive dominions; the Mahāyāna seems to have originated beyond the Indus, among people, possibly, o Indian origin, but still not subjects of any purely Indian state.

Yet As'oka is of importance in the study of the Mahāyāna. For, first, he enables us to correct a great error as to S'akyamuni's date, still commonly made by many of the official defenders of Buddhism in Japan. The Mahāyāna books place the date of S'akyamuni's birth in B.C. 1027, and his death, consequently, about B.C. 950 —a chronological misstatement which vitiates all their other calculations. For if this be true, then Aśvaghosha, who lived 500 years after the Nirvana, and Nāgārjuna, who lived in the sixth century after the same occurrence, must be supposed to have flourished respectively about the years B.C. 450 and 400, and the whole Mahāyāna system predates the Christian era by some centuries.[1]

[1] It is said that the falsification of the date was made in China, where the Buddhists were anxious to show that their religion was much

Fortunately As'oka is well known to us, not only from books, but also from the edicts which he has left engraved in stone in various parts of his former dominions, and the data thus furnished enable us to give both As'oka's exact year, and approximately that of S'akyamuni's entrance into Nirvana. From the materials at hand, Dr. Fleet[1] has been able to fix the dates for the principal events between the death of Buddha and that of As'oka. We may accept them with confidence. As'oka was anointed king on the 25th of April, B.C. 264, 218 years after the death of Buddha, which consequently took place in B.C. 483—in the interval, it is well to remember, between the battles of Marathon and Salamis.

Again, As'oka's monuments give us data whereby to gauge the extent of his influence. Edict No. 2, translated by Dr. V. A. Smith,[2] is on the subject of comforts for men and animals, and runs thus : "Everywhere in the dominions of King Priyadarśin, and likewise in the neighbouring realms, such as those of the Chola, Pandya, Sattyaputra, and Keralaputra, in Ceylon, in the dominions of the Greek king Antiochus, and in those of the other kings subordinate to that Antiochus—everywhere, on behalf of his Majesty King Priyadarśin, have two kinds of remedies been disseminated—remedies for men, and remedies for beasts. Healing herbs, medicinal for man and medicinal for beasts, wherever they were lacking, have everywhere been imported and planted. On the

more ancient than anything of native Chinese origin, it being claimed that Laotze, in particular, had borrowed much from S'akyamuni. It may also be that, supposing the Buddhists of North-West India and Afghanistan to have had any acquaintance with Judaism, there may also have been a desire to antedate Isaiah's prophecy of the Virgin Birth. See Hultzsch, "The Rupnath Edict," in *J.R.A.S.* for July, 1909.

[1] Fleet, "The Day on which the Buddha died," *J.R.A.S.*, January, 1909.

[2] V. A. Smith, "Asoka," pp. 115 ff.

roads, trees have been planted, and wells dug for the use of man and beast."

Edict No. 5 concerns the Censors of the Law of Piety: "They (*i.e.* the Censors) are engaged among people of all sects in promoting the establishment of piety, the progress of piety, and the welfare and happiness of the lieges, as well as of the Yonas, Kambojas, Gandharas, Rashtrikas, Pitenikas, and other nations on my borders."

(*c*) Edict. 13 is on the subject of the "True Conquest" (*i.e.* the Conquest of Self): "Even upon the forest tribes in his dominions, His Majesty has compassion, and he seeks their conversion, inasmuch as the might even of His Majesty is based on conversion." . . . [It has been communicated] "even to where the Greek King named Antiochus dwells, and beyond that Antiochus, to where dwell the four kings severally named Ptolemy, Antigonus, Magas, and Alexander; and in the south, to the Kings of the Cholas, and Pândyas, and of Ceylon,—and likewise here, in the King's dominions, among the Yonas, and Kambojas, in Nābhaka of the Nabhitis, among the Bhojas and Pitenikas, among the Andhras and Palindas, everywhere men follow the law of Piety as proclaimed by His Majesty.

"Even in those regions where the envoys of His Majesty do not penetrate, men now practise and will continue to practise the Law of Piety. . . ."[1]

(*d*) Minor Rock Edict No. 1, if accurately translated by Senart, speaks of 256 missionaries who have gone forth to proclaim the law.[2]

---

[1] V. A. Smith, "Asoka," p. 132.

[2] Smith translates this Edict to the effect that "256 years have elapsed since the Tathāgata, a statement which, if correct, would make S'akyamuni's death to have been B.C. 508. Kern gives many details about these missionaries and their spheres of labour. I have not dwelt at any length on them, as I think what I have given in the present chapter will suffice for showing the expansion of Buddhism.

We have here a picture of As'oka's missionary activity. It embraced his own subjects, those living in his capital, those living in the remote provinces and dependencies of his empire within India, the Yonas or immigrant Greeks, the Chōlas, Pāndyas, and Andhras, the degraded tribes of the forests, the King of Ceylon, the Greek kings who ruled as the Diadochi of Alexander the Great, and last, but not least, the unmentioned lands to which As'oka had sent no envoy, but in which Buddhism was nevertheless being actively and piously pursued. These sovereigns and peoples As'oka addresses, mainly on two subjects— care for the health and welfare of the people, and " True Conquest " over themselves and their passions— a lesson which was surely not superfluous in those troublous days.

The Indian states and peoples need not delay us long. The mention of Chōlas, Pāndyas, etc., serves to show how widely spread, in India itself, was the Buddhist faith which As'oka strove to promote and reform. Nor need we linger over Ceylon.[1] That island is said to have owed its conversion to the labours of Mahendra, the son or son-in-law of As'oka, and, whoever may have been its apostle, it has remained true to the faith which it then received. The mention of the *Yonas* or *Yavanas* (*i.e.* the Ionians or Greeks; we have the authority of Aristophanes that by the Oriental the name "Greek" was pronounced *Iaonau*, which is very near to *Yavana*) is a little ambiguous; for it may refer to the Greek kingdom of Bactria, which set up for itself a few years after the publication of the earlier

---

[1] Japanese writers assert that Buddhism was preached at this time in Further India and Burma. There is nothing in As'oka's inscriptions to justify this assertion, for the Kamboja mentioned there have nothing to do with Cambodja. The list given in the Singhalese books (see Kern, ii. 287) of the apostles sent forth after As'oka's Council is somewhat vague in its statements.

Rock Edicts, or it may refer to the Greek merchants trading and travelling in India, whose votive inscriptions have been found in ancient Buddhist temples in the peninsula. It is possible, though we cannot make a positive assertion on the point, that some of the nations on his borders, to whom As'oka refers, may have dwelt on the frontiers of what in later times became the Parthian kingdom.

The ruler of Syria at the time when As'oka published his Edicts was Antiochus II. (Theos), the unfortunate monarch who inherited the splendour but not the genius of his more illustrious father, Antiochus I. (Soter). He had only just come to the throne when the Edicts containing his name were published, and we must therefore, I believe, refer the allusions to the state of the Syrian Kingdom to his father's reign rather than to his own. It was to Antiochus I. that As'oka had applied for assistance as to medical herbs and trees, and whom he had consulted as to wells and fountains in streets and by roadsides, and for trees to give shade to man and beast. In Antiochus I., the Founder of Cities (the Syrian kingdom was dotted over with them), many bearing his name, and one of them, Antioch in Syria, justly famed as one of the most beautiful cities of the ancient world, As'oka's request would find a sympathetic welcome. The ideas of municipal and civil government encouraged by Antiochus Soter were just such as would commend themselves to As'oka. How far Antiochus profited by As'oka's suggestions, we cannot say, but Antiochus styled himself $\beta a\sigma\iota\lambda\epsilon\grave{\upsilon}\varsigma$ $\beta a\sigma\iota\lambda\acute{\epsilon}\omega\nu$, and amongst his " subordinate kings " mentioned in the Edict on " creature comforts " were Philetærus (B.C. 281–263) of Pergamus, Nicomedes of Bithynia, and, for a short while, Magas of Cyrene, who was availing himself of assistance from Antiochus in a revolt against Egyptian

suzerainty. In the wars which Antiochus I. waged against
the Gauls and Celts, who had invaded Asia Minor at the
invitation of Nicomedes, a rebel against the suzerainty of
the " King of Kings," he had used elephants, which he,
like his contemporary, Pyrrhus of Epirus, had obtained [1]
from As'oka's father, Bindusara, King of Magadha, a
favour which, it may be, As'oka was expected to continue
in the case of Antiochus II. The kings of Pergamus were
famous for their collections of books and parchments (the
latter a *pergamene* substitute for the papyrus which the
Egyptian government would not allow to be exported);
also for the botanical gardens of medicinal herbs, which
antedated the more famous collections of Alexandria, into
which they were afterwards merged; and Cyrene was
noted, the whole world over, for a medicinal plant called
silphium (a kind of *asafœtida*), which formed one of the
staple articles of its extensive commerce. The plant was
almost extinct in the West in Pliny's time (though it is
still, I believe, to be found in India),[2] but it is to be found
engraven on the coins of Cyrene as the emblem of the
city, and there has been found a silver cup from Cyrene,
with a representation of the king himself personally
superintending the packing, weighing, and dispatching of
the precious herb.[3] We can imagine that Antiochus Soter
would have much pleasure in forwarding As'oka's memo-
randum touching medicinal herbs to his subordinate kings.
We can also imagine that Antiochus II., who surnamed
himself " the God," would not be equally pleased to
receive the sermon about the " True Conquest." And yet
As'oka would have us believe that the Dharma was being

[1] There was absolutely no other monarch in the world from whom
elephants could be obtained.

[2] And, significantly enough, in the neighbourhood of the ancient
Pataliputra, according to the " Encyclopædia of India."

[3] See Haeser, " Geschichte der Medizin," vol. i. p. 101.

observed and practised in the territories of the Syrian
king. Stoicism was already a power in the world of
philosophy and morals, and Stoicism is notoriously a semi-
oriental mode of thought.[1]

Antigonus Gonatas, King of Macedonia, claimed
possession of the European dominions of Alexander the
Great. Macedonia must have been full of men who had
been in Central Asia and India in those days of constant
coming and going, and there must have been a great
interest taken in things Indian. When Alexander took
Babylon, he had the books in the library sent to his old
tutor Aristotle, who, we may be sure, appreciated the gift,
and found some way of discovering the contents of the
books before they reached their final resting-place in the
library of Alexandria. One of Alexander's successors,
Cassander, who thoroughly disapproved of Alexander's
policy of adopting Oriental habits and ways of life, had,
living at his court, a philosopher named Euhemerus, who
had travelled in Asia, at Cassander's request, and had
returned with stories which had gained for him the reputation of a liar. And yet much that Euhemerus related
accurately described what must have been going on in
Buddhism at the time of his visit. The island of Panchaia
may have been an Utopia; the history of the earthly life
of Zeus before he became a god, which he brought back
with him, may have been a fabrication; still, the process
described was exactly the process which was going on in
Buddhism.[2] S'akyamuni had been just such a man as

---

[1] Kirchner, "Geschichte der Philosophie," p. 137.

[2] Müllach, "Fragmenta Philosophorum Græcorum," vol. ii. (Paris,
1831). Müllach gives a passage from Sextus Empiricus (adv. Math. ix.
17): Εὐήμερος δέ φησιν · ὅτε ἦν ἄτακτος ἀνθρώπων βίος, οἱ περιγενόμενοι τῶν
ἄλλων ἰσχοΐ τε καὶ συνέσει ὥστε πρὸς τὰ ὑπ' αὐτῶν κελευόμενα πάντας βιοῦν,
σπουδάζοντες μείζονος θαυμασμοῦ καὶ σεμνότητος τυχεῖν, ἀνέπλασαν περ'
αὑτοὺς ὑπερβάλλουσαν τινα καὶ θείαν δύναμιν, ἔνθα καὶ τοῖς πολλοῖς

Euhemerus described. He had towered high above his compeers in wisdom, if not in strength, and had possessed that magnetic influence which compelled men to walk according to his precepts. He had certainly demanded personal loyalty to himself from all his followers, for he had only received them into his Order after a threefold expression of belief—in the Law, the Order, and the Buddha. His relics, divided up after his death, had become the nucleus around which grew up the worship of the whole Buddhist community. S'akyamuni was undergoing the process of deification when Euhemerus visited India (indeed, that process may already have been popularly accomplished), and the process was already being applied to other Buddhas as well. The Mahāyāna had not yet taken definite form, but the ideas underlying it were in the air, and when, later, we get our first definite literary acquaintance with, e.g. Amitābha, he comes as a god deified after a long succession of holy lives, led in the fulfilment of his tremendous vow for the salvation of mankind. That the same process was taking place in the case of S'akyamuni himself may be seen from the development of the *Saddharma pundarika* and kindred Sūtras,[1] and from the more certain testimony of Buddhist art. The process, in the case of Buddhism, may not have been

ἐνομίσθησαν θεοί. There is also another quotation given from Eusebius ("Praep. Evang.," ii. 59) in which Euhemerus says that there are some deities, e.g. Sun, Moon, Winds, etc., which are ἀΐδιοι καὶ ἄφθαρτοι, but that there are others who are called ἐπίγειοι θεοί.

[1] Whilst I think we must hold most of the developed Sūtras of the Mahāyāna (and certainly the *Saddharma pundarika*) to be posterior, and in some cases much posterior, to the Christian era, the process of the gradual deification of S'akyamuni may, I believe, be fairly inferred from many of the Agama Sūtras which record the events of his actual life. Certainly, the sculptures, even of the earliest topes and temples of India, would have been different in style, had it not been that he, in whose honour the shrines were raised, was coming to be looked upon as more than an ordinary man.

completed in the days of Euhemerus; it was also going on in Brahmanism and other forms of Indian religion. But certainly Euhemerus described it accurately.

Antigonus Gonatas of Macedon had an ambition, which he realized, for a while, after many years of conflict, of uniting Greece and Macedon under one sceptre. He had opponents in the Achæan league, and a rival in Alexander, the son of that Pyrrhus of Epirus who had defeated the Romans with the aid of elephants obtained from As'oka's father, Bindusara. Alexander and Gonatas are both mentioned in As'oka's Edict on the "True Conquest." We can imagine that the peace-loving As'oka, who was fully in touch with what was going on in the West, must have been distressed beyond measure at the desolations of Greece during this period of "False Conquests."

I have already mentioned Magas of Cyrene, in connection with the medicinal herbs. I need only mention, as another link in the chain showing the extent of Indian influence in the West, that among the dialogues of Aristippus, the founder of the Cyrenaic school of philosophy, there was one which bore the name of *Porus*, a name well known among Indian kings.[1] Aristippus, born B.C. 435, was prior in time to As'oka, but amongst the later Cyrenaics was Hegesias, surnamed Peisithanatos, from the strenuousness with which he advocated suicide as the highest form of self-immolation. This is a truly Buddhistic notion. S'akyamuni's well-beloved disciple, Ananda, is said to have ended his life by voluntary self-cremation, and the *Saddharma pundarika* speaks of it as the highest expression of devotion and gratitude from one who has learned the truth.[2]

[1] Diogenes Laertius, ii. 83–85, quoted by Müllach, *op. cit.*, p. 403.

[2] Cf. *Saddharma pundarika* in "Sacred Books of the East," vol. xxi. p. 378, etc. The same is affirmed of two more of the patriarchs of the Northern Succession.

The mention of Hegesias brings us to Alexandria.
The ruler of Alexandria, Ptolemy Philadelphus, is also
one of the sovereigns mentioned in As'oka's Edict. Philadelphus and his predecessor, Soter, were both much
concerned in carrying out Alexander's great scheme of
effecting the Hellenization of the East through the
instrumentality of the newly founded city of Alexandria.
Alexandria was connected with India by at least three
routes. A certain amount of the overland traffic from
China came into Alexandria *viâ* Palestine (which was in
the Egyptian sphere of influence), and even the superior
attractions of Antioch could not kill this commerce, which
was, however, more Central and Eastern Asian than
Indian. A further contingent of caravans brought in
Indian goods *viâ* the Persian Gulf, Palmyra (later), and
Palestine. The Egyptian ports on the Red Sea had direct
communication, without any serious rivals, with the
Indian ports at the mouth of the Indus. The early
Ptolemies took a great deal of interest in religion. Soter
imported the god Serapis from Pontus, and both he and
Philadelphus interested themselves in the (LXX.) translation of the Hebrew Scriptures into Greek. They were
notoriously ready to welcome any new lights on religious
subjects. It is perhaps, therefore, more than a mere
coincidence that, about the days when As'oka was sending
envoys to the kings of Egypt, and speaking of the keeping
of the law in distant countries, we get—first, the so-called
Hermetic literature (*e.g.* the Κορὴ Κόσμου preserved for
us by Stobæus), with its many Buddhist echoes;[1] and,
secondly, the semi-Buddhistic communities of monks as
the Essenes and Therapeutæ described for us by Philo.
How far Philo and Aristobulus, the Jew, may have been

[1] Flinders Petrie. See *Transactions* of the Congress of the History
of Religions (Oxford, 1908), vol. i. pp. 185 and 224.

influenced by Indian thought is an inquiry beyond our present limits.[1] But it is evident that the relations, tradal or otherwise, between Alexandria and India were close and constant. The influence was not all on one side. Alexandria had its influence on Indian philosophy, medicine, and mathematics,[2] and a time came when the religions of the Far East felt the power of its mystic (not to say cryptic) thought. In the mysterious Shingon system of Japan, the term "RA" occurs as the name of the deity of Fire, and the word for God, *Abraxas*, used by Basilides, is the fundamental conception of the Shingon system of Philosophy, which also uses certain hieratic hieroglyphics for the conveyance of its teachings.[3]

It may be asked, what precisely were the teachings which As'oka exerted himself to spread amongst other nations and amongst his contemporary sovereigns? The one conclusive answer to this question will be found in the study of the monuments themselves, with the

[1] Cf. Ueberweg, "Hist. of Philos. Jewish Alexandrian Philosophy," sect. 63.

[2] Cf. *Ibid.*; and Haeser's, "Geschichte der Medizin," vol. i. p. 103.

[3] I am sorry not to be able to give more clear indications of the source from which I have drawn my information. The Japanese article on Abraxas, on which I have relied, is a long treatise of over fifty pages in a collection of Buddhist essays entitled (佛教疑問解答集) and was written by a man who certainly had no knowledge of Egyptian history or thought. He takes the word *Abarakakia*, to which he adds a final syllable *un*, as representing the sum-total of the Universe, the Five Elements, with *un* (= *alaya*, the Spirit). He says that the whole word is sometimes abbreviated by taking the first syllable *A* and the last syllable *un*, thus making *A-un* (= *om*). Corresponding to the six elements (including *alaya*) there are six skhandhas, six colours, six geometrical forms, etc., all of which are expressed by six hieroglyphics, which are not Chinese ideographs, but evidently of Egyptian origin. *Abarakakiun* also comes in certain *Wasan*, or hymns, belonging to various Buddhist sects. There is an evident allusion to the "Holy Name of the Six Letters." The Gnostic word *Caulaucau* is also found in Japanese Funeral Rites.

inscriptions, that he has left us. In them we shall find Buddhism as it existed in As'oka's mind, and as As'oka believed that it had existed in the mind of S'akyamuni. I cannot do better than summarize the contents of the inscriptions.

I. In the first, As'oka speaks of his care to provide medicines and medical herbs for the use of the sick, trees for shade, and fountains for men and cattle, and calls attention to the fact that he has done this not only within his own dominions, but also in those of his neighbours, *e.g.* in the territories of King Antiochus and in Taprobane (Ceylon).

II. In the second, he speaks of the killing of animals, exhorts his subjects to abstain from such evil practices, and explains his own custom. He was once in the habit of allowing many animals to be killed for the royal feasts : during late years the number of animals thus killed has been very small. Henceforward, there shall be no killing of animals in the royal kitchens.

III. He exhorts provincial and city governors, and all teachers of religion, to be diligent in inculcating obedience to parents, kindliness and courtesy, respect for Brahmans and Buddhist monks, and moderation in speech and conduct, upon all who come under their authority.

IV. He speaks with gratitude of the good effects upon the people at large of the religion which he has been teaching throughout his dominions. He is glad to find that civic and social virtues, filial piety, respectfulness, kindliness, and toleration are everywhere on the increase.

V. In order to spread further the virtues inculcated by his religion, he appoints superintendents of morals for all creeds throughout his dominions, as well as in the neighbouring countries of the Yavanas, Kambojas, Gandhāras, etc. (these were probably subject or tributary states). It shall be the duty of the superintendents to take especial care of prisoners and captives, particularly when they are married men with families dependent on them, or when they have been the victims of malice, spite, or fraud.

VI. He speaks of his constant care for the welfare of his people.

VII. It is his great desire to secure religious liberty and toleration for all religions practised within his dominions.

VIII. Royal progresses throughout the country have hitherto been made occasions of feasting and revelry. It is his intention henceforth to give them a religious character, and use them for the advancement of religion and morals.

IX. What is religion? It is the Way by which men learn to be truly human and humane, and it has its stimulus in the hope of a future life.

X. The hope of the rewards of a future life has been the motive power of his religious life. [*N.B.*—Nothing is said about a past Karma influencing the present, nor yet about Nirvana after death.]

XI. True religion—*i.e.* to help the fatherless and widow, and to keep one's self unspotted from the world— has the promise of this life, as well as of that which is to come.

XII. The sectarian spirit should be avoided. We should never decry the followers of a religion other than our own. Nor should we think that we are serving our own creed by constantly puffing it.

XIII. A survey of his own life. He describes the horrors of the war against the Kalingas, and his own remorse when he realized the cruelties attendant upon it. He resolves henceforth to eschew the *rôle* of a conqueror.

The true conquests are those of religion. He has communicated his sentiments to his brother sovereigns—to Antiochus, Ptolemy, Antigonus, Magas, Alexander Balas, to the Codas and Pandyas as far as Taprobane, and even to the King of the Huns.[1] It gives him great happiness to contemplate the success which has attended his efforts, but present contentment is as nothing when compared with the joys of future bliss.

XIV. An abridged edict containing the points on which Piyadasi, the beloved of the gods, wishes to insist. His empire is an extensive one, but he has done his best, by means of inscriptions, to arrange that every part of the empire is provided with the required moral teaching. He wishes all his subjects to be acquainted with the religious law.

The above fourteen Edicts form, as it were, a continuous series, and are to be found in several recensions in several parts of India. There are also isolated Edicts, the contents of which are somewhat as follows:—

1. *a* and *b*. To the officials at Tosali and Samāpā, urging them to greater diligence in the care of the people committed to their charge, so that those who stand may not fall, and those who fall may be restored. The most essential thing in religion is perseverance and patience in what is good. Officials should take care to guide men in the right way, so that they may live without fear and follow their religion. These edicts are to be read publicly before the people at the monthly festivals of the full moon, and privately whenever necessary. His Majesty has taken care to have a solemn assembly in his own territories every five years, and the princes of Ujjain and Taxila will do the same.

---

[1] Again see Prof. Pelliot's article in *Bulletin de l'École Française de l'Extrême Orient*, viii. 3-4.

2. The king regrets that hitherto, as a layman, he has not been very diligent. He has now, however, been for a year a member of the Order, and has worked with such zeal during that time that the ancient gods of Jambud-vīpa (India) have been almost driven from their places.[1] It is a great truth that the Kingdom of Heaven is really within the reach of all men, even the humblest, and no effort should be spared to spread this Gospel by missionary labours. The King is much gratified by the fact that already 256 missionaries have gone abroad. [This last sentence has been differently translated, as though it referred to the date of the Edict, 256 after the Nirvana of Buddha.]

3. [The Bhābhrā Edict.] To the clergy of Magadha. All that the Blessed One has said is well said, and should be studied with reverence. The king especially commends the following books: "Vinayasamukasa," book on discipline; "Aryavasāni," on the supernatural powers of the Aryas; "Anagātabhayāni," on dangers to come; "Munigatha," stanzas in honour of the Muni; "Upatishya pasina," questions of Upatishya; "Moneya sūtra," Sūtra on Perfection; and the Sūtra, in which the Blessed One instructs Rahula.[2]

---

[1] For this see Chap. V. on "Pushyamitra."

[2] Vincent Smith translates these titles as follows:—

 a. The Exaltation of Discipline.

 β. The Supernatural Powers of the Aryas.

 λ. Fears of what may happen.

 δ. The Song of the Hermit.

 ε. The Dialogue on the Hermit's Life.

 ζ. The Questioning of Upatishya.

 η. The Address to Rahula, beginning with the subject of False-hood.

He points out that these "passages" have all been identified, with the exception of *a*, by Rhys Davids in *J.R.A.S.* for 1898, p. 639. It has been contended that these books were not written, but handed down memoriter, and recited by men who knew them by heart. But if

What I have hitherto said does not by any means exhaust the question of the expansion of Buddhism in As'oka's days, for, leaving aside the subject of As'oka's apostles sent forth by the Council, we have also As'oka's own testimony as to the countries in which Buddhism (as he understood it) was practised, though his envoys had never reached them.

In the days of As'oka the Parthians revolted against Antiochus, and, under the family of the Arsacidæ, carved out for themselves a small kingdom to the north of the Seleucid Empire. They were by origin Sacæ or Scythians, and their earlier home had been in the plain country between the Caspian Sea and the Oxus. Their religion was that of Zoroaster, or rather, perhaps, that of the Magi. What the precise tenets of that religion were, it is hard to say; they do not seem to have been precisely those of the Persians before the fall of the Persian Empire, nor yet those of the restored Zoroastrianism of the Sassanid period. They probably worshipped the heavenly bodies, paid a great deal of attention to astrology and astronomy, and in other points were not very unlike the Buddhists in their belief and practices. That Buddhism obtained some hold among them is shown by the fact that Parthian missionaries in later days took part in the evangelization of China; but when that influence began it is impossible to say. At a much later date, when the Buddhist evangelization of China was well established, we find Zoroastrian monks treated as brethren, and we read of Buddhists in Persia presenting a Chinese Emperor with a tooth-relic of the Buddha. And in the Shiite and Sufite forms of Mahometanism we may, it is said, see the ancient Buddhism of Persia still asserting itself.

As'oka could write his edicts, why suppose that the monks could not write their books?

Next to Parthia came Bactria,[1] the reputed home of Zoroaster himself. Bactria asserted its independence in the same year as Parthia. It had Greek kings, and a small percentage of Greek settlers, the residue of the Macedonian invasion; but its main population was probably of S'akyan origin. Indian writers speak of the Bactrian people as Vrijji,[2] the same name that we found amongst the Nepaulese S'akyans of S'akyamuni's time, and recognized them as being Kshatriyans by caste, though their standing was defective by reason of inter-marriages with other nationalities. Their religion was a mixed one, Parthian, Brahmanic, Buddhist, with probably a slight preference for the last.

Bactria marches on the Pamirs. East of the Pamirs, and north of what is now Thibet, dwelt the S'akyas, separated from the S'akyan brethren of India and Nepaul by the common pasture lands of Thibet. When they afterwards emerged from their mountain fastnesses they were divided into four tribes, Asii, Pasiani, Tokhari, and Saka-rauli (Strabo, ix. 8), and it is recorded (Kern, " Buddhismus," ii. 272) of the Northern Patriarch Dhītika that he made conversions by his labours among the Tokhari, who eventually gave their name to the whole of that tribe of S'akyans. As'oka's envoys did not reach these tribes, but there were many traders who carried the faith.

East of the S'akyans, in the valley of the Tarim, lay the Uighurs, the most civilized and literary of all the Scythian tribes; beyond them, to the south of Lake Lob,

---

[1] I have constantly made use of M. Drouin's exhaustive article on Bactriane in the " Grande Encyclopédie."

[2] It is to be remembered that, according to the northern books, it was the Vrijji-putrakas who, at the Vaisali Council, demanded a relaxation on some points of Buddhist discipline, and who, being unable to get their request granted by the Sthavisas, " trekked " over the frontiers of Magadha into the lands beyond the Himalaya.

were the Usuns, who bordered on the Chinese Empire. We know that Buddhism reached these districts at a very early date.[1]

When it first reached China we cannot say,[2] for the unofficial introduction must have long preceded its official acceptance under Mingti. In As'oka's time, *Hwangti*, who had assumed the title of " King of Kings," in imitation of Seleucid magniloquence, had begun the erection of the Great Wall that was to isolate China from disagreeable neighbours. The break-up in Central Asia had already begun; Scythian hordes were already on the move, and had troubled the Bosphorus, Macedonia, Asia

[1] Buddhism was introduced into Khotan B.C. 125. The King of Western Yarkand was converted in B.C. 122. Kashgar was already Buddhist in B.C. 122. The Buddhism of Kashgar was Hīnayāna, that of Khotan Mahāyāna. Stein ("Ancient Khotan," vol. i. p. 57) says that the Kashgar Buddhism came from Bactria, a statement which, if true, would imply that the Yuetchi of Bactria had been converted to Buddhism at a still earlier period. In the 1908 volume of the *Transactions* of the Imperial Russian Academy of Sciences there are two articles, one by Radloff, the other by von Stael-Holstein, treating of the newly discovered Central Asian languages. In the latter article it is shown that Language I. has been found mostly in the Khotan district, while written fragments of Language II. have been found chiefly in Turfan. In both languages Buddhist books (fragmentary) have been found, and both languages show distinct traces of Sanskrit influence on their grammar and accidence, the resemblance being stronger in Language I. than in Language II. But, Baron Holstein observes, the fragments themselves do not seem to be direct translations from the Sanskrit. The word used in the colophon in one case implies " compilation" or "working over," from which we might almost infer a special recension of Buddhist books for Central Asian readers. In such a case, a later manufacture of Central Asian Sūtras does not seem to be out of the question. No Sanskrit text has been found for (*e.g.*) the " Amitāyur dhyāna Sūtra."

[2] If any reliance can be placed on the statement in the Thibetan History already mentioned, that China was first evangelized by Manjuśri, we must place that mysterious personage during the centuries of silence between As'oka and Kanishka. The temple especially connected by tradition with Manjuśri is the Wu-tai monastery near Peking.

Minor, and Rome with their presence,[1] the Hiungnu were already restive in their places in Western China, when Buddhism plunged, at the death of As'oka, into a dark night which lasted for over two centuries. Before it took the plunge it had already shown its ambition to become a world-religion. When it emerged it had somewhat changed its character, though it still retained its ambitious projects. It had, moreover, gained for itself a most relentless and formidable rival.

[1] Irish records sometimes speak of Scythia as the cradle of their race, and Druidism traces itself vaguely to Taprobane, i.e. Ceylon.

CHAPTER V

PUSHYAMITRA

PUSHYAMITRA was an important factor in the development of the Mahāyāna, whose claims to distinction have generally been overlooked.

As'oka, it is evident, ruled over a very extensive kingdom, and was one of the great monarchs of the day. It has always been a matter of wonder how his empire, so great, and apparently so firmly based on righteousness and judgment, should, after his death, have come to such a speedy ruin that the Mauryan family practically disappears from the annals of India.

A recent writer in the *Journal of the Asiatic Society of Bengal*[1] calls attention to the fact that As'oka's policy was one of unmerciful antagonism to the Brahmans, whose most cherished prejudices he took a pride in shocking. As'oka had, by precept and example, discouraged the taking of animal life, and had thereby put an end to much of the worship of the Brahman rites. He had appointed "superintendents of morals," Dharma Mahāmātās, whose functions necessarily superseded those of the Brahmans as expositors of the law. He had proclaimed the principle of Vyavahāra Samatā, "equality of punishment," "equality in lawsuits," which did away with the peculiar privileges

---

[1] See *Journal and Proceedings of the Asiatic Society of Bengal*, vol. vi., No. 5 (May, 1910), "Causes of the Dismemberment of the Maurya Empire," by Mahamahopadhyaya Haraprasad S'astri.

of the sacerdotal caste, and secured fair treatment for all subjects, irrespective of caste, creed, or colour. Above all, he had boasted that he had, in a short period of time, reduced " those who were once regarded as gods," *i.e.* the Brahmans (whose privileges as the twice-born seemed to entitle them to a quasi-divine position in the eyes of India), to the position of false gods whose claims to respect he had demonstrated to be baseless.

It could not reasonably be expected that the Brahmans should acquiesce without any feelings of resentment in such drastic changes. They were not fighting men, however, and their only course of action was to bow before the storm and wait for a good opportunity.

The opportunity came about B.C. 185, in the reign of one of As'oka's weakling successors, the last of the Mauryan house. The Greeks were still active, pushing their conquests further and further to the east, and founding principalities, some of which seem to have been still in existence at the beginning of the first century A.D. As'oka had lived on good terms with his Greek neighbours ; his successors found it necessary to fight against them for the defence of their own shrunken territories, and the commander-in-chief of the Mauryan army was a certain Pushyamitra. It has been conjectured, from the termination of this man's name, that he was of Persian stock. He was certainly a very determined enemy of the Buddhist religion, and he had the confidence of the Brahmans, who had been biding their time and quietly growing in numbers and influence.

After a successful campaign against the Greeks, who had advanced into the very heart of the Mauryan country, Pushyamitra returned in triumph to Pataliputra. A review of the troops was held ; in the midst of the festivities, the Mauryan emperor suddenly fell dead, slain by an arrow from an unknown hand. The successful general, whose triumph was being celebrated, was at once proclaimed emperor in his stead—and the hour of vengeance had come for the Brahmans. In the very city where As'oka had prohibited animal sacrifices, Pushyamitra celebrated (B.C. 184) the Hindu rite of As'vamedha, the "sacrifice of the horse"; the equality in the eyes of the law, which As'oka had established, disappeared once more. Hinduism was once more the dominant faith, though a Hinduism more elaborate, more philosophical than it had been, and one that had come into fertilizing contact with foreign influences. Buddhism was in its turn downtrodden and oppressed.

But beyond the limits of the kingdom ruled over by the new dynasty, there were principalities and kingdoms in which Buddhism found a welcome and a home, the principalities of the Greeks, the Parthians, the Yuetchi, S'akas, who come and go round the north-western confines of India during the two troubled centuries which precede the Christian era.

It is here, rather than in India itself, that must be sought those germs of thought which ended by making the Mahāyāna so very different from its more southerly and more purely Indian sister. Buddhism has always been a faith that has readily taken into itself whatever in its immediate surroundings it has found suitable for its purposes. Even Jewish influences would not necessarily be excluded. "Woe is me," says the Hebrew pilgrim, "that I am constrained to dwell in Mesech." [1] There

[1] The Jewish diaspora went as far as China. The Chinese Jews at Kaifongfu, in Honan, seem to have entered China between B.C. 170 and the Nativity of Christ, though laying claim to an even earlier date. But it is clear that they must be post-Captivity Jews. They are acquainted with the name of Ezra, and they possess portions of the books of Daniel, Zechariah, Malachi, Esther. They reckon time

E

were Buddhists in Mesech as well as Israelites; there were also Zoroastrians and Greeks, and the remnants of the old Babylonian cults.

Presently, with Kanishka, this Buddhism returns to India, and in As'vaghosha's time appears as a conqueror before the walls of Benares. And in process of time As'vaghosha is converted to the Mahāyāna.

by the Seleucid era; they are ignorant of the name of Jesus, and equally so of the Rabbinical traditions. They know of *Shiloh*, which they interpret as the "great one descending man" (which is practically the Buddhist *Nyorai*). And they wear a veil over the face in reading the Law (*Chinese Recorder*, vol. xiv. p. 325).

CHAPTER VI

THE NEW TESTAMENT IN TOUCH WITH THE EAST

THERE are a few passages in the New Testament which seem to bear on the subject we have in hand. I propose to touch upon them in this chapter.

The visit of the Magi will at once occur to the mind of every Christian reader as having (or as being intended to have) some bearing on the relations of Christianity to the country or countries from which the Wise Men came. The account given in St. Matthew presents many difficulties owing to the apparent impossibility of giving a scientific explanation of the star which is said to have guided these Eastern sages to the cradle of the Infant Saviour, and many, even devout, Christians are disposed in consequence to treat the visit as unhistorical. We have not at the present day the evidence required to prove the historicity of the story, and it would not therefore be wise to lay too much stress on the account of the Gospel record. But certain deductions are evidently legitimate. It is quite clear that St. Matthew believed the story when he inserted it in the forefront of his narrative. Or, if it be maintained that the narrative forms no integral part of the original Gospel, it is evident that the later interpolator recognized the story as having some important bearing on the preaching of Christ in the Orient. St. Matthew's Gospel—thanks, it may be, to the Jews of the Dispersion, for whom he wrote quite as much

as for the Jews of Palestine, early met with favour in
the remote countries where the Mahāyāna took its birth.
Pantænus of Alexandria[1] found it in India when he went
to that country as a Christian missionary at the end of
the second century, and the story of the visit of the
Magian pilgrims to Bethlehem evidently had a vogue of
its own in Central Asia. An expanded version of the
story has but recently been recovered from a sand-buried
ruin in Turkestan, and given to the world of students.[2]
It is true, it may be argued, that the Magi were Parthians,
and that the Parthians have had but little proveable
connection with Indian forms of religion;[3] but we know
that there were Parthian Buddhists, and must remember
that, besides the great Parthian Empire with which the
Romans of the period so often came into conflict, there
were at the time the Indo-Parthian satrapies in the
Indus Valley, which were almost as good as independent
sovereignties, and in parts of which the followers of
Zoroaster lived side by side with those of S'akyamuni.

The   second   point   is   evidently   the   selection   of

[1] Cf. Eusebius, "Eccl. Hist.," V.

[2] By Dr. Müller in the *Transactions* of the Berlin Museum für
Völkerkunde.

[3] Amongst the Sūtras translated into Chinese by the batch of
Buddhist missionaries who arrived at Lōyang in A.D. 147 is one on
Astrology, of which an English translation was given in the *Contemporary Review* for February, 1876 (vol. xxvii. pp. 417–424), by the
late Prof. Childers. It is directed against the practice of astrology as
a useless and misleading superstition, and shows how foolish it is to
suppose that the stars can possibly have any influence on the welfare
or happiness of man. This would seem to show that the particular
form of Buddhism preached by these men (which seems to have been
a kind of undeveloped Amidaism) was strenuously opposed to fortune
telling and astrology. Nevertheless, it will be seen, there were some
sects of Buddhism which allowed their followers to have recourse to
the soothsayer. There are such in Japan to-day. But see what I have
to say in my chapter on the Han translators.

Capernaum as the centre of our Lord's ministerial activity. "Galilee of the Gentiles" was a country with a mixed population. It lay on, or near, some of the greater trade-routes between Rome and the unknown Orient; it must have been constantly visited by strange figures from the lands of Asia. The custom-house at Capernaum must have been frequently called upon to appraise, and to pass through, bales of precious merchandise from Persia, India, and beyond, and he who, before his vocation to be an evangelist, had served as head of that establishment must have had many opportunities of making the acquaintance of travellers from distant countries. The silk trade between Asia and Europe was in the vigour of its early development. Varro is the first Roman writer to mention the subject. As'vaghosha,[1] the first great teacher and inspirer of the Mahāyāna, is honoured in Japan as the patron saint of the silkworm culture, and it was the Jews[2] who were the active promoters of this trade all along the lines of the trade routes from Antioch and Alexandria to their outpost colony in Kaifongfu,[3] in the province of Honan. It is evident that the tradal affinities of Galilee of the Gentiles lay much more with the East than the West, and the personal influence of the evangelist who sat at the receipt of customs at Capernaum must have tended to spread the gospel he was commissioned to preach amongst the Jews of Babylonian, Indian, and Central Asian Dispersions, and, through them, to the heathen amongst whom they dwelt.

---

[1] "Bukkyō Mondō Shū," p. 33 ff.

[2] I believe it is Dr. Graetz, in his "Geschichte der Juden," who brings out this point. The Jewish Diaspora must have been a great means of spreading a knowledge of Christ in remote regions. Think how Arab traders carry Mahometanism in Africa.

[3] This little colony of Chinese Jews still exists, though on the verge of extinction.

I find a third point of possible contact in St. John xii. 20. We are there told that the Feast of the Passover at Jerusalem was visited not only by Jews, but also by Greeks ("Ελληνες, not 'Ελληνισταί),[1] and that, on the occasion of the great Passover which saw the consummation of Christ's work, some of these Greeks came to Philip with the request that they might see Jesus. We are not told that Jesus saw them, but St. John tells us how Jesus recognized in the coming of these Gentile inquirers a sign that His work was drawing near to its accomplishment. "The time has come," He said, "for the Son of Man to be glorified. In most solemn truth I tell you that unless the grain of wheat falls into the ground and dies, it remains what it was—a single grain; but if it dies, it yields a rich harvest. . . . Now is My soul troubled. . . . Father, save Me from this hour. . . . Father, glorify Thy Name. . . ." Then followed a voice from heaven, which they that heard it failed to comprehend. "It is not for My sake," said Jesus, "that the voice came, but for yours. Now is the judgment of this world : now will the prince of this world be driven out. . . . And I—if I am lifted up from the earth—shall draw all men to Me."

Who were these Greeks, and where did they come from ? After Pentecost, and still more so after the subsequent dispersion of the Apostles and the recognition of St. Paul as the Apostle of the Græco-Roman world, the gospel of Christ spread rapidly throughout the bounds of the Roman Empire. Nay, it is clear that the zeal of unofficial preachers of Christ outran the slower movements of the authorized evangelists, and that the good news reached the extreme West, Spain, Gaul, and Britain, long before the arrival of Christian missionaries.[2]

[1] The Hellenists (Acts vi.) were Jews who spoke Greek; the Hellenes were Gentiles not in connection with either Judaism or Christianity.

[2] See J. W. Taylor, "The Coming of the Saints."

But there is no trace or sign of any interest taken in Christ, during His earthly life, by any European Greek. The centurions mentioned in the Gospels and Acts were Romans, not Greeks, and the Greek influence exercised in Palestine through Herodians and Sadducees was notoriously and actively opposed to Christ's claims and teachings. It is evident that the Greeks of whom St. John tells us were of a different kind from the friends and abettors of Herod.

We will call to mind the statement made by Irenæus [1] that the Gospel of St. John was written for the purpose of combating the heresy of the Nicolaitans, and we will anticipate matters a little by stating that there is very good reason for believing that the Nicolaitans professed a form of Buddhism almost identical with the still-existing Shingon sect of Japan, a sect which pins all its faith on the mercies of an abstract and eternal Buddha of the name of Vairoc'ana, and which, significantly enough, gives to S'akyamuni the title of the " Lord of this World." [2]   We will also remind ourselves of the fact that there existed an Asiatic colony of Greeks [3] in the valley of the Indus,

[1] See Irenæus, " Adv. Hær.," iii. xi.

[2] The Japanese Shingon hold that S'akyamuni was only a partial manifestation of Vairoc'ana, and that his value as a teacher of religion is entirely confined to the things of this world. For all higher truths, they say, we must have recourse to the Supreme Buddha Vairoc'ana. See next chapter.

[3] These Greek principalities were the remnants of the Greek kingdom of Bactria, established by Diodotus in B.C. 248, and recognized by Antiochus B.C. 208. It was divided in B.C. 175, Eucratides retaining Bactria, and Demetrius ruling in the Indus valley, which he had conquered. The Bactrian portion, broken into many principalities, was overrun by barbarians in B.C. 130, Heliocles being the last Greek ruler north of the Hindu Kush. The Greeks of the Indus valley continued to hold to their little principalities for two centuries longer, though much troubled by the Indo-Parthian sovereigns, who robbed them of much territory. The last Greek prince in India, Hermaios, finally succumbed to the Turkish or Scythian invader Kadphises I. about A.D. 50. See Smith, " Early History of India."

who professed Buddhism as their religion, and who were still under the rule of their own Greek princelets during the time of Christ's earthly life.

It is quite clear to all students of the history of North-West India and the lands around the Hindu Kush that things were in a state of religious ferment at the period of which we are speaking. Some change was imminent. The Mahāyāna was approaching the end of its period of gestation; the vague prophecies of a teacher to come had filled men's minds with anticipation. The Greeks of Asia had felt it; they had also heard, from the hearsay stories of caravan travellers, of the great Teacher who had appeared in the neighbourhood of the Sea of Galilee, and some of them went to the Passover at Jerusalem, "desiring to see Jesus," not from any idle curiosity, but because they had been taught to look for some such solution of their difficulties.

And Christ recognized the significance of their appeal. There was nothing yet to differentiate Him from him whom the East worshipped as the "Lord of this Saba-world," but He knew the lurking potentiality. His death, His uplifting, would give Him the magnetic power He needed. He would then begin to draw all men to Himself.

Two further points of contact between the infant Church of Christ and the East will be found in the Acts of the Apostles.

Men from many lands heard St. Peter's first Christian sermon on the Day of Pentecost. If the Acts are a genuine record of facts, Parthians, Medes, and Elamites, as well as Jews of Libya and Cyrene, and proselytes from Rome, listened to that great announcement of the gospel of Christ. It is hard to believe that the men who heard and believed, and were pricked to the heart by what they heard, should not have told their fellow-townsmen of the great events that they had witnessed at Jerusalem. There is also something peculiarly significant in the selection of Antioch as the headquarters of Gentile Christianity. No town, not even Alexandria, was more advantageously situated in this respect than Antioch. I shall reserve to the next chapter what I have to say about these two great cities.

I find one more point of contact with the Far East in the Book of the Revelation, in the vision of the man with the bow, who rides on a white horse and goes forth conquering and to conquer. Again I must content myself here with a bare mention of the fact. It will require a chapter to itself if the point is to be so put as to carry conviction to the mind of the reader, to whom it may possibly come with a shock of surprised horror.

CHAPTER VII

ALEXANDRIA AND ANTIOCH AT THE TIME OF CHRIST

THERE are two words which connect the Japanese Mahā-yāna, in one of its many aspects, with the Gnosticism of Alexandria and Antioch, and through it with the Christianity of the Apostolic age. These words are *Abraxas* and *Caulaucau*.

I have already, in a previous chapter, spoken of Alexandria and Antioch, of their mixed populations, of the extent of their commercial relations with Central Asia and India, and of the fact of As'oka's emissaries having been sent to both these cities during the course of the third century B.C. It is not necessary for me to repeat what I said then. What is of present importance is that these two cities, the two organs, so to speak, through which the commerce between Asia and Europe was effectuated in the early days of the Roman Empire, were the native homes of that syncretic miscellany of religious ideas, known as Gnosticism. Alexandrian Gnosticism is connected with the name of Basilides,[1] that of Antioch (or, rather, Syria) with Valentinus.[2]

Gnosticism is derived from the Greek *gnosis*, which is identical in meaning with the word *Bodhi*, from which we get *Buddha*, "the Enlightened One," and it is akin, both etymologically and in signification, with the word *Prajñā* (Jap. *Hannya*), "Knowledge." The first of these Sanskrit

---

[1] Basilides, A.D. (*circa*) 110.   [2] Valentinus, A.D. (*circa*) 130.

words, personified and used in the singular, has supplied Mahāyānism with its nearest approach to the idea of God, such as we know Him, "above all, in all, through all"; the second, likewise personified, in that vague manner which the Mahāyāna delights to use, has been identified with Nature, with the Hindu goddess Prithivī, with the spirit which animates the Kosmos, the "universal Pan."

The Gnostics, like the Mahāyānists, claimed to have the key of wisdom or knowledge, and, like them, tried to interpret the various religions of the world, with the help of the key which was in their hands. There seems to be no doubt that the fact of Christ was the impulse which spurred them to activity; it is equally certain that the outward form of Gnosticism varied according to the country in which it made its appearance. It is this that makes Gnosticism such an extremely puzzling subject to the student of philosophy and religion.

Gnosticism, like Proteus, claimed to be "thrice excellent;" it "knew not only things to come, but even things past as well as present;" it had great "skill in divination;" "it was (or claimed to be) the messenger and interpreter of all antiquities and hidden mysteries." But it was at liberty, nevertheless, "to turn itself into all manner of forms and wonders of nature." [1] The underlying matter was always the same; the form differed from country to country and from age to age. The Mahāyāna exhibits a precisely similar Protean power of assuming the most varied shapes.

The existence of Buddhism in Alexandria has often been suspected. Scholars have seen Buddhists in the communities of the Essenes in Palestine, in the monastic congregations of the Therapeutæ described by Philo, in the Hermetic books of Egypt, and especially in the κορὴ

[1] Bacon, "Wisdom of the Ancients," ch. xiii.

κόσμου preserved for us by Stobæus. The identity of
these with Buddhism has never been clearly established.
It has also been often suspected that Gnosticism was
derived from Buddhism. Again, the identity has never
been clearly established, possibly because Western scholars
have devoted their attention almost exclusively to the
Hīnayāna Buddhism of Ceylon and the Pali books. It
would not readily occur to any one to look for traces of
Egyptian Gnosticism in remote Japan. Yet there can be
little doubt that the system known in Japan as the
Shingon, and introduced into that country about A.D. 804,
by the celebrated Kōbō Daishi, must be looked upon as a
system which is not Indian in its origin, but which has
been foisted upon Buddhism from some extraneous quarter,
and that it is essentially Egyptian and Gnostic.

The Gnosticism of Basilides was based on the religions
which that thinker found to his hand in Alexandria, and
the task to which he set himself was apparently to
reconcile the fact of Christ with the preconceived notions
of the Alexandrian people. The religions were mainly
two, the ancient Egyptian cults, and Judaism. The
mythologies of Greece and Rome did not apparently count
for much in Alexandria, the philosophies in vogue were
not those of the schools of Athens, nor were they such as
Seneca or Pliny would have delighted in. The Judaism
of Alexandria was of a far more liberal type (or shall we
call it " broad "? to be " broad " is not always to be
" liberal ") than that of Jerusalem, and the " broad "
school of Jewish thought which eventuated in the Cabbalah
looked to Alexandria as its nursery. Egypt lay outside of
St. Paul's province—on no other hypothesis can we explain
his neglect of a city of such importance to an Apostle to
the Gentiles—and all early notices of Alexandrian
Christianity show it to have been for many years of a

very vague and mixed character.[1] Evidently the spiritual
soil of Alexandria was different from that of Jerusalem,
Ephesus, or Rome, and required a different treatment.

Basilides is spoken of by Clement of Alexandria, who
had better opportunities of judging than Irenæus, as a
worthy man and an earnest Christian, and his efforts to
adapt the fact of Christ to the spiritual prejudices of the
Egyptian or Egyptianized Alexandrians were probably
quite praiseworthy. A missionary religion must adapt
itself to the circumstances and thought of the people to
whom it comes.[2]

The system of Basilides was, like the system of ancient
Egypt,[3] and like that of the Japanese Shingon, dualistic.
It represented two Worlds ($\beta\acute{v}\theta o\varsigma$ and $\zeta\acute{\omega}\eta$), the World of
Light and the World of Darkness. The former—like the
glaring noon of an Egyptian summer's day—was still,
immovable, fixed, the world of permanent ideas; the
other, like the streets that are filled with life at sunset, is
the world of motion, of birth, of death—in short, the
world of Nature.

In the centre of the World of Light—the Diamond-
World (*Kongo Kai*), as the Shingon well calls it, to denote
its fixed and permanent nature—the Egyptians placed
God, the unknown I AM, whose name the priests of
Pharaoh would not pronounce. The Gnostics called him
Pater Innatus; in the Japanese Shingon it is *Roshana*, the
Buddha of Light, Eternal. From that central and eternal
Deity emanate, or proceed, four Beings—Æons in
Gnosticism, Buddhas in the Shingon—who surround the
central God on the Four Quarters. The Gnostics termed

---

[1] See *Church Quarterly Review*, October, 1909.

[2] This thought is constantly expressed in the Saddharma pundarika.
It was one of Nichiren's favourite topics.

[3] I have taken my matter mainly from Irenæus and Epiphanius.

them Logos, Phronesis, Sophia, Dynamis.[1]   The Shingon
personifies them as Ashuku, Hōshō, Amida, Fukūjōjū;[2]
but it treats Ashuku as representing that reason (λόγος)
by which a man is capable of faith, Hōshō as the sense
(φρόνησις) which enables a man to regulate his conduct,
Amida as the Wisdom (σοφία) which enables a man to
understand and explain the divine laws, and Fukūjōjū as
the practical power which manifests itself in salvation
(δύναμις).

Emanating from this central God, with his four modes of
manifestation, we have, in the Gnostic system, a number
of minor Æons and other mysterious beings, evidently
borrowed from the gods of Egypt.   They numbered 365,
which number written in Greek numerals spelled the word
Abraxas or Abrasax, and this name was consequently
given by the Basilidean and other Gnostics to the Deity,

[1] See "Dissertationes Præviæ in Irenæi Libros," in Migne's edition of
Irenæus, p. xxxviii.

[2] In Sanskrit Akshobya, Ratnasambhava, Amitâbha, Amogha-
siddhi.   These, with the Central Roshana or Vairoc'ana, form the
Five Dhyāni Buddhas, the Gochi Nyorai of Japan.   It is to be noted
that Fukūjōjū is identified with S'akyamuni.   Millioué ("Cat. Mus.
Guimet," 1883, p. 204) identifies Amida with the Egyptian Amenti.   In
the funeral ritual of the Shingon he appears as Amṛita, "The Immortal."
I believe that it must have been this personage whom the Gnostics
identified with Christ.   There was evidently, from the case of Fukūjōjū,
a disposition to identify the Dhyāni Buddhas with actual teachers and
saints, and it is quite evident that the Alexandrian Gnostics did not
look upon Christ as the only Saviour.

It is interesting to compare St. Paul's treatment of a somewhat
similar problem in the Epistle to the Ephesians, which, like Colossians,
is treating of some Gnostic or quasi-Gnostic difficulties.   In it (Ephes. iv.)
we have Christ the centre of all ministerial authority; and, issuing from
Him, a fourfold ministry: Apostles, centres of authority, who appeal to
the will; Prophets, whose sphere lies in the imagination; Evangelists,
who appeal to men as reasonable beings; Pastors and Teachers, who
guide men through the emotions and affections.   Men do not always
express themselves alike; in this case, however, the underlying thought
is the same.   God has many ways of saving lost mankind.

as a whole; not to the central Pater Innatus of the
World of Light, but to the whole fulness or pleroma
made up of all the Æons within that world. It is
evidently in opposition to this splitting up of the Godhead
amongst many minor and unsubstantial beings that St.
Paul insists that there is but one God, the Father, one
Lord (and not four)—and that in that one Lord dwells
the whole Pleroma of the Godhead in a bodily manner.[1]
St. Paul scarcely seems to be conscious of the gods of
Greece and Rome; he never speaks against the great
goddess of Ephesine superstition. He is keenly alive to
the dangers which may beset the Faith which he is
commissioned to preach from Gnostic foes disguised as
friends.

In Japan, the Shingon creed fills up the *Mandara* or
pleroma of the Diamond World with many Æons, whom
it calls sometimes Buddhas, sometimes Bodhisattvas, and
sometimes *Myō-O*, or "mysterious kings." As a term for
the whole it employs two words, *Abarakakia* and *Kha-la-
ka-ba-a*.[2] The one is used in the Shingon funeral rites,
where it is invoked *first*, before any invocation of personified Buddhas. The second is written in Sanskrit
characters on the wooden post which is erected over a
Buddhist grave immediately after the funeral. Both
words are found in Gnosticism—Abraxas and Caulaucau;
both are identical in meaning, both with one another and
with the corresponding words in Japanese. I shall have
to mention Caulaucau again in this chapter.

We now come to the Womb-world—as the Japanese
call it—the World of moving Life, of Darkness, and of

---

[1] *E.g.* Col. i. 19.
[2] Japanese has no *l* sound. Hence I write here *mandara*, not
mandala. This word has become naturalized. But *Kha-la-ka-ba-a* is
always written in Sanskrit letters, hence I write it with an *l*.

Death. (It is worth while noticing that the expression
" womb-world " is not confined to the Japanese Shingon.
It is also found in Epiphanius in his description of the
Basilidean conception of the World of Darkness.[1]) In
the centre of the Womb-world we have, in the ancient
Egyptian religion, Osiris ; in the Gnostic system, the Pater
Innatus ; in Shingon, Vairoc'ana or Dainichi. All three
systems identify this central Deity with the Sun.[2] From
Him, in all three systems, emanates an " ogdoad," or
eight-petalled flower, known in Sanskrit as *ashtapattra
vriti*, in Japanese as *hachi-yō-in*, and composed in
Gnosticism of various Æons, in Shingon of Eight Ideal
Buddhas and Bodhisattvas, whose names we need not
enter into. Thus the Ogdoad *plus* the Pater Innatus
becomes an Ennead, or group of Nine, and the Shingon
hachi-yō-in plus Vairoc'ana becomes a similar ninefold
constellation.[3] The three systems are strikingly alike.

[1] I have consulted, for the purposes of this comparison, (i.) the chapter
on Shingon in Dr. Nanjo's " Short History of the Twelve Japanese Buddhist Sects ; " (ii.) Dr. Wallis Budge, the " Gods of Egypt ; " and (iii.)
the accounts of the Gnostic sects given by Hippolytus, Irenæus, and
Epiphanius. The Greek word used is μήτρα. See Bousset on Gnosticism.

[2] This gives us the point of contact with the Japanese Shinto. It
was the policy of the Shingon and other early sects to identify the
Japanese Sun-goddess Amaterasu with Vairoc'ana. Amaterasu is the
fabled divine ancestress of the Imperial House, and the sixteen-petal
chrysanthemum, which is the Imperial crest, is said to be a Buddhist
emblem, an expansion of the *Hachi-yō-in*, adopted *circa* A.D. 1120 at
the suggestion of a courtly Buddhist monk by the Emperor Toba, who
was an ardent Buddhist. Strangely enough, Dr. N. G. Munro, of
Yokohama, has found the sixteen-petal chrysanthemum on an Egyptian
tomb. It is also found in " Pistis Sophia."

[3] Dr. Nanjo (p. 91) speaks of the " Mandala of nine Assemblies of the
Vajradhatu, which corresponds to the *nine* Beings of the *Hachi-yō-in*."
It is also noteworthy that there are nine stages in our knowledge of
Amida, who is accordingly sometimes represented by nine figures, each
a little different from the rest. There are also nine forms of Osiris.

When an Egyptian died, his soul descended to the realms of Tuat, or Hades. Here it passed through thirteen kingdoms, each with its own guardian deity, until it finally obtained emancipation at the end. The same thirteen kingdoms are to be found in the Gnostic book, "Pistis Sophia," and the soul is represented as passing through them in a similar manner. Only he who plays the part of Osiris in the Gnostic version is Jesus. In the Shingon sect there are thirteen Buddhas [1] and Bodhisattvas, who take charge of the soul at death, the two last, Vairoc'ana and Kokūzō, remaining its permanent guardians. The whole conception of the state of the dead in Shingonism is Egyptian. It is certainly not Buddhist.

I might multiply examples, but I must content myself with one or two. In Egypt, the guardian deity of the first of the mansions in Tuat bears a name which signifies the " Crusher of the forehead of the enemies of *Ra*." In Japan it is Fudō Sama, the fierce-looking, but essentially kind-hearted, Being, who stands amidst the flames, and bears in his hands a sword wherewith to slay the enemies of man's soul. The Shingon astronomy speaks of twenty-eight *chiku*, or constellations, seven in each quarter of the heavens ; the Egyptian astronomer knew the same, and spoke of them as the "gods of the twenty-eight finger-breadths of the Royal cubit." The Shingon astronomer uses the Egyptian signs of the Zodiac,[2] the same as ours,

[1] The thirteen Buddhas of the Shingon are Fudō (one week after death), S'akyamuni (2nd week), Manjus'ri (3rd week), Samantabhadra (4th week), Kshitigarbha (5th week), Maitreya (6th week), Bhaishajya-guru (7th week) ; Avalokites'vara (100 days), Mahāsthāmaprāpta (1 year), Amitābha (3 years), Akshobya (7 years), Vairoc'ana and Kokūzō, for ever. To these correspond a series of thirteen planets and heavenly deities. See "Catalogue of Musée Guimet," p. 191 (1883).

[2] The Shingon signs of the Zodiac are : (1) Hōbyōgū, *Aquarius ;* (2) Suigyōgū, *Pisces ;* (3) Byakuyōgū, *Aries ;* (4) Go mitsugū, *Taurus ;* (5) Nannyōgū, *Virgo* (though this is bisexual) ; (6) Būgegū, *Cancer ;* (7) So-

F

and not the Turkish cycle in ordinary use in Japan. The opening chapter of the " Saddharma pundarika Sūtra " (the *Hokekyō* of Japan) is so like the opening chapters of the "Pistis Sophia"[1] that it is impossible to resist the conclusion that the author of the latter work must have had before him either the " Saddharma pundarika Sutra " itself or a Sūtra of a very similar type. The latter alternative is the more probable one. The Hokekyō is a composite work based on something that has gone before; and it is indeed most likely that the " Ur-evangelium " in its case was a Mahāyāna Sūtra by some early Mahāyānist writer. There are grounds for such a conjecture. In the list of Scriptures taken to China in A.D. 147 by Anshikao the Prince of Parthia, and translated by him into Chinese during the Han period, there is one, the " Marghabhūmi Sūtra " (Jap. Dōshikyō[2]), the last three chapters of which are said by Nanjo to be based on the " Saddharma pundarika." Nanjo's statement is denied by some Japanese students, still the fact remains that there are portions of this Sūtra which

nyōgū, *Gemellæ* (not *Gemini*) ; (8) Shishigū, *Leo* ; (9) Hyōryōgū, *Libra* ; (10) Kattchengū, *Scorpio* ; (11) Kūgū, *Sagittarius* ; (12) Makatsugū, *Capricornus.*

The ordinary signs are the Rat, Bull, Tiger, Hare, Dragon, Snake, Horse, Ram, Monkey, Cock, Dog, Boar. This is the Turkish cycle. In some of the trades, such as the building trade, which abounds in ancient customs, I have found an occasional use of the Buddhist cycle.

[1] The resemblances between these two books are extremely striking. I have called attention to the subject in a lecture delivered before the Asiatic Society of Japan. The resemblances lie principally in the structure and conception of the two dialogues, in certain mannerisms of speech and action, and in the light that emanates from the Teacher in either case. There is also a strong similarity between the two books in respect to the use of *gāthās* and songs.

[2] In Nanjo's "Catalogue of the Tripitaka," No. 1326. Another Han book, the earliest edition of the *Sukhāvati Vyūha*, differs largely from the versions made in the fourth and fifth centuries which are now current in Japan.

strongly resemble the spirit and tone of the longer
Scripture, which, in its longer and completer, form is
evidently of later date.

There is also the statement made concerning the Manichæan books by Cyril of Jerusalem,[1] whom, as a bishop,
we must credit with trying to speak only what he believed
to be truth, and who, as Bishop of Jerusalem, probably
knew a good deal about the earlier history of his own
diocese.   Cyril tells us of a certain Scythianus who lived
in Alexandria and wrote books which pretended to be the
gospel, but "had not the acts of Christ but the mere
name only," to which the " Acta Archelai " adds that he
founded his sect during the lifetime of the Apostles, and
came to Jerusalem in the hope of getting them approved.
Scythianus had a disciple named Terebinthus,[2] who
apparently came to Jerusalem for the same purpose, but
was rejected by the authorities and retired to Persia,
where he assumed the name of Buddas. These books
were the basis upon which Manes founded his teachings.
The resemblances between the "Saddharma pundarika"
and the "Pistis Sophia" give probability to the story. There
must have been in circulation in Alexandria, during the
latter half of the first century A.D., a Buddhist book or
collection of books which was the "Ur-evangelium" of
several heresies.

How far was the Gnostico-Shingon system which I have
described influenced by the speculations of the mystic
school of Judaism which eventually blossomed out into
the Cabbalah ? [2] And how far was the Cabbalah influenced
by the thoughts of the Mahāyānists ? It would take us
too long to investigate the problem here. A thorough
investigation of this subject would necessitate a long

[1] Cyril, "Cat. Lect.," vi. 22.   Also "Acta Archelai," c. li.
[2] See, below, the chapter on Manichæism, p. 147.

excursion into the realms of theurgy and magic, and I must therefore content myself with a few brief remarks. Theurgy was practised by the Egyptians; it was a prominent feature of Gnosticism;[1] it is at the present moment the main and distinctive element of the Shingon worship, which consists very largely of manual gestures and the repetition of certain meaningless Sanskrit formulæ.[2] The mystic formulæ are Greek or Coptic in the one case, Sanskrit in the other; but the manual gestures are much the same in both. It is probable that the Gnostic system was taken by Alexandrian merchants to Southern India, a district which had intimate trade relations with Alexandria during the whole of the first century,[3] though it fell off in volume after the death of Nero in A.D. 68; and it was in Southern India, according to the Shingon story, that Nāgārjuna found the mystic books which lie at the base of their system.[4] This migration from Egypt to South India would account for the Sanskritizing of a system mainly Egyptian, and there is a certain amount of historical probability in the story as related by the Shingon authorities; for Nanjo tell us that Nāgārjuna (whom we may place anywhere about the middle of the second century) received the Shingon doctrine from a teacher of the name of Vajrasattva (Jap. Kongōsatta), and that Vajrasattva had received it, along with the mystic Baptism, from Vairoc'ana himself through the hands of S'akyamuni, at an assembly called the *Joshōe*

[1] See, *e.g.*, " Pistis Sophia," cap. 64.

[2] I have worked out many of these in an article on the " Care of the Dead," written for Hasting's " Encyclopædia of Sects and Religions," and one of the publications of the Musée Guimet is entirely devoted to them.

[3] See article by Sewell on " Roman Coins found in India," in *J.R.A.S.* for October, 1904.

[4] Nanjo, " Twelve Buddhist Sects," p. 79.

("self-nature-assembly").[1] If we may apply to a Buddhist
assembly the ordinary rules of chronological computation
(which is perhaps a little hazardous), that "self-nature-
assembly" must have taken place about the end of the
first century A.D.

We must not forget that Antioch as well as Alexandria
was a great centre of trade with the Orient. Antioch
was the centre of much Christian life. From it went
forth St. Paul and all that missionary activity which
laboured in Asia Minor, in Greece, and in Italy. From
it, likewise, went forth, Eastward, the missions to Edessa,
to Nisibis, to Armenia,[2] to Persia and beyond. From it
came the churches which were cut off in consequence of
the quarrels over Nestorius, and through the Nestorians
Antioch became the grandmother of the earliest missions
—at least as far as definite records are at hand—to
China.

Antioch originated the word "Christian;" the first
Christian from Antioch whose name is recorded in the
Acts of the Apostles, was a certain Nicolas,[3] a proselyte of
that city, who was chosen to be one of the Seven Deacons.
The term "proselyte" would seem to imply that Nicolas
was a Gentile by birth, converted to Judaism, and again to
Christianity. He must have been a fickle person, for he
subsequently left the Christian Church, and became the
founder of a heretical sect mentioned by the writer of the

[1] This points to a belief, of which I have found traces elsewhere in
Japan, of a reappearance of S'akyamuni somewhere about the beginning
of the Christian era.
[2] In an article by J. Kennedy in *J.R.A.S.*, 1904, we learn that there
was an Indian colony in Armenia from B.C. 130 to A.D. 300, when it
was broken up by St. Gregory the Illuminator. They were snake-
worshippers ("Nāgas") from Nāgpur, and may thus have had some
connection with Ophitism.
[3] Acts vi. 5; Rev. ii. 15

Apocalypse. His teachings are described by Irenæus, Hippolytus, Epiphanius, and others. They were of the general Gnostic type, and we note with interest that he and his followers used the word *Caulaucau* as a term apparently for God. Now, *Caulaucau* is that Buddhist term which is found along with Abraxas in the system of Basilides and in the Japanese Shingon. It brings the Japanese Mahāyāna very near to the holy ground of the New Testament—too near, perhaps, for some people.

One more point remains to be noticed. It is said both of Nicolas and of Basilides that their followers speedily lapsed into wild immoralities, quite at variance with the austere strictness which these two heresiarchs affected. I am not personally aware of any immoral practices amongst the Japanese Shingonists, but the Rev. Ekai Kawaguchi, the Buddhist priest who has travelled so long in Thibet, speaks of the immoral doctrines of the old sect of Lamas in that country, and likewise of an immoral sect of the Japanese Shingon which had to be suppressed on account of its filthy practices. So I conclude that the Shingon, like its parent Gnosticism, has, at some period in its history, presented the same sad contrast of the pure and the impure.[1]

[1] Ekai Kawaguchi, "Three Years in Tibet," pp. 409-411.

CHAPTER VIII

The Legend of St. Thomas

THE last chapter will, it is hoped, have prepared the mind
of the reader for accepting the idea that the beginnings of
Christianity and of the Mahāyāna were nearly related in
time, in place, and in idea. Nicolas of Antioch, who became
a worshipper of Caulaucau, was certainly a contemporary
of the Apostles; the testimony of St. Cyril and others, to
say nothing of the Buddhist Sūtra of which we have
found a chapter embedded in the "Pistis Sophia," may be
taken as evidence of local connection in Alexandria, and
the testimony of the same two books may be taken to
show that there was a connection (some might call it a
confusion) of thought in Gnostic minds between S'akyamuni and Christ.

An early Christian legend, given in the Apocryphal
Acts of St. Thomas, and supported by the testimony of
Eusebius and others, connects the Apostle St. Thomas
with the valley of the Indus. The legend has undoubtedly
been much embellished by later additions, but competent
scholars have concluded that it is quite possible that it
may rest on a substratum of fact. Let us examine the
story.[1]

Eleven of the original Apostles (Matthias is not
mentioned) are supposed to have been together in Jeru-

[1] "Acts of the Holy Apostle Thomas" in "Ante-Nicene Fathers,"
vol. viii. p. 535.

salem. They were, we may presume, in possession of their Master's commandment to go into all nations, and were considering how to fulfil the commandment. "We portioned out the regions of the world in order that each one of us might go into the region that fell to him, and to the nation to which the Lord sent him." They then proceeded to cast lots, a procedure quite in accordance with what we know from the Acts, and " by lot, then, India fell to Judas Thomas,[1] also called Didymus or the Twin."

But Thomas did not wish to go. He pleaded " the weakness of the flesh," " and how can I, being a Hebrew man, go among the Indians to proclaim the truth ? " What we know of St. Thomas from the Canonical Gospels makes his hesitancy on this occasion quite natural—in him.

Then Christ appears to him in the night. " Fear not, Thomas," He says; " go away to India, and proclaim the word ; for My grace shall be with thee."

But Thomas is not to be moved: " Wherever Thou wishest to send me," he says, " send me elsewhere; for to the Indians I am not going."

But Christ overrules the obstinate refusal of his doubting Apostle. A merchant has arrived from India, with a commission from a certain King Gundaphorus, to buy him a carpenter, and for three pounds Christ sells him His servant Judas, " who also is Thomas." The slave-dealing need not stop us. It only amounts to saying that Thomas came to be sold as a slave to an Indian merchant, and that people saw in the circumstance the overruling finger of God. But Gundaphorus is a historical personage, whose identity has been brought to light by the industry of the pioneers of modern historical research, and was an

---

[1] Cf. Eusebius, " Ecc. Hist.," i. 13.

Indo-Parthian king, ruling in the Indus valley. Thus
St. Thomas goes, according to one story, to India; according to another, to Parthia. Both stories may be true,
supposing that he went to Indo-Parthia. Gundaphorus
had a long reign, from A.D. 21 to A.D. 60, and he ruled
over the districts of Arachosia, the lower Indus, Herat,
and Peshawur. He was a great ruler, for the Scythian
hordes of the Yuetchi had not yet swept down upon his
territories, and, like great rulers, he immortalized himself
in stone. He was a mighty builder, and his buildings
were artistically adorned. We shall see in discussing
Gandhāra art, which is the art of North-West India at
the beginning of the Christian era, that it is dominated
by Græco-Roman conceptions, and a recent discovery at
Peshawur has given the world the name of a Greek
architect for the stūpa erected by the Scythian King
Kanishka in honour of S'akyamuni's relics. It is, therefore, an altogether possible story that St. Thomas should
fall into the hands of kidnappers, and be taken, as a slave
skilled in building and architecture, to the court of a
great Indian king, thus fulfilling, in spite of himself, the
desires of his Master.

The Indian merchant, Abbanes, having made his
purchases, returns to his master in Indo-Parthia. "They
began, therefore, to sail. And they had a fair wind, and
they sailed fast until they came to Andrapolis, a royal
city." The Syrian trade with India went overland as far
as the head of the Persian Gulf, and thence by sea to the
mouth of the Indus. If St. Thomas was sold as a slave
and taken to India, it would be by that route that he
would be taken. Andrapolis means the "city of the man,"
and Purushapura, the modern Peshawur, has the same
meaning. Purushapura was, as the legend says, actually
the royal city of Gundaphorus.

After being for some time in the service of Gunda-phorus, at Andrapolis, or Purushapura, where he did much preaching of the gospel, St. Thomas goes to a neighbouring kingdom, the sovereign of which appears as Misdeus or Basdeo. The second of these names gives us an Indian form, Vasudeva, and it is known that a king of this name was reigning, contemporaneously with Gundaphorus, at Matharā on the Jumna.

It is on the strength of evidence such as this that scholars such as Fleet, Smith, Dahlmann, and others have concluded that it is quite possible that the story of St. Thomas the Apostle having preached the Gospel of Christ in North-West India is well within the bounds of probability, though the same cannot be said of the other story, which tells us that he preached in South India, and was buried at Mailapûr, near the coast of Madras. This much, however, we can say of it. There is a constant tradition in South India which for centuries has connected the shrine of Mailapûr (or Meliapore) with the death, not the preaching, of St. Thomas; and the so-called Christians of St. Thomas can be traced, not certainly to Apostolic times, but to a period of great antiquity. In A.D. 78 there is a Pallava king reigning at Mailapûr and its neighbourhood, and Ceylon tells of another king, named Shálivahana,[1] who was a *Takshaka-putra*, "son of a carpenter," *i.e.* a Christian—a follower of Christ, or a follower of Thomas the Carpenter. The phrase is a Gnostic one; at some later time I shall show traces of a Gnostic connection between the Alexandrian Gnosis, a Tamil poet from Mailapûr, and Kōbō Daishi.

---

[1] *J.R.A.S.*, vol. xvii. The Pallavas, or Parthians, seem to have carried on an extensive commerce both with the West and the East. It seems probable that Gondopharus and Vasdeo were both Parthians and if so, the Pallava king at Mailapûr may have been Vasdeo.

For present purposes, I shall assume that the earlier portion of the St. Thomas legend is at least so far true that there actually was Christian preaching at a very early period in North-West India.   What I have to say in the next chapter may (or may not) be found to confirm the truth of the ancient legend.

CHAPTER IX

THE CALL FROM CHINA

WE will assume, then, that Christian preachers visited
India somewhere about A.D. 45, and that the story of
St. Thomas having been martyred near Mathura, on the
Jumna, in Central India, or at Mailapûr, on the Tamil
coast, about A.D. 51 (this being the year traditionally
assigned for his martyrdom), is not an absolutely im-
probable one. These men would have brought no Christian books with them; they would have their own
memories of the things that they had seen or heard,
and they may have had, or have made, *logia*, or short
pithy sayings of or about Christ, such as have recently
been found in Egypt, and such as St. Matthew is supposed to have jotted down before composing his Gospel.
And they possibly had some converts.

Now, in the year 64 A.D., the Chinese Emperor Ming-ti
had a dream. On several successive nights there stood
before him a man in golden raiment, holding in his hand
a bow and arrows, pointing him to the west. The
emperor was much moved by his vision, and, divining its
purpose, determined to send men to the west to seek for
the *mabito* [1] (眞人), "the true man" of his vision. There
was at this moment no commanding figure in Buddhism
to whom the words could apply. As'vaghosha might have

[1] Murakami, "Handbook of Buddhism," p. 290. The story will be
found in the S.P.C.K. "Handbook of Chinese Buddhism."

been such a man, but As'vaghosha is connected with the reign of Kanishka (*circa* A.D. 120), and his days were not yet. But there had lately been, and in the faith of his followers there still spiritually was, such a Man, and it is quite within the bounds of reason to suppose that rumours of such a person had reached the Chinese court at Lôyang. We have only to consider that the active silk trade between China and the luxurious early empire of Rome was in the hands of the Jews, whose headquarters were in Antioch; that these Jews had colonies and trade posts all along the route to the distant East; that their furthest outpost was at Kaifongfu, in Honan, where a miserable colony of their descendants still subsists to bear witness to a buried past; that Jews from Parthia were amongst those who were impressed by the events of the day of Pentecost;—we have only to consider these things to understand how extremely probable it was that rumours of the *mabito* should reach China. The Roman Empire had good roads; the Parthians had inherited good roads from the Persians and the Seleucid Greeks; China under the Han was a progressive military power, and must have had them. The journey from Antioch to the Chinese capital at Lôyang would not occupy more than a year and a half, and already thirty years had elapsed since the Crucifixion and Pilate's testimony to the *mabito*—Ecce Homo!

Further, although it was not until the year A.D. 75 or so that the great Chinese general Panchao started on the great military expedition which brought the Chinese arms victoriously to the shores of the Caspian Sea, and made the Celestial Empire for a few years almost the next-door neighbour of Rome, it is certain that the Central Asian troubles which caused that expedition were already brewing, and the solution of them was already occupying the

minds of Chinese statesmen. We can hardly imagine such
a great expedition being planned without some previous
study of the actual conditions of the countries concerned,
and we can readily understand that such an inquiry might
bring the fact of Christ to the cognizance of the officials.
The inquiry might have led them to an explanation of
the "Great One Descending Man," looked for by the Jews
of Kaifongfu.[1]

At any rate, Ming-ti, warned by his dream, sends his
commissioners to the West. There were eighteen of them,
their names, or at least some of them, are given, and they
start for India. According to the most authentic form of
the story,[2] they never reached India, for on the road they
met two monks toiling over the mountain passes, and
leading a white horse laden with the *impedimenta* of their
journey. The names of these two travellers were Kaśyapa
Matanga and Dharmaraksha, or Gobharana. The white
horse was laden with Scriptures and Buddhist images, and
they were on their road to China to preach the gospel.
Buddhism had now been in the world for five centuries
at least, and had, as we have seen in a previous chapter,
amply recognized its calling as a world-religion. One is
tempted to ask with wonder, Why should China, so nearly
related to northern and north-western India, have been
left so long without a preacher ?

There was something about these men—possibly the
white horse—which satisfied the Chinese commissioners
that they had found what they wanted. They turned
back with their newly made acquaintances to the Chinese
capital, where the missionaries were well received and
lodged in a monastery which still exists, the oldest in
China, the celebrated *Pomash* (Jap. *Hakubaji*), the oldest
existing temple in China, "the Monastery of the White

---

[1] See above, p. 50.   [2] "Bukkyō Kakushu Kōyō," vol. i. chap. i. p. 4.

Horse." It is evident that the White Horse made a great impression on China, an impression which apparently reached Japan as well.[1]

Kaśyapa Matanga and Dharmaraksha reached China in A.D. 67. Three years later, in A.D. 70, they both died. They had had but a short sojourn in China; but it was not altogether a fruitless one. The "Bukkyō Mondō Shū" gives us, in the chapter from which I have already quoted, certain particulars of their workings. They at once attracted many inquirers (coming as they did in answer to an Imperial dream, they could not well have done otherwise), and the Taoists and Confucianists were at once stirred up to jealousy. Their enemies applied to the emperor, and Ming-ti, desirous of doing what was right, appointed a day for a public discussion. Not much could be done in that line, however; for the one side knew no Chinese, and the other no Sanskrit. But there were other tests which the missionaries and their friends stood triumphantly. Buddhist relics refused to be broken by sledge-hammers, Buddhist books emitted a gentle light and refused to be burned in the fire, and the two Buddhist monks compelled the attention of a large audience by speeches in Sanskrit, which, strangely enough, every one understood. There are echoes, as it were, in this story, of Elijah and the priests of Baal, of

[1] In "Bukkyō Mondō Shu," vol. i. p. 34, in a discussion on As'vaghosha as the patron saint of silk-culture (he is so considered in the provinces of Shinshu and Echigo, and perhaps elsewhere in Japan), there is a mention of As'vaghosha in connection with the White Horse. He is said to have appeared as a thousand white horses, to have made a thousand white birds sing, to have assumed the forms of countless silkworms, to have spun thousands of cocoons, to have saved many thousands of living creatures. The Shingon speaks of him as an incarnation of Vairoc'ana, who, in the days of his flesh, was the Eighth Patriarch of Buddhism. There are several temples in Japan in which a white horse is constantly kept.

the Children in the Furnace, of the Pentecostal experience, which are very strange. We shall find the same story as to the relics in Japan, and the Buddhists of Ceylon claim the same thing for their Tooth of Buddha.

Four books are put to the credit of these two missionaries in Nanjo's "Catalogue of Tripitaka," of which, however, only one survives. One of the best books is said to have been a life of Buddha, which some have identified with the "Buddha carita"[1] of As'vaghosa, an impossibility, seeing that the day of As'vaghosha had not yet come. The book that survives, that has weathered the many vicissitudes of Chinese history, the fires[2] and other catastrophes, is known as the "Sūtra of the Forty-Two Sections." It is not in the form of a dialogue as are most other Sūtras, but is merely a collection of short pithy sayings of "the Buddha," loosely strung together, and provided with a short introduction setting forth the place and time at which Buddha is supposed to have spoken them. It has been conjectured (though I believe there is no definite authority for the conjecture) that the missionaries, finding handbooks in use with short extracts from the writing of Confucius, conceived the idea of composing a similar book with extracts from the Buddhist Sūtras, and that the "Sūtra of the Forty-Two Sections" was the result. It may be so. The book has undergone many editions and revisions, and any one who knows the East knows that the Chinese are adepts in the culinary

---

[1] In "Sacred Books of the East," vol. xlix. Bukkyō Mondo Shu (l.c.) correctly gives As'vaghosha's approximate date as "during the sixth century after the Nirvana."

[2] Chinese history has several "bibliothecal catastrophes," as they are termed, when, by order of the Government, all books were burned except a few favoured ones on practical subjects. But these catastrophes sometimes occurred at a time when China was divided into several kingdoms, and then of course they did not apply to the whole empire.

art. It is a possible belief that we have in the "Sūtra of the Forty-Two Sections" a collection of *logia*, containing short pithy sayings of the Master, and prepared for the use of missionaries such as were Kaśyapa Matanga and Dharmaraksha, working in a new land without proper books in the vernacular; but a conjecture has before this been made that these two men were not Buddhist missionaries, but Christians, disciples of St. Thomas, who is still, I believe, to this day commemorated in Nestorian liturgies as the Apostle of India *and China*. *Qui per alium facit per se facit.*

The reasons available are as follows :—

1. It is known that there were such *logia* among early Christians. I believe I am right in saying that there are no similar *logia* in the whole range of Buddhist Sūtra literature, except those which were compiled about this period for like purposes.

2. The fact that we have in the "Pistis Sophia" the introduction of a Buddhist Sūtra, taken by some Gnostic *cordon bleu* and served with suitable garnishings as the introduction to a book concerning Christ, seems to suggest the feasibility of the reverse process, and that a Christian book might similarly be taken by some Chinese literary cook and served up to the devout in China as a Buddhist book, with a suitable introduction to give local colour and tone.

3. The *main* contents of the book will be found, *on the whole*, to be not in disagreement with Christian doctrines, and far more suitable for Christian purposes than the Epistle of St. James (which has been claimed as a Buddhist writing) would be for the use of disciples of S'akyamuni.

4. We shall see, from a study of Buddhist art, that whereas the early Buddhist sculptures invariably treat

G

the Master as absent, thus carrying out the spirit of the
Sanskrit title for Buddha, *i.e.* the *Tathāgata*, "the one that
went thus (as he said)," in the post-Christian art of Gandhāra, he is always represented as a Being that is present
amongst his disciples, and, being present, very often
depicted in Greek or Græco-Roman costume. The "one
that had gone" had been changed to "the one that had
come," whose Presence (παρουσία) was recognized by his
followers. This first mission to China, the first *official*
introduction, be it remembered, of a new faith to China
(for whatever Buddhism there had been before this time
must have been quite unofficial), must be held responsible
for the invention of suitable " characters " through which
to introduce to the Chinese literati the idea of the Tathāgata. And the characters they chose (如來), the Chinese
Julai, the Japanese *Nyorai*, convey the idea of the pa-
rousia. "He that comes thus (as was expected)," the
Great One Descending Man of the Kaifongfu Jews. It
is a very significant change.

5. Still more significant is the character which must
have been introduced to represent Buddha (佛), the
Chinese *Fo*, the Japanese *hotoke*. The component parts
of this character are said to represent a man (亻) with a
bow (弓) and arrows (丨丨); and we may suppose the two
missionaries to have said to the people of Lôyang (the
ancient capital of China), "We have come to tell you of
the *Mabito*, of the true man, of the man with the bow and
arrow whom your Emperor saw in his vision." It is
possible (for there were Greeks living in India, as we have
seen) that under the Indian names of these two missionaries there may have lurked a Greek nationality. At
any rate, the character they chose is capable of another
signification, besides the one usually given—the three first
letters of the *name* of the Perfect Man, our cherished

Christian monogram, $\overline{IHC}$, the man with the bow and arrows![1]

6. We may suppose this character for Buddha to have been introduced to China about the year 68 A.D. There are many competent scholars who assign to the year 67 A.D. the composition of the Book of Revelation. In that book the author, after a rapid survey of the Churches under his immediate Apostolic guidance, and after a vision of God in His glory, proceeds to tell his readers the things that must shortly come to pass. The immediate future is a sealed book with many seals which none but the Lamb may open. The first seal is broken (Rev. vi. 2), and St. John is told to come and see "*a white horse, and he that sat on it had a bow, and a crown was given unto him, and he went forth conquering and to conquer.*"

There are Christians who say that the New Testament is a book that is all fulfilled, that the end of which Christ spoke in His discourse on the Mount of Olives was accomplished at the siege of Jerusalem, and that we should think of the saints who took part in that first resurrection as already gathered around Christ in the heavenly places. One of the signs given was that the Gospel of the Kingdom should be first preached unto all nations for a witness, and then the end should come. It is certain that Christianity reached England and Spain and the lands of the furthest West about the same time that the White Horse reached China. If we could trace the Ethiopian Eunuch or the labours of other Apostles, we might be astonished to find how far to the south the gospel travelled in those early days. For a thing which is really a gospel requires no elaborate machinery or organization to push it

[1] Compare what has been said above of the "Divine Name of the Six Letters."

on. It is recognized as "good news," and it travels from mouth to mouth.

The White Horse in the Apocalypse was followed by others, red, black, pale, the symbols of War, of Famine, of Death. Nothing was done by the Buddhists of India to follow up this mission of the White Horse—a fact which seems to point to its not having been a Buddhist mission at all, for the Buddhists would surely not have neglected to follow up so gracious an invitation from so powerful a monarch as Ming-ti. But suppose it to have been a Christian preacher that went to China, and we may, in the confusions that followed in Europe and Asia, find abundant reasons for the cessation of Christian missionary effort. The seed had been scattered very widely —the testimony had been delivered, by St. Paul before Nero, by some unknown preacher before the Great Han Emperor. Then the labourers fell asleep, and the enemy came to sow the tares. Those first men were sent forth only to give a testimony, and when the testimony had been delivered the End of the Age came.[1]

[1] A good translation of the Sūtra of the Forty-Two Sections will be found in "Sermons by a Buddhist Abbot." Chicago, Open Court, 1905.

CHAPTER X

Buddhism just before the Coming of Christianity

It is my intention in this chapter to estimate as far as I can the condition of Buddhism just before the coming of Christianity to India, and consequently just before the first visible development of the Greater Vehicle. This will clear the ground for the consideration of the Mahāyāna itself in later chapters.

Our most trustworthy guides for the dark period between As'oka and Christ are the remains of ancient Buddhist temples of the earlier or Persian period of Indian art. From these [1] we may gather that long before the dawn of the Christian era Buddhism had, for all practical intents and purposes, formulated for itself a demi-god in S'akyamuni, whom it worshipped with far more fervour than the Greeks worshipped Herakles, whom in Asia they identified with S'akyamuni. Round Herakles in Greece many myths formed themselves ; the person of S'akyamuni was likewise enveloped in a robe of legends and sayings, and it comes to a Christian reader as an unpleasant and unwelcome shock to find S'akyamuni provided with stories very similar to those which have always endeared to us the Nativity and Infant life of Christ our Saviour. There is

---

[1] *E.g.* those at Amarâvati, Ajânta, Sanchi, Barhut, Gayā, Nalanda, etc. For a convenient summary reviewing all that has been written on the subject, see Grünwedel, " Buddhistische Kunst in Indien " (Museum für Völkerkunde, Berlin). Also Rhys Davids' " Buddhist India."

no use for us to try and blink the fact.   It stands there in
the clear-cut stone monuments of India that pre-Christian
India believed in Buddha as a Being whose Birth was
supernatural, the result of a spiritual power overshadowing
the mother ; as one whose Birth was rejoiced over by angels
and testified to by an aged seer; as one who had been
tempted by the Evil One and had overcome ; as one whose
life had been one of good deeds and holy teachings ; as one
who had passed into the unseen, leaving behind him a
feeling of longing regret for him who had thus gone away.[1]

Buddhism was also by this time provided with books,
or at least with a body of doctrines orally embodied in set
forms, and recited by the monks with that verbal exact-
ness for which the Indians have always been so famous.
On one of his rock inscriptions, in the edict at Bairât in
Rajputâna, As'oka mentions the names of seven such
Sūtras, of which five have been identified as still existing
in the Pali Sutta Pitakam,[2] while the sixth and seventh
have been with considerable reason supposed to be,
respectively, the germ of the Vinaya Pitakam, or books
of Discipline, and the First Sermon delivered by Buddha
after his Enlightenment.   Shortly after As'oka's death,
about B.C. 200 (and therefore before the accession of
Pushyamitra), on the rail around the stupa of Barhut,[3] are
inscribed the " names of pious Buddhists, who are described
as " reciters," " versed in the Dialogues," " versed in the
Baskets," and " versed in the Five Collections,"[4] and

---

[1] See, e.g., " Buddhist and Christian Gospels," by A. J. Edmunds.
I have used the Tokyo (1905) edition with notes by M. Anesaki.

[2] Edmunds and Anesaki, l.c., p. 2. See above, p. 42.

[3] Ibid., p. 3.   The writers also refer to Ferguson's " History of
Indian and Eastern Architecture " (London, 1876), p. 5, and to Cunning-
ham, " The Stupa of Barhut."

[4] I.e. The Five Nikayas, or, as they are termed in the Mahāyana,
the Five Agamas.   Professor Anesaki has given the Asiatic Society
of Japan an exhaustive comparative study of the Pali Nikayas and
Sanskrit Agamas.

these inscriptions bear witness to the continual tradition
of these oral records. And, finally, if we may trust the
Ceylon Chronicles, these oral records were committed to
writing in Ceylon about 40 B.C., and thus the Hīnayāna
books assumed their stereotyped form.

We may assume, further, that the pre-Christian Buddhism, possessing the books, possessed also the doctrines
of Hīnayāna Buddhism, such as it is still to be found in
Ceylon and other Buddhist countries of the Southern
School. It does not fall within the scope of this work to
give an account of these doctrines. The student will
find them admirably summarized in books like Hardy's
"Manual of Buddhism," or Warren's "Buddhism in
Translation." [1] But it is also certain that while the
doctrinal standards had been faithfully handed down until
the time came for them to be committed to writing, there
had also been a steady downward tendency in the life
of the Buddhist Church, accompanied by a corresponding
relaxation of the firmness with which the doctrines of
Buddha were held. This downgrade movement has been
graphically described for us in the "Ten Dreams of Kaśyapa," which may be taken as coming to us from the
latter end of this period of Buddhist decay. [2]

According to that book, the great disciple Kaśyapa,
who is reckoned by north and south alike as the first
Patriarch of Buddhism after the death of S'akyamuni,
had ten dreams : (1) An elephant, having squeezed its
body through a narrow door, failed to get its tail through.
(2) Thirsty men were seen running away from a fountain

---

[1] Cf. also Neumann's "Die Reden Gotamo Buddhas." I have also
learned very much from Léon Feer's Buddhist articles in the *Journal
Asiatique.*

[2] See *J.R.A.S.* for 1893, p. 512. The dreams are found in Thibetan;
also in Nanjo's Catalogue, 543, 631, 632 (connected with Prasenajit).
They have likewise made their way into Russian folklore.

of water which pursued them. (3) A measure of pearls was given as payment for a mess of porridge. (4) A load of costly sandal-wood was sold at the price of common fuel logs. (5) A garden full of flowers and fruits was stripped by thieves. (6) Elephants during the rutting season, when they are usually fierce and pugnacious, were driven away by a knot of little children. (7) A dirty monkey was seen covering another monkey with dirt. (8) A monkey was crowned and anointed as king. (9) A piece of cloth was torn into eighteen pieces. (10) A crowd of people were quarrelling in the streets.[1]

The dreams had their interpretations, and in those interpretations we may see the gradual decay of the institutions which S'akyamuni had founded, and which As'oka had been at such trouble to propagate. (1) The disciples had, in obedience to their master's commands, left their homes to follow him, but the surrender had not been complete. The elephant's tail had refused to pass through the door, and presently the monks made new homes for themselves, and became attached to their comfortable monasteries, as they had once been to their mansions and villas. (2) The disciples were like a well, bubbling over with the water of life; but the laity had no thought of religion, and possibly a contempt, more or less openly expressed, for the comfortable recluse. So the fountain had to pursue thirsty men, who, while perhaps craving for the truth, were yet unwilling to quench their thirst at that particular fountain. (3) Thus there resulted a

---

[1] It is a testimony to the early existence of a schism in Buddhism that the two lists of patriarchs of the Northern and Southern Schools respectively agree only in one name—that of Kaśyapa, the immediate successor of S'akyamuni. This implies that the two parties went each its own way immediately after Kaśyapa's death, which occurred not long after that of S'akyamuni. As'oka possibly tried to effect a reunion, and may indeed have had some temporary success.

cheapening of religious instruction. In their anxiety to win adherents, the preachers tickled the ears of their audience with the highest truths, when the simpler ones would have been more suitable; and in return for the measure of pearls they offered received but a poor meed of gratitude—a mess of porridge. (4) In the same way, the fear of losing disciples caused the monks to tolerate the existence of heresy in the community; the teachings of heretics were esteemed as highly as those of the orthodox —sandalwood was sold at the same price as common fuel. (5) The monasteries were rich and well endowed with lands and estates. The revenues should have been for the poor; the monks used them for their own profit. (6) Good disciples (the rutting elephants) were driven away by worthless ones (children). As early as the days of As'oka complaints were made of this, the better sort of monks preferring to retire rather than be forced into religious contact with worthless and evil brethren. (7) These worthless men were like dirty monkeys, covered with mud. They threw the dirty mud of slander at their fellows, and so made them appear as dirty as they were themselves. (8) Then, having got rid of the worthy monks, they proceeded to elect superiors of their own type in the monasteries, till it came that the monkey was anointed as king. (9) Thus it came to pass that the Buddhist community, which, like Christ's garment, had once been a seamless vesture of whole cloth, had been torn and rent into eighteen pieces, corresponding to the eighteen sects [1]

---

[1] I here give the eighteen Hīnayāna sects as found in Japanese books. There were two main divisions which were made very early, some would have it as early as the Council of the Grotto immediately after S'akyamuni's death, others at the Second Council of Vais'āli, a hundred years later. According to this view, the Mahāsānghikas, who were the liberally inclined amongst the monks, being unable to communicate any longer with the conservative Sthaviras, broke loose and

into which the Hīnayāna had been torn. (10) And the
result of sectarianism was religious strife.

formed themselves into separate communities outside the limits of the
Magadhan kingdom.   In this way the germs were planted out of which
later grew the two Vehicles.   The *Mahāsānghikas* (*Daishūbu*, 大衆部)
were divided into (i) *Issetsubu* (一説部), (ii) *Sesshusebu* (說出世部),
(iii) *Kei-in-bu* (鶏胤部), (iv) *Tamonbu* (多聞部), (v) *Setsu-ge bu*
(說假部), (vi) *Seitasanbu* (制多山部), (vii) *Seisanjubu* (西山住部),
(viii) *Hokusanjūbu* (北山住部).

The *Sthaviras* (上座部) were not so numerously subdivided.   Their
sub-sects were (ix) *Setsuissaiubu* (說一切有部), (x) *Tokushibu*
(犢子部), (xi) *Hōjōbu* (法上部), (xii) *Kenchōbu* (賢胄部), (xiii)
Shōryōbu (正量部), (xiv) *Mitsurinsanbu* (密林山部), (xv) *Ketabu*
(化他部) (xvi) *Hōzōbu* (法藏部), (xvii) *Onkōbu* (飯光部), (xviii)
Kyōryōbu (經量部).

Murakami enumerates twenty sects by reckoning in a parent
Sthavira and a parent Mahāsānghika sect.   Some of these sects, *e.g.*
those in which the character 山, *san* ("mountain"), appears, were
most probably local.   No. ix., known in Sanskrit as Sarvāstivādins, were
the most powerful.   It was for this sect that Kanishka erected the
great stupa for Buddha's relics lately unearthed near Peshawur.
No. xvi, the Dharmaguptas, were very strong on the Vinaya, and
through it exercised much influence in China.   Nothing is known about
the majority of the sects here enumerated.   It must not be supposed
that the Hīnayāna disappeared before the rising Māhāyāna.   It continued side by side with its rival, not only in India, but also in China
and Japan.   It seems probable, however, that the Mahāyāna ultimately
absorbed many of the Mahāsānghika subjects.

The following extract from a Burmese book (quoted by Edmunds and
Anesaki, *op. cit.*, p. 5) deserves a thought :—

"In the time of the king named Nāgo the Robber, when the whole
of Ceylon was vexed by the fear of the bad monks, the monks who kept
up the Tripitaka went to India (compare No. 6 of Kaśyapa's dreams).
Those monks who did not go thither, but stayed at home, being vexed
by fear of famine, tightened their waistbands, encased their bodies
in sand, and kept up the Tripitaka. . . .   When the fear of bad monks
was appeased, the monks came back from India, and, together with the
monks who had stayed in Ceylon, they reconciled the Tripitaka with
the recension of the Great Minster (Mahāsānghikā), and when the two

One of the most important books for the study of the Dark Period is the so-called "Questions of King Milinda," of which there is an English version by Professor Rhys Davids in the "Sacred Books of the East." Menander (for that is the proper reading of Milinda) was one of the Greek princes that ruled in India during the last century before Christ. The book fixes its own date, for it alludes to S'akyamuni's prophecy that his religion would not last for more than 500 years after his death, and yet betrays no consciousness of the fact that it had already lasted beyond that period. We may take it, therefore, that the five centuries had not quite elapsed when the book was written, and may place the composition of it somewhere about the time "of the Flavian Emperors of Rome." [1]

The book has been called the "Irenæus" of Buddhism. The Pali Pitakas are "immanent" in its pages, just "as the New Testament is immanent in the pages of Irenæus." It bears a strong testimony to the existence and nature of the Hīnayāna books, as also to the Hīnayāna doctrine, and, better than any other book, enables us to see what was the state of Buddhist thought at the end of its first period, when the Age of the Upright Law (as it has since been called) was all but over, and the Age of Image Law was about to be introduced.[2]

The author of the book speaks of the period of Five Hundred years as being the duration of S'akyamuni's teachings in the world. The Five Centuries were just elapsing, when the new faith of Christ came into the

were made harmonious, they established them. Then when they were established, they kept them up in Ceylon."

From this it would seem that the Mahāsānghika (Great Minster) School of the Hīnayāna has continued itself in Ceylon.

[1] Edmunds and Anesaki, p. 4. The date coincides with the dawn of the new era in the religious history of the world.

[2] This is the chronological theory adopted by Japanese Buddhism.

world. There was everything to fill a Buddhist monk possessing a statesman's mind, one capable of taking a wide outlook over the world, with anxiety as to the future. India was a political cypher, divided among weakling princes. On its north-western frontier lay the dreaded Scythian, whose invasion of the land would certainly not be delayed for many years to come. He was very possibly a Buddhist, but his Buddhism, already mixed with alien elements, was not of the same type as that of Magadha. If he came, he would not help the poor distracted Hīnayānist; if he only threatened to come, he was still a Buddhist and an alien enemy, and the patriotism of India was asserting itself by a return to the old Indian gods whom A'soka had persuaded it to lay aside. Go away he certainly would not. Is it to be wondered at that at such a time our monk should turn his thoughts to him that had " thus gone "? I have already, in a previous chapter, spoken of the change that comes over the Buddhist architecture, and of the significant change in the Chinese word for the Tathāgata. I will now quote from another of the Pali Sūtras, one which surely referred not merely to the Buddha that once was and now had gone, but much more to him that was to come, and whose coming was to give new hope of life.[1]

" Ananda, the future Buddha, is mindful and conscious when he is born with the Tushita Body. . . .[2] (he) is mindful and conscious when he vanishes from the Tushita Body and descends into his mother's womb. . . When he vanishes from the Tushita Body and descends into his

---

[1] I quote from the " Dialogue on Wonders and Marvels," given by Edmunds and Anesaki, pp. 54–60.

[2] The Tushita Heaven, one of the lower heavens in the Buddhist cosmology, is one in which beings with *form* can appear. The Highest Heaven is beyond form, and consequently beyond thought.

mother's womb, then, in the world of the angels, of Māra, of Brahmā, unto the philosophers and Brahmans, princes and peoples, there appears a splendour, limitless and eminent, transcending the angelic might of the angels," etc.

Words such as these, written in all probability before the birth of Christ, and applicable to the Nativity of S'akyamuni as it lives in Buddhist legend and belief, do not at all necessarily imply that the Nativity stories of the New Testament are merely faked-up fables, borrowed from an older cycle of fiction. Rather they show that when He was born, in the way in which His birth is recorded, He was fulfilling more than one prophecy. It is thus that it behoves a Divine Saviour *to be born;* that is the testimony of Isaiah, of Virgil, of the Buddhist Sūtra, of many another great teacher that has appeared. It was part of the stock-in-trade (if I may so call it) of S'akyamuni; it was also a part of the stock-in-trade of Christ. If Christ's superhuman credentials had gone no further than the Nativity cycle, Christ would in no sense have differed from S'akyamuni. But Christ's claim of supernatural testimony went farther than S'akyamuni's. He claims our allegiance not merely because " He was conceived of the Holy Ghost, and born of the Virgin Mary," but more especially so because, having been crucified and slain, He rose again the third day from the dead. It is on the Resurrection that St. Paul bases Christ's claim to be the Son of God; it is this that makes Him unique in religious history. This places Christ at the head of all things in the religious world; its absence puts S'akyamuni into his proper place, a place in which he may yet claim the ungrudging respect of Christian people. It constitutes him a great witness and forerunner of Christ, and no Japanese can be offended at having him placed in such a seemingly humble position, for it is the place which they themselves assign to him when they say, with their own poet, that the sole reason for S'akyamuni's appearance in the world was that he might point men to Amitābha.[1]

[1] See my "Shinran and His Work" (Tokyo, 1910), p. 47.

A good instance of the moral bankruptcy of the Hīnayāna at this period will be found in the "Katha Vatthu," translated by Rhys Davids in *J.R.A.S.*, 1892. Also in the *Jātaka* stories (published in English by the Cambridge University Press). Æsop esteemed these rightly in making them the basis of many of his fables, and they have left their traces in much of the folklore of many peoples in Asia and Europe. But the religion which produced them must first have lost a large part of its moral vigour. They do not speak the language of men who are terribly in earnest about some teaching of faith. One cannot imagine Tertullian or Augustine gravely telling a Jātaka story. The "Katha Vatthu" contains a discussion, from the standpoints of the various Hīnayāna sects, of certain questions concerning Buddhist philosophy, ethics, and discipline. On very few of these questions were the answers given unanimously in the same sense. Here are some of the questions—

"Is there, in the truest and highest sense, a soul?" "No." [To this question two sects gave an affirmative answer. One of these sects must have been that of the Sarvāstivādins, for the existence of the soul was one of their tenets.]

"Does the universe exist?" "No; there is nothing that is not transient." [But here again the Sarvāstivādins affirmed the real existence of the universe.]

"Can an Arhat fall from grace? Can he be guilty (unwittingly or through diabolic temptation) of indecency? Can he have ignorance, doubt, or error? Is there moral restraint among the gods?" "To all these questions, No" [unanimous].

"Is the Noble Path self-existent? or the Chain of Causation? or the Four Noble Truths? or Nirvana?" Again "*No.*" [And yet these four things are the very groundwork of S'akyamuni's| personal teachings. The very foundations of the Buddhist Faith had gone!]

"Is Nirvana a virtuous (moral) state?" "No."

There are also some, very interesting points raised in what we may perhaps call "Buddhology."

"Was Buddha a true man?" Yes," [said most of the sects; but one sect affirmed that this was not so. The Buddha had remained all the time in the Tushita Heaven, and that which appeared upon earth was only a phantom. It was exactly what, at that very moment, heretics further west were saying about Christ !].

"Did Buddha himself preach the Law?" "No," said one sect; he never preached. It was Ananda that preached. [It was Ananda, it will be remembered, whose memory supplied so many of the Sūtras after the death of S'akyamuni].

"Did the Councils alter S'akyamuni's doctrines or make it afresh ? " [With one dissentient voice they all agreed that they had so tampered with the deposit of the Faith.]

"If there should be another Buddha, would it be possible for him to be born out of India ? " "Impossible," said they all; "a Buddha can only be born within the limits of Jambudvīpa." [And accordingly the Japanese, who want to have their share in everything that is great, have extended the limits of Jambudvīpa (Ichi-Embudai) to include China and Japan as well.]

The lowest depth was reached by the question, "Were the Buddha's excretions of exceeding sweet savour ? " And to this some answered one thing, and some another.

CHAPTER XI

As'vaghosha

EVERYBODY in Japan reckons As'vaghosha as the founder of the Mahāyāna Faith, and yet there is not a single Mahāyāna sect in Japan which traces its official lineage back to him. They all go back to Nāgārjuna, who is made to be responsible for very great varieties of doctrine; and one or two of them will then add, in a parenthetic and half apologetic manner, that As'vaghosha said something of the sort.

The Zen teachers give him in their list of Patriarchs [1] of the Mahāyāna, but do not in any way treat him as one of the pivots of their system. The mystic Kegon, now practically non-existent, spoke of As'vaghosha as their founder, in the sense that the germ of their teachings may be found in him who first roused his fellow-religionists to faith in the Mahāyāna, then coming into the world; but their doctrines they derived, through Nāgārjuna, from some mysterious books said to have been brought by that saint from some " Dragon's palace under the sea." And the believers in salvation by faith in the vow of Amida,

---

[1] It is noteworthy that there are great discrepancies in these lists. Suzuki (" Awakening of the Faith," p. 33) quotes five lists. In most of them As'vaghosha comes about eleventh or twelfth, with Nāgārjuna thirteenth or fourteenth. But in the list given by the Sarvāstivādins As'vaghosha is 12 and Nāgārjuna 34.

while acknowledging that the first signs of that faith are to be found in As'vaghosha's treatise, yet make Nāgārjuna the first in their list of Patriarchs.[1]

There is a great deal of uncertainty about As'va-ghosha's life. His advent is said to have been foretold by Buddha himself, but Suzuki,[2] who has written a very full and candid account of As'vaghosha, quotes a passage from a book claiming to be written by Nāgārjuna, in which it is stated that, in order to fulfil all the prophecies concerning him, there must have been six As'vaghoshas, each of whom "appeared to fulfil his mission according to the necessity of the time, and there is no contradiction in them." (Nāgārjuna's book was translated into Chinese in A.D. 401.) According to the first of these prophecies, As'vaghosha had been a disciple of Buddha in his earthly life. When the Buddha was telling his disciples of his approaching Nirvana, he had asked to accompany him, and then, "gazing at the pupil of Buddha's eye, had passed out of life." In the next prophecy, Buddha is said to have told As'vaghosha that *three hundred* years after the Nirvana, he would obtain an inspiration from him which would be for the happiness of mankind. According to another, he was to come *six hundred* years after the Nirvana to confute the heretics. A fourth prophecy places him in the *eighth century* after the Nirvana; a fifth brings him back to *one hundred* years. A sixth represents him as having appeared to Buddha, seventeen days after his Enlightenment, in the form of a monster serpent with 86,000 heads and 86,000 tongues, and to have asked the Tathāgata 86,000 questions all at once. This sixth legend was evidently invented to bolster up the pretended revelations of the Kegon Scrip-

---

[1] See translation of the *Shōshinge* in " Shinran and His Work."
" As'vaghosha's Awakening of Faith." Chicago, Open Court.

tures, but it is not without its significance for the contemporary Ophite Gnosticism.

A similar uncertainty hangs about the name and place of birth. As'vaghosha[1] is the most common of his designations; but in Chinese books he is sometimes Punyaditya, or Punyaśrika, while in Thibetan he has at least eight other names. His place of birth is sometimes Ayodhya, sometimes Pataliputra, but Benares puts in a claim, and so do South India and Khorta.

All accounts agree in saying that he was a Brahman by birth; that he wandered through many parts of India searching for knowledge; that he eventually fixed his residence at Benares, where he acquired considerable reputation as a deep scholar and skilled reasoner. He was a pillar of Brahmanism, when, for reasons unknown, he was converted to the Hīnayāna. As a Hīnayāna monk he acquired a great reputation for sanctity.

The latter half of the first century was a period of trouble, and not for India only. The Scythians, who had long threatened the north-western frontiers, at last made their anticipated invasion. The year 50 saw the overthrow of the last Greek princelet by the Scythian king, Kadphises I., who also a little later overthrew the power of Gundaphorus of the St. Thomas legend. His successor, Kadphises II., extended his power down the valley of the Ganges as far as the gates of Benares, which he reached between 85 and 90 A.D.[2] The whole of India was in the tumult of war. The Scythians were on the move from Bactria to Benares, the Chinese under Panchao were

---

[1] Chinese, *Maming*; Japanese, *Memyō*. As'vaghosha means the Neighing Horse, and it is striking that he is in certain Japanese books connected with the "White Horse," which is one of the forms he is said to assume, *e.g.* in amulets.

[2] Smith, "Early History of India."

marching to the shores of the Caspian Sea, the Parthians were restless, there was war on the eastern frontiers of the Roman Empire. The White Horse of the vision had been succeeded by the red, black, and pale steeds.

Benares, it is said, was saved by the sanctity of As'vaghosha. The Scythian king lay at its gates. He was willing to spare it, but he wanted money, and he also desired to impoverish the Magadhan kingdom. So he laid upon Benares a fine of enormous dimensions. The King of Benares declared himself unable to pay it. "Then," said the Scythian king, "give me Buddha's Begging-bowl and the person of your great sage As'vaghosha." (An alternative story adds a "compassionate fowl" which would not drink dirty water for fear of killing the insects in it.[1]) Thus As'vaghosha and the Begging-bowl of Buddha saved Benares.

It has been said that it is unlikely that the Scythian king should thus accept a monk and a bowl in lieu of the heavy ransom which he had at first demanded from the city of Benares. Yet there is a good deal to be said in favour of its probability. The Scythian king had, by virtue of his recent conquests in Afghanistan, the Indus valley, Punjaub, and the Northern-Western Provinces, become the ruler of a great Buddhist kingdom, and the Buddhist provinces of his empire were about to be increased by the conquests in Central Asia which took place a few years later. Kadphises II. (if it were indeed that

---

[1] The "compassionate fowl" I have found in Japanese sources, besides those mentioned by Suzuki. It is said that As'vaghosha not only appeared in the forms of a thousand white horses, but that he also caused a thousand white birds to sing, *Issen no hakuba to genji, issen no hakuchō wo nakashimu*. It is said of him that he was a manifestation or temporary incarnation of Dai Kōmyō Nyorai, "the great Tathāgata of Light," an expression which some explain as Vairoc'ana, others as Amitābha

monarch) was, in fact, the greatest Buddhist monarch of the world. The Begging-bowl, however, which is the prototype of the Holy Grail of the Arthurian legend,[1] was the holiest of all relics of the Buddha, and its possession, like the Sacred Sword[2] and Mirror of the Japanese Imperial House, brought with it the recognized spiritual headship of the whole Buddhist world. Neither Balkh, nor Peshawur, nor any other city that the Scythian king might choose for his capital, could hope to be the centre of Buddhism so long as the Bowl remained at Benares. With the Begging-bowl in his possession, the Scythian king might safely assert that the headship of the Buddhists had been transferred to him. The Bowl meant very little to the King of Benares, for the Hīnayāna was losing its prestige, and already that Hindu reaction had set in which well-nigh expelled Buddhism from the soil of India. To the alien ruler of recently annexed Buddhist provinces, its possession was beyond all price important.

As'vaghosha's conversion to Buddhism has been variously described. According to one story, he was converted by the singing of a bird, whose notes sounded like the praises of Buddha. According to another, he found, in a Buddhist book, a prophecy of Buddha's in

---

[1] I will remind Celtic readers of the Welsh tradition preserved in *Barddas* that their ancient religion came to them from Taprobane, or Ceylon. In that case, it is within the bounds of possibility that the Arthurian legend may have been an adaptation of the Indian one, with Arthur as S'akyamuni, and Modred as Devadatta.

[2] In Japan, the possession of the sword, mirror, and jewel makes their owner the legitimate sovereign. When the empire was for a few years divided between two rival lines, the legitimate line was recognized by these tokens, though it was the other line which eventually won the day. The Huns had the same tradition about the sword. But theirs had been lost for centuries (can it have been in Japan?), and was discovered accidentally and brought to Attila. The possession of this sword made Attila the recognized chieftain of all the Huns.

which his own name was mentioned. According to a third, which comes from Thibet, he was converted by Āryadeva, a prominent disciple of Nāgārjuna's, not by argument or reasoning, but by a liberal display of magic arts. According to a fourth, which agrees with Thibetan as well as with Chinese authorities, he was reasoned into belief by Pārśva, or Punyayaśas. These two men were As'vaghosha's immediate predecessors in the list of Patriarchs. Of the five lists given by Suzuki, three have Pārśva, Punyayaśas, As'vaghosha as consecutive Patriarchs ; two omit Punyayaśas, and go straight from Pārśva to A'svaghosha. It is possible that Pārśva and Punyayaśas are one and the same person.

It may be that there is some truth in each of these stories. As'vaghosha was a poet,[1] and his poetical imagination may have been awakened and turned to Buddhism by the song of a bird. He would be neither the first nor the last man whose conversion has been due to a bird's song or a beautiful piece of scenery. Thus converted, he passes over from the Hindu worship of Mahes'vara to the faith of S'akyamuni, only to find that the Hīnayāna, seen from within, was not all that his fancy had painted it from without. He would not be the first idealist that has found his dreams destroyed by the disappointments of the actualities. And yet we may imagine that in this period of his life he may still have done good service to his new faith by the publication of the *Vajrasuci*,[2] in which he combats the mistaken Hindu theory of caste.

So far we may presume his literary activity to have gone in his Benares days. But following in the train of the Scythian monarch, he finds himself, in the dominions

---

[1] As'vaghosha's great poem is the *Buddhacarita*, of which there is a translation in *S.B.E.*, vol. xix., but there are some other minor poems as well, in praise of Amida.

[2] See *Journal Asiatique*, Ser. X. vol. xii. p. 1 (July, 1908).

of the conqueror, among what M. Sylvain Levi[1] calls "des cultes, des rites, des usages inconnues." His new companions are still Buddhists, but they have brought with them from Bactria, Turkestan, Khotan, new ideas, foreign to the Hīnayānists of Benares. Again his imagination is kindled; he recognizes in Pārśva a dialectician greater than himself, in Aryadeva, the master of a magic more powerful than any that he knows of, and he accepts the new and enlarged faith, and becomes its first great exponent.[2]

In truth, there were, in germ, in the new Buddhism which was then coming into shape in the Indus valley, three modes of expression which must all be taken into account, if we would understand the Japanese Mahāyāna of to-day. They not confined to Buddhism: they are found in Gnosticism, in Hinduism, in Christianity; they are, in fact, universals of religion. They may, for brevity's sake, be termed the Way, the Truth, and the Life; the appeal to the affections, the intellect, the spiritual imagination of Faith.

The new Life imported into Buddhism, connected, as we have seen, with the Gnosis of the Egyptians, and profoundly influenced by the Magianism of Bactria, was quite ready to assert its claim to supernatural powers. It rested with As'vaghosha, while re-asserting the half-forgotten claims of S'akyamuni, to provide a philosophic basis for the polytheistic conceptions of the mixed multitude of the North-West, and thus to commend to the people of Hindustan the spiritual authority of the new Truth proclaimed by the new possessors of the Buddha's Begging-bowl.

---

[1] See *Journal Asiatique*, Ser. X., vol. xii. p. 1.

[2] As'vaghosha's great works are the "Awakening of Faith" and the "Book of Great Glory." See Suzuki, *op. cit.*

It is noteworthy that in doing so he opens the Way to Life, which a large and constantly increasing school of Northern Buddhism has from the beginning interpreted as being Faith in one who is greater than S'akyamuni.

"Therefore" (these are almost the last words of his Discourse on the Awakening of Faith), "it is said in the Sūtra that if devoted men and women would be filled with concentration of thought, think of Amitābha Buddha in the world of highest happiness in the Western region, and direct all the root of their good work toward being born there, they will assuredly be born there. Thus always seeing Buddhas there, their faith will be strengthened, and they will never relapse therefrom. Receiving instruction in the doctrine, and recognizing the Dharmakāya of the Buddha, they will by gradual discipline be able to enter upon the state of truth." [1]

It is surely significant that at this particular period in the world's history the very first book which describes itself definitely as belonging to the Mahāyāna should end with a recommendation to faith in one who bears such a strange resemblance to Christ.

[1] Suzuki, *op. cit.*, p. 145. It is not known what Sūtra is here mentioned, but it is generally supposed to be the Sukhāvati Vyūha. If so, this is the earliest mention of the book, as it is also the earliest mention of the name of Amitābha. For the development of the doctrine of Amitābha, I will refer the reader to my "Shinran and His Work"; also to Haas, "Amida unsere Zuflucht" (Leipzig: Dietrich, 1910). The allusion to "seeing Buddhas" is capable of two interpretations, for the word for Buddha may be singular or plural. If singular, then it refers to Amitābha; if plural, it refers to the many inferior Buddhas, who are treated as so many "members" (*bunshin*) of the True Buddha Amida, who in the Sūtra of Forty-two Sections is treated as superior to all Buddhas. The Japanese Shingonists, who make Vairoc'ana to be the Supreme, say that Amida is identical with him.

The Dharmakaya is that spiritual body of Buddha which is capable of being spiritually present everywhere. The conception is not unlike that of the Christian "Real Presence" of Christ.

The name of Pārśva who converted As'vaghosha to the Mahāyāna gives a clue to As'vaghosha's date. For Pārśva was the chairman, or at any rate an active member, of Kanishka's Great Council which took place at Jhālamdara early in the second century. We may therefore, with a certain amount of confidence, place As'vaghosha about the year A.D. 80 or 90, some twenty or thirty years after St. Thomas, and about the same period before Kanishka's Council.[1]

---

[1] I would refer my readers to Professor Anesaki's article on As'vaghosha in vol. i. of Hasting's Encyclopædia of Religion and Philosophy, and to a long article by M. Sylvain in the *Journal Asiatique* for July and August, 1908.

CHAPTER XII

NĀGĀRJUNA

WE may consider that As'vaghosha, a native apparently of Saketa, and for many years a resident of Pataliputra or Benares (probably the latter), brought into the newly formed, or reformed, Mahāyāna a certain Magadhan or Central Indian element. We may suppose that a sage of his wisdom, learning, and reputation would do much to strengthen the dying cause of Hīnayāna Buddhism in the very land of its birth, by raising it to a higher level of aim and endeavour, and to nobler because truer views of life and duty.

But the Kushan or Indo-Scythian rulers, in their newly awakened zeal for the propagation of a religion with which seemed to be bound up their hopes of the over-lordship of the fair peninsula of Jambudvipa, where they might rule in peaceful possession, no matter what might be the disturbances raised by Huns and Alani on their far distant Central Asian frontiers, were by no means contented with spiritual influence on the Ganges plains alone. All India, they might reasonably argue, ought to be won to the reformed Buddhism of which they were the acknowledged heads, as the possessors of Buddha's Begging-bowl. If India could thus be won to spiritual allegiance, the temporal allegiance would not be far off. Only, to win all India, there must be a religious platform which all India could accept.

In Nāgārjuna they found a man admirably suited for the carrying out of their designs of recommending their enlarged faith to the spiritual conscience of India. A Brahman by birth, he was born, somewhere about the beginning of the second century,[1] in Southern India. As a Brahman, he was one of the hereditary exponents and custodians of religion and faith, but seems at first to have had but scanty reverence for his privileges. He went the way of "gilded youth," threw himself into a life of dissipation, and thoughtlessly profaned his birthright. But one night he and three of his companions broke into the palace of the Rajah, partly for robbery, partly for intrigue with the ladies of the princely harem, and were discovered. Nāgārjuna managed to escape in safety, but his three companions were taken and killed.

This was the turning-point in his career. Why had he been saved, while his companions, no more culpable than himself, had been overtaken by the vengeance of man, if not of Heaven? He recognized in his escape the hand of some unseen Providence, and from that moment determined to walk worthy of his sacerdotal birthright.

But the Brahmanism of the day (we must remember that it was not yet the reformed and elevated Brahmanism which at a later date drove Buddhism out of India) failed to satisfy him, and he turned to Buddhism. This too— it was the distracted Hīnayāna—failed to give him rest. He read books without end, yet arrived not at the truth, until at last he went as a wandering religionist to the country of the Nāgas, among the Himalayas, where he found peace and guidance.

---

[1] There is no definite date to be given for Nāgārjuna, about whom, as about As'vaghosha, there are many legends. But he took part in Kanishka's Council (so it is said), and in that case his birth must have taken place about the time I have assigned for it.

A Japanese writer,[1] in whose conscientious scholarship I have learned to put much confidence, says that his first journey was to a shrine of Ādi-Buddha (一 佛), whom Japan looks upon as Amitābha, the Supreme and Original Buddha, from whom, as from a source, comes everything that is called Light in the human mind. Ādi-Buddha is essentially a Himalayan cult, and it would be among those mountains, if anywhere, that Nāgārjuna would meet with such a teaching. At this shrine he made the acquaintance of a Bodhisattva of the name of Mahānāga (Dai-ryū), who taught him the faith in Amida Buddha, and finding him an adept in spiritual understanding, conducted him to the Palace of the Dragons (Nāgas) under the sea, and there revealed to him treasures of wisdom and doctrine which had been kept hidden for long generations, but which could now be communicated to men, inasmuch as the destined [2] expounder of the secret doctrine had at length appeared.

From the Himalayas Nāgārjuna went again to the south of India. Here he had a similar experience, one which we should be justified in treating as being the same as the one mentioned in the previous paragraph were it not that the treatment of the Japanese Mahāyāna requires that we should consider them as separate phenomena. In Southern India he is said to have found an Iron Tower (a shrine of some sort, we may suppose, like the shrine of St. Thomas at Mailapûr) in which dwelt an aged Bodhisattva of the name of Vajrasattva (Jap. Kongōsatta). Vajrasattva was the authorized exponent of a teaching which emanated from a Buddha named Vairoc'ana, who was greater than S'akya-

---

[1] Tada Kanae, "Shōshingekōwa," p. 225.

[2] In the *Lankāvatāra Sūtra* (Jap. Ryōgakyō) Shaka is made to prophesy the appearance of Nāgārjuna six hundred years after his Nirvana.

muni. Vairoc'ana claimed to be the *one*, the *original* Buddha, just as Amitābha did; and yet the two seemed to be different. Nāgārjuna listened with sympathy: Vajrasattva recognized that his spiritual successor had arrived, committed the secret Teachings to him, and gave him the rite of Abhis'ekha, a rite which is half Baptism and half Ordination.

We shall presently come back to these points. For the present we will merely summarize what we have said, and remind the reader that Nāgārjuna had personally "sampled" very much of the religious thought of India. He had been a Brahmanist and a Hīnayānist. He had then become a Mahāyānist, and since his conversion to that faith he had come into contact not only with the faith in Amitābha, but with faith in Vairoc'ana, with the Dragon's Palace, with the Iron Tower, with the Nāgas, and with the religionists whose special symbol is the Vajra.

He then retired to South India, where he spent the rest of his days in writing books and evangelization. The Japanese historians whom I have read say nothing about his connection with Kanishka's Council; they say that after long and successful labours he died at Kosála, in the northern portion of South India.

He was a voluminous writer (the reader will find a long list of his works in the pages of Nanjo's "Catalogue of the Tripitaka"), and his influence on Northern Buddhism has been so great that one is not astonished to read that he was revered by many as a second Buddha, a teacher whose authority equalled that of S'akyamuni himself.

He may be said to have settled, for Buddhism, the long-disputed question of the existence of the soul, which had troubled generations of Buddhist thinkers.

Buddhists had long been divided into *Astikas* and *Nāstikas*, the one party maintaining, with the Sarvāstivādins and others, the existence of the soul, the reality of life after death, the existence of an Oversoul, and the other denying all these things, and in some cases even allowing to material substances no more than a phenomenal existence. Nāgārjuna's philosophy mediated between the two views. The Madhyamika system, of which he was the interpreter, taught that the soul might be said to exist or not to exist, according to the way in which you looked at it. The soul of the individual is like the wave of the sea, it has an apparent separate existence for a moment, then it disappears in the body of the ocean once more. It was never a distinct entity. So with the Buddhas: they appear in the world, and we look upon them as individual Beings. But that is all only apparent. Buddhas and Saviours are but waves that appear on the surface of the ocean of God's love. They come and they go, and men talk of their deaths or their Nirvanas; but the ocean of God's love is unchanged. Only the surface waves have changed. It was thus that Nāgārjuna was able to recognize the essential oneness of Amitābha, of Vairoc'ana, of S'akyamuni. It was thus that the Mahāyāna faith, of which he was the great doctor, was able to adapt itself to the Taoism of China, to the Shinto of Japan. It was thus that the Buddhist gnosis of the second century tried to overthrow the Christian faith of the Catholic Church. Docetism is nothing but the Madhyamika doctrine applied to the problem of getting rid of the offence of the Cross and the uniqueness of Christ.

Nāgārjuna did not reject the teachings of either Astikas or Nāstikas. He divided Truth into two parts, an apparent truth and a true truth, a distinction which is constantly cropping up in Japanese Buddhism. The one, *Zokutai*, is

" truth by general consent," the truth as held by Nāstikas, who believed that nothing existed. The other, *Shintai*, is " true truth," the fulfilment of truth, which was to make perfect that which the Astikas held in part only. The one is the absolute Truth, the other is the Truth adapted to the mental and spiritual circumstances and capacities of the hearers. The distinction is to be found in every Buddhist sect in Japan; it underlies the distinction between the two classes of hearers in Manichæism. Was it not the whole contention of the Gnostics that ordinary Christianity was but a form of *Zokutai*, a " truth by common consent," and that they themselves were the possessors of the *Shintai*, " the true Truth," the perfect Gnōsis ?

Nāgārjūna is further credited in Japan with having taught that there are two ways of life, the one a road of difficulty and pain (*nangyōdō*), the other one of ease and pleasure. In the first, the aspirant after salvation takes the hard road of asceticism, of fastings and penance, etc., and thus labours to work out his own salvation; in the second, he throws all his own efforts aside, puts his faith in One who has effected salvation for him, and so, like a ship with a stout sail and a favourable wind, attains the haven of his hopes.[1] It is for this reason that Nāgārjuna is considered by all the Amitābha sects in Japan as the great Founder, after S'akyamuni, of their Faith. For, in deed, the " Faith in Another " is Faith in Amida. Amida is the One Original Buddha (*ichi-Butsu*, *hon-Butsu*), besides whom there is none other, and who has had no beginning. He has manifested himself time and again to men ; in the *Sukhāvati Vyūha*, for instance, there is a list given of eighty-one such manifestations. At the last

[1] See my "Shinran and His Work," p. 51. I have in that book very fully discussed the doctrinal bearings of the Faith in Amida.

he manifests himself as a person whom the Japanese call
Hōzō Biku, makes a vow for the salvation of man, and
works it out until he has established a Paradise where he
himself reigns in power, and into which all may enter
who have the faith to call upon him. Nāgārjuna does not
claim to have invented this doctrine. He claims to have
found it, and we know that the doctrine must have existed
in India before A.D. 147, for we know that in that year
the Sukhāvati Vyūha was taken by two men, Anshikao and
Lokaraksha, to China. We may safely say that Amidaism
was a portion of the faith of Mahāyāna Buddhism from
the middle part of the second century. Before that time
our notices of it are somewhat vague. Nāgārjuna may be
considered, by his clearly announced doctrine of salvation
by Faith, to have laid, as far as Indian Buddhism is concerned, the foundation of that Third Vehicle which may
be said to be the One and True Mahāyāna.[1]

---

[1] Japanese very often divide the doctrines of S'akyamuni into three
Vehicles. These are sometimes called the Hīnayāna, the Apparent
Mahāyāna (*i.e.* of the Abhidharmas), and the True Mahāyāna (in which
there is always salvation by faith, though the object of faith may be
Amida, Vairoc'ana, S'akyamuni, or all the Buddhas). At other times
they are also spoken of as the Vehicles of S'ravakas, Pratyekabuddhas,
and Bodhisattvas, and this is the view taken in the Saddharmapundarika.

If we turn to Irenæus, whom we may consider a somewhat younger
contemporary of Nāgārjuna's, we get the first mention of the Ophites,
a Buddho-gnostic sect, known by various names, such as Naassenes,
Peratæ, Marcosians, etc., all of whose doctrines are very similar. Perhaps
the best account of these sectaries will be found in Hippolytus, "Ref.
omn. Hær.," bk. v. These men, he says, assert that the beginning
of all things is "a Man and the Son of Man" (a term which will apply
either to Amida, or to Christ, or to S'akyamuni); that he has three
bodies—spiritual, psychic, material (which is true both of Amida and
of S'akyamuni); that he has three natures—one that of the blessed
man above, of Adamas (Sans. Ajita), which is true of Amida; a second
a mortal one, below on earth; and a third, which is above and has no
king over it (Hippolytus, *op. cit.*, bk. v. pp. 150–151, ed. Migne). This
"Man and the Son of Man" has appeared in various parts of the

Nāgārjuna is also treated by Japanese Buddhists as having been the first man to bring into Buddhism a set of doctrines known as the Avatasaṃka or Kegon. The Kegon no longer exists in Japan as a separate organization, but its views still influence a great many writers, and the Kegon Sūtras have had more influence on Japanese and Chinese religious art than any other set of the Sūtras of the Mahāyāna.

According to the Sanron[1] traditions (the Sanron is another sect, now extinct as a separate organization, which claimed Nāgārjuna for its founder), there were three collections of the Buddhist Scriptures made immediately after S'akyamuni's death. The orthodox party made one, within the cave of Rājagriha; the Mahāsanghikas made another, outside the cave or in another cave-monastery not far off. In the meantime, Manjuśri (or Ananda? *supra,* Chap. III.) and Maitreya, who never appear in Hīnayāna books as disciples of S'akyamuni, but who are very active debaters in the Mahāyāna Sūtras, formed a third collection which contained true Mahāyāna books. The volumes of this collection had been gradually coming down into the plains for some years, from their hiding-places among the Himalayas and by the Anavatapta Lake, and thus, little by little, had been sown in men's hearts, as they were able to bear them, the doctrines of the Mahāyāna as expounded by the Kegon. To Nāgārjuna the honour had been reserved of bringing the whole collection to light

earth, each part having its own gods and saviours and godlike men. Such a one was Jesus, surnamed Christ, a Man with three natures, three bodies, three powers, who came upon earth in the days of Herod (pp. 176-7).

The Ophites also maintained that there were three churches — spiritual, psychic, material—an arrangement which again suggests the three Vehicles of the Mahāyāna.

[1] Nanjo, "Twelve Buddhist Sects," p. 51, etc.

through the kindness of the great Nāga sage at the Shrine of Ādibuddha.[1]

But the world was not worthy of this high doctrine collected by Manjuśri and Maitreya. The Avatamsaka Scriptures consist of six different texts. Two of these have never been written. They have been "kept," says Nanjo,[2] "by the power of the *dharani* or holding of the great Bodhisattvas, and not written down upon palm-leaves." The third and fourth were kept in the Dragon Palace under the sea,[3] and not "committed to the men of Jambudvîpa." The fifth was taken from the Dragon Palace by Nāgārjuna and transmitted to the men of India. A portion of it was taken to China by Anshikao and his companions.[4] The sixth reached China between

[1] See Introduction to Saddh. in *S.B.E.*, vol. xxi. p. 1. The Gandhavyūha is another name for Kegon. The Nāgas were tribes of Indians who worshipped the serpent (*nāga*), and always appear as the protectors of Buddhism. The terms *Ophite* and *Naassene* are etymologically the same as Nāga; and it is noteworthy that while Nāgārjuna is getting his inspiration from a Nāga sage, the Ophites in the Roman Empire (see Irenæus, p. 110, ed. Migne) should be proclaiming in a like manner the "Wisdom of the Serpent." In "Asiatic Researches," vol. x. p. 83 foll., mention is made of a Christian king in India, Vijaya, who lived A.D. 77, and was very possibly a Gnostic. He is spoken of as a Takshaka, a caste connected with the Nāgas. Christ is also spoken of as a Takshaka, "a carpenter," and the Takshaka Brahmans are supposed to have been Christians originally. That there were Christians in India we know from the fact that Pantænus, the predecessor of Clement in the Catechetical School at Alexandria, found Christian communities and the Gospel of St. Matthew there in A.D. 189.

[2] Page 57.

[3] In the Manichæan Acts of Thomas, Thomas builds a celestial palace, which is fully described in a poem by Sarug (see *Z. d. m. G.*, xxv. 321, xxviii. 584). It is apparently a palace in the sea, for the words occur, "Ist es möglich ohne Grundlagen im Meere zu bauen?" The connection of the word Takshaka (see previous note) with Christians on the one hand, and Nāgas on the other, suggests the possibility that the poem is dealing with some of the common folklore material used by Buddhists and Gnostics alike.

[4] Nanjo's "Cat. Tripitika," No. 102.

I

317–420 A.D., having been translated by Buddhabadra. It is said that As'vaghosha knew something about it, and that Nāgārjuna fully understood it. No other Indian teacher is connected with it, nor does it appear in China in a developed form until the commencement of the Tang period. In the same period, early in the eighth century, the Kegon reached Japan, where it had considerable vogue, but was afterwards swallowed up and amalgamated by the all-embracing Tendai.

The Kegon claims to be the first of S'akyamuni's preachings. It purports to have been delivered, during the first week after his Enlightenment, to seven assemblies in Heaven and Earth, all of which he addressed simultaneously without leaving his seat under the Bo-tree. It was delivered in a supernatural manner, and thus it came to pass that S'ariputra, Maitreya, Manjuśri, and other disciples of a much later date, came to be spiritually present at it. It was followed by teachings adapted to ordinary people, whom he led by five stages to the perfection which he had found in the spiritual hearers of his first teachings. The five stages are (1) "smallness," the doctrines of Hīnayāna, based on the Four Truths and the Twelvefold Chain of Causation, as explained in the Agamas; (2) "beginning," i.e. of the Mahāyāna, in which the disciple is shown the unreality of things; (3) the "perfection," i.e. of the Mahāyāna, which consists in the realization of the existence of the Bhūtatathāta, or the impersonal God; (4) "suddenness," i.e. the direct attainment of the knowledge of God by straight and direct intuition; and (5) "completion," or the absolute identity between God and the soul.[1] Thus step by step, according to the Kegon doctrines, were the believers led

---

[1] These stages are Sho (小), Shi (初), Jū (充), Ton (頓), En (圓). they are of considerable importance in the study of Tendai.

to the accomplishment of that perfection which S'akyamuni had seen before him at the moment of his Enlightenment. The doctrine was certainly held in China and
Japan. It has a Gnostic flavour. Whether Nāgārjuna
actually held it or not, I am not prepared to say.

The story of the visit to the Iron Tower is rejected by
all sects in Japan except the Shingon, who make it the basis
of their own teachings, and Nichiren, who was always plain-
spoken, did not hesitate to call Kōbō Daishi the "prize-
liar of Japan" (*Nihon no dai mōgo*) for maintaining the
truth of the story. I have already advanced reasons for
believing that the Shingon is a form of Egyptian Gnosticism, closely allied with Basilidianism and the ancient
religion of Egypt, and brought to Southern India by
Egyptian merchants during the first century of our era. I
need not repeat what I said. I should, however, add that
the Japanese Shingon retains what many other sects have
discarded—the practice of a species of Baptism, known as
Kwanjo. It is administered with water, it may be re-
iterated; it is considered efficacious against disease; it
may be administered vicariously on behalf of the dead.[1]
As regards its mode of administration, if the student will
give himself the trouble to read what Irenæus (lib. I.
cap. xxi.) says of the Baptism administered by the Marcosians, he will see a picture of the Shingon administration, with its manual gestures, its mystic incantations,
and even its opobalsamum or liquid unguents.

The truest disciples of Nāgārjuna [2] were to be found in

[1] I think this will be found to throw much light on St. Paul's words
in 1 Cor. xv. 29. The Sanskrit word is Abhis'ekha.

[2] Perhaps it would be profitable to note that, according to Shingon
writers, Nāgārjuna lived to be three hundred years old. For one century
he was a heretic (*i.e.* Brahmanist and Hīnayānist) : for one century he
taught the exoteric Mahāyāna ; for another century he was the apostle
of the esoteric Buddhism of the Shingon. A man who lives for three

the *Hossō* sect, founded by Hiouen Thsang after his return
to China from his pilgrimage tours in India.   Hiouen
Thsang was a worthy follower of S'akyamuni, a painstaking scholar, and a man of judgment.   We shall have
to consider his personality and doctrines later on.   The
sect which he founded has ceased to have any organic
existence in Japan.

hundred years may have several opportunities for radical changes of
opinion.

CHAPTER XIII

THE MISSIONARIES OF THE HAN

IF we could construct a comparative Chronological Table of the religious phenomena of Europe and Asia during the first two centuries, we should see that the next Buddhist mission (A.D. 147) coincided with a mission sent by the Kushan sovereigns to the Han emperors, partly, it may be, to carry out negotiations for a matrimonial alliance, and partly, no doubt, to arrange for concerted action for defence against the Huns and other barbarians who were threatening both China and India. Political negotiation and religious propaganda would seem to have gone hand-in-hand.

The two pioneer missionaries were Anshikao (who, from his rank as Prince of Parthia, may well have had some political commission) and Lokaraksha. The two arrived simultaneously at Lôyang, or, at any rate, with only a comparatively short interval between them; the rest came at intervals during the seventy years that still remained for the Han dynasty to rule. Six of them are mentioned by Nanjo,[1] but none of them can be compared for industrious translation with the first two. There must have been other missionaries as well: there are sixteen translations by unknown hands, and there must surely have been some missionaries whose methods were not literary. In all, ninety-six Sūtras were translated during the latter years of the Han dynasty, of which Anshikao

[1] Nanjo, "Catalogue of the Tripitaka," Appendix II.

claims fifty-six and Lokaraksha twelve. The other six men only produced twelve Sūtras between them.

The first notable point with regard to these pioneer missionaries is that none came from India proper, and, in particular, none from Magadha and the plains of the Ganges. Two were Parthians; three are described as coming from Thibet; one from the country of the Yuetchi; the others vaguely as from the Western region. They were all subjects of the Kushan kingdom, and had therefore all been more or less influenced by the Gandhāra Buddhism which had come in with the new era.

The leader of this successful mission to China was a Parthian prince known to us as Anshikao. His real personal name is not given (Anshikao merely means " Prince of the Ansi," *i.e.* Parthians), but it is said that he resigned his throne to his uncle in order to become a monk, and that he was the son of a famous king who had been the enemy of Trajan and the friend of Hadrian. All this enables us to identify him with Axidares, the son of Pachorus, whom his father had nominated to the Armenian throne, shortly after A.D. 100, thereby giving much offence to the Emperor Trajan. Pachorus' successor on the Parthian throne, his brother Chosroes, at once apologized to Rome for the error in judgment that Pachorus had made, deposed Axidares in haste, nominated his younger nephew Parthamasiris in his stead, and wrote to Rome begging for investiture on his behalf. But Trajan refusing to listen, Parthamasiris surrendered himself, and was at first treated with clemency, but was afterwards murdered about A.D. 115. There seems to be little doubt that the prince Axidares, deposed about A.D. 108 by his uncle, and ousted from his Armenian kingdom, after his brother's death, by a distant relative, retired to a cloister, as others have done who have experienced the sorrows of a vain world, and eventually, as an elderly man and a tried ecclesiastic, became the leader of the Buddhist mission to China.

But Axidares (may we call him by his title Anshikao?) was the nephew of Chosroes, and the son of Pachorus. He was therefore the nephew of King Tiridates, and consequently the nephew of that King of Armenia who had sent an invitation to the Apostle Thomas to preach the gospel in the Parthian dominions.[1]

"And here comes in the most remarkable incident in a remarkable story:—Tiridates had been a Mazdean priest, and was so strict an observer of Mazdean rites and ceremonies that, to prevent any possibility of defiling the element water, he, instead of taking the ordinary route and embarking at Antioch direct for Rome, insisted on making the long journey overland through the entire length of Asia Minor to the Hellespont, and thence round the head of the Adriatic to the Capital. His grand-nephew, Axidares, or Vargash, had taken orders in Buddhism. In his desire to quit the vanities of a life of royalty, whose instabilities mocked him at every step, he had found no refuge in Mazdeism and no place in which a sorely tried spirit could find relief. The preaching of the sage As'vaghosha had thrown a bridge over the chasm between Mazdeism and Buddhism, and the doctrines of Christianity as taught by St. Thomas had shown how superior to the bondage of the ceremonial law was the freedom inculcated by it as well as the new Buddhism. Buddhism, without breaking away from Mazdean tradition, offered in its conventional monasticism just that escape for which the soul of the sorely tried

[1] This and the following paragraphs I take from a kind review of my book "The Wheat amongst the Tares," published in *The Anglican* (Shanghai, June, 1909) by the late Mr. T. W. Kingsmill. See also *East and West* for July, 1911.

prince was longing; was it any wonder that it, with the prospect that it offered of converting a world, should have prevailed." [1]

"Already before the time of As'oka the logical void involved in the acceptance of Nirvana had led to the evolution of a Maitreya Buddha, the "Future Buddha" of Kindness, who was to mitigate the ills of an inflexible Karma; but the movement did not here end, and once started, its mere *vis inertiæ* carried it on. Pratyeka Buddhas, those who had without regard to others attained an individual Buddhahood, and Bodhisattvas, those whose progressive Karma was insensibly leading them along the "path" to Buddhahood, were the natural outcome of the movement, and of these, two—Manjuśri, the Gracious-one, and Avalokiteśvara, the Pitiful-one—gradually came to the front. At first only mental abstractions, the inevitable tendency was to segregate from the magma, and condense as personal Buddhas. In the process they came under the influence of the school of As'vaghosha, when Manjuśri easily was found to take the place of Çpenta Ârmaita, *Holy Wisdom*, and Avalokiteśvara in like manner of Khshathra Vairya, *Perfect Sovereignty*, both lieutenants of Ahura Mazda in ruling mundane affairs. So it was that when Amida came to take in the celestial hierarchy the place of The Buddha, seats beside him were found for the two great Bodhisattvas, Avalokiteśvara and Manjuśri."

Yet it is noteworthy that a very great portion of this literature thus early translated into Chinese is Hīnayāna.

---

[1] I quote another passage from Mr. Kingsmill's essay, because it seems to throw some light on the origin of that remarkable Trinity— Amida, Seishi, Kwannon, which plays such an important part in the later developments of the Mahāyāna. He traces the origin of these ideas to the religion of Parthia during the Arsacid sovereigns, a theory not at all inconsistent with the few traces we get of the worship of Amida in the time of Anshikao and his brother translators.

Many of the extra-Indian provinces of the Kushan Empire, Khotan to wit, and portions of Bactria, had been converted to Buddhism long before the commencement of the Mahāyāna movement, and, having been converted to Hīnayāna, remained constant to their allegiance, though sectarian differences, as well as the nature of the mountainous countries between them, cut them off from their Hīnayāna brethren on the southern slopes of the Himalaya. Besides, the dividing-line between the two Vehicles was hardly as yet sharply drawn.

We may therefore safely conclude that the second-century Buddhist mission to China was mainly an effort made by the Kushans to gain the friendship of that portion of the Chinese people that was predisposed to religion; that its members came from extra-Indian countries which had long since been Buddhist, and which had now passed under the sway of the Kushans; and that, whilst it contained the beginnings of Mahāyānism, it was in the main Hīnayāna.

The next thing that strikes us is the very elementary character of the Hīnayāna Buddhism that these men taught. There are some extremely elementary treatises amongst the Sūtras translated — tracts, for instance, on the Four Truths, the Twelvefold Chain of Causation, the causes of Pain, the duty towards parents, the punishments of sin, the rewards of Virtue. The publication of these tracts seems to show that the Buddhist missionaries were doing pioneer work on untouched ground. The previous mission of Kaśyapa Matanga and Dharmaraksha (if indeed it had been a Buddhist mission at all) had evidently died out completely, and these men had to begin again. It is only thus that we can account for the necessity of publishing these elementary treatises. It is not yet more than fifty years since the re-introduction of

Christianity into Japan, but the day for elementary
treatises is past already. We have our Bibles, our Testa-
ments, our Prayer-books, our Catechisms—all standard
books, in fact—in Japanese translations, and it would be
next to an impossibility that they should be swept away
even by a wholesale " destruction of books " such as the
Chinese indulged in.

Had the " Heralding of the Son of Man," [1] as I venture
to call it, been a permanent or successful Buddhist
mission, it would have left behind it literary memorials
which would have made it unnecessary for the successors
of those men to insist so much on the elements of
Buddhism, the more so as both missions seem to have
laboured in the same city of Loyang and its immediate
vicinity.

There are, however, certain very distinctly Mahāyānistic elements to be found in these ninety-six books of
the Han translators, and notably in the twelve books attributed to Lokaraksha, who comes from the country of the
Yuetchi, the very heart of the Kushan Empire. There
are likewise Mahāyānistic traces to be found in the
writings of Anshikao, who was very possibly a Parthian
hostage at the court of the Kushan kings.

Thus we find the use both of *mudrā* and of *mantra*, of
mystic gesticulations and of apparently meaningless

---

[1] I have already pointed out that the character for *Fo* or *Butsu* (佛)
consists of three elements, " man," " arrows," " bow."—a reminiscence
of Ming-ti's Vision, which bears a striking analogy to the three first letters
of our Lord's name. But the symbols for " arrows " and " bow " (弗)
are also used in combination, *e.g.* in translating the name S'ariputra
into Chinese, as an equivalent for the Sanskrit word *putra*, "a son."
Bearing this in mind, we shall see that the addition of the element
" man " (亻) which completes the whole compound (佛), produces a
word which may mean " Son of Man." See the Sūtra on the *True
Man* (Nanjo, " Cat. Trip.," No. 565).

formulæ of incantation.[1] These formulæ and practices, which have not as yet received much attention from scholars, are valuable to the student of religion as showing how far-spread was the use of cognate practices during the second century. We find the *mudrā* and *mantra* in Egypt; we find them in the Gnosticism of Asia Minor, *e.g.* amongst the Marcosians mentioned by Irenæus, in North-Western India, in China, and, in process of time, in Japan. The sacred language used for the mantras differs; in the West it is Hebrew, in the East it is Sanskrit; but the manual signs made by the worshippers are the same, as are also the seals or characters used conventionally to denote certain objects. One most interesting case in point is the so-called sixteen-petalled Imperial Chrysanthemum of Japan. Dr. Munro of Yokohama [2] has, as I have said, found it in Egypt on a tomb. It is also given in the newly discovered book of Jao [3] as a "seal," with its appropriate though meaningless mantra : it comes to Japan *viâ* China and appears at Kyoto as the "seal" of the god of Peace. In the twelfth century it appears as the *mon* or crest of the Emperor Toba, who was a religious-minded person, much devoted to the worship of the "god of Peace." It is to-day the Imperial Crest, sacred to the uses of the Imperial House. No subject may have it on anything that belongs to him; and yet, for the modest outlay of a halfpenny, he can procure at the (modern) Heian-Jingū, or Temple of the God of Peace, at Kyoto, amulets and charms, protective against evil, which bear the Imperial Chrysanthemum Crest.[4]

[1] Nanjo, "Cat. Trip.," Nos. 451, 478.

[2] In a lecture delivered before the Asiatic Society of Japan, in April, 1910.

[3] I. Book of Jao., cap. 12; in Schmidt's German translation, p. 269.

[4] Heian was the old name of Kyoto; it means "the city of peace," the haven of refuge to which Kwammu fled from the turbulence and intrigues of the Nara monks.

Another Mahāyāna trace will be found in the Sūtra on the use of Images of the Buddha, ascribed to Lokaraksha.[1] That it was not until the inauguration of the Gandhāra Buddhism that images were made to represent the Buddha and other prominent personages, is shown in Japan by the use of the term "Image Law" to denote the second phase of their religion. For five centuries after the Nirvana, so they say, the "Upright Law" continued. This was to be followed by a thousand years of "Image Law," after which should come the Age of the Destruction of the Law in which we now are. It was, apparently, the Image Worship of the Buddhists that incited the Confucianists to make images of their own revered master. The Buddhists were inspired by Gandhāra art, that art was Greek and Roman in its ideals, and thus it has come to pass that the art of China, and eventually that of Japan, has drawn its inspiration from Antioch and Alexandria.

Another trace, again, of the Mahāyāna teachings may be found in the presence of Buddhas and Bodhisattvas other than S'akyamuni. The Hīnayāna knows of S'akyamuni's predecessors, Five Previous Buddhas, as they are called. The Mahāyāna has many of them. In the "Sukhāvati Vyūha," for instance, which is one of the Han versions, there are eighty-one Buddhas previous to Hōzō Biku, who is afterwards known as Amitābha, besides a large number of Buddhas exercising their functions simultaneously with and independently of S'akyamuni. One of these is Akshobya, another Amitābha, the one representing the East, the other the West; the one that perfect wisdom which is unmovable because it rests firmly on the thought of Buddha, the other that same perfect wisdom which has run its course and destroyed its doubts, and so is at rest. Many new Bodhisattvas appear: S'ariputra,

[1] Nanjo, "Cat. Trip," No. 289.

Maudgalyâyana, Kâtyâyana, have not attained to Buddha-hood, but Samantaprabha, Manjuśri, Avalokiteśvara, Maitreya, Bhadrapāla, are all mentioned. Some of these are evidently human Bodhisattvas. Bhadrapāla, said to have been one of the few laymen to attain to the Bodisattvaship, is now sometimes installed in Japan as the patron-deity of a temple bathroom. Manjuśri and Maitreya, once fabled as disciples of S'akyamuni's, appear again in re-incarnations. The one appears in China at Wutaishan; the other, while dwelling permanently in the Tushita Heaven, is fabled at a later time to have come down on earth to preach for Asangha. Only Avalokiteśvara is an eternal Being. He is the son of Amitābha. He has no earthly history; he has come down to earth at divers times and in sundry manners, but always to help man. He is intimately connected with Maitreya, the Buddha of the Future, for whose coming Japan still waits.[1]

[1] It is said that the great Kōbō Daishi is still awaiting in his tomb at Kōya San the coming of Maitreya, the friendly one, to restore the old Faith to Japan. His body, it is said, does not decay, though from time to time he requires a new suit of clothes. Thousands of devout Buddhists lie buried round him at Kōya San. They want to be present when Maitreya comes to wake Kōbō from his sleep. That Maitreya and Avalokiteśvara are connected may be shown from the following mantra in debased Sanskrit, which I do not pretend to be able to understand, but which evidently contains both names : *Nobaratanno Tarayāya nōmaku Aryāvalokitei jimbaraya Bodhisattvaya Mahasattvāya Mahākiyaronikyāya taniyata on, Maitareyi, Maitararano sei maitarakiu babei maitrōto banbei mahamammaya sovaka. Om Maitreya sōvaka.* Christian imagination has always fixed itself on Maitreya as the type of Christ; but the Buddhist sees more clearly the analogies in Avalokiteśvara. Avalokiteśvara, they say, is the spiritual son of Amitābha, and it is only through Avalokiteśvara that Amitābha can manifest himself. Thus when Amitābha came down to fulfil his vow, he came as Avalokiteśvara under the earthly name of Hōzō Biku. And many Japanese have told me that Christ is an incarnation of this same Avalokiteśvara, the son of Amida, who is the one, self-originated, Buddha.

It is no longer the old canon of the Tripitaka that is in use. Kaśyapa's collection of the Tripitaka is discussed, as are also the charges against Ananda which kept him outside the first Council of the Sthavira held in the Rājagriha Cave after S'akyamuni's death. But Anshikao to some extent, and Lokaraksha almost exclusively, uses the third canon of the Scriptures, the collection fabled to have been made, independently of Sthaviras and Mahā-sanghikas, by S'ariputra and Maudgalyayana, parts of which were brought back to India by Katyāyana at the close of the last century B.C., and the remainder by Nāgārjuna from the Dragon's Palace. There is also some mention of the books which Nāgārjuna is said to have received from Vajrasattva at the Iron Temple in South India. There are selections from the Prajñāpāramitā, from the Avatamsakas, from Abhidharma S'āstras, all of which are books of late origin.

Five accounts are given of S'akyamuni's life. The Mahāyānists were as busy with the life of their Founder as were the Gnostics with their Apocryphal Lives of Christ. (The most advanced of higher critics will, I think, allow that the received Gospels had all been written before the latter half of the second century.) There is a striking resemblance between the Apocryphal Gospels and the Mahāyāna Lives of S'akyamuni. In both, the whole stress is laid on the events connected with the infancy. Only one of the Apocryphal Gospels, that of Nicodemus, deals with the Death of Christ. Not one of the lives of S'akyamuni taken to China by the Han missionaries touches on the Nirvana of the Buddha. The silence is not without its significance. Gnostic and Mahāyānist alike were by this time face to face with the higher claims of the Resurrection. The insistence on the mysteries of the Nativity of the Buddha may have seemed to be the right way to offset the Crucifixion of the "Son of Man" and the Gospel of His Resurrection.[1]

A great number of the Sūtras deal with quite practical subjects—the curse of drunkenness, the evils of impurity, the twelvefold chain of causation, the causes of death, the duty of kindness to children, etc. Many of this class are to be found in the various Agama Collections. Of those which deal with the life of S'akyamuni, from his birth to the commencement of his ministry, one especially, the *Adbhūta-dharmapariyaya* by an unknown translator, treats the whole subject in a theological and supernatural manner. Some introduce Bodhisattvas unknown to earlier Sūtras, *e.g.* Maitreya and Manjuśri, sometimes as interlocutors, and sometimes as principal exponents of the doctrines taught, and we may notice the gradual development of the Mahāyāna in the fact that whereas the Sūtra of Forty-two Sections constantly speaks of *Arhats*, the books translated by the missioners from Central Asia often speak of *Bodhisattvas*,[2] and there is a Sūtra given which contains an explanation of the office, duties, and

[1] In connection with the A.D. 67 Mission to China, it must be remembered that early in the first century a rumour was current in China that Sū Wang Mu, the goddess of the West, had given birth to a child who should be the Saviour of the world. This event is, as it were, crystallized in Buddhism, in the female *Kwan-yin*, the goddess of Mercy, who is so constantly represented with a babe in her arms. It is said of this babe that he was originally an enemy to Buddhism, but was afterwards converted. I seem to see in this a trace of that very early "heralding of the Son of Man" in China. It was merely a heralding, merely a preaching for a witness. The remaining converts of that early mission, or their descendants, may have offered some resistance to the Buddhist onslaught, and then in the end agreed to some compromise.

[2] *Arhat* is the Hīnayāna term for the full-blown disciple. In the Mahāyāna, such a person is termed a Bodhisattva, the distinction between the two consisting in the fact that the Bodhisattva's faith is the more altruistic.

privileges of a Bodhisattva. The new school of Prajñā philosophy is represented by a translation of the Prajñā Parāmitā Sūtra [1] in 10,000 couplets, but without Nāgārjuna's commentary, which was possibly not accepted until the following century (say about A.D. 220). Little is apparently said about the Previous Buddhas, but two of the Dhyāni Buddhas are mentioned, Akshobya and Amitābha, although the whole system of the Five Dhyāni Buddhas does not yet seem to have been elaborated.

Akshobya appears in the completed system of the Dhyāni Buddhas as the Buddha specially connected with the East. There is practically only one Sūtra devoted to him either in the Chinese Tripitaka or in the Thibetan Collection. I believe the Sūtra has never yet been translated into English, but a translation into modern Japanese has recently been published, which is, however, in its modern form, almost as obscure as the Chinese original.[2] Akshobya is especially connected with Manjuśri. He is the author of long life, and much worshipped by means of *Dharani*.

Amitābha we have mentioned before. It is claimed by the Buddhists of Japan that he was preached about by S'akyamuni himself during the last years of his ministry. After S'akyamuni's time he apparently vanished from Buddhist consciousness ; possibly he was taken across the Himalayas along with some travelling Buddhists, and so disappeared from the eyes of India. As'vaghosha [3] and Nāgārjuna both worshipped from afar ; with Anshikao and

---

[1] This work forms one of the great books of the Nepaulese Canon, which does not, however, seem to have been finally drawn up before the time of Vasubandhu, *circ.* A.D. 300.

[2] In a popular book called " Jusan Butsu no Yūrai " (Tokyo, 1908).

[3] For As'vaghosha, see Suzuki's " Awakening of the Faith," p. 146. Nāgārjuna is said to have died with his face directed to the Western Paradise.

Lokaraksha he reappears in a literary form, fully developed. As'vaghosha and Nāgārjuna would only know him by repute, as being natives of India proper; Anshikao and Lokaraksha, as coming from Central Asia, knew him more fully.

The doctrine of Amitābha is more fully developed now. When S'akyamuni consoled the Queen of Bimbisara he merely pointed her to Amitābha, whose mercies are Infinite, and who is ever near to comfort the distressed.[1] In the Sukhāvati Vyūha, nearly every Chinese translation of which is by Central Asian hands, Amitābha is strangely and significantly changed. He has (*more Buddhico* again) been *euhemerized*, so to say; his genealogy is given; he is practically God Almighty; but he was once a man, and his present high station as the Lord of the Western Paradise, the Father and Saviour of them that trust in him, the ψυχοπομπός meeting the soul at death and placing it in the mansion prepared for it, is all the result of a vow made countless centuries ago by a mere man, and pursued diligently through many lives, till it has resulted in the formation of a Paradise, and the opening of a salvation through Faith for them that invoke his name.

And, again significantly strange, more than a century after the Christian revelation, in a country in which Jews, Israelites, and Christians dwelt side by side with Buddhists and others, Amitābha is produced in literary form, developed into the first member of a quasi-Trinity. He is accompanied by his son, Avalokiteśvara, the bisexual expression of his mercy, who in many forms and as many persons, was manifested upon earth to save the suffering,[2]

[1] In the "Amitāyur-dhyāni Sūtra," *S.B.E.*, vol. xlix. With the help of some Buddhist friends, I have nearly completed an English translation of Lokaraksha's edition of the S.V.

[2] I have a small Japanese "Catechism of Kwannon," which states the doctrine about this deity very succinctly.

just as in the account of Peratæ and other Gnostics, given in the "Philosophumena,"[1] the Christ is manifested, in many forms and characters, with the Birth at Bethlehem among them, to give expression to the mercy of His Father. Avalokiteśvara (the "Lord that looked down") descended even into Hell to manifest the mercies of Amitābha; his companion Mahāsthāmaprāpta[2] is the embodiment of Amitābha's strength, the Spirit of Might, and the three together are a significant shadow of the Persons of the Christian Trinity. It is hard to avoid drawing an inference.[3]

[1] "Philosoph.," vi. 12.

[2] The Japanese *Seishi*. He is sometimes spoken of as having "destroyed death." He is not a very popular deity.

[3] I would strongly recommend, in connection with this chapter, a perusal of a paper by the late Dr. Rehatsek on "Christianity in the Persian Dominions," published in the Journal of the Bombay Branch of the Royal Asiatic Society, vol. xiii., 1877. It shows very clearly the knowledge of Christianity which Anshikao and his companion must have had.

CHAPTER XIV

DHARMAGUPTA [1]

ONE of the most important services that S'akyamuni rendered to his immediate disciples, as well as to posterity, was to supply them with a set of disciplinary rules of life. This discipline, known as the *Vinaya*, was not given in any formal manner. As the occasion arose the Master spoke his mind, and thus, little by little, during the long years of his ministry, there was formed as it were a *corpus* of miscellaneous rulings delivered without any definite plan or system. Yet there was no contradiction among these rulings, for it was one mind that gave them all, and that mind a singularly consistent and clear-seeing one.

What the Vinaya rulings lacked in system was, furthermore, more than compensated by the definiteness which came to them from the fact that in every case they were based on some real fact or some concrete difficulty. If the Sūtras—those I mean, such as most of the Agamas, which can be distinctly traced back to the life of the Master—give us a true picture of S'akyamuni's life, we cannot but conclude that his mind vacillated at times between two or more alternative sets of speculative doctrines. Is there a god? Is there such

[1] I take this chapter mainly from Gyōnen's sketch of the Eight Buddhist Sects in Japan ("Revue de l'Histoire des Religions," vol. xxv. p. 341).

a thing as a soul? Does the physical universe really exist, or is it all a mere illusion? On these points he spoke in such a way as to leave his followers the largest room for speculative differences, and if we are disposed (not being metaphysicians) impatiently to throw aside the speculations of Sarvāstivādins, Sautrāntikas, and all the babble of Hīnayāna sectarianism, if we find it difficult to see how the term "Buddhism" can be stretched wide enough to cover all the variations of the so-called Mahāyāna, we must remember that it was the studied vagueness of the Master's own teaching that gave his followers the boldness to wander so far afield in the wide daring of their later speculations.

From all this vagueness of the Sūtra pitaka the Vinaya pitaka was saved. When the Master gave rules to his communities for the sabbath meetings, for the confession of sins, for the admission of women, for the regulation of dress, etc., he was obliged to be terse, clear, and definite. The Vinaya rules, therefore, give us a more trustworthy picture of the Master's mind than do any of the Sūtras. They make us feel that we are dealing with the real Buddha, with the real community of monks.

It fell to the lot of Upali, the barber, to record, from his memory, at the orthodox Council at Rājagriha, the disciplinary decisions of his Master, and to form them into a connected whole. His collection met with favour, was adopted, and for more than a century was the authorized canon of discipline enforced by the successive Patriarchs—Kaśyapa, Ananda, Madhyantika, S'ānavasas, and Upagupta. Upagupta was a contemporary of As'oka's, and we know from some of As'oka's monuments that many corruptions had come into Buddhism by then, and that the monks were beginning to form cliques and

schisms and to withdraw from communion with their
brethren. Dharmagupta, Upagupta's successor, whom
we place, therefore, somewhere about B.C. 240 or a little
later, reformed the Vinaya by a new recitation,[1] and
thus withdrew his followers formally from communion
with the others. This, says Gyōnen (p. 343), was the
first schism.

After this the process of sect-forming went on very
rapidly, and each sect feeling itself justified in drawing
up a modified discipline of its own, it was not long before
there were twenty disciplines where originally there had
been but one.

We need not stay to inquire what these twenty
disciplines were. Only four of them reached China,
and these four were ultimately merged into one, the
survivor being a reformed edition of Dharmagupta's
reformed code.[2]

According to the Dharmagupta system of discipline,
a system which is still largely in vogue in Japan, though
the old Vinaya or Ritsu sect has long ceased to have
a separate corporate existence of its own,[3] the faithful
here on earth are divided into seven classes. At the
bottom of the scale come (i) the *Ubasoku,* and (ii) the
Ubai, laymen and laywomen, who, without leaving their
homes, desire to lead a life of religion. Of these persons
it was required that they should keep the five precepts—
not to kill, not to steal, not to be guilty of any form of

[1] The Sacred Books had possibly not yet been committed to
writing; they were orally recited, and the oral recitation must have
been a frequent cause of inadvertent error.

[2] These four were : (a) *Jūbunritsu,* the Vinaya (in Ten Recitations)
of the Sarvāstivadins ; (b) *Shibunritsu* (Four Recitations), of the
Dharmaguptas : (c) *Gobunritsu* (Five Recitations), of the Mahis'akas ;
and (d) *Sōritsu,* the Vinaya of the clergy.

[3] Early in the Meiji era the Government forced the Ritsu sect to
amalgamate itself with the Shingon.

lewdness, not to lie, to abstain from intoxicants. Further, on the sabbath day,[1] the prohibition of lewdness became the prohibition of even lawful sexual intercourse, and there were added a prohibition of the use of perfumes and oils, of dances and spectacular shows, of luxurious couches—of all things, in short, that might prove an incitement to the passions. To these was added as a counsel of perfection, not to eat at odd hours.

Above the Ubasoku and Ubai came (iii) the *Shami*, and (iv) *Shamini*, whom we may call the Buddhist *Endeavourers*.[2] These persons undertook to keep all the above rules permanently. They further added a rule which forbade them to receive gold, silver, or precious objects of any kind; they made a vow, that is, of Perpetual Poverty. Higher up in the scale came (v) the *Shiki Shamana*, a higher grade of ascetics, who added what are known as the Six Doctrines. They would not kill even a mosquito; they undertook to be scrupulously honest, even in regard to the smallest sums of money; they would not touch a woman; they would not tell even a white lie; they never drank fermented liquors; and they never took meals out of hours.

Finally came the full-fledged monks and nuns, (vi) the *Biku*, and (vii) the *Bikuni*. These, as the Vinaya came to be influenced more and more by Mahāyānistic ideas, were looked upon as candidates for the rank of Bodhisattva, and were consequently called upon to undertake the *Bosatsu Kai* or *Gusoku Kai*, the rules of the Bodhisattva, or the Complete Rules.

The Bodhisattva, in the Mahāyāna Conception, is the

---

[1] The observance of the weekly sabbath was one of the primitive features of Buddhism. The Buddhists of Japan are beginning to observe the day; perhaps in time to come they will do so still more.

[2] The Sanskrit word *S'ramana* has the idea of "endeavouring."

man who has arrived at the "jumping-off place" of life, if we may so call it. He might enter into Nirvana if he chose, but he does not choose. He is freed from the necessity of life and death; there is nothing to force him back to the monotonous wheel of life; but of his own free will, and moved by compassion for the ignorance and misery of his fellow-creatures, he deliberately chooses a continuance of his earthly existence in order that he may live for others and not for himself. Such is the by no means unworthy aim that is set before the Buddhist follower of the Mahāyāna Discipline.[1]

In order to reach to that end the candidate for Bodhisattvaship must observe a multitude of rules (250 for a man, 348 for a woman),[2] of which we may give the following summary account, taken, however, from sources posterior to the Wei period, and representing the system in its fuller developments.

There are four deadly sins for which there is no forgiveness in this life: sexual intercourse, theft, murder,

---

[1] It must be remembered that there are two kinds of Bodhisattvas and Buddhas—human and superhuman. *Ningen no uchi ni mo Hotoke ga ari, Bosatsu ga aru. Ningen igwai ni ni mo Hotoke ga ari, Bosatsu ga arimasu.* The superhuman Bodhisattvas, such as Avalokiteśvara and Mahāsthāmaprāpta, have no human history; they are essentially extra-human and unborn, and, though they may from time to time assume human or other forms, are incapable of death. But S'akyamuni is the example *par excellence* of a human Buddha or Bodhisattva. After his Enlightenment he might have passed at once into his Nirvana of Rest; but for the sake of suffering humanity he remained where he was. During the whole of his ministry he was a Bodhisattva, with power to lay down his life and to take it again whenever he chose. At his Nirvana he became a Buddha. The Japanese use the phrase *sokushinjōbutsu,* "'attainment of Buddhahood in the present body," to describe the state of the Bodhisattva who "need not return again" (*fu tai ten*).

[2] The 250 *Bosatsu Kai* are explained in the Bommōkyō (Brahmajālasutra).

falsehood. He who commits these sins forfeits all hope of the Bodhisattvaship for the present. These sins are known as *harai* (Sans. *Parājikā*).

Another set of sins, thirteen in number, are considered as very grave, though they do not altogether destroy the spiritual character of the sinner. They are (i) self-defilement; (ii) coming into contact with a woman; (iii) slander; (iv) self-praise, with a view to getting an increase of alms; (v) acting as a go-between in arranging a marriage; (vi) speaking evil to the clergy; (vii) calumnies against the clergy; (viii) disobedience to the orders of a religious superior; (ix) exciting another monk to such disobedience; (x) going to the house of a layman to cause quarrels; (xi) to disregard the wishes of the community and to cause divisions. Two more rules (xii and xiii) concerned the building of a house, with one's own money, or with the contributions of the faithful.

Another set of offences against the law of Poverty could only be removed by purificatory ceremonies. These concerned the prohibition of two coats, the one garment that is always to be worn even at home, unnecessary dishes, importunity in asking for alms, etc.

Again, others would necessitate a sojourn in Purgatory (*Jigoku*) before emancipation could be accomplished : white lies, duplicity, digging the earth, cruelty to animals, intoxicants, meals at unseasonable hours, etc.

Then followed minute rules for the deportment of the monks and nuns. The Vinaya sects laid great stress on the observation of these rules, for they said, again with a certain amount of truth, that if a man would follow the discipline of Buddha he would come to know of his doctrine.[1]

The Han translators had spoken only on *Sila*, or

[1] See Nanjo, " Twelve Buddhist Sects," p. 20.

Morality. Anshikao had translated a Sūtra, said to have been spoken by the Buddha himself, on "the lightness and heaviness of the sin of transgressing the *Sila*;" [1] and Ch' Huen had translated another which illustrated the Mahāyāna conception of the Sila by showing how the Bodhisattva (*i.e.* S'akyamuni in his earthly ministry) had kept the Six Parāmitās, or Cardinal Virtues of the Mahāyāna.[2] He, whose life was a pattern for the Buddhist monk, had shown (i) liberality and generosity; (ii) the morality of self-restraint and chastity; (iii) patience; (iv) steadfastness of purpose and energy in the pursuit of Truth; (v) self-collectedness and the power of meditative concentration of self; (vi) the power of applying to daily life the lessons acquired by the steadfast and thoughtful pursuit of the truth by a generous and pure mind.

But the Han translators had apparently been contented with a mere sowing of Buddhistic seed—another indication of the fact that they were truly the pioneers of Buddhism. They said nothing about discipline, and they had made no attempt to introduce into China the order of monks.

The great Han dynasty came to an end in A.D. 214, having held China in one way or another under its continuous sway ever since B.C. 206.[3] The assassination of the last Han ruler led to a prolonged civil war, at the conclusion of which we find China divided into the kingdoms of the Wei, the Wu, and the Shū. Buddhism had been before the people for several years now — fully seventy, if we reckon only from the time of Anshikao's

[1] Nanjo, "Cat. Trip.," No. 1112.
[2] *Ibid.*, No. 435.
[3] The Former or Western Han were in power from B.C. 206 to A.D. 25; the Latter or Eastern Han from A.D. 25 to A.D. 214.

mission. Several important events had taken place in China during that time. Perhaps the most significant was the arrival in China of a Roman mission which reached Lôyang by way of the sea, in A.D. 166, thus opening another route to China of which the Indians and Arabs soon learned to avail themselves.

The gradual desiccation of Central Asia, the process of the drying up of the waters, which laid waste the fertile plains of Khotan, Ferghana, Bokhara, and Transoxiana, and which drove forth to more happy lands the hosts of the barbarians, was in full swing. The Hans in China, the Kushans in India, were equally concerned in defending their territories against these dreaded invaders, and many embassies passed between them during the last half of the second era. It was the age which saw Pao Chao's noble sacrifice and his victory over his barbarous foes.[1]

After the fall of the Han dynasty and the division of China into three hostile camps, the Kushans sent no more embassies. It was useless to appeal for help to the helpless kingdoms of China. The Kushans themselves had suffered from the inroads of their enemies. In spite of temporary successes during the first decade of the third century, they lost ground rapidly and steadily; by 221 A.D. they were confined to Sind, Punjaub, Kabulistan, and Kashmir. Several of their fairest Buddhist provinces had been lost, and the hegemony of Hindustan was passing into other hands. The Andhras were in possession for the time being; the rise of the Imperial Gupta Dynasty was already a " coming event."

The short-lived Chinese kingdom of Shŭ has no

---

[1] Pao Chao's wife and mother fell into the hands of the barbarians, who placed them in the van of their army, and threatened to put them cruelly to death unless Pao Chao withdrew his forces. Pao Chao was in great distress, but the exhortations of his wife and mother prevailed, and he resolved to do his duty by his country.

importance for the Buddhist historian. It contained within its boundaries no already established centre of Buddhist teaching, and apparently attracted no missionaries. The southern kingdom of Wu will require a special note ; [1] to the translators of the Wei dynasty (A.D. 220–265) I will devote a few words as a fitting conclusion to this chapter.

There are only five names, responsible for seven Sūtras, and there are, besides, two Sūtras by unknown hands. Of the five men, two (Thân-ti and Ân-fah-hien, A.D. 254) come from the country of the Ânsi, *i.e.* Parthia, one (Po-Yen) from the Western Regions (Khotan), one (Dharmakâla) from Central India, and a fifth (Sangha-varman) from India *viâ* Thibet, or *vice versâ*. Three of these men brought with them the Vinaya of the Dhar-magupta School, which I have been explaining in this chapter, and thus laid the foundation on which in later years the Chinese and Japanese orders of monks were erected.

Of other subjects, outside of the Vinaya, they give us two volumes of the dialogues of which Buddhists are so fond, the Questions of Ugra (No. 23) and those of Surata (No. 43), a translation of the Sūtra of the Great Decease (No. 5, now lost); one on the Names and Surnames of the Seven Buddhas (No. 626) ; a treatise on Immortality as contained in the Abhidharma (No. 1278), and three translations of the Sukhāvatī Vyūha, of which only Sanghavarman's (No. 27) has survived.

It says much for the opinion that the Doctrine of Faith in Amitâbha is the true representative of the

[1] It was from the kingdom of Wu that Japan obtained its first acquaintance with Chinese letters, and especially with Confucianism. To this day the ordinary pronunciation of Chinese words in Japan is called *Go-on*, the *Wu pronunciation*. The Buddhists have a pronunciation of their own, known as *Kan-on*, "the pronunciation of *Han*," *i.e.* Northern China. The numbers are from Nanjo's Catalogue.

Japanese Mahāyāna.[1] We have already seen it dimly
in As'vaghosha; we have seen Nāgārjuna learning it
from the Nāga chieftain. In A.D. 147 the book containing that doctrine is taken to China ; before A.D. 250 *five*
versions of that book had been made. It looks as though
the Han and Wei missionaries were using the historical
S'akyamuni as a means whereby to point men to the
unhistorical Amitābha and his spiritual son, in whose
story there lies enshrined the essence of the story of man's
redemption as preached by St. Paul. The story of Amitābha was needed by those early missionaries of the faith
of S'akyamuni to give life to the otherwise dead rules
of the Dharmagupta Vinaya. Its historical counterpart
is now changing and quickening the dead bones of
Japanese Buddhism and preparing the way for what will
be one of the most remarkable conversions in the religious
history of the world.

From the fall of Han in A.D. 220 to the rise of the
Tang in A.D. 618, China was rarely united. For the
greater part of this period of four centuries, two, three,
four, even five or more dynasties ruled side by side, as
rivals and competitors, within the empire. It is almost
impossible to write a history of the China of the fourth
and fifth centuries ; it · is still more difficult to give
anything like an adequate description of the religious
policy of the conflicting states, or to trace, step by step,
the gradual growth or decline of Buddhist doctrines in
the whole empire during this period.

Some of the dynasties were influenced mainly by the

[1] The Japanese and Chinese Vinaya sects afterwards adopted Vairoc'ana as their central deity, and it was for this reason that they were
forced to join themselves with the Shingon. But Vairoc'ana and Amitābha are in idea identical. They both represent, in idea at least,
the "Son of Righteousness with healing in His wings," preached to the
Far East by Gnostics who used Buddhist terminology.

literati, who were, to a man, the followers of Confucius, and the enemies of everything that called itself a religion of the supernatural. Others, again, were Taoists from conviction, and others Buddhists or Taoists from conviction or policy. Occasionally attempts were made to unite these conflicting faiths. Thus we have, about A.D. 240, an attempt at unifying Confucianism and the Mahāyāna, by introducing the images of the *Wuti*, or Five Rulers (*i.e.* the five Dhyāni Buddhas), into the Temples of Confucius, made without success. An equally unsuccessful attempt forcibly to effect an amalgamation of Buddhism with the religion of Tao, in A.D. 555, was probably the measure which gave to the Japanese a few years later the idea of the *Ryobu-Shinto*, or amalgamation of Buddhism with Shinto, which lasted until the restoration of Meiji.

India, in the meanwhile, was undergoing many a political and religious convulsion, and the monks, persecuted by the Brahmans at home, took refuge in China, bringing with them each the books that had affected him in his native land, and translating them into Chinese for the benefit of the native peoples. It is interesting to turn over the leaves of the Appendix to Nanjo's Catalogue and analyse the lists of translators by dynasties, by books, and by the countries from which they came. Thus the translators of the *Wei* dynasty, which ruled at Lôyang from 220 to 265, come either from Central India or Parthia, but all bring with them the Vinaya books of the Dharmagupta sect of the Hīnayāna. Under the *Wu* (222–280) at Nankin, we get none but Central Indian monks, and scarcely any but Hīnayāna books, or at least books which, like the Dharmapada, belong equally to both Vehicles. The Western Tsin at Lôyang (265–316), with Dharmaraksha, as *facile princeps* of the band, give us mostly theological treatises of the Mahāyāna, from the pens of translators who come from Ansi, Khotan, and the western provinces of China proper. The former Lian, with capital at Kutsan (302–376), furnish but one book, translated by a man from the Yuetchi country. The Eastern Tsin (at Nankin, 317–420) give us a long list of translators from Kabul, Kharachar, Central Asia— one of them a descendant of S'akyamuni's uncle—and some translate works of a practical rather than a religious character : spells for relieving toothache, bad eyes, crying babies, and people suffering from summer sickness.[1] The Lian (502–557) at Nanking have translators who come by sea from Siam. It would be unprofitable to continue this list any further. Suffice it to say that books came in by the thousand, representing all the conflicting schools of Buddhist thought, and hailing from every country, north, west or south, in which Buddhism was represented. Buddhism itself almost died under the weight of its own books, and of the institutions which it had brought with it from India.

Several practical reforms ought to be noticed. In A.D. 335 a monk named Buddhoganga persuaded King She-hu of the Posterior Chow dynasty to institute ordinations and allow Chinese natives to take monastic vows.[2] This permission greatly changed the nature of Chinese Buddhism. In India it had been the custom for kings to support the Order by their royal bounty, and the custom obtained at first in China also, thus keeping the Order as an exotic and aristocratic institution. But when Chinese natives took the vows, the Order increased very rapidly, and Buddhism became a thing belonging to the people rather than to the sovereign.

[1] In the popular *Bukkyōgimon Kaitōshū*, vol. iii., there is an exposition of several of these short "spell-sūtras."

[2] This I touch on again in my chapter on Heian Buddhism.

In A.D. 401, Kumarajiva was brought to China, and was welcomed at Chang-an by the sovereign of the Latter Tsin Dynasty. Kumarajiva suggested, and carried out, a revision and retranslation of the older works, some of which had been but roughly translated by the earlier missionaries. This secured a large measure of popularity for the revised versions of the Tripitaka. In 520, Bodhidharma, the then patriarch of Mahāyānism, left India and came to China to avoid the persecution of the Brahmanists, where, finding the block of literature, he swept the whole of the Tripitaka aside, declaring that the essence of Buddhism is to find the "heart of Buddha" by meditation, as Buddha himself had done. In 399, Fahian started on a journey to India, to investigate Buddhism at its fountain-head.

It is noteworthy, says M. Ch. Pithon, in an article in the *China Review* (vol. xi.), on the History of China under the Tsin Dynasty, that the Posterior Chow and the Tsin, who did so much for Chinese Buddhism, were really Huns, and ruled over a large proportion of Hiungnu subjects. The Huns all over the world stood by one another, and the chief of all the Huns was Attila (A.D. 445), whose word was law from the frontiers of Gaul to those of China. How much of Buddhist teaching came into Christian folklore and superstition through Hunnish soldiers in the regiments of Attila, it would require a large treatise to investigate.[1]

In 372 a Chinese monk preached Buddhism in the

---

[1] The annexed quotation may possibly throw some light on these Buddhist ordinations. The reader will remember that the period with which we are now dealing was the period when Europe was being over-run by barbarian hordes from Central Asia. Eunapius, "Historia," pp. 82–83 (in "Scriptores Historiæ Byzantinæ"), has an interesting paragraph relating to this subject. It deals with the year 376, and speaks about the Goths. If these are to be identified with the Yuetchi,

Korean kingdom of Koma, or Kaoli, and thus at length, after a long and eventful history, the Way was brought to Japan in the year 545 A.D.

they may (must?) have been Buddhists before entering Europe. (See Flinders Petrie on " Migrations " in *Journal of Anthropological Inst.*)

φυλαὶ μὲν γὰρ τῶν πολεμίων τὴν ἀρχὴν διαβεβήκεσαν ἄπειροι, καὶ πλείους ἐπιδιέβαινον, οὐδενὸς κωλύοντος · ἀλλ' ἐν τοσούτοις κακοῖς κέρδος ἐδόκει γνήσιον τὸ δωροδοκεῖσθαι παρὰ τῶν πολεμίων. εἶχε δὲ ἑκάστη φυλὴ ἱερά τε οἴκοθεν τὰ πάτρια συνεφελκομένη, καὶ ἱερέας τούτων καὶ ἱερείας · ἀλλὰ στεγανή τις ἦν λίαν καὶ ἀδαμάντινος ἡ περὶ ταῦτα σιωπὴ καὶ τῶν ἀπορρήτων ἐχεμυθία, ἡ δὲ εἰς τὸ φανερὸν προσποίησις καὶ πλάσις εἰς τὴν τῶν πολεμίων ἀπατὴν διηρτυμένη. καί τινας ὡς ἐπισκόπους αὐτῶν ἐς τὸ θαυμαζόμενον σχῆμα καταστολίσαντες καὶ περικύψαντες, καὶ πολλῆς αὐτοῖς τῆς ἀλώπεκος ἐπιχέαντες, εἰς τὸ μέσον προεφίεσαν, πανταχοῦ τὸ ἀφύλακτον διὰ τῶν καταφρονουμένων ὅρκων παρ' ἐκείνοις, παρὰ δὲ τοῖς βασιλεῦσι σφόδρα φυλαττομένων, ὑποτρύχοντες καὶ κατασκευάζοντες. ἦν δὲ καὶ τῶν καλουμένων μοναχῶν παρ' αὐτοῖς γένος, κατὰ μίμησιν τῶν παρὰ τοῖς πολεμίοις ἐπιτηδευόμενον, οὐδὲν ἐχούσης τῆς μιμήσεως πραγματῶδες καὶ δύσκολον, ἀλλ' ἐξήρκει φαιὰ ἱμάτια σύρουσι καὶ χιτώνια, πονηροῖς τε εἶναι καὶ πιστεύεσθαι, καὶ τοῦτο ὀξέως συνεῖδον οἱ βάρβαροι τὸ θαυμαζόμενον παρὰ Ῥωμαίοις εἰς παραγωγὴν ἐπιτηδεύσαντες · ἐπεὶ τά γε ἄλλα μετὰ βαθύτητος καὶ σκέπης ὅτι μάλιστα στεγανωτάτης τῶν ἀπορρήτων τὰ πάτρια ἱερὰ γεννικῶς τε καὶ ἀδόλως φυλάττοντες, οὕτω δὲ ἐχόντων τούτων, ὅμως εἰς τοσαύτην ἄνοιαν ἐξεπτώκεσαν, ὥστε συμπεπεῖσθαι σαφῶς καὶ ἅμα ἐλαχὼς τοὺς δοκοῦντας νοῦν ἔχειν, ὅτι χριστιανοί τε εἰσι καὶ πάσαις ταῖς τελεταῖς ἀνέχοντες.

In the above extract, note (i) that the religion is τὰ πάτρια ἱερά, a faith brought with them from Central Asia ; (ii) that the institution of quasi-bishops seems to be spoken of as a recent innovation, and that it corresponds in point of time with what we know of Chinese ordinations ; (iii) that *black* (φαιός) suits what we know of Shinshū and Jōdo monks ; (iv) that it corresponds with what we know from other sources about the confusion between Buddhist arhats and Christian " saints." The object of the ruse was to deceive the Romans into believing that the barbarians were already Christians. The work of Ulfilas came later, at any rate in its influence, and his institutions could not be described as being " ancestral rites " of the Goths.

CHAPTER XV

MANICHÆISM

WHEN we reach this point in our history of the Mahāyāna, it behoves us to turn a glance to that great religious movement which began in the middle of the third century.

Mani, or Manichæus,[1] to give him the name by which he was generally known, was born in A D. 215, almost contemporaneously with the fall of the Han Dynasty. He was descended from a distinguished Persian family which had emigrated from Ecbatana in Persia, and had settled in Babylonia. His early days were spent amongst the Mugtasilahs, or Baptizers,[2] a sect which his father, Fathak,

[1] *Mani* means a painter. I have often wondered if there can be any connection between the name *Manichæus* and the famous Buddhist monastery of Manikyala. I draw my materials for this chapter mainly, though not entirely, from Kessler's article on Mani in the "Schaff—Herzog Encyclopædia." It is probable that in the course of a few years our knowledge of Manichæism will be much increased as a result of recent finds in Central Asia.

[2] The Mendæans or Mandæans still subsist, in a very small community, on the eastern banks of the Tigris. They are sometimes called the Christians of St. John, on account of the great veneration they pay to St. John the Baptist, whom they consider to have been a true prophet, in contradistinction to Abraham, Moses, Solomon, Jesus the Sorcerer, and Mahomet, all of whom they consider to have been false prophets. The true religion, they say, still existed in the days of Moses, and was in the possession of the Egyptians, and was brought back into the world by St. John. It was this, doubtless, that turned Mani's thoughts towards Egypt in his travels in search of religion. The official name, among themselves, for their religion is *Mandā*, which is Gnosis. But Mandā is personified, as it is among the

joined shortly after Mani's birth, a sect out of which sprang in later years the sect of the Mandæans, and which was undoubtedly a form of Gnosticism. But the boy separated himself from this body when he was about fourteen, choosing to spend the next eleven years in travelling in search of a religion. I believe I am right in saying that some of the recently discovered Central Asian manuscripts now in the Berlin Ethnographical Museum show conclusively that his travels at this period embraced Egypt.

It was from Egypt, though indirectly, that he obtained the books which eventually gave a definite shape to his religious speculations. The story is told by St. Cyril of Jerusalem ("Cat. Lect.," vi. 22). It has been almost uniformly rejected by modern scholars; but I hope that what I have been able to show of the existence of Buddhism in Alexandria during the first century of our era may lead some scholars to reconsider their verdicts. I will give St. Cyril's own words, which are mainly taken from the Acta Archelai.

"There was in Egypt one Scythianus, a Saracen [1] by birth, having nothing in common either with Judaism or with Christianity. This man, who dwelt at Alexandria and imitated the life of Aristotle, composed four books— one called a Gospel which had not the Acts of Christ, but

Buddhists, and so becomes a sort of counterpart of the personified though indefinite *Butsu* of which many Japanese Buddhists speak (especially the followers of the old Ritsu or Vinaya sect, now amalgamated with the Shingon). They also talk of themselves as "Subbâ," *i.e.* "Baptists," and their Baptismal rites, oft repeated, are again, like those of the Marcosians mentioned in a previous chapter, very similar to those of the Shingon *Kwanjo*. Like many Japanese Buddhists, they have a special veneration for the Polar Star (Jap. *myōken*), towards which they turn when praying.

[1] I have already shown how widely, even in As'oka's days, was the expansion of Buddhism among non-Indian peoples.

the mere name only; and one other called the Book of Chapters; and a third of Mysteries; and a fourth, which they circulate now, the Treasure. This man had a disciple, Terebinthus by name. But when Scythianus purposed to come into Judæa[1] and make havoc of the land, the Lord smote him with a deadly disease, and stayed the pestilence. But Terebinthus, his disciple in this wicked error, inherited his money and books and heresy, and came to Palestine, and becoming known and condemned in Judæa, he resolved to pass into Persia;[2] but lest he should be recognized there also by his name, he changed it and called himself Buddas.[3] However, he found adversaries there also in the priests of Mithras; and being confuted in the discussion of many arguments and controversies, and at last hard pressed, he took refuge with a certain widow."

Here Terebinthus died. "The books, however, which were the records of his impiety, remained; and both these

---

[1] In the "Acta Archelai" we read, "Scythianus thought of making an excursion into Judæa, with the purpose of meeting all those that had a reputation there as teachers." And this is said to have been in the days of the Apostles. See my paper on the "Formative Elements of Japanese Buddhism," in *Trans. As. Soc. Japan*, vol. xxxv.

[2] In the "Acta Archelai" it is "Babylon, a province which is now held by the Persians."

[3] Does the name of some great Mahāyānist doctor—for instance, Nāgārjuna—lurk behind Terebinthus? Nag is the name of a tree, "the *arjuna* tree sacred to the worship of the Nagas," and always appears in Japanese as *Ryū ju*, the "tree of the Dragon" or Nāga. Can it be that the name of Nāgārjuna was similarly translated into Greek, and that the *terebinthus* was the "sacred tree of the Nāgas"? Nāgārjuna's date corresponds roughly with that assigned to Terebinthus. There is a great similarity of ideas between Nag. and Manichæism; the "Thibetan Life of Nāgārjuna," translated by Mr. Das in *J.A.S. Bengal*, speaks of a journey westwards undertaken by Nāgārjuna, and Nāgārjuna, like Terebinthus, was known amongst his contemporaries as "Buddha." The establishment of this conjectural identification would clear up many difficulties.

and his money the widow inherited. And having neither kinsmen nor any other friend, she determined to buy with the money a boy named Cubricus; him she adopted and educated as a son in the learning of the Persians, and thus sharpened an evil weapon against mankind. So Cubricus, the vile slave, grew up in the midst of the philosophers, and on the death of the widow inherited both the books and the money. Then, lest the name of slavery might be a reproach, instead of Cubricus he called himself Manes, which in the language of the Persians signifies 'Discourse.' " [1]

In the year A.D. 242, at the coronation of King Sapor I., Manes, now twenty-four years of age, and fed upon the doctrines of the Baptizers, and of the Aristotelian and Buddhist philosophy of the Scythianus books, as well as on the varied experiences of his *Wanderjahre*, proclaims his new religion. It was an auspicious moment. King Sapor was the successor of Ardashir, who had driven out the Parthian dynasty and restored a Persian Empire under the Persian dynasty of the Sassanid House. It was a strictly nationalistic movement, encouraged by the Magian priests, and the new rulers were bent on restoring that ancient faith of the land which had been overthrown when Alexander burnt its sacred books and proscribed its sacred rites. Manes apparently thought it a favourable opportunity for proclaiming a new religion. So he announced himself as the prophet of God to his own people of Babylonia. "What Buddha was to India, Zoroaster to Persia, Jesus to the lands of the West, that am I to Babylonia."

In its first form, his preaching was a protest against the forcing of Zoroastrianism on his own people of Babylon

---

[1] The name also means "painter." The Greeks, not unnaturally perhaps, nicknamed him the Maniac.

by the victorious Sassanid House, and it is probable that, had he been left alone, his religion would have had nothing but a mere local importance. But the Magians did not want to see Babylonia aroused to national enthusiasm by the preaching of a new national faith, and Manes was driven into exile. His exile, followed later by his martyrdom, changed his system from a merely local cult to one of world-wide significance. He wandered as an exile through the countries north, north-east, and east of the newly constituted Persian kingdom, from which he was an outcast, and when, venturing to return to Persia, he was cruelly put to death by his enemies, his disciples seized upon his memory with enthusiasm, and carried his teachings far and wide through Europe and Asia. Manichæism was for many centuries a serious menace to the Christian Church.

Manichæism may most properly be described as the completion of the Gnostic systems. It seems to have swept them all together, and to have joined them into one cohesive whole. We hear no more of Gnosticism after the rise of Manichæism. It was not a Christian religion, yet it had its Christian side. It could speak to Christians in Christian language, and it made claim for Manes that he was the Paraclete, the Comforter whom Christ had promised. We have but to read the Anti-Manichæan treatises of St. Augustine, or any of the notices of Manichæism in the Greek or Latin Fathers, to understand that Manes could talk, when he pleased, as a Christian. But he faced many ways, and in China the Manichæan clergy rather seem to have aimed at identifying themselves with the Buddhists.

Manichæism did not, like Christianity, "present itself to man as a power to save him by cleansing his heart from sin; but, like Gnosticism, it simply proposed to gratify man's craving for knowledge by explaining the very problem of his existence."[1] It had a phrase in China which well sums up its principal teaching—a word pronounced in Japanese as *Dai-un-Kōmyō*, "the Light on the Great Cloud."[2] It recognized two elements—the Light and the Cloud; and the Light, which is all good, is God. The personality of God comprises five spiritual and five material sub-elements, a division clearly corresponding to the five Dhyāni Buddhas and Bodhisattvas. "But God is not alone in the light: His fulness comprehends an air of light, an earth of light, and numberless glories and magnificences. Upwards and sidewise this realm of light is unbounded; but from below it is met by the realm of darkness, the Cloud." Thus "Light resting on the Great Cloud" becomes the symbol of the Manichæan system. The term is found in China and Japan, often as a name for temples. I believe that in every case it can be traced back to a Manichæan origin or connection.

The ethical system of Manichæism is more clearly allied with Buddhism. Whether Manes, coming to India, found the Dharmagupta system at work and incorporated it into his own, or whether the later Vinayists borrowed from the Manichæans, I cannot tell. It all depends on the date to be assigned to books like the Brahmajāla Sūtra. But there is no doubt that the "Perfect" of the Manichæan system are remarkably like the candidates for Buddhaship who take upon themselves the 250 Rules of the Bodhisattva. In both systems there is the same threefold arrangement of sins according as they concern the hand, the mouth, or the heart. In both there is the same prohibition of marriage, and of every sort of sensual pleasure; Bodhisattvas and "Perfect" are alike forbidden

---

[1] Kessler, *l.c.*
[2] See my "Shinran and His Work," p. 166.

to dig the earth, to build houses, to engage in industry or commerce. The Bodhisattva and the Perfect alike are forbidden to partake of the "five strong herbs," known in Japan as "Go Shin."[1]

It is impossible to deny the influence exercised upon the plastic Mahāyāna by Manichæism. From the middle of the third century onwards the two religions were constantly side by side, and whatever person we consider after that date, we must always take into consideration the fact that most probably he knew something of Manichæism. Zoroastrianism also comes into account, but the Zoroastrians were not a proselytizing community like the Manichæans, and it is not until the Tang period that we find them side by side with Buddhism.

Manichæism did not set itself to work to preach Christ, but it had its Christian aspect, and wherever in Central Asia we find, as we often do, a Manichæan temple almost side by side with a Buddhist monastery, we may safely infer that there must have been some indirect knowledge among the Buddhists of the fact of Christ.

[1] Cf. "Shinran and His Work." The lower class of Manichæan disciples, the "Hearers," corresponds, even philologically, with the S'ravakas of Buddhism. The distinction lies at the basis of the distinction, common in Japanese sects, of *Shintai* and *Zokutai*.

CHAPTER XVI

CHINA IN THE THIRD, FOURTH, AND FIFTH CENTURIES

IT is very difficult for the mind to frame for itself a distinct picture of China from the middle of the third century A.D. to that of the sixth. The three kingdoms of the Wei, the Wu, and the Shu, of which I have spoken in a previous chapter, came to an end in A.D. 265, when Szuma I. established himself as the first ruler of the Tsin dynasty on the ruins of the Wu and the Shu, which he annexed to the Wei. The Tsin dynasty formally united China under one sovereign, but the unity was apparent rather than real. There were many semi-independent principalities, which were extremely reluctant to acknowledge the supremacy of the Dragon Throne, and the unification of the empire was not carried out without considerable difficulty. Many of these border principalities were Buddhist, and it was from them, more even than from India, that came that overwhelming flood of Buddhist books and translators which has served to make the history of Buddhism in China such a hopeless chaos. Many of these translators brought their books from Khotan. Khotan, about the year A.D. 270, was a semi-independent state, tributary to China, with which it had very close trade relations. Buddhism was practically the only religion of the country, the common language was an Indian dialect, and the script a form of Sanskrit known as Kharoshti. There were other principalities of the same sort. How small was the intercourse with India proper may be inferred from the fact that, during the years 317–439, out of thirty-six translators mentioned by Nanjo, twelve came from the western regions (including Khotan), eight from Kubhâ (Kabul), ten from various parts of China proper, two from Turkestan and Bokhâra, and only four from India.

The Emperor Wu-ti (for this was the name that Szuma I. assumed on his accession) was an extremely able ruler. He not only unified the country and saved it for the time from foreign invasion, but he also did much for literature and the general development of the empire. He encouraged travel (we read of a Chinese scholar, Tsushi, or the "Red Teacher," being sent to India), and in the year 284 he received at his capital (more probably at Nanking) an embassy from a Roman emperor. It was the year of Diocletian's accession : the embassy, which may have been some time on its way, must have been sent by Probus (276–284), or by Aurelian, the "Restitutor Orbis" (270–276). Possibly it was not an embassy at all, but only a company of traders whom the vanity of the Chinese raised to the dignity of ambassadors.

Wu-ti died in 290, and was succeeded by his son Hweiti, a simpleton "who could not distinguish pulse from wheat," and who was entirely in the hands of an unprincipled wife. The country was immediately a blaze of rebellion from one end to another, and the Tartars on the frontier set up a rival kingdom in Shansi, with a pretender on the throne who claimed descent from the great family of the Han. The Han had not yet been forgotten, and the great Wu-ti had after all only been a successful usurper. The feeble Hweiti was poisoned in 306, his successor was killed in battle against the Tartars in 311. Mingti, who succeeded him, was compelled to remove his capital from Lôyang to Singanfu, and in 317 Mingti's successor, Yuanti, was obliged to make another remove, and to bring his capital to Nanking. From 317 to its extinction in 420, the dynasty was known as the Eastern Tsin. Thus China, remaining united in name, was divided into two portions, the line of division being the Yangtze river. In the south the Chinese ruled, in the north the Tartars. India had its own troubles, and concerned itself very little about its missions to China.

It will easily be understood that the sympathies of the Buddhists would be more with the Buddhist principalities on the north and west than with the Confucianist Chinese State of Tsin.[1] The " Bibliothecal catastrophe," or " burning of the books," instituted by Hweiti in A.D. 306, must have been directed against the Buddhists and their importations, and appears to have been well deserved. It also possibly affected the Taoists. It would almost seem as though something had for a while driven Taoists and Buddhists into a common camp. About the year A.D. 240, Taoist sectaries began to live as Buddhist monks in bamboo-groves and caves, and to cultivate the philosophy of the Void, as did many of the Buddhists : nay, even the Confucianists were tempted to follow suit by erecting images of " the Five Rulers " in the Temples of the God of Heaven. The literati saved Confucianism from this stupid imitation of the Five Dhyāni Buddhas ; shortly after Hweiti's " bibliothecal catastrophe," the votaries of the Void were forcibly put down, on the ground that their doctrines and practices were subversive of public order. But it is evident that these measures

[1] There is a long and painstaking article on the history of the Tsin Dynasty by Ch. Pithon in *China Review*, vol. xii. p. 401. He shows that during this period the illegitimate states were the true props of Buddhism, just as in Germany it was the small states that favoured the Reformation.

were limited to the dominions of Hweiti and his Tsin successors.

In the year 335 A.D. an Indian monk, of the name of Buddhoganga, persuaded the Emperor She-hu of the Posterior Chow to allow Chinese subjects to take monastic vows. The Chow were Huns,[1] in touch with the main body of their tribe, whose vanguards, driven from their homes by the same process of desiccation which had sent the Chow against China, were now on their way to Europe. The permission obtained by Buddhoganga enabled Buddhism, at any rate in the Chow dominions, to become a native growth instead of an exotic. This is the first sign that Buddhism was becoming an object of serious study to the Chinese people.

Buddhism was also much furthered by the establishment at Singanfu of the Empire of the Anterior Thsin. This dynasty was of Tangut or Thibetan origin, and had extensive trade relations both with India and the West. They were very zealous Buddhists, and did much for the spread of their faith. Cave temples, after the manner of the celebrated holy places of India, were established in this kingdom about A.D. 370, and it was from the kingdom of the Anterior Thsin also that, in A.D. 372, the first Buddhist missionary was sent to the Korean kingdom of Koma.

In 366 there was translated into Chinese a portion of the Avataṃsaka, or Kegon Scriptures. The reader will remember that these were the Scriptures fabled to have been brought by Nāgārjuna from the Dragon's Palace

---

[1] In 375, the Huns, with the Alani and Ostrogoths, crossed the Volga and attacked the West Goths. The latter applied for help to the Emperor Valens, and it was on this occasion that they brought into prominence the bishops, priests, nuns, etc., whom they had according to their ancient rites. See the quotation from Eunapius at the end of the preceding chapter.

at the bottom of the sea. How suitable those weird books must have seemed for reconciling the occupants of the Dragon-throne to the faith of the great Sea-dragon! In the year 381 Hiao-wu-ti, Emperor of the Anterior Thsin, was the first ruler of China openly to profess the Buddhist faith.[1] He built large monasteries and did much for the spread of Buddhism in his extensive dominions. He was not a great gain, perhaps, to his new religion. He was a very sensual man, and was smothered by one of his concubines whom he had offended.

The Thsin dominions extended far to the West, possibly as far as Bokhara, with which country they had, at any rate, many trade relations, and from which they received Buddhist missionaries. In 375, two Christian missionaries, Palladius, a Goth, and Musæus, Bishop of Aduli, were sent from Galatia to India. Palladius turned back, Musæus went on from India to Bokhara, and there established a mission.[2] It was probably not without some results.

Communications with India were restored. The peninsula was now under the sway of the later Gupta sovereigns. Samudragupta (326–375) ruled over an empire larger than any that had acknowledged a purely Indian sovereign since the days of As'oka. He was paramount in the peninsula, and his alliances extended from Ceylon to the Oxus, where he came in touch with the Thsin. Neither he nor his successor Chandragupta II. (shall we call him Vikramāditya?) were Buddhists. They were both worshippers of Vishnu, but both were tolerant men and gave free liberty to Buddhism and Jainism. What wonder is it that, the way being once more open to the Holy Land of Buddhism, devout Chinese pilgrims

---

[1] *China Review*, vol. xi. p. 308.

[2] Mentioned by Cosmas Indicopleustes.

should have flocked to visit the places associated with the birth, life, and death of S'akyamuni? And what wonder that the net result of the journeys of these pilgrims was to give them, and, through them, their countrymen, a juster appreciation of the religion of the Master? Much strange matter had come into China by all manner of by-paths and highways. True it all claimed to be Buddhist, but it was not all such as Pataliputra, or even Peshawur, would have recognized.

The first of these pilgrims was Fah-hian, who started in 399 and returned by way of the sea in 414, four years after Alaric had sacked Rome, and the year after the accession of Kumaragupta I., whose reign was likewise to be disturbed by the inroads of the dreaded Huns. Fah-hian found Buddhism flourishing in Khotan, Yarkhand, and Kashgar, in Kashmir, Punjaub, and the valley of the Indus. At Pataliputra he found two monasteries, one for the followers of each Vehicle, but many of the holy places connected with the life of S'akyamuni— S'ravasti, Kapilavastu, Kus'inagara, and even the Bodh Gaya itself—were in decay. Men did not trouble themselves about the historical Buddha; they were too much occupied with his deified aspects. Whilst Fah-hian was still in India, the Buddhist monk Buddhaghosha reached Burma, but there was no sign of Buddhism to be seen in Java.

But before Fah-hian returned to China, there had arrived at Singanfu a man whose activity constitutes an epoch in the history of Chinese Buddhism—the celebrated Kumarajīva.

Kumarajīva came of a family that had long been domiciled at Kharachar, a town and kingdom in Eastern Turkestan, at the foot of the Tien Shan mountains. Entering the Fraternity at the age of seven, he was sent for his education to Kubhā (Kabul), where he was put under the charge of a famous Hīnayānist priest, who was cousin to the king of that country. At the age of twelve, *i.e.* in 352, he returned to Kharachar, where he remained until 383, spending the thirty years of his sojourn there in the prosecution of his theological studies. He was admirably suited for the work of an interpreter. An Indian by descent and by education, he was familiar with all the twists and turns of Sanskrit; in Kharachar he had been forced to familiarize himself with Chinese and one or more Turkish dialects. There are vague hints to be found here and there of sporadic Christian communities in that part of Central Asia.

In 383 the town of Kharachar was attacked and destroyed by Chinese from Thsin, and Kumarajīva, still in the prime of life, was taken prisoner, and carried, first to Liancheu, and thence, in 401, to Singanfu, where he was attached to the court of Yao Hing, second ruler of the Posterior Thsin. His fame as a scholar had preceded him; he had established his reputation as a Saint by a very successful resistance to a fleshly temptation thrown in his way by his Chinese captors, and was received by the Thsin court with much honour. His opinion was at once asked with regard to the numerous translations of Buddhist Scriptures with which the country was flooded. Travellers to India had already brought back stories of how the Buddhism being introduced into China differed from that of India; it was certain that the translations into Chinese offended the literary tastes of the educated classes. What guarantee was there that they were even accurate translations?

Kumarajīva's verdict was that the translations made hitherto were neither accurate nor elegant, and that he had better be set to the task of revision. This work occupied him for the rest of his lifetime, and was the joy and pride of his declining years. The proper conversion of China had been laid upon him as a charge by his teachers both in Kabul and in Kharachar, and he was glad to be able to set himself to the task. " I have translated many books," he said to his disciples on his death-bed, " and ye shall know by a sign that I have done my work well. When my body is cremated, it will all be consumed, but the tongue only will remain untouched by the fire." So his disciples knew that his written words were true and correct.

Among Kumarajīva's most notable translations were the Smaller Sukhāvati-vyūha,[1] the Saddharmapundarika, and the three S'āstras[2] which form the basal teaching of the Sanron sect. These last he had studied under Suryasoma in Kharachar, and it was to the expounding of them that he devoted the greater part of his energy. The result of his labours was the formation of a sect— the so-called Sanron—the first definite sect in Chinese Buddhism, a sect which was brought to Japan in A.D. 625 by Ekwan, where it flourished for some time before being finally merged into other schools.

[1] See note on the three Amida books at the end of this chapter.

[2] The three S'astras are (i) " the Madhyamika-s'āstra, or " Book of the Mean " (Chūron); (ii) the S'ata sūtra, or " Collection of one hundred Essays " (Hyaku-ron) and (iii) Dvādas'anikāya s'āstra, or " Book of the Twelve Gates " (Jūni mon ron). They were composed by the Bodhisattvas Nāgārjuna and Deva to clear the confusion arising in men's minds from the distinctions between entity and non-entity. They expound, from a Mahāyānistic standpoint, the whole teachings of Buddha's long life, with special emphasis perhaps on the " Twelve Gates " that lead to the Inmost Shrine of Perfect Enlightenment. They accepted the Kegon, the Âgamas, the Saddharmapundarika as three periods in S'akyamuni's ministerial career, and placed the Saddharmapundarika last as being the crown of Buddha's personal teachings. It is not the object of this book to explain Buddhist philosophy. I leave these questions for discussion in a later volume.

Kumarajíva died about the year 420, just as the Thsin Dynasty was being replaced by the Sung. Four years before him died Eon (Chinese Hwui-Yin), the Founder of the White Lotus Society. Eon is not reckoned among the patriarchs of the Amitābha sects in Japan, but he is surely deserving of such honour, for he was the first to gather into a distinct body a band of monks and laymen combined for the sole invocation of Amida's name. There is a great deal to be said for the contention of the Amidaists that their beliefs are of the essence of the Mahāyāna; that they are, in fact, the one true form of that religion. We have seen the faith in Amida with As'vaghosha in the first century A.D., with Nāgārjuna, Anshikao, Lokaraksha, and other Han missionaries in the second. In the third there was Sanghavarman (252), whose translation of the larger Sukhāvatî Vyūha is still much used. In the fourth century we have Dō-an (Thâo Ān, ob. 390), of whose faith we know from a story that is told of him. A certain very conceited Indian monk entered into conversation with him. "I am Shūsakushi," said the Indian (I give the Japanese equivalent for his name) ; "I am well known within the four seas." "Oh, are you?" said Dō-an. "My name is Dō-an, and I am well known in the Paradise of Amida." The repartee shows Dō-an's faith quite clearly. Eon was a disciple of Dō-an. Like his master, he lived south of the Yangtze, in districts where there was not so much Buddhism, perhaps, as in the dominions of the Thsin. He does not seem to have troubled himself very much about the Amida Scriptures (of which only one was accessible to him in a Chinese dress), but to have led a monastic life constantly devoted to the worship of Amida. His writings had a great influence on the Amidaist Patriarch Zendō. It has been said that he was a Manichæan : the

White Lotus Society still exists in China, I am told, and its members sing hymns which it is hard to distinguish from Christian ones.[1]

With Kumarajíva commences the period of Saddharmapundarika influence. That remarkable book (the connection between which and one of the Gnostic books I have already pointed out) may be spoken of as a species of Buddhist Apocalypse.

The Master, on the Vulture Peak, awakes from his trance to show his auditors that, though men may think there are three forms of saving doctrine, there is really only one, the apparent differences arising from the fact that the One Truth has to be adapted and modified to suit the needs of those to whom it is delivered. This is illustrated by various parables, and the hearers have the lesson impressed upon them that the ultimate goal of all endeavours must be to reach All-knowingness. And to know everything is the same thing as to know nothing.

The Master is endowed with all knowledge and with all power. He knows the past, the long record of his own existences, and the future, the destinies of his hearers, both of which he describes. His knowledge is so great that even the Buddhas made Perfect in the past are anxious to hear his Wisdom, and he proposes himself, made one with a great Buddha of previous times, for the adoration of the congregation.

[1] I have had no opportunities of verifying this statement, nor have I been able to find any account of the White Lotus Society in any publication accessible to me. The statement may be capable of verification by persons residing in China. I have discussed the question in the appendix to "Shinran and his Work."

A book of dialogues, mainly religious, between Eon and Kumarajíva exists in the library of the *Shinshu Daigakko* at Sugamo near Tokyo. The work is said to be unique, no other exemplar being known to exist. Through the kindness of the librarian of that institution, a copy is now being made for me.

M

Then he sends forth his disciples to preach his gospel. He promises them his protection, and he encourages them by showing the wonderful success of their preaching. It will really be He that preaches, and not they. Every one of their countless myriads of converts has been somewhere at some time his personal disciple. He gives them rules for their conduct in preaching.

At the head of the bands of those that shall believe are four great Bodhisattvas. The later chapters make us infer that "the Four" are Yakushi, Kwannon, Fugen, Myō-On.[1] Nichiren claimed that he himself was one of the Four. Whoever they are, they are beings of great power, and they stand around the Master, who is supreme, and uncircumscribed in time or space.

If Professor Takakusu is right, we must assign to this period the two brothers Asangha and Vasubandhu, who play such an important part in the development of the Mahāyāna. Takakusu places them about A.D. 445, and gives reason for so doing. But Vasubandhu, on the list of the Mahāyāna Patriarchs given by Nanjo, comes just halfway between Nāgārjuna and Bodhidharma. We know Bodhidharma's date, A.D. 520; if we place Nāgārjuna about A.D. 120, we shall find that a halfway date will place Vasubandhu about A.D. 300, which fits in better with what one can judge of the effects of his work. Vasubandhu, like Nāgārjuna, is claimed by many sects. He belongs to the Kusha, the Hossō, and the Jōdo, the latter, especially, esteeming him to be one of the most powerful advocates of Faith in Amitābha and Rebirth in the Pure Land.

His brother, Asangha, who was a Mahāyanist before him, is looked upon as the founder of the Hossō or

[1] Their names in Sanskrit are Bhaishajyarāja, Avalokites'vara, Samantabhadra, and Gadgadasavara.

Dharmalakshana sect. A story is told of him which throws an interesting light on the superstitions of his day. He was delivering a course of lectures in a preaching-place in Ayodhya, his place of residence. The lectures were not his own. Every evening he ascended to the Tushita Heaven and was coached for the next day's lesson by the Great Maitreya himself, the Buddha of the Future. One day a student doubted his word. "You must not do that," said the Professor; "what I am giving you I obtained from the Tushita Heaven, from Maitreya himself." With an incredulity which would have done honour to a class of Japanese students his auditors refused to believe him. "Very well, then," said Asangha, "I'll bring my Maitreya with me next time!" And the lessons thus delivered were the foundation of the doctrines of the Hossō Sect!

A. Note on the Chinese Sects.

The following notes on Chinese sects will be found useful for reference, as some of them will occur again in the Japanese chapters. Many of them were extremely superstitious and corrupt; but few professed much real reverence for the teachings of S'akyamuni, and in none, except in the Jōdo, do we find any of the enthusiasm that uplifts its followers. I take my information mainly from Nanjo and Murakami.

1. The *Abhidharma* sect. This in India was reckoned as one of the twenty sects of the Hinayāna. It was based on the Commentary on the Abhidharma treatises written by Kātyāyaniputra, and was brought to China about A.D. 394 by three Indian monks, Sanghadeva, Dharmanandin, and Sanghabhūti. It seems to have prospered until about A.D. 440. 1 have found no traces of it in Japan.

2. *Jōjitsu*, based on Harivarman's "Satyasiddhis'āstra" (Nanjo No. 1274), and brought to Singanfu by Kumarajīva in 401. It was opposed to the doctrines of the Sarvāstivādins. It prospered in China until the beginning of the Tang period, when it was absorbed by the Tendai. It appeared in Japan only to disappear again.

3. *Sanron*, based on three S'āstras, two by Nāgārjuna, one by

Deva, with commentaries by Asangha and Vasubandhu. It was severely metaphysical, and was in high esteem in China during the Sui dynasty (589–618). Under the Tang it lost its prestige. It was brought to Japan during the time that the Sui influence was strong, and its first recognized head was Ekwan (624), but was ousted from favour by the Hossō and Kegon.

4. *Nirvana* (Nehan). May be said to have flourished from A.D. 386 to A.D. 589, first among the Lian, and afterwards at Nanking under the earlier Sung. It was one of the first sects to construct a " Harmony " of the numerous miscellaneous Sūtras. It divided Shaka's life into five periods, and considered the Sūtra of the Great Decease (Nehangyō) as representing the highest and final teachings of the Master. The Saddharmapundarika and the most of the Amida books had not yet come to the fore in China when this sect was started. It was absorbed under the Tang by the *Tendai* sect, and reached Japan under that name.

5. *Jiron*, based on the Das'abhūmika, with Vasubandhu's (not Nāgārjuna's) commentary. Introduced by Bodhiruci A.D. 508, it flourished under the Northern Wei (386–534). It was eventually absorbed by *Kegon*.

6. *Jōdo*. This sect is an effort at simplification. It tries to present *one* object of Faith to its followers. Its best-known teacher is Zendō, a contemporary of the Nestorian missionaries at Singanfu. He advised his followers (and in this he was followed by the Japanese Hōnen) to throw away the other books of the Canon, and to pin their faith on the central clause of Amida's vow. His writings contain some wonderfully striking echoes of Scriptural phrases, *e.g.* " the turning of the hearts of the children to the Fathers, and *vice versâ*," and the warning against adding to or taking from the words of his book. Haas (" Amida Buddha unsere Zuflucht ") gives quotations from his works, as well as from those of Donran and Dōshaku.

7. *Zen*, another effort at simplification. Bodhidharma, who arrived in China in A.D. 527, advised his followers to throw away all books, and to strive to attain to Enlightenment by way of Meditation. Bodhidharma taught in the Kingdom of the Lian, and afterwards among the Northern Wei. This sect, like the Jōdo, has had a great influence in Japan. I have a chapter on it in my " Wheat among the Tares." See also " Sermons by a Buddhist Abbot," published by the Open Court, Chicago. It was not taught much at Singanfu, and was consequently slow in reaching Japan.

8. *Ritsu*, founded as a separate organization by Dōsen, at the beginning of the Tang period. But the Vinaya discipline had been taught long before that time, and came very early to Japan (see chapter on Dharmagupta), "If a man does not practise the Dhyāna and Samādhi, *i.e.* meditation and contemplation, he cannot understand the truth. If he does not keep all the precepts, he cannot accomplish his excellent practice." This would seem to show that the Ritsu is in some ways an amplification of the Zen. The sect in Japan was ultimately merged in the Shingon.

9. *Hossō, i.e.* "the sect that studies the nature of things," also known as the Dharmalakshana, or Yoga sect. This is the doctrine contained in the lectures given by Maitreya for Asangha to which I have already alluded. It was established in China by Hiouen Thsang, about A.D. 640. It was brought to Japan in 653 by Dōsō, who transmitted it to Gyōgi, and again, independently, in 712 by the notorious Gembō. It was the Hossō that brought about in Japan the system known as Ryōbu Shinto. It cannot be accused of having done much for the bettering of humanity in Japan.

10. *Tendai*, so called from the mountain on which its chief founder, Chisha Daishi, had his monastery. It is based on the Saddharmapundarika, and is one of the harmonizing sects. Emon (A.D. 551) is the first man to grasp the full significance of the Lotus Scripture. He was assisted in his work by Eshi and Chi-ki, the latter of whom, under the name of Chisha Daishi, becomes the actual founder of the sect. This sect sets out to be all embracing. Its supreme Buddha is Vairoc'ana, who transmitted his teaching to S'akyamuni, who transmitted it to Maitreya, and thus through Asangha's lecture-hall to the world. It divides the period of S'akyamuni's life into five. It admits Amida as another name for Vairoc'ana. It practises Yoga, and charms like the Hossō and Shingon do, but rejects the Shingon claim of a revelation to Nāgārjuna through the sage of the Iron Tower. Chisha Daishi died in A.D. 597.

11. *Kegon* (Avatamsaka). The basal scriptures were translated in A.D. 418 by Buddhabhadra (Kakugen). It had a great vogue under the Tsin (557–589) and throughout the Tang period. In Japan it arrived later than the Hossō, but was swallowed up by the Shingon (see below on Namudaishi) and Tendai.

12. *Shingon*. We have seen that this sect (as also the Tendai) contains doctrines very similar to those of the Gnostics of Alexandria. The Secret Shingon was not, however, brought to China

till 716, when it was brought by Subhakarasinha (Zenmui), Vajra-
bodhi, and Amoghavajra. The Tendai claims to have. the true
Shingon, which it obtained by another route. There was a Syrian
Gnosticism as well as an Egyptian one.

B. Note on the Three Amida Books.

The three books are—

1. The Larger Sukhāvati Vyūha, translated by Lokaraksha,[1]
Anshikao, and numerous other translators during the first three
centuries. The translation most in use now is that made by
Sanghavarman in A.D. 252. "This Sūtra gives a history of the
Tathāgata Amitābha, from the first spiritual impulses which led
him to the attainment of Buddhahood in remote Kalpas down to the
present time when he dwells in the Western world called Sukhāvati
(Goku-raku), where he receives all living beings from every direction, helping them to turn away from confusion and to become
enlightened " (Nanjo). The Sūtra is known in Japanese as the
Muryōjukyō.

It should be noticed that, in spite of what is said in the Sūtra,
Amidaists always speak of Amida as an Eternal Being without
beginning or end. Also that very little attention is paid to any

---

[1] With regard to the earliest extant Chinese translation of this work,
the one made by Lokaraksha in A.D. 147, it is worthy of notice that
Hōzō Biku, the earthly phase of Amida, there makes his vow before not
the last, but the first of his eighty-one predecessors, and that the Name
of that Being is Lokeśvararāja, " the King, the Lord of the World." In
the description of his Vow, the conditions of salvation are faith and
obedience, not faith only, and the obedience required embraces the ordinary morality, which is largely common to all religions. In Sanghavarman's translation the twenty-four paragraphs of the original vow have
been expanded to forty-eight; the chief stress being laid by subsequent
teachers on the paragraphs which accentuate the importance of Faith
alone as a means of salvation. But even in the earliest version it is laid
down most distinctly that, though there are many Buddhas (as there
are gods many and lords many), yet they all are summed up in Amitābha,
the Buddha of Infinite Purity, whose vow was made countless ages ago
in the presence of the Buddha whose name is "the King, the Lord of
the World."

If we judge by the dates of the translations, the other Amida books
clearly do not belong to the first stages of the Amida cult.

portion of Amida's Vow except to that portion (eighteenth section) which relates to Salvation through Faith in Amida's Name.

2. The Smaller Sukhāvati Vyūha (Japanese *Amida Kyō*), brought to China by Kumarajiva soon after A.D. 400, and by him translated. It is not certain whether Eon had access to this Sūtra or not. Probably not. "It is taught in this Sūtra that if a man keeps in his memory the name of Buddha Amitābha one day or seven days, the Buddha together with Bodhisattvas will come and meet him at the moment of his death in order to let him be born in the Pure Land Sukhāvatī; and that this matter has equally been approved by all the other Buddhas of the Universe." Eon's ceaseless devotion to the Sacred Name seems scarcely necessary in view of the words of the Sūtra, "one day or seven days."

3. *Amitāyur-dhyāna-sūtra* (Jap. *Kwammuryōjukyō*), translated by Kalayas'as in A.D. 424, eight years after Eon's death. In this Sūtra, Queen Vaidehi is weary of this wicked world, and is comforted by S'akyamuni, who teaches her how to be born in the Pure Land, and instructs her in the three kinds of goodness. These are (i) worldly goodness, *e.g.* filial piety, loyalty, respect for parents, etc.; (ii) morality, of that internal and unworldly kind which is the first foundation of the religious life; and (iii) the goodness of practice, which includes the practical application to life of the Four Great Truths and the Six Pārāmitas or Cardinal Virtues. A good seed produces good fruit in abundance. If we sow the seed of the three goodnesses we shall reach, as a fruit, the ninefold bliss of the Pure Land.

CHAPTER XVII

Buddhism reaches Japan

Buddhism reached Japan from Korea, and not at first from China.

Korea, in the age which we have been considering, was not as large a country as it is now. The whole of the district, from the Yalu river, which forms the present boundary of the Korean Empire, to the Tatong river, halfway between Wiju and Seoul, belonged to China. The rest of the peninsula was divided into three independent kingdoms : Koma, which occupied the eastern slopes, from the Tumen in the north down almost to the extreme south of the peninsula ; Kudara, which occupied the whole of the western slopes from the Chinese frontier to the extreme south ; and the small kingdom of Shiragi in the south-eastern corner of the peninsula, on the side nearest to Japan. The southernmost province of Shiragi was the province of Mimana, which may be said to have been at one time practically a Japanese colony.

Buddhism had reached the kingdom of Koma in A.D. 372, the missionary having been sent from Singanfu by the ruler of the Former Thsin (A.D. 350–394). A ruler of the Eastern Tsin (317 to 420) had sent an Indian priest, Marananda, to preach the Gospel of Buddha in Kudara in the year 384. Shiragi had received the doctrine from the neighbouring kingdom of Koma in

A.D. 424. The well-known propensity of the Buddhist priesthood for political intrigue and amateur statecraft makes it highly probable that the rival rulers of the Thsin and the Tsin, casting about for any straw with which to support their tottering dynasties, made use of the Buddhist missionaries for political purposes to gain allies for themselves in Koma and Kudara, both of which kingdoms touched the Chinese frontiers. As to the exact nature of the Korean Buddhism we have no accurate information. The division into sects in China was still new, and sectarian lines were not very clearly defined. The doctrine still wore its Indian and predominantly Hīnayānistic character; Vasubandhu, Asangha, and other great teachers of Mahāyāna had possibly not been born when Buddhism reached Korea.[1] There are indications to show that much attention was paid to the Vinaya discipline, and that whatever speculation there was ran along the lines laid down by the Kusha, Sanron, and Jōjitsu sects (see Chapter XVI.).

Korea and Japan were by no means strangers to one another. As early as B.C. 32 (if there is any confidence to be put in the early records of Japan) the little province of Mimāna or Kara, oppressed by Shiragi, had appealed to Japan for aid. The reigning emperor, Sujin Tennō, became its protector, and the prestige of the Japanese name was so great that Japan was able not only to turn Mimāna into a Japanese dependency, but to keep it as such for several centuries. Korean influence upon Japan may have begun even then, for in the reign of the next emperor, Suinin, about the dawn of the Christian era, we find the beginnings of rice culture in Japan, and an attempt to elevate and ennoble the native worship of the Kami, which may have been due to the influence

[1] Takakusu gives for Vasubandhu's date A.D. 445.

of a foreign religion.[1] In A.D. 2 Suinin is said to have
abolished the custom of burying alive the wives, concubines,
and retainers of deceased rulers and nobles, and to have
substituted the burial of clay figures, a practice which led
to the Japanese pottery industry.

In the year A.D. 202 the great Japanese heroine, Jingu
Kōgō, made her famous expedition to Korea, and established the Japanese ascendency not only over Shiragi,
but likewise over the sister kingdoms of Koma and
Kudara, an ascendency which it would probably have
been impossible to establish had it not been for the fact
that the great dynasty of the Han was at that period
tottering to its fall. In the confusions which followed
that catastrophe (A.D. 220), none of the transient Chinese
kingdoms was powerful enough to be able to pay much
attention to Korea.

Jingu Kōgō's son and successor, Ōjin Tennō, subsequently deified by his countrymen as Hachiman, the
God of War, and at a still later period adopted into the
Buddhist Pantheon as an incarnation of one of the great
Buddhas, made great use of his suzerainty over Korea by
importing from that country horses and arms, tailors and
sempstresses, smiths and artisans. His successor, Nintoku
(311–399), who was obliged to fit out an expedition to
Shiragi in order to maintain his rights, followed in the
footsteps of his father. He had been instructed in the
doctrines of Confucius and Mencius by the Chinese sage
Wani, whom his father had engaged as a tutor to the
Imperial family, and Japanese historians always speak

---

[1] It is not impossible that this may have been Buddhism. A.D. 64
marks the *official* recognition of Buddhism in China, not its popular
acceptance, and there is an early Japanese tradition that at a very
early period certain *Ratai no hito* brought an image of Kwannon to
Japan, which they set up at Kumano-ura for worship ("Bukkyo Seiten,"
App., p. 12).

of Nintoku with deep respect as a man of singular virtue and nobility. Nintoku introduced silkworm breeding into Japan, and it is a significant fact as showing a possibly earlier existence of Buddhism in this country that in the silk districts the patron deity of sericulture is the Buddhist saint As'vaghosha.[1]

In the year A.D. 522, a Chinese priest named Shiba Tatsu, a subject of the Liang (502–557), made an attempt to establish a mission in Yamato, which failed. The Liang ruled in the south of China. Their first emperor, Wu-ti, was a powerful ruler who extended the dominions of his house to the sea-coast on the east, and did much to foster trade and commerce. In his reign the Chinese began to be a seafaring people, and Chinese ships visited the Bay of Bengal, Ceylon, the west coast of India, and even penetrated as far as the Persian Gulf.¹ Wu-ti, during the earlier years of his reign (502–549), was a great patron of Confucianism; in his later years he alienated his Confucian subjects by his zeal for Buddhism, which he adopted with all the ardour of a convert. In the north of China, his most powerful rival was the kingdom of the Wei, ruled over by a queen, Hushi, who, like Wu-ti, was a zealous Buddhist, much to the disgust of her Confucianist subjects, who objected to the worship of S'akyamuni on the ground that he was only a deified man, and not a god like Tientei, the ruler of Heaven. In the end they dethroned their queen and threw her into the Hoangho.[2]

The Wei [3] influence (386–584) would naturally be great in the Korean states which touched their boundaries.

---

[1] See "Bukkyō Mondō Shū," pp. 14–24.

[2] Kaeuffer, "Geschichte Ostasiens," vol. ii. p. 397.

[3] There were three Wei dynasties, all in the north of China: (1) Northern Wei, 386–534; (2) Western Wei, 534–557; (3) Eastern Wei, 534–550.

Shiba Tatsu passed through Korea on his way to Japan. It is highly probable that he came on a semi-political mission which failed. Neither Korea nor Japan cared for an alliance with the distant Liang, whose fortunes were apparently bound up with the personality of one man. Wu-ti's death in 549 was practically the end of his house and dynasty.

But Shiba Tatsu's mission may very possibly have suggested a reason why the Korean kingdoms should seek to strengthen themselves by an alliance with Japan. Korea was practically a Buddhist realm. Both Wei and Liang, though ruled over by sovereigns with Buddhist propensities, had powerful aristocracies which were strongly anti-Buddhist. Had either of these kingdoms gained the ascendency in the Peninsula a grievous persecution would have followed, ending perhaps in the overthrow of Korean dynasties.[1] Japan was as yet neither Buddhist nor Confucian. If she could be won over to the faith, the immediate future at least would be secured from danger.

Accordingly, in 545, and again in 552,[2] King Seimei of Kudara sent presents to the Emperor of Japan—images of Buddha and Sacred Books—together with a recommend-atory letter in which he pointed out the excellences of the Buddhist religion, as well as its evident destiny to travel constantly eastward from the land of its origin. The presents received but a doubtful welcome. One

[1] The straits to which Buddhism in China was at this time reduced may be seen in the fact, noticed by Kaeuffer, that about 555 an attempt was made forcibly to unite Buddhism and Taoism, in a common enter-prise against the powerful Confucianists—a foreshadowing of Ryōbu Shinto. The attempt failed because the Taoist priests objected to having their heads shaved, and the failure only made things worse.

[2] This must be considered as the date of the official introduction of Buddhism.

noble family, that of Soga no Iname, whose household had possibly been already converted to Buddhism, advised the sovereign to accept the gift. Another section of the nobility, headed by Mononobe no Okoshi and Nakatomi no Kanako, was furiously opposed to having any dealings with a new religion which could not be brought into the country without offence to the national gods. The Emperor temporized. He entrusted the care of the images and books to Soga no Iname, as though to allow those who would to adopt the new religion,[1] without committing himself to any definite line of action in this respect. Soga housed the idols in his own villa, which he converted into a place of worship. Soon after this a pestilence broke out, which was taken to denote the anger of the native gods. Soga's temple was destroyed by a mob, and the great statue of the Buddha thrown into the canal at Naniwa. Then followed another portent—a flash of lightning from a cloudless sky, which set fire to the Imperial Palace. This was clearly a token of the anger of the Hotoke.[2] The offending statue was fished out of the river, and reverently placed in a suitable abode, and the Emperor, as a further act of reparation, caused two images to be carved in wood and set up at Hoshino. This was the first beginning of the glyptic arts in Japan. At the same time he sent a prudent message to the King of Kudara, asking him to send no more Buddhist bonzes or images, but requesting to be supplied with physicians, apothecaries, soothsayers, almanack-makers, and artisans, and promising in return to supply him with munitions of

[1] The Emperor would scarcely have adopted this course had not Iname been backed by a considerable number of influential sympathizers.

[2] *Hotoke*, the Japanese term for a Buddha.

war.[1] This last clause looks very much as though an offensive and defensive alliance had been really the aim of the King of Kudara.

The bonzes and images, however, continued to come. It cost a civil war and many a riot before Buddhism became a permanent institution. It possibly cost even more, for there was something suspicious about the death of the Emperor Sujun (592), if not about those of his predecessors, Bidatsu (586) and Yomei (587); but the proselytizing zeal of the Korean Court and their supporters in Japan (whose numbers may have increased with the opposition raised by the Kami-worshippers) knew no discouragement. Architects, wood-carvers, and almanack-makers came. Books on geography and astronomy, which the Buddhists, from their wide-reaching connections, were most fitted to teach, books on magic, and almanacks, of which they had almost a monopoly, came, and were eagerly received by the Japanese, who have always had a desire to know. But priests came too, and nuns, and in their hands were books, relics, and sacred images of Maitreya, of Amitābha with his two companions,[2] of Kwannon the Deity of Mercy, so that by the death of Shōtoku Taishi there were 46 temples and nearly 1400 monks and nuns composing the staff of Buddhist missions. Many sacred books came also, for

[1] In preparing this chapter I have largely consulted the historical sections of Rein's " Japan," which remains a standard work. For the Buddhist part I am much indebted to the painstaking chronology published by my friend, Dr. Hans Haas, of Heidelberg, in *Mitteilungen der Gesellschaft für Natur und Völkerkunde Ostasiens*, vol. xi. 3 (Berlin: Behrend & Co., Unter den Linden 16).

[2] The statue of Amitābha, with Avalokiteśvara and Mahāsthamaprāpta, sent over by the King of Kudara, in 552, is said to be now at the Zenkōji Temple at Nagano. See Satow and Hawes, "Handbook of Japan," p. 289.

we find Shōtoku Taishi lecturing on the "Hokekyō, Yuima Kyō," and "Shomangyo" (the last two, books of the Vinaya), and there must have been many others.

During the whole of this period of Korean influence the cause of Buddhism in Japan found a doughty champion in the Crown Prince, Shōtoku Taishi (572–621), a rare personage, who united in himself the qualities of a general, a statesman, a theologian, and a mission-preacher. A more important factor in the progress made by the religion was the fact that Buddhism in Japan soon attracted the enthusiastic adherence of the women. In 577 the King of Kudara sent over a nun, who must have been a very good mission worker. In 584 several Japanese women were admitted to the Order. In 588 a band of Japanese nuns went over to Korea to study. In 590 they returned, bringing with them the disciplinary rules of the Vinaya, and were well received by the people of Naniwa (Ōsaka), who built them a convent and allowed them to receive many postulants. It is probable that these pious women, teaching the comparatively simple doctrines contained in the Vinaya books, did much more to recommend the faith of Buddha to their countrymen than did the Mantra priest with his incantations and magic, or the ordinary bonze with his Kusha, Sanron, or Jōjitsu speculations.

The Vinaya books are divided into four sets. They represent the disciplinary books of the four Hīnayāna sects, Sarvāstivādins, Dharmaguptas, Vibhās'ikas, and Mahis'akas—which alone had any connection with Chinese missions. What the precise differences between these traditions were we know not, and which tradition found its way through Korea to Japan, we cannot tell. Possibly there was not much to choose between them; but the lesson to be learned from the four divisions is worth remembering. For, if the Discipline might be altered a little, it might also be altered much, and if it might be altered much, it might also be abolished entirely. In later years, Shinran Shōnin's reforms practically swept away the whole discipline, and we may presume that it was by arguments such as these that he justified his action. But be that as it may. The pious women of Japan took kindly to the definite rules of Vinaya Buddhism, and their adherence to the new religion was of immense importance. There were not wanting signs of the need of discipline amongst religious communities, even in those early days.[1]

The fashionable form of religious metaphysics was that adopted by the Sanron sect, which commenced its Japanese existence in the year 624, three years after the death of Shōtoku. This sect professed to accept the whole of the Buddhist Canon so far as it existed in China in those days.[2] The diseases of the human mind were many and various, so they said, and the prescriptions for so many diseases must be many also. The object of Buddha's teaching was to destroy error and establish the truth: the one implied the other, for the destruction of error left truth in its place, and when all errors were destroyed truth would have the field all to itself. But to set to work to establish positive truth would of necessity involve the establishment of error. [There can, therefore, never be such a thing as a positive and infallible Revelation of Truth.] Truth was of two kinds, absolute (眞) and apparent (俗), and error, though infinite in its possibilities, might all be summed up under eight great heads. There

---

[1] See Haas, "Chronology of Buddhism, A.D. 623 and 628," in *Mitteilungen der deutschen Gesellschaft für Natur und Völkerkunde Ostasiens.*

[2] See Nanjo, "Cat. Trip.," Introd., p. xviii.

were errors connected with positive views of Life and Death, about Oneness and Multiplicity, about the Determinate and the Indeterminate, about Going and Coming.[1] Place the word "No" (不) in front of each of these eight notions, and the Truth would be clear. "No Life and No Death, No Oneness and No Multiplicity, No Determinate and No Indeterminate, No Going and No Coming." The Universe and the Microcosm, Man, are nothing but negations.

Speculations such as these, the products of the hair-splitting Indian mind, had no charm for the practical Japanese intellect, and the Sanron sect[2] was never more than a shadow among the Buddhist denominations in Japan. If it had not been for the simple faith of the Japanese women, who took the Buddha of the Vinaya books as their model, with his plain, straightforward directions as to the religious life of the believer, it is possible that Buddhism might have had to wait some years longer before gaining the ear of the Japanese people. The lesson is one not to be thrown away.

---

[1] "Murakami," p. 446. The words are Shō-metsu-ichi-i-dan-jō-ko-rai (生, 滅, 一, 異, 斷, 常, 去, 來).

[2] For the meaning of *Sanron* see previous chapter.

CHAPTER XVIII

THE CROWN PRINCE SHŌTOKU TAISHI

THE Emperor Kimmei, who had received from Korea the gifts of Buddhist images and sacred vessels which had caused so much disturbance among his subjects, died in A.D. 570. His reign had not been a very happy or glorious one. In addition to the domestic confusions arising from the introduction of the new religion, there had been disappointments in the foreign policy of the country. His ally, King Seimei of Kudara, had been defeated by the troops of Shiragi and taken prisoner (about 557), a Japanese army in Korea had been defeated by the Shiragi armies in 562, and the province of Mimãna had been entirely lost to Japan. When Kimmei lay a-dying in 570, he charged his successor, Bidatsu, not to rest until Mimãna had been recovered.

It was not Bidatsu's good fortune to recover the lost province, and when he died, in A.D. 585, he laid on his successor, Yōmei, the same solemn injunction that his predecessor had laid upon him. But the year following his accession, the wife of his brother Yōmei bore a son who was destined to restore the fallen prestige of the country. The child thus born was at the first called Umayado, "the Stable Prince," a name which has been explained by the story (surely a fiction) that his mother, while going the rounds of her house and grounds, was suddenly seized by labour pains, and gave birth to her son in the stable.

He had another name, Toyoto-mimi, which may convey some reference to his personal appearance; but at any rate personal defects had no effect on his intellectual powers, and he was early distinguished both for wisdom and for virtue.

His early youth was a troublous one. Bidatsu continued to receive presents (and appeals for help) from the King of Kudara, hard pressed by Shiragi and scarcely able to hold his own. Without becoming a convert, the Emperor did all in his power to help the new religion, and, to give but one instance, instituted the practice of releasing animals on the eighth, fourteenth, fifteenth, twenty-third, twenty-ninth, and thirtieth of every month— an institution not unlike the primitive *uposatha*, or the Christian and Jewish sabbath. No civic disturbances marked his reign; but once, when a pestilence broke out shortly after the erection of a pagoda, built to contain a Buddhist relic that had, it was claimed, been found in some rice, there must have been many doubtful heads shaken over the untoward event. But the Buddhists were not to be moved. They met the pestilence with the weapon of prayer, and when the Emperor himself miraculously recovered from an attack of the plague, they felt that they had triumphed.

In 586, Prince Umayado's father, Yōmei, came to the throne, and the Prince became, in expectation at least, Heir-Apparent. Yōmei went further than any of his predecessors, for he was the first Imperial convert to Buddhism, and the first emperor to be baptized with the Buddhist ceremony of Kwanjo. His conversion possibly cost him his life, for he died in the following year, and his death was the occasion for the outbreak of a civil war, which ended with the Battle of Shigisen, in which the Prince Shōtoku and his staunch friend, Soga no Umako, were victorious. It would seem that the Prince's Buddhism was of too pronounced a type for him to be a suitable occupant of the throne, which went to his uncle Sujun, a younger brother of Bidatsu and Yōmei. Sujun must have been the candidate favoured by the conservative Kami worshippers, or at least acceptable to them. He made preparations for an expedition against Shiragi, but he was apparently unable to preserve the loyalty of the advanced party of the Buddhists, for he was murdered in 592 by the ally of the Prince, Soga no Umako.

The Prince was again passed over—voluntarily, it would seem. Sujun's successor was his elder half-sister, Suiko, the widow of Bidatsu—for marriages between half-brothers and half-sisters were always allowed in ancient Japan. Suiko reigned from 593 to 628; for all but the last seven years, her nephew, now known as Shōtoku Taishi, acted as her deputy and vice-gerent, so that what was nominally the reign of the Empress Suiko was in reality the reign of the Crown Prince Shōtoku.

Shōtoku's life-work falls under three heads. We must judge him by his foreign policy, his domestic administration, and his religious achievements.

His foreign policy was eminently successful. His uncles had dreamed of conquering Shiragi, and an expedition was actually on the point of starting when the Emperor Sujun was murdered. Shōtoku tried a more conciliatory line of policy, and one more in accordance with the religious professions of a Buddhist. He sent embassies to Shiragi, in 597, and again in 600, with the result that tribute was sent to Japan, not only from Shiragi, but from Mimāna as well, showing thereby that, thanks to the Regent's wise policy, Shiragi had recognized the independence of the state of Mimāna protected by the

Japanese. Shōtoku even went further in asserting the dignity of his country. He dared to claim for Japan an equal Imperial dignity with China, which Wen-ti of the Sui Dynasty had just united once more under one sceptre. Wen-ti had stretched his dominions from the frontiers of Koma in the east, to those of the Turki kingdoms in the west, and his successor, Yangti, who ruled from 606 to 618, had extended his power still further. Shōtoku's Korean policy brought him into collision with Yangti, who also had designs on the peninsula, and in 609 a letter came from the Chinese sovereign, which the Japanese Court received. Shōtoku answered it, but in a tone of equality, " The Eastern Emperor begs respectfully to speak to the Emperor of the West." The Chinese Court did not altogether appreciate the tone of the letter ; but in 610 Koma sent presents to the Court of Japan, and Shiragi in 616. Bluff, or rather the proper assertion of dignity, is at times a very paying line of policy for a statesman to adopt.

Shōtoku's home administration is chiefly connected with an attempt made in 603 to arrange the official ranks of persons in Government service according to the model of the Chinese Court,[1] and the Constitution of the Seventeen Articles issued in the following year. The newly graded official ranks were named after the Confucianist virtues, as though to remind the holders of the paramount importance of virtue above all things else ; in the Constitution we have traces of Confucianist influence, together with an outspoken advocacy of Buddhism, as being, in the writer's mind at least, the sole religion for a wise man to follow.

[1] The grades are as follows: *Daitoku, Shōtoku, Daijin, Shōjin, Tairei, Shōrei, Daishin, Shōshin, Daigi, Shōgi, Daichi, Shōchi. Toku, Jin, Rei, Shin, Gi, Chi* (virtue, benevolence, propriety, sincerity, justice, wisdom) are the basal Confucianist virtues.

The seventeen Articles of the Constitution throw a very bright light on the conditions of the country which Shōtoku sought to amend. It was a period of disunion and discord, dating probably from days prior to the introduction of Buddhism, but also probably accentuated by the same. The results of this discord were visible in the loss of Mimāna and of almost all prestige in Korea, and in the backwardness of Japanese culture. Shōtoku appeals to the country on behalf of concord, in his first Article: in the second, he points his countrymen to what he feels to be the best and truest way of arriving at the same—the whole-hearted acceptance of Buddhism. We cannot but admire the boldness of his words, in view of the still constant opposition to foreign doctrines. Neither can we forget that, just about this time, an Emperor of China was coming to the conclusion that, whenever a ruler showed himself too partial towards the doctrines of Buddhism, he always brought ruin on his dynasty.[1] In Shōtoku's eyes, Buddhism wore a very different aspect.

In Article III., Shōtoku dwells on the dignity of the Emperor, who stands above his people, covering them with his protection, just as Heaven stands over and protects the earth beneath it. The Article was probably directed against the nobles, whose respect for the sovereign in those days of civil strife and confusion was not always as great as it should have been. The Article must, moreover, be read in reference to the murder of the Emperor Sujun by Shōtoku's ally, Soga no Umako. Had Shōtoku felt himself in any way to be blamed for his continued friendship for the man who had committed that deed, he would scarcely have ventured to speak as he did of the respect due to the Emperor.[2] It would seem as though

[1] Taitsung of the Tang Dynasty, A.D. 627.
[2] Aston's "Nihongi," vol. i. p. 129, etc.

Sujun had been a usurper, possibly with the aid of the opponents of Buddhism; that Soga no Umako, as the supporter of Shōtoku's claims, had opened the way for the Prince to succeed, and that the Prince, declining to come to the throne in this way, had secured the nomination of his aunt. He was conscious of his own rights as the son of Yōmei, yet he stood back in order that he might be in a position to speak with greater emphasis of the duty that the subject owes to his sovereign. It is evident from the Article that Shōtoku did not share the subsequently formulated and now officially accepted doctrine as to the origin of the Imperial House.

The following Articles deal with the duties of ministers and functionaries. If subjects have certain duties towards their rulers, rulers and magistrates have certain responsibilities towards those beneath them, which must be discharged with decorum and the observance of due proportion. Such observance cannot fail to have a good influence on the country at large (Art. iv.). But if, on the other hand (Art. v.), the magistracy allows itself to be bribed with gifts, if the judge is remiss in the administration of justice, if he gives his decisions to suit his own interests, or without clearness, the poor will no longer know whom to look to for support, and the country will lose its prosperity. Lying and flattery (Art. vi.) have been evils in every country and age; Shōtoku's age was certainly not free from them. It was exposed to another peril, that of hereditary office (Arts. vii. and viii.). Men were promoted to dignities and high charges, not for any special capacities that they had shown in inferior positions, but because these offices were considered to be the perquisites of certain families. And the hereditary office had but too often been treated as a sinecure. The result of all this (Art. ix.) was the loss of public confidence.

In Arts. x.–xiv., the evils arising from the want of a feeling of responsibility, on the part of these hereditary holders of offices treated almost as sinecures, are laid out more in detail. The magistrate would allow himself to lose his temper on the bench, and bully the accused or the witnesses. He should remember that it was always possible that he himself might not always be the perfection of wisdom ; that it was also possible that the prisoner in the dock, and the witness under cross-examination, were reasonable men (Art. x.). He should listen, therefore, to the opinions of others, should give his decisions with sobriety and fear, and be very careful to administer praise and blame in strict accordance with the results of a severe and impartial investigation (Art. xi.). He should be careful to levy no arbitrary taxes, on his own authority, in the district over which he was called to rule, so as not to provoke the people to resistance (Art. vii.). He should know the working of every detail of his own office, and the regularity or slackness of the members of his staff. If something had gone wrong, because a subordinate was absent from his post, the chief of the bureau must not excuse himself by saying that he did not know the man was absent. It was his duty to know it, and to provide for the public service being properly attended to (Art. xiii.). Mutual jealousies have often brought ruin upon a State. Saints and sages appear but rarely in the world ; jealousy and envy are the main obstacles which hinder their more frequent development. And what would become of the government of a country without sages or saints ? (Art. xv.). A sage or a saint, he continues, showing the identity of both Confucianist and Buddhist teachings in this respect, is one who sacrifices his own will, and devotes himself to the service of others. This principle produces self-sacrifice in the governors, obedience in the people, and makes for peace and harmony (Art. xv.). It shows itself in the way in which orders are given.

For instance, Government has the right to demand a certain amount of forced labour from the people. But times and seasons must be observed. If the governor makes the people work for the State during the summer months, the farmer will suffer, and distress will ensue. If the governor exercises patience and self-control, and waits till winter comes there will be no friction (Art. xvi.). " Never act," he concludes, " on your own private initiative or authority ; and never take any step of importance without consultation. In a doubtful case, consult the more " (Art. xvii.).[1]

Such were the principal defects which Shōtoku found in the administration of the country after he had had his hand at the helm of State for several years. For these evils he had two great remedies. The one was the reform of the judiciary and magistracy according to Chinese [2]

---

[1] This passage may possibly have inspired one of the recent poems of her Majesty the Empress—

> *Ayamatan*
> *Koto wo omoeba,*
> *Karisome no*
> *Koto ni mo mono wa*
> *Tsutsushimaretsutsu.*

> " Should we fear
> To slip or err, we take good care ourselves,
> And e'en the smallest deed, do heedfully."

[2] P. Balet (" Mélanges Japonais," vol. iii. p. 287) points out that when Shōtoku, in 607, sent students to China (Sui Dynasty, 590–619) to study actual conditions, he chose only the descendants of Chinese families naturalized in Japan. All bear the designation *Ayabito*, which denotes a Chinaman naturalized in Japan.

models; the other was the inculcation and propagation of Buddhism, as the best religion he knew, and as eminently fitted, in his judgment, to supply to his countrymen that firm ethical basis which the Shintoism of the time lacked, plus the religious enthusiasm which comes from a definite theological system. We will now pass on to the consideration of Shōtoku's religion.

Shōtoku has been much blamed by modern Shintoist writers as wanting in patriotism, because he laid no stress on the national gods of the land, and because, in the second article of his Constitution, he emphasized Buddhism as the sole religion worthy to be adopted by his subjects. It is true that the saying once currently attributed to him, that the religion of Japan was like a tripod standing on three legs, Buddhism, Confucianism, and the Shinto, cannot be sustained, because, as Dazai truly observes, Shinto did not exist, *i.e.* was not elevated into a system, until long after the Crown Prince's time.[1] But it is also true that there is no sign of his having forced his beliefs on the consciences of his people against their wills. He confined himself to preaching the faith which he had adopted with all his heart and soul; for other forms of faith and religion, he had no thoughts left.

He had no reason to love the Kami-worshippers. The adherents of that system were not only conservatives in religion, but probably obstructionists in the path of popular progress, and were opposed not only to Buddhism, but to Confucianism as well. His whole early life had been embittered by the antagonism of a Conservative party, which was not even loyal to the throne; it can hardly cause wonder if, on his accession to power, he did

---

[1] See Mr. Consul-General J. C. Hall, "A Japanese Philosopher on Shinto," in *Transactions of the Third International Congress for the Study of the History of Religions* (Oxford, 1908).

not go out of his way to recommend a system which had always stood in the way of the reforms and the progress he was so anxious to inaugurate. Besides, the Shinto of his day needed no commendation from him. It was already well established in the hearts of the people. It had not yet been systematized—that came later, as a result of the opposition to Buddhism—neither had the amalgamation between the two religions yet been carried out. But we can well imagine that Shōtoku saw no reason why it should not be quietly absorbed by the all-embracing Buddhism which he preached. There was no need for mentioning the subject. He would preach Buddha, and trust to coming events for the result.

Shōtoku, like As'oka, whom he very much resembled in character, was a preacher. The fact facilitates the task of the historian, for we fortunately know the texts from which he preached to the ladies and gentlemen of his aunt's court. In the year 606, two years after the promulgation of his Constitution, he lectured in his palace at Naniwa on three books, the " Saddharmapundarika Sūtra," the " Vimāla-Kīrtti-nirdesa-sūtra," and the " S'rimāladenī-simhananda-sūtra." [1] In the same year he decreed the observance of S'akyamuni's birthday. We may sum up the three Sūtras by saying that the first furnished Shōtoku with a manual of theology ; the second, with texts on the duties of the devout layman ; the third, with homilies on the duties of faithful women. On these three Sūtras he preached and also composed commentaries.

The Hokekyō is an extremely well-known Sūtra. It is one of a comparatively late date, for, when the five subdivisions of the Mahāyāna Sūtras were made, it was not in existence, and Dr. Nanjo gives it to us under a

[1] In Japanese, "Hokekyō," " Yuima-kyō," "Shomangyō." In Nanjo's Catalogue, Nos. 134, 144, and 23 (48).

separate heading as one of the Sūtras of the Mahāyāna not included under any of the previous five classes. It is post-Christian in its structure, and betrays acquaintance with the New Testament scriptures, an acquaintance which it may have derived through Manichæism.[1] It represents S'akyamuni, but not as he was in the guise of his historical life, preaching a simple life to simple persons, and bringing to the searcher after Truth in India the gospel of a relief from the fetters of caste and the possibility of attaining to a Nirvana of rest and freedom, without penances or austerities, by a simple placing of trust in Himself and a following along the noble Eightfold Path of Right Actions, Right Views, Right Aspirations. It represents Him as the Eternal Buddha, without beginning and without end, manifested in India as Gotama, but manifested often both before and since. It represents him spiritually present with his people, giving them His spiritual Body for their worship, with four great Ministers before Him, and surrounded with a glorious company which no man can number, of perfected saints who rise to greet Him out of the clefts of the earth. And, if we may judge from the fact that all the images which came to Japan in those early days were images of Amida, with or without his great son and representative Kwannon (Avalokites'vara) and his other minister Seishi (Mah'āsthāmaprāpta), we shall infer that Shōtoku identified the glorified S'akyamuni of the Hokekyo, the counterpart, to use no stronger expression, of our Christ, with the Great Buddha, Amitābha, as do the Shinshuists to-day.[2]

The other two Sūtras are not so well known, neither

[1] See my "Wheat among the Tares."

[2] The oldest Image in Japan, the one sent by the King of Kudara in 552, is said to be at the Zenkōji, in Nagano. It represents Amida, Kwannon, and Seishi. See my "Wheat among the Tares," *passim*, and Dr. Tada Kanae's "Shoshinge Kâwa" (in Japanese).

has the Commentary by Shōtoku ever been made accessible
to Western scholars. All I know of the "Shomangyō,"
the Sūtra treating of the duties of women, is that it is
classed by Nanjo among the Avatamsaka Scriptures
which formed the Canon used by the Yogāchārya sect, the
Japanese Hossō. It is therefore a writing of a comparatively late date.[1] Of the "Yuimakyo," which deals with
the duties of the Buddhist layman, there is fortunately
an English translation, published in 1897 in the columns
of a now defunct periodical, the *Hansei Zasshi*. It is too
lengthy to be reproduced here, but it is very practical,
and contains a very full summary of the religious life as
viewed by the Mahāyānist. A man who should fashion
his life according to its precepts would come very near to
being a holy man. He might, however, be a prig.

Shōtoku was also a man who believed in the power
and efficacy of prayer. When his friend the Ōmi, Soga
no Umako, lay ill, he instituted formal intercessions for
his recovery, and a thousand persons took temporary
vows to lead a monastic life until the sick man should
recover. Shōtoku's limitations were due to his exalted
position. Had he been born a prince of a long-dethroned
house, like Christ, with no thoughts before him of temporal
power, or had he been able to make the renunciation of
earthly position, which is such a touching and prominent
feature in the life of S'akyamuni, he would have accomplished even more than he did. It was his misfortune
that, like As'oka, he had to combine the offices of priest
and prince in his own person. When a ruling prince
takes to preaching, there is always a danger lest the

[1] It would be almost impossible for any single-handed historian of
the Mahāyāna to translate all the Chinese texts he is obliged to
mention. It requires time, money, and many sets of brains and hands
to lay bare all that is contained in the vast Mahāyāna Canon.

doctrine, becoming superficially popular, should become perverted. It was so in As'oka's case; it was so in Shōtoku's. Three years after his death stringent measures had to be taken to enforce discipline amongst an immoral clergy, and the Nara age, to which we are now coming, was a very corrupt and superstitious one. There is no healthy religion of any kind that does not involve the bearing of a cross of some sort or other.

It is a true instinct that has led the Shinshu or "True Sect" believers in Japan to place Shōtoku on a pedestal of honour as the firstfruits of Amidaism in Japan. For undoubtedly he was inspired by the idea of that great Being, the counterpart of our Western Christ, who humbled himself that he might save man, who was exalted when he had accomplished that salvation, and from whom so much of comfort and strength has flowed out to suffering humanity in Japan and the Far East.[1] A further study of Comparative Chronology, one of the most important branches of the study of religion, will show us that Shōtoku was the contemporary of that religious move- ment which took place in the capital of the Chinese Tangs, when the victories of Mahometanism brought Christian and Zoroastrian exiles to the court of Singanfu, to rub shoulders together in the sympathy that came to them from the participation in a common misfortune.

[1] And yet Shōtoku preceded Zendō and the great development of Amidaism which originated with him. See next chapter.

CHAPTER XIX

BUDDHISM DURING THE NARA PERIOD [1] FROM A.D. 621–782

THE activities of Kumarajiva seem to have led to the dismemberment of the Mahāyāna, which, in spite of the variety of doctrines it contained within its ample folds, had hitherto contrived to preserve a united front. The sectarianism of Chinese Buddhism was aided by the distracted state of the Chinese Empire, broken up into many kingdoms, each striving for the mastery; and we have seen some of these rival states casting about for supporters, and trying to enlist sympathy for themselves in the Korean peninsula and in Japan. We have seen Korea similarly divided into warring kingdoms, some of which—Kudara and Mimāna—looked to Japan for aid, while Shiragi, relying on Chinese support from the kingdom of the Wei, boldly resisted Japanese intervention; and Koma, too weak for independent action, sat on a fence and vacillated between Japan and Shiragi, according to the interests of the hour. And, lastly, we have seen Japan under Shōtoku Taishi gradually inclining more and more towards a following of China, and taking the Empire of the Sui (590–618) as its model, both in religion and in secular politics.

[1] The town of Nara was actually the capital of Japan only from 710 to 784, there having been no definite capital before that date. But Nara became so distinctly the dominating centre that its name may well be given to the whole period.

Shōtoku died in 621. Three years before his death, the dynasty of the Sui, in China, with its costly ambition and magnificence, had been obliged to make way for the family of the Tangs, who ruled till 907, and who inaugurated a period of greatness and prosperity such as China had not known since the downfall of the great House of Han in 220 A.D.

The Tangs began badly for Buddhism. Kaotsu (618–627), their first ruler, broke up Buddhist monasteries right and left, and sent 100,000 bonzes back to lay life where they would be obliged to work, and neither his successor Taitsung nor his wife Ch'angsun[1] had any sympathies for the faith. But the Buddhists knew how to win their way back to favour in the course of a few years, and the Tangs had not been fifty years on the throne in China ere Buddhism was once more in full force, and on a far more splendid basis than before. Under the Tangs it became essentially a Chinese faith; it had, as it were, discarded its Indian waistcloth and adopted the flowing robes of the Celestial.

In the selfsame year that Shōtoku Taishi died, there was erected at Singanfu, at that time the capital, the first Zoroastrian temple ever built in China. The Tangs had owed very much to the support of the Turkish tribes on the western frontier of China in the days when they were busy winning their crown, and it was probably due to this

[1] When Ch'angsun was dying she addressed her son in words somewhat to this effect: "Our life is in the hands of Heaven, and when it decides that we shall die, there is no mortal power that can prolong it. As for the Taoist and Buddhist faiths, they are heresies, and have been the cause of injury both to the people and to the State. Your father had a great aversion to them, and you must not displease him by calling on them on my behalf." She requested to be buried with great simplicity, exhorting her son to associate with good men and to avoid extravagance, especially in hunting and building.

connection between the Empire and the tribes on its borders that the Magians took the opportunity of preaching in China itself. Singanfu, which lies in the province of Shensi, is not far removed from the then abodes of the Turkish tribes; indeed, it was once suggested to Kaotsu, by some pusillanimous advisers, that he should remove his capital to some safer spot in the province of Honan, where he would be free from the danger of incursions from the barbarians.

The year of Shōtoku's death was also the year of the Hejirah, the year in which Mohammed fled to Medina and announced his divine mission to the astonished world. Ten years later, Izdegerd, King of Persia, was fighting for his very existence against the victorious Arabs who had gone forth conquering and to conquer, and by the year 640 the whole of Persia, with Merv, Balkh, Herat, everything as far as the Indus and the Oxus, had submitted to the sword of the new-born enthusiasm. That Persia, in the pangs of her last crisis, appealed to China for help is known. After Izdegerd's death in 651, his son fled into Turkestan, from whence he made his way to China. He succeeded in persuading the Chinese to take over the administration of the whole country between their frontier and that of the Arabs, and it was as Chinese Viceroy of that district that he was attacked and defeated by the Arabs in 670, and obliged once more to flee to Singanfu.[1]

Was it chance, or was it the design of Heaven, that, in the year 636, shortly after Izdegerd had entered upon his last fatal war against the Arabs, there arrived in Singanfu a Christian mission hailing from Persia ?

When the Nestorian protest against the use of the word Theotokos as applied to the mother of Our Lord

[1] E. H. Parker, "China: Her History, Diplomacy, and Commerce."

O

had been condemned by the Council of Ephesus in A.D. 431, the followers of Nestorius, finding themselves liable to unjust persecution in the Roman Empire, withdrew into Persia, where they were well received, and enabled to establish flourishing communities, not only in Persia, but in Balkh, Merv, Central Asia, and India. They were loyal to the country of their adoption, as well they might be; that country was now in distress, and was looking to China for help; a Christian mission in China might be productive of much good, both spiritually and politically. The mission was, therefore, sent;[1] it arrived at Singanfu in 636, and was well received by the Emperor and his successors, some of whom issued edicts in favour of the faith, or gave money for building "temples of felicity," as they were called, whilst one went so far in his patronage that,

[1] It purported to come from a certain Potolik, King of Fulin. Professor Hirth gives reason for saying that Potolik = Patriarch, and that Fulin is to be pronounced as Pat-lam, the birthplace of Christ being taken as = to Christendom, just as Magadha to the Chinese stood for India.

That the Nestorian mission was as much political as religious may e seen in the fact that an *Olopen* (was it a name or a title?) visited the court of the great Indian ruler Siladitya Harsha in 636. It is clear that the Nestorians, making common cause with their Persian protectors and friends, were actively engaged in trying to procure allies for them in their warfare against the Arabian invaders. Many Nestorian dioceses were destroyed when the Arabs annexed Merv, Balkh, Herat, etc., in A.D. 644. Hiouen Thsang, the Chinese traveller, was also in India at the time, returning to China in A.D. 645. It is also noteworthy that from this date both Siladitya Harsha and Taitsung now become more favourable to Buddhism. Neumann ("Asiatische Studien," i. 166) quotes, out of a Chinese work published about A.D. 502, a description of Persia, in which it is stated that there were many Buddhist temples in the Persian capital. Buddhist survivals are still to be traced in the doctrines of the Shiite, and still more so in those of the Sufite, sect of Mahometanism. It is quite probable that both Zoroastrianism and Manichæism were looked upon as legitimate variants of Buddhism. There were Nestorians in China before Olopen—some are mentioned as early as A.D. 508.

without becoming a Christian, he would still keep the Christmas festival with his Nestorian subjects. There were times of persecution, to be sure ; but the Nestorian missions survived them all. In the year 1293 the Franciscans under John of Montecorvino arrived at Peking, and found the Nestorians in full force; in 1304, the Nestorian Patriarch of Baghdad, the head of the whole Nestorian Church, submitted himself to Rome, and the Chinese Nestorians seem to have thought it best to follow his example. In 1305, John de Montecorvino reported very large accessions to his flock, and the Nestorians of China disappear from history.

There was also in Singanfu and its neighbourhood the zeal of Buddhism, aroused by the sense of its new dangers. The luxury of the Sui, and of many of the sovereigns of the illegitimate states, had been suffered by the Buddhists to go unreproved. Nay, they had profited by the distractions and evils of the times, and had secured for themselves wealth, position, and exemptions from taxation as the price of the support they gave to luxurious and ambitious princes. All these things had brought upon them the hatred and contempt of the lettered classes, and the undisguised hostility of powerful sovereigns, like Kaotsung and others, must have warned them to set their house in order if they would continue in their former prosperity. We can see many signs of this movement of reform produced by fear. The new school of translation inaugurated by Kumarajīva, the suggested amalgamation of Buddhism with Taoism, the new revelations (for they amounted to that) of the Hossō and the Kegon, and the wide-embracing system inaugurated by Chisha Daishi of the Tendai, all point to the same conclusion.

Bodhidharma and Zendō [1] alone aimed at simplification,

---

[1] For Zendō, see note at the end of this chapter.

but the former was not represented at the capital of the Sui and Tang. Zendō, however, was there, and his preaching of salvation by faith was welcomed by the poor. He was the popular preacher of the hour, and the popularity of his preaching drew upon him the hostility of the other sects. Tendai, Hossō, Kegon have always been the enemies of the simple faith preached by Zendō. They have always treated it as something alien to Buddhism, and so perhaps it was. At any rate, there it was in Singanfu, side by side with many alien faiths, during that momentous half-century which meant so very much for the religious development of the Far East.

It was probably about this time also that the Manichæan missions reached China proper. They had long ere this time been in the Turfan and Khotan districts, but probably never reached China itself until the time of the Tangs. The recent discoveries of German and other explorers are likely in a short time to add so much to our knowledge of Manichæism that it is not worth while here to dilate upon the subject. Let us content ourselves with noting that Manichæism was in China, and was one of the rivals of Buddhism.

Magians, Christians, Manichæans, three rivals, and the old enemies to boot, Confucianism and Taoism. With Kaotsu and Taitsung on the throne of the united empire, and putting down Buddhist monasteries with a strong hand, things looked very dark indeed for the Chinese Mahāyāna. Hiouen Thsang was the man who saved it in this crisis. Born in 602, and admitted to the priesthood in 622, Hiouen Thsang determined to travel to India and collect accurate information and materials from the original home of Buddhism for the defence of the faith which he saw threatened from within and from without. It is quite possible that he mistrusted the Central Asian traditions. Starting in 629, he made a tour of such Buddhist countries in Central Asia as had not yet fallen a prey to the Arabs, and in India, where he was royally treated by the great king Siladitya Harsha, one of the last of its Buddhist sovereigns. When he returned to China, the movement hostile to Buddhism had for the time spent its strength, and when, about 646, he published translations of some of the new books he had brought with him, the Emperor himself deigned to write a preface.[1]

Hiouen Thsang, the Max Müller of his day, was in direct relations with Japan. In 655, about the time of the accession of the Empress Saimei, a priest from Kawachi, a Sōzu[2] of the name of Dōsō, went over to China with the ambassadors sent to announce the new sovereign's accession, and there, meeting with Hiouen Thsang, learnt from him the Hossō or Dharma-lakshana doctrines, which the great doctor was preaching. Five years later, in the same reign, two more priests, Chitsū and Chitatsu, crossed to China in a ship of Shiragi, and were initiated into the Hossō mysteries by Hiouen Thsang and his coadjutor Jion daishi. In the third year of Taihō (704), another batch of these priests went to China, armed with letters from their sovereign, and studied the doctrines

---

[1] *Hiouen Thsang* gives us the best contemporary picture we possess of Buddhist India. If it were not for him and the other Chinese pilgrims who visited India, we should know nothing of the history of that country for several centuries. Hiouen Thsang, in addition to his own contributions to the theology of Buddhism, brought back the materials with which the purely Chinese sects, such as *Tendai* and *Kegon* (Avatamsaka), were afterwards established.

[2] *Sōzu*, a Japanese ecclesiastical title equivalent to our *canon* or *archdeacon*. The lawlessness and want of discipline among the monks, whose numbers were very large owing to the indiscriminate patronage of the faith by devotee sovereigns during this period, gave rise to many attempts to regulate the Buddhist clergy by the appointment of overseers or superintendents.

of the Unity (*Yuishiki*) under Chishō Daishi. Thus three[1] distinct strains of Hossō teachings came to Japan, and blended there, and though the Hossō sect, *quâ* sect, disappeared shortly after the close of the Nara age, it left permanent traces in the religious history of the country. For Dōsō and Chitatsu had as their principal disciple the celebrated Gyōgi Bosatsu[2] to whom is attributed the invention of the Ryōbu Shintō,[3] which made it possible for Buddhism to strike deep roots in the religious consciousness of Japan.

If we trace back this teaching to its earliest origin we shall see what it meant, and how powerfully it was likely to affect the situation in Japan. We shall also see, incidentally, how far the Mahāyāna had by this time travelled from the simplicity of S'akyamuni's teachings.

---

[1] There were actually *four* strains of the Hossō in Japan.

[2] *Gyōgi Bosatsu*, a celebrated Korean priest (670–749), who enjoyed great influence in Japan. It was he who administered Baptism (Kwanjo) to the reigning emperor.

[3] *Ryōbu Shinto*, an amalgamation of Buddhism and Shinto, which was not done away with officially until the beginning of the Meiji period.

One of the natural consequences of the adoption of the system known as *Ryōbu* ("two parts") was that, by treating the native gods of Japan as merely incarnations of one or other of the Buddhas, and as therefore entitled to the worship of the Buddhists, the Japanese were enabled to introduce into their Buddhism many non-Buddhist elements. Thus Amida and Vairoc'ana, both of them symbolized by the Sun, came to be identified with *Tenshōkōdaijin*, the "Heaven-shining-mighty goddess," from whom the Imperial house claims descent. (The change of sex is unimportant, for many of the Buddhas and Bodhisattvas, *e.g.* Kwannon, are bisexual.) Thus, too, Buddhism, which absolutely forbids the taking of life, gained a Buddhified god of war in Hachiman, and Buddhist monks, who worshipped the god of war, could with quiet consciences take to fighting. Nichiren ("Seigoroku," p. 132) speaks of Tenshōdaijin and Hachiman as the true lords of Japan, revealed in later times as Buddhas, and Hideyoshi, who openly avowed his desire for deification, built for himself a temple in which he intended to be worshipped after his death as Shin Hachiman, the new god of war.

The Hossō sect traced itself back to the brothers Asangha and Vasubandhu, whom we may place at the beginning of the fourth century A.D. It was an age of syncretism and eclecticism. Mani, the founder of Manichæism, had already worked out his great religion, which was destined to spread so widely and to have so extended and varied an influence, and Mani had laboured in India, as well as studied in Alexandria and Babylon. The Buddhists in India, hard pressed by the arguments of Hindu philosophers, such as the doughty Sankarāchārya, were casting about for new ways of putting their principles before the Hindu world. The Dharmalakshana or Hossō teachings of Asangha and Vasubandhu were intended to build a bridge between Hinduism and the Mahāyāna, of such a nature that the Buddhist might, as it were, invade the territory of Hinduism and conquer without seeming to do so.

The teaching was based, as I have said, on a revelation or quasi-revelation. Whilst Asangha was lecturing in Ayodhya, the present Oude, in India, he received a heavenly visitor, the great Bodhisattva Maitreya,[1] the disciple of S'akyamuni, who had received the promise of becoming the future Saviour of the world, and who was waiting in the celestial regions for the fulness of the times to come. Maitreya, appearing in the lecture hall, expounded for Asangha a secret and mysterious doctrine which he had been commissioned to deliver. He had come from a Buddha greater and wiser than S'akyamuni, from the great Buddha *Loc'ana*, or *Roshana*, whose colossal statue is now known as the Daibutsu of Nara, and who is not to be confounded with the Vairoc'ana of the Shingon sect, introduced later by the Kegon doctors and Kobōdaishi;

[1] For this, see the chapter on *Hossō* in vol. i. of " Bukkyō Kakushū Kōyō."

Roshana, said Maitreya, was the Supreme Being, invisible but all-powerful. When He showed Himself upon earth, it was through the personality of two great spiritual Beings, Maitreya Himself, and Manjuśri, the potent Bodhisattva of China.[1]

One of the keynotes of the Hossō teaching (it would require a large volume to describe it all) is the doctrine of Oneness from which the other name of the sect, the *Yuishikikyō*, or Oneness sect, is derived. A Christian would say, " God is One, and besides Him there is none other." But the Hossō sect (if we may use the word " God " for Buddhist speculations) would put it a little otherwise. " God is One, and besides Him there is nothing." The Universe, or God (for the two were treated as identical) was looked upon as a mighty ocean, unfathomable and unlimited, and the phenomena of nature and life, trees and plants, birds and beasts, sun and stars, men, angels, and even the gods whom men worshipped, were but the waves which appear for a moment on the surface, vanish, and reappear in a different shape. The wave I look at now is but a rearrangement of the drops in the wave which appeared in a different shape in another part of the bay. The god I worship now, on the Himalaya slopes, I call by the name of S'akyamuni ; rearrange the particles that compose him, and he will appear presently on the plains of the Ganges as the Hindu Vishnu. The name and the form have been changed, the essence which is a part of the great Ocean of the Universe, which is God, is unchanged, and remains identically the same. Thus it came in India that men passed from one cult to

[1] It is interesting to note how the different schools of the Mahāyāna nearly all present us with a Triad or Trinity. Between this Trinity of Locana, Maitreya, Manjuśri, and the Pure-land Trinity of Amitābha, Avalokites'vara, and Mahāsthāmaprâpta there is only a difference of names. The concepts are identical.

the other, and that the Hindus, to this day, look upon S'akyamuni as one incarnation of their god Vishnu.

This was the doctrine which enabled Gyōgi Bosatsu, and other leading priests of the Nara period, to propound the doctrine of Ryōbu-Shinto (or *Ryōbu-Bukkyō*, as it is also called). According to this doctrine, the ancient gods of Japan, Amaterasu, the goddess of the Sun, and the other divinities whom the Japanese had brought from their unknown original homes on the continent of Asia, were not independent spiritual Beings, but merely fresh incarnations of that same divine Essence which had moved for a while on the surface of things, as this or that one of the great Bodhisattvas and Buddhas of the Indian religion. Buddhism had not come to destroy the faith of Japan, but to strengthen it with the additional light that was shining forth from India and China. How far the movement was a popular one, may be doubted. The common people counted for very little in those days; it was an oracle, issuing from the Temple at Isé, that authoritatively proclaimed the identity of Amaterasu and Vairoc'ana.[1] A few years before, in the year 616, the great god of Miwa[2] had very obligingly let it be known throughout Japan that the proper ministers to take charge of funeral rites were the Buddhist clergy.[3] This amounted practically to an endowment of Buddhism.

[1] Nichiren (see "Sei-go-roku," *passim*) was very scathing in his denunciation of this spurious oracle, as he termed it. Nichirenism had no official connection with Ryōbu, and yet, on occasions, it too would turn to Hachiman and Tenshōdaijin.

[2] *Miwa* is a town in Yamato, with a well-known Shinto temple. The oracle is mentioned by Dr. Murakami on p. 859 of his handbook.

[2] Most of the present funeral customs of Japan date from the Nara period. Strange to say, most of them imply the continuance of the soul after death. This is absolutely contrary to the original doctrines of Buddhism; but the Japanese belief in immortality was too deeply engrained to be easily eradicated.

Another sect which made its appearance in Japan during the Nara period was the Kegon, or Avatamsaka sect, which was introduced in 736. It was one of purely Chinese origin, though the books on which it was based came originally from India, and had been founded at the end of the Sui and beginning of the Tang dynasties, between 600 and 660, by a priest whose name the Japanese pronounce as Tojun (杜順). It represented, when it arose, one of the latest developments of Chinese Buddhist thought (it came into prominence a little after the Hossō). The Japanese have always wanted to have the very latest in every department of human thought.

Like the Hossō, the Kegon went back for its origin to the very beginnings of the Mahāyāna. When Nāgārjuna, in his wanderings, had reached the Himalayas, he was taken to the Dragon Palace under the Sea, out of which he fetched the wonderful book known as the Avatamsaka Sūtra,[1] which was to form the basis of the new sect. It is a very difficult book, and very long : many translators in earlier times had tried their hands at it, but had only produced fragmentary versions of individual chapters.[2] Now at last, in the Tang period, a version of the whole was accomplished. The enterprise had the warmest encouragement from the Court, and one of the Tang empresses early in the eighth century, not only sent to Khotan to procure a complete copy of the Sanskrit Sūtra,

[1] See Nanjo, No. 87.

[2] The list of Avatamsaka Sūtras given by Nanjo gives us some data for fixing the age of Nāgārjuna. One of the chapters was translated by Lokaraksha of the Han Dynasty who reached Loyang in A.D. 147. It would follow that Nāgārjuna must have lived before that date. Again, all Buddhist authorities in Japan place him 600 years after the Parinirvana. If we fix that at about 500 B.C. we get Nāgārjuna's date about 100 A.D., which agrees very well both with the translation of the chapter by Lokaraksha and with the year assigned by Eusebius and other writers for the *terminus a quo* of Gnosticism.

but also wrote a preface for the Chinese version when it came out.[1] It may have been that, in view of the close proximity once more of Christianity, Buddhism felt the need of advancing supernatural claims.[2] The Avatam-saka Sūtra is full of the supernatural. In the days of S'akyamuni's life, immediately after he had, under the Bo-tree, attained to Enlightenment, he had (so it was said) remained in a trance of awe and wonder for the space of two weeks. It was now alleged that during that time he had in spirit ascended to the highest heaven, where, in a kind of Transfiguration, he had conversed with the two great Bodhisattvas—Manjuśri and Samanta-bhadra—in the very presence of the Supreme and Ever-lasting Buddha Vairoc'ana.[3] The doctrines thus delivered had been of a very deep and mysterious character, too deep for the ordinary mind of men to comprehend. S'akyamuni had therefore laid them aside for a while, and had not reverted to them again until towards the close of his ministry, when the disciples were sufficiently advanced to receive them.

We have thus, as it were, three different Buddhist

[1] Nanjo, "Cat. of Tripitaka," Nos. 87, 88.

[2] Mr. G. Sakurai, in the now defunct *Hansei Zasshi*, vol. xiii. p. 12, says that in A.D. 781 one of the Indian translators of the Tang period, Prajnā by name, who had come to China in order to get near the scene of Manjuśri's labours, was actually collaborating with the Nestorian priest King Ching, or Adam, the man who erected the Sin-ganfu monument. Between them they made a translation of the "Shat-pāramitā Sūtra," which they offered to the Emperor Tetsung. The Emperor, however, refused to receive it, saying that King Ching should devote himself to preaching the doctrines of *Meshiho* (Messiah), leaving the Buddhists to propagate the teachings of S'akyamuni. The book therefore appears in Prajnā's name only.

[3] Vairoc'ana is said to be distinct from the Roshana of the Hossō, though in practice he is almost always identified with him. I have drawn my materials from the chapters on Hossō and Kegon in "Bukkyō Kakushū Kōyō," vol. i.

Trinities—the Trinity of the Hossō, namely, Roshana, Maitreya, and Manjuśri; that of the Kegon, Vairoc'ana, Samantabhadra (*Fugen*), and Manjuśri; that of the Pure Land, Amitābha, Kwannon, and Seishi—all claiming to come from the beginnings of the Mahāyāna, all supposed to have appeared simultaneously in China, just at the time when Christian missions first made their way to that empire, and all three brought over to Japan during the early years of the Nara period. At bottom the three sets meant pretty much the same thing, and the ethics of Buddhism were much the same whoever preached them; but the three represented sectarian differences, and there speedily appeared rivalries between jealous monks competing with one another for the favour of the court and nobility. This was one of the characteristics of the Nara age.[1]

The student who has the time, inclination, and opportunity to prosecute further the study of this period, will find it full of very valuable historical material which throws a flood of light on the present life and thought of the Japanese people. Such a research lies far beyond the scope of the present work.[2] We may, however, refer to one or two points of importance.

[1] It is very interesting to trace chronologically the workings of the different Buddhist sects in the early years of Japanese Buddhism. Of the rival Trinities, the first to reach Japan is undoubtedly that which has Amitābha as its central figure. A century later comes the Trinity of Roshana, and still later again that of Vairoc'ana. For a while syncretism prevails, and an attempt is made to treat the three as identical. Geshin is the first to see that this syncretism is impossible. Finally, Hōnen and Shinran, in the twelfth century, get the courage of their convictions, and proclaim Amida as the True and only Refuge of the Buddhist believer.

[2] I would call the attention of the European reader to the very suggestive work "Le Japon," by M. de la Mazelière, of which, I believe, three volumes have appeared. The author brings out very clearly the

Amongst a number of sovereigns of no special importance Kōtoku Tennō (645–654) is distinguished for the zeal with which he worked along the lines of political and civil reform laid down by Shōtoku. The Taikwa reforms (so called from the *Nengo*[1] or year-period in which they were issued—an institution then first borrowed from China) brought the institutions of Japan very near to the Chinese models. The old offices of the *Ōmi* and *Ōmuraji*[2] were abolished, and three new officers, with Chinese titles, *Sadaijin, Udaijin, Naidaijin*, appointed to take their place. Exact reports were demanded from the governors of the provinces as to the conditions and needs of the people, a simple but (for the time) sufficient Court of Appeal was instituted, in the shape of a box placed at the palace gates to receive the complaints of the people, provincial boundaries were fixed, and the *Handen shuja-hō*, whilst providing that each peasant family should have a minimum allotment of rice land (two *tan* for a man, and a little more than one tan for a woman), also provided for the revenues of the State by taking one-twentieth of the produce for State purposes. Thus the State became the universal landlord, and the people paid a single tax inclusive of rent. The reforms were not carried out without opposition. Soga Ishikawa-maro, who held the office of Udaijin, was falsely accused

points of Japan's indebtedness to China and India for the materials of much of her religious thought.

[1] The practice of reckoning time by certain periods of years arbitrarily fixed from time to time, for the purpose of worrying the historian, had been long in vogue in China. Kōtoku introduced it in Japan, and there have been over 240 such periods since that time.

[2] The Ōmi and Ōmuraji were in ancient times the ministers of the Emperor. The offices were hereditary. The new offices were not so in intention, but the Japanese is an oligarch by constitution, and the new offices gradually came to be monopolized by certain families.

by his enemies and unjustly done to death in 649.[1] Less than fifteen years later the Emperor Tenji (662–671) found it necessary to extirpate the Soga family, and to call to his assistance the family of the Fujiwara,[2] who have contrived to hold their great position, in one form or another, down to the present day. Tenji Tennō outlined the great Taihōryō[3] Code of Laws, which, promulgated in a subsequent reign, in A.D. 701, remained in force, with but few modifications, right down to the commencement of the Meiji era.

The Nara period also saw the publication of the two great chronicles of ancient Japan—the "Kojiki" and the "Nihongi,"[4] published, the one in 712, and containing the history of Japan from the creation to the close of the reign of the Empress Suiko (A.D. 628); the other, published in 722, and covering very much the same ground. In estimating their value, it must be remembered that they are chronicles and not histories, and that, even so, the writers were obviously inspired with a desire to assert for Japan an antiquity, and consequently a dignity, equal to that claimed by the empire of the haughty Tangs. The lives of early sovereigns have therefore been in some cases extended beyond all bounds of probability, and

[1] That is the Buddhist version. It is claimed by Soga's enemies that he, true to family traditions, was aspiring to the crown.

[2] To estimate the greatness of this aristocratic family, which has supplied such a long list of imperial consorts, the student is referred to the pages devoted to the subject in Fr. Papinot's "Dictionnaire d'Histoire et de Géographie du Japon."

[3] For the Taihōryō, see *Transactions Asiatic Society of Japan*, vol. viii. p. 145.

[4] Of the "Kojiki" there is a translation by Chamberlain (*Asiatic Society of Japan*, vol. x., Supp.); of the "Nihongi," one in English by Aston (*Japan Society*, London, Supp. I.); and one in German by Florenz (*Mitteilungen der deutschen Gesellschaft für Natur and Völkerkunde Ostasiens*. Tokyo).

there are inconsistencies (not to say falsifications) which modern writers (even Japanese among them) have not failed to note.[1] There is practically no credible history of Japan and Japanese events before the introduction of Buddhism.

For the rest, the age was uncritical, superstitious, and therefore credulous. When the Kegon Scriptures were being expounded in the palace a pink cloud hovered over the building, which was taken to denote the presence of a celestial audience. A priest in the mountains of Tamba, who served a temple dedicated to Kwannon, was snowed up one winter's day, and, being cut off from access to the outer world for nearly a week, was in danger of starvation. As he prayed he heard a sound in the veranda, and, going out, found a joint of venison placed there. He ate it and lived, though by eating it he broke the laws of Buddhism. Some time after this, whilst cleaning his temple, he discovered the giver of the venison. From the thigh of the statue of Kwannon had been cut a piece of—wood, shall we call it? or flesh?—the exact size of the venison that had been placed on the veranda.[2] The deity himself, at the cost of a painful self-sacrifice, had saved the life of his worshipper.

Wonder was in the air, and therefore when the Goddess of Isé proclaimed her identity with Amitābha, or Vairoc'ana, it was believed; and when the strange tales of the "Kojiki" came out, they also were accepted in faith. It is easy to sneer at the ages of credulity; it would be wiser, perhaps, to look back at the strange stories current in Europe during the same period, which our forefathers

[1] See, e.g., vol. i. of Murdoch's "History of Japan."

[2] I specially notice this particular instance, because the mention of venison seems to connect it with the deer Jātaka, which reappears in Christian folklore as the legend of St. Eustathius, and afterwards as that of St. Hubert.

believed with simple credulity. People who live in glass houses cannot afford to throw stones. At the same time no one could possibly hold up the Buddhism of the Nara age as a model for any one's admiration or imitation.

ADDITIONAL NOTE TO CHAPTER XIX.

(Extracted from " Shinran and his Work," as showing the great importance of Zendō in the history of the Jōdo Mahāyāna.)

KŌMYŌJI (光 明 寺).

In the year 614 A.D. a boy was born in China. By what precise name his parents first knew him I do not know. Judging from the analogy of other men similarly situated, he had many names at different periods of his life. The name by which he was last known was Zendō (善 導), but that was almost certainly not the name of his childhood. His family name was Shu (朱), and he was born in the district of Shishū (泗 州).

When he was born the Sui [1] dynasty was tottering to its fall, and had in fact only four years more of life. Already, we may believe, was the Duke of Tang, on the extreme north-west boundaries of the Empire, conspiring with Turkish and other chieftains, and meditating that great *coup d'état*, which put his master at his mercy and seated himself firmly on the Celestial

---

[1] The *Sui* dynasty ruled in China from 589–619 A.D. They came to power at the close of a long period of division, the Empire having been previously divided into many small kingdoms, with Chinese rulers south of the Yangtse, and Tartar or Turkish chieftains in the northern districts. Such were the Wei (Tartars), the Hsia (Hun), the Northern Yen (Tartar), the Western Liang (Turkish), and the Western Tsin (Thibetan). These smaller kingdoms are of great importance in the History of Buddhism, for it was in them rather than in China proper that Buddhism flourished before the Tang period. The Sui family had but two Sovereigns—Wenti (589–606), who united China and carried the Chinese name far among the Turks in the North and East; and Yangti (605–617), a man of violent temper, prone to debauchery and extravagance, who brought the Empire to the verge of ruin. He was overthrown by Li-yüan of the Tang family, who ascended the throne in A.D. 618, as Kaotsu.

Throne, as the founder of a Dynasty, the most magnificent China had ever yet seen, and which was to continue for well-nigh three centuries.[1] The miseries of the people, heavily burdened and harassed to support the luxurious and ostentatious extravagance of the Sui monarchs, tended to encourage his hopes, and with the practised eye of the statesman he could see that it only needed a strong man at' the helm to make China a world-power with very widely extending influence. For the inland states on the Western frontiers were already looking to China for aid against the terror of the Arab, shortly to be kindled to victory by the enthusiasm of the new faith inspired by Mahomet, and only a few years were destined to elapse before Persia, at war with Constantinople, and overrun by the Arabs, should come to China in the vain hopes of an alliance against the new foe.[2] To give another note of time, Shōtoku Taishi,[3] the greatest of Japan's early statesmen, and as

[1] It will be well to remember that under the earlier Tang Emperors, Chinese Viceroyalties extended as far as the frontiers' of the Persian Empire, and that even monarchs like Siladitya Harsha of Kanauj acknowledged Chinese influence. It must also be remembered that Kaotsu suppressed Buddhist monasteries, sending 100,000 bonzes and nuns about their business, being stimulated thereto by petitions from Chinese literati. Buddhism had many enemies : e.g. in India, where Harsha's predecessor had likewise (in 601) dissolved the Buddhist monasteries, and even uprooted the famous Bodhi-tree. V. A. Smith, " Early History of India."

[2] It will be well to keep a few dates in mind. The first Persian Temple (whether Zoroastrian or Manichæan is not quite clear) was erected at Singanfu, in 621, three years after Kaotsu's accession. The Persian Empire, under Chosroes II., was at the time at war with Rome (or rather Constantinople), a Persian army was on the Bosphorus. This war was a great strain on the Persian dominions, and there were other causes for anxiety. Mahomet, born 570, had announced himself as a prophet in 610, and the Hejira, from which all Mahometans date their years, took place in 622. Siladitya Harsha, whose Indian Empire extended over the whole basin of the Ganges, and who began as a war-like monarch, came to the throne A.D. 606. He, too, received an Embassy from the Persians, which he housed in a monastery near Multan, and massacred after entertaining them liberally. This must have been before his conversion to Buddhism, which seems to have been about 645 (V. A. Smith, " Early History of India "). The Persians were evidently looking everywhere for helpful allies.

[3] Shōtoku Taishi's political activity may be said to have begun with

P

great in the religious world as he was in the political, was already busy with his celebrated reforms. The Constitution of the 17 Articles had already been in force some ten years when Zendō was born; the ruler of Japan had already given offence to the vainglorious Sovereign of the Sui by the letter in which the "Eastern Emperor" sent his greeting, as an equal in rank, to his brother the "Emperor of the West," and Korea, which had already done so much for Japan in the way of religious and civilizing influences, was giving Japanese statesmen a good deal of political anxiety.[1]

In matters of religion, Confucianists and Taoists were apparently going on much as usual; but the Buddhist world, distracted partly by the immense volume and bulk of its own religious books, and partly by the multiplicity of the new ideas which the growing commercial activity of the people was importing from foreign countries, was in a state of apparently fermenting chaos.[2] Bodhidharma's attempts at reform (A.D. 520) [3] were already a century old, and his way had already lost some of its prestige : new sects,

---

the battle of Shikisen in 587, when the Shinto supporters were crushed. He became Crown Prince in 593, proclaimed Buddhism in 595, promulgated his Constitution of 17 Articles in 604, sent his celebrated letter to the "Emperor of the West" (Yangti of Sui) in 609, and died in 621. With him may be said to end the Korean period of Japanese Buddhism.

[1] Korea, divided into several small states, was fluctuating in allegiance between China and Japan. Yangti of Sui sent an expedition to Korea (A.D. 615), and Shōtoku was much concerned to preserve Japanese influence in the peninsula.

[2] With a few exceptions, the early books translated by the Buddhist missionaries of the Han period (ended A.D. 220) and of the era of confusion which followed, were so badly done as to be practically unintelligible. Kumarajiva, a native of Karachar, with apparently both Chinese and Indian blood in his veins, arrived at Changan in A.D. 406, and inaugurated a new era of translation. Amongst the books of which he provided fresh translations were the Sukhāvati Vyūhas and the Hokekyō. Kum. therefore marks a new period in the history of the Chinese Buddhism.

[3] Not even with Kumarajiva's efforts could Buddhism in China be brought into a satisfactory condition. Bodhidharma's efforts were devoted to introducing a form of Buddhism which should not depend upon books, but teach men by contemplation to get straight to the Heart of Buddha.

e.g. the Sanron, Jōjitsu, and Tendai, were already in process of formation, if not actually formed, and Hiouen Thsang had already (A.D. 611) entered the order of monks,[1] and was now preparing for the celebrated journey to India for the purpose of studying at first hand the doctrines of his faith.

Some reform was certainly needed. In the year 618, the Duke of Tang deposed his master, and took his seat on the Imperial throne as Kaotsu, the Founder of the Tang dynasty. One of the most striking incidents of his reign was the presentation of a petition to the throne against Buddhism. It was presented by leading men among the *literati* and Confucianists, and was strongly worded.[2] Kaotsu accepted the petition and acted upon it, He ordered a general dissolution and suppression of Buddhist monasteries, and sent 100,000 monks and nuns back into lay life. It was probably a necessary measure. The monks were very numerous and very powerful, and they claimed exemption from State control. Abuses of many kinds are apt to spring up in institutions the members of which claim not to be placed on the same footing with ordinary citizens.

Zendō entered the Buddhist order at a very early age. I cannot find whether it was before or after the suppression of the monasteries by Kaotsu; but it was most probably before that event, and his teacher was a certain Shōshō (明 勝) of Misshu (密 州), a prominent person in the then newly-formed Sanron sect. This sect, which is also called the *Ichi-dai-kyōshu*, or "Sect of the Teachings of Buddha's whole life," made it a feature of its teachings that it professed to accept every one of the many thousand volumes of the Mahāyāna Canon as of equal authority, without assigning to any single one a pre-eminent place among its compeers. It aimed at the most complete and glorious compre-

---

[1] Hiouen Thsang, born A.D. 602, enters the Order 622, about the time of Kaotsu's edict against the monasteries; unable to satisfy his mind, starts for India, 629, meets Silabhadra in India and enters the Nalanda monastery in 638, returns to China 645. The Emperor Teitsung writes a preface for his translation in 648. Hiouen Thsang is regarded as the founder of the Hosso sect, and it shows how close was the connection between Japan and China that the same sect appears in Japan 653, having been brought over by Dōshō, a student under Hiouen Thsang. It is noteworthy that H. T. did not bring Amidaism of the Zendō type back from India. Perhaps he did not find it there.

[2] Kaeuffer, " Geschichte Ostasiens," vol. ii. p. 659.

hensiveness (a comprehensiveness, which, I fear, can only be attained by the sacrifice of the critical faculty). Zendō's Buddhist biographer [1] adds that he also studied the Vinaya discipline (a fact which may be taken as showing traces of a somewhat practical turn of mind), and notices further that, during these student days, he was continually restless, that he sighed for greater definiteness, and expressed a longing for that simpler doctrine of Salvation by Faith in Amida, which has always had its exponents in China as well as in Japan.

At last, weary of the confusion, he went into the library, prayed for guidance, closed his eyes, and put out his hand for the book which was to simplify his Creed. The same story is told of others in Chinese Buddhism : in Zendō's case, his hand fell upon the volume of the Kwangyō (the Amitayurdhyāni Sūtra),[2] which relates how S'akyamuni comforted Queen Vaidehi in her distress

---

[1] Tada, " Shōshingekōwa," p. 347.

[2] The Kwangyō, which is the second longest of the three Jōdo books, was not translated into Chinese until A.D. 424, its translator being Kala-yasas, a contemporary of Kumārajiva. The Larger Sukhāvati Vyūha was translated as early as A.D. 147, by Anshikao and also by one of his companions, there being two later translations, one in 252 by Sanghavarman, and one of the Smaller Sukh. Vy. by Kumārajiva about 420. This would seem to point to the fact that Eon's teaching must have been based entirely on the earlier translations of the Larger Sukhāvati Vyūha, if, indeed, it was based on the present Amida books at all. Eon's spiritual father was Dōan (d. 390), a native of Ch'angshan in Chekiang, who moved to Jōyō (襄 陽), where he was besieged and taken prisoner by a king named Fu Ken (苻 堅), who ruled over one of the Central Asian principalities. During Dōan's lifetime, the Tsin Emperor Hiao-wu-ti was converted to Buddhism, chiefly owing Tangut influences. Dōan professed to have the aid of Pindola (Jap. Bindzuru), and was devoted to all the Buddhas, though perhaps especially to Amida, as may be inferred from his nickname *Miten no Dōan*, " Doan of Mida's Heaven." Eon, who followed him, seems to have been entirely devoted to Amida, as was also the Society which he founded, and which, there is some reason to suppose, was Manichæan. In the lifetime of Eon and Dōan began the streams of Chinese pilgrims to India, Fahian being the first. It is noteworthy that none of these pilgrims seem to have brought back anything definite about Amida from India. This is especially noticeable in the case of Hiouen Thsang, and it seems to point to the Central Asian origin of the Amida cult.

by reminding her of the mercies of Amitābha, " who is ever near thee." Zendō read and received comfort; but he could not understand all he read, and where he was there was none to explain it.

But he heard that, south of the Yangtze, at Rozan (盧山), there were traditions and books which might explain what he wanted. It was here that Eon (慧遠), who died A.D. 416, had worked for thirty years, and had founded, in connection with a body of friends known as the " eighteen sages of Rozan," a guild known as the White Lotus Society, which was the first association of Buddhist monks and laymen for the joint adoration of Amida Butsu. Zendō learned all that he could at Rozan, and then recommenced his travels, consulting as many religious teachers as he found likely to be able to give him helpful advice and counsel. What he learned from these teachers induced him to adopt a rule of life, known as *han shu sammai* (般舟三昧), which reads almost like the stern rule of some Christian ascetic, still more so, perhaps, of that of some Manichæan fanatic. *Mi tsune ni butsu wo raishi, kuchi tsune ni butsu wo tonae, kokoro tsune ni butsu wo omou.* "His body ceaselessly engaged in the worship of Buddha, his mouth ceaselessly engaged in the recital of Buddha's praises, his heart ceaselessly meditating Buddha." With this in mind he retired to the Temple of Goshinji (悟眞寺) in Shunnan, where, amidst beautiful mountain scenery, and in the solitude of retirement, he "beat out his music." It is quite evident that this retirement, which lasted for some years, was of great value in the formation of his religious ideas. The name of the temple signifies, not inaptly, the "Temple for the Instruction of Truth." He remained here until his 29th year, returning to Singanfu in the year A.D. 643.[1]

---

[1] It is said of Eon that he was so strict in his observance of Buddhist discipline that when, on his deathbed, he was ordered to take honey, he first set his pupils to find out whether the Buddhist rule permitted it. While they were still examining, he died. Once he broke his rule of retirement by mistake, being so engrossed in conversation that he inadvertently went outside the bounds of his hermitage. This is a favourite theme for artists. We may here mention another theme, frequently found in Buddhist pictures, which may be called the "Narrow Way." A pilgrim, pursued by wild beasts, demons, and evil spirits, arrives at the edge of a precipice. In front of him are two lakes, the one of water, filled with sharks and other monsters of the deep, the other of fire and peopled with devils. Between the two is

His stay, however, was for a short time only. Ever since his first conversion to Amidaism in the library, he had evidently been searching for any traces he could find of Amida followers in China. He had been to Rozan to examine Eon's literary remains and to get into touch with the White Lotus Society. We may presume that the Goshinji to which he retired was a place at which he would find persons in sympathy with his religious sentiments. Now he heard that Dōshaku (道綽), the monk who is reckoned as Zendō's predecessor in the list of Shinshu patriarchs, was teaching in the district of Shinyō (晉陽, Chinyang in Kiangsi), and he set off at once to visit the aged man.

Dōshaku, who is reckoned by the Jōdo Buddhist as the fourth patriarch of the Amida Doctrines, and therefore as Zendō's immediate predecessor, was born in Heishū (幷州) in the year A.D. 553, and died in 636. He had experienced the persecution which the Buddhists had undergone during the reign of Wu-ti of the Chow (周) Dynasty,[1] and he was one of the few brave ones who remained faithful in spite of the violence of the storm. His predecessor, the third patriarch, Donran,[2] had taught with con-

a very narrow strip of precipitous rock, necessitating the wariest of walking, the first false step meaning instant destruction on the one side or the other. It is dark; but on the other side of the narrow pathway stands Amida, who has accomplished salvation. A ray of light issues from him, and the legend above him is *Namu Amida Butsu*, which Zendō taught men to translate "Trust ME, for I will save you"—the meaning of the word *Jesus*, but not that of the Buddhist legend.

[1] The *Chow* [*circ.* 560) were a northern Kingdom, a rival, of the *Wei*, whose territories and powers they gradually usurped.

[2] *Donran* died in 533. Like all the Amidaists, he was not a pure Chinaman, but a subject of one of the small northern kingdoms. Wu-ti, of the Liang, *circ.* A.D. 528, was a great admirer of Donran's. It is interesting to note that shortly after Donran's death, within the lifetime both of Dōshaku and Zendō, an attempt was made (the forerunner of the Ryobu Shinto in Japan) to amalgamate Buddhism with Taoism). I quote it to show that this was an age of syncretic aspirations. Donran may almost have been a contemporary of Vasubhandhu. Some trace of the tendency to make common cause with Taoism may be perhaps found in the syllable Dō (道) in the assumed names of *Dōan*, or *Dōshaku*. Donran was certainly a Taoist before becoming a Buddhist. The *Dō* in Zendō's name is slightly different (導), as though to emphasize some new principle that had come into his teaching.

siderable effect in the district in which Dōshaka was born, and though he had been dead twenty years when Dōshaku came into the world, his influence was still felt in the neighbourhood. It was kneeling before the stone pillar erected to Donran's memory that Dōshaku made his vow to propagate the Doctrine of Salvation by Faith in Amida. Dōshaku was forty-eight years of age when he thus enrolled himself as a posthumous pupil of Donran's; but he is said to have developed the doctrine beyond what Donran had done. Donran had been drawn by the hope of eternal life, and it was this hope, set before him by the Indian monk Bodhiruci, that had made him burn his Taoist books of magic and set himself to the study of Amidaism. In Dōshaku's hands the Amida doctrine had developed in the direction of personality. He taught (if we may believe his latest biographer, Mr. Tada)[1] that Amida must be considered to be a personal Being and not a mere abstract ideal, and the book which he placed in Zendō's hands was the Larger Sukhāvati Vyūha, the book which gives the account of Amida's life, of His Incarnation in the person of Hōzō Biku, His labours undertaken for the Salvation of men, the successful accomplishment of His Great Vow, and His return to glory as King of His Western Paradise. This doctrine Zendō accepted and preached. He may be said to have carried the doctrine a stage further. The followers of Hōnen Shōnin (otherwise known as Genkū) form three communities: (i) the Shinshu, founded by Shinran, and (ii and iii) the two sub-sects of the older Jōdo sect, the Chinsei-ha and the Seizan-ha.[2] The Chinsei-ha, agreeing in this respect with the Shinshu, differ from the Seizan-ha in the matter of reciting the Nembutsu. The latter community treat the Nembutsu as an act of adoration addressed to all the Buddhas; the Chinsei-ha and Shinshu treat it as addressed to Amida alone, as being the only Buddha, and the one to whom everything else is subordinate and subservient; and this practice, according to Murakami,[3] is due to the teachings of Zendō. To Zendō, there-fore, the doctrine of faith became a doctrine involving a belief in a single Being, without beginning of days or end of life, unbounded

---

[1] Tada, "Shōshinge Kōwa," p. 349.

[2] This is Mr. Murakami's division in *Bukkyo Hyakkwa Hōten*. But there are other disciples of Zendō in Japan, who do not trace their descent through Genkū and Shinran, notably the *Yūdzūnembutsu* and *Ji* sects, concerning whom a note will be given later on in this chapter.

[3] Murakami, "Bukkyo Hyakkwa Hōten," p. 493.

in every respect, who, for man's salvation, had become a man, had accomplished a scheme of salvation, and had returned to his original glory.

Zendō's biographers relate how, when the patriarch was on the way to visit Dōshaku, his road lay through forests and mountains, so rough and impassable that, at last, worn out with fatigue, he had to lie down to rest in a cave. He was fainting with hunger and weariness, and it was two days before he could raise himself. Then it seemed to him that a voice sounded in his ears : "Pull yourself together, and struggle on : your difficulties will disappear." We may perhaps inquire what these difficulties were and how they disappeared.

Dōshaku is said to have died in the year A.D. 637. The date cannot be implicitly trusted, for it is also said that Zendō was twenty-nine years old when he visited Dōshaku and accepted Amidaism, an impossible age, if Zendō was born in A.D. 614. The explanation probably will be found in another statement to the effect that Dōshaku died five years after the visit of Zendō. That would make Zendō twenty-three years old when he visited Dōshaku, and we may easily believe that the conversion to Amidaism, as he came to learn it, may have been a slow process, not fully accomplished for several years. But, whichever way we look at it, the conversion of Zendō to the full faith in Amida must have taken place about the year A.D. 636 (if anything a little later than that year), and in, or near, the capital city of Singanfu. From that date, and in that city, he began his preaching activity.

China under the Tang dynasty had many dealings with Central Asia. The ruling family, as dukes of the dependent principality of Tang, had been much mixed up with Tartar and Turkish tribes, and it was apparently by their help that the family had been seated on the throne of China. From the moment, therefore, that the Dynasty was established, the new Empire became the cynosure of Central Asian eyes.[1] A Persian mission was sent by Chosroes II. praying for an alliance, and in 621 the first Zoroastrian temple was erected in Singanfu. The leader of this mission seems to have been a Magian of the name of Holu ("le fils du feu," as P. Gaubil calls him), who was very active in stirring up China against the Mahometans. Of Manichæans in China proper there seems to be no mention for many years to come,[2] but in 636,

[1] P. Gaubil, " Mém. des Chinois," vol. xv. p. 399.

[2] Acc. to the authors of *Mem. Conc. la Chine* (see xvi. 227, also

almost synchronizing with the commencement of Zendō's preaching activity, arrived the Nestorian mission under Olopen, which
has left behind it an enduring memorial in stone. Is it possible
that the " difficulties " with which Zendō was troubled, when he
lay wearied in the cave on his way to Dōshaku, were difficulties
connected with the relations between the Buddhist Faith and the
Faith which the Nestorians preached ?

We can trace the development of Zendō's thought. Confused
by the multiplexity of the popular Buddhism of his day, he turns
to the scripture in which S'akyamuni is represented as comforting

Kaeuffer, ii. 663) the first mention of *Moni* or Manichæan monks
among the Tartar tribes occurs in 786. I am indebted to my friend
Mr. S. Tachibana for the following data concerning the Manichæans,
which somewhat modify these statements. In the fifth year of the
Jōkwan (Chih Kwan) period of the Tang dynasty, *i.e.* A.D. 632, a Manichæan named Boku-go-ka-roku obtained from the Emperor Taitsung
permission to erect a Tatsin Temple (Jap. *Taishinji*) at Singanfu.
Tatsin was a generic name for Persia and Syria, and the name Taishinji
was at first applied indifferently to all temples, Christian, Manichæan,
or Zoroastrian, devoted to the propagation of faiths coming from those
regions. In 734, the Emperor Hiüan Tsung ordered the destruction of all
Manichæan Temples (probably of all Tatsin Temples), and forbade the
promulgation of Manichæanism. In 746, the same emperor removed the
prohibition and ordered that all temples belonging to religions of Persian
nationality should be called *Taishinji*, whether in the two capitals or in
the neighbouring country districts. In the third year of Daireki (Chin.
Ta-lai), *i.e.* 768, Taitsung authorized Persian subjects to erect *Dai Un Kōmyōji* (大雲光明寺), evidently as something distinct from the Tai-
hinji, also as distinct from Buddhism. Again, in the third year of the
Emperor Wutsung, A.D. 843, all Manichæan Temples were closed and
many of their priests, nuns, and laity put to death or sent into exile.
In the meantime the Kōmyō doctrine had reached Japan. It had
been brought to China in the reign of the Empress *Wu*, in the first
year of Yen Tsai, in 694 by a Persian of the name of *Pu-ta-tan*
(拂多誕). The Empress Jito was then on the throne. She was a
zealous Buddhist. In the year 692, she received from the Chinese
Ambassador a statue of Amida, and copies of a Sūtra called *Kon Kōmyō
Kyō*, which she caused to be preached throughout her empire. It
is difficult not to connect this with the Faith that Zendō had preached.
(Mr. Tachibana quotes from *Bussotōki*, fasc. 39–42. See also Haas,
" Annalen des Japanischen Buddhismus," p. 318, and Dévéria, *Journal
Asiatique*, ix.-x. p. 445).

Vaidehi with the proximity and tender watchfulness of Amida. Then he goes south of Rozan, to the remnants of Eon and his White Lotus Guild, after which, in the solitude of the Goshinji Temple, he works out his problem. In the meantime he hears of Christianity (by no means an impossibility if we remember the story of the introduction of silkworms into Europe a century before). What is he to do or say? He goes to Dōshaku to resolve his doubts, and Dōshaku tells him of "Eternal Life," and gives him the Sukhāvati Vyuha, which tells of Amida as a Person who came down upon Earth, who opened the door of salvation, and has gone to the place He has prepared for us.[1]

[1] I would like to call attention to an excellent article entitled the "Mystery of Fulin," by Dr. Hirth, of Columbia, which has just appeared in vol. xxx., part 1, of the *Journal of the Am. Oriental Society*. Dr. Hirth has long maintained (and gives reasons for so doing) that this embassy came from the Patriarch of Antioch as head of the Nestorian Church. There is also a great deal of information in Mrs. Gordon's recent work on the Messiah, a book which, despite its superabundant mysticism, is full of valuable information and most suggestive in the many hints and indications it gives for further investigation and research. It is interesting to observe that Olopen and his missionaries emphasize the fact that they come, not from the King of Persia or any political power, but from the Patriarch of Antioch, a purely spiritual personage with no political influence at all. Perhaps they did this on purpose to avoid being mixed up with Manichæans and Zoroastrians, who were more closely connected with the Persian State. Dr. Grierson, in his article on Bhakti-marga, in vol. ii. of Hasting's "Encyclopædia of Religions," shows us the same Olopen, three years later, in India, at the Court of Siladitya Harsha, where he is well received. This will show us how Nestorianism was at work, quietly and unobtrusively, in India as in China. We know that there were Christians in China before Olopen, for the Emperor Justinian (527-565) received a present of silkworms brought to him by monks who had been living for some years either in Singanfu or in Nanking, These missionaries can scarcely have been Nestorians, seeing that Justinian had a great dislike to that body of Christians. On the Singanfu monument, erected 781, Olopen is described as Daitoku (大德). In the year 771, the Emperor Taitsung appointed ten Daitoku, men of recognized virtue and merit. The erectors of the monument would scarcely have ventured to give Olopen this title unless it had been (posthumously perhaps) conferred on him by the Emperor (see Murakami, *op. cit.*, p. 804 ; and E. A. Parker, "Notes on the Nestorians," *J.R.A.S.*, North China Branch, vol. xxiv. p. 297).

After 636, then, we find, in Singanfu, two men preaching almost similar doctrines, the one preaching them in connection with Christ, the other in connection with Amida. It is further said of Zendō's activity that he was constantly helped by a mysterious priest who came to visit him every evening and helped him with his commentaries (see Tada, " Shoshingekōwa," p. 359). This mysterious collaborator may have been a Christian, and if so, the strange coincidences, the almost Pauline echoes, which are constantly to be found in Zendō's writings, would be amply accounted for. Nor is the supposition a baseless one ; for we have one clear instance of such collaboration between a Buddhist and Nestorian about a century later, when the Nestorian priest King Tsing (or Adam, as he is called on the Singanfu monument) collaborated with the Indian monk Prajna in the translation of a book on the Six Cardinal Virtues (*Shat Parāmitā Sūtra*).[1] The original was not in Sanskrit, but in the Hu (胡), *i.e.* the Persian, or, more probably, the Uigur language. At any rate, not much came of this attempted collaboration, which probably caused much jealousy and opposition. It was after a while forbidden by the Emperor Taitsung, who, in a published decree, ordered the Nestorian King Tsing to confine himself to the teachings of *Mishiho*, and to leave the followers of S'akyamuni to propagate the teachings of their master.[2]

The suggestion of opposition raised against such collaboration, on the part of friendly disposed believers of the two religions, by more strait-laced partisans, brings me to another point of contact between Zendō and the Nestorians. It is said (my authority again is Mr. Tada) that great opposition was made against Zendō for his preaching. A butcher, whose customers had left him to turn

---

[1] It is to be found in the Buddhist Canon. See Nanjo's Catalogue, No. 1004.

[2] Prof. Takakusu called attention to Prajnâ in his Translation of I-Tsing's " Record of the Buddhist Religion," (Oxford, 1896). *Mishiho* is Messiah. Among the Jews in Kaifongfu, in Honan, are preserved portions of the prophets Zechariah and Malachi. A phrase which Zendō uses more than once is *Fushi Sōgō*, " the turning of the hearts of parents and children to one another," a phrase which at once suggests Malachi to the mind. Zendō's phrase was later made the title of the well-known Japanese Jōdo book, the *Fushi Sōgō*. I am much indebted to Dr. Haas, of Heidelberg, for calling my attention to this matter.

Buddhists, tried to murder the persuasive [1] monk who injured his trade. And not only did persons of low degree set themselves against them. The *literati* persecuted him and his followers, as did also the priests of the other Buddhist sects. When the Emperor Kaotsung died in 684, the reins of the Government fell into the hands of the Empress-Dowager Wu-hu, who was under the influence of a Buddhist monk named Hwai-yi, a monk of one of the sects opposed to Zendō's teaching, and Hwai-yi in 694 caused much popular discontent among the lower classes by burning a favourite temple, which may have been Zendō's. For the common people heard Zendō gladly, and it was his preaching of a Gospel to the poor and outcast that annoyed the literati and the " Salvation-by-knowledge " Schools of Buddhists.

Strange to say, the Nestorians, well received and honourably treated by Taitsung and Kaotsung, fall into disgrace, and are persecuted, as soon as Kaotsung's death leaves the supreme power in the hands of the Empress-Dowager Wu-hu, and her adviser Hwai-yi. The persecution of the Nestorians is instigated by the same people as that against the followers of Zendō, and much the same pretexts are alleged. Moreover, the persecution of the two bodies goes on for the same time, and relief comes to them simultaneously. Of the Nestorians we read that Huantsung (723–756), succeeding Wu-hu, rebuilds the " Temple of Felicity," as the Nestorian Church is called, that Huantsung's successor, Sutsung (756–763), coming into a disordered inheritance recovers Singanfu which was in the hands of rebels, and erects " luminous " temples in various parts of his Empire, and finally that the Emperor Taitsung (763–780), the same who discouraged the

---

[1] Tada says that Zendō's preaching was so persuasive that many of his hearers committed suicide by burning themselves alive. Mr. Tada rightly feels called upon to apologize for this ; but no student of the Hokekyō will need to be reminded that to make a holocaust of *oneself* is set forth in the Hokekyō as the highest form of grateful adoration. But the word " holocaust " is also a good Christian expression, spiritually interpreted, and I venture to suggest that the holocausts in Zendō's time may have been of this kind. I am encouraged to think this by the fact that in the short biography of Zendō which appears in *Shinshu Seikun*, the word *nyūjō* (入 定) is used to describe the occurrence. *Nyūjō* literally means " to enter into the state of determination," though Hepburn in his Dictionary, explains it as meaning voluntary suicide by fire.

collaboration of King Tsing and Prajnâ, not only celebrated the Bon Festival with the Buddhists in the seventh month, but kept Christmas in the twelfth with the Nestorians, "burning incense" in a "luminous temple" with the "luminous multitude." As to Zendō's followers, we find them gathering round a teacher named Ekan, not very long after the master's death. Ninety years after that event, a monk named Hossō is mentioned as acquiring great fame, and in 793 Shōkō makes Uryūsan (鳥 龍 山) the headquarters of the teachings promulgated by Zendō. But by that time the Emperor Taitsung was already dead (ob. 780), and the collaboration between Amidaist and Christian had already been prohibited.

When the Nestorian mission first arrived in China in A.D. 636, they procured from the Emperor Teitsung a decree authorizing the erection of a *Tatsin* (*i.e.* a Syrian) temple. This name, however, may have led to confusion, for both Zoroastrians and Manichæans might conceivably have claimed the title (loosely construed), and in fact did so. When Huantsung, soon after 713, rebuilds the Nestorian Church, it is called a "Temple of Felicity." When Sutsung, in 756, recovers Singanfu, the Nestorian Churches are "luminous (景) temples," and this name has come to be identified with Nestorianism ever since, both in China and Japan.

When Zendō died, the Emperor Kaotsung (650–683) granted to the temple in which he resided the honorific title of Kōmyōji (光 明 寺), which is only another form of "luminous temple." The popular explanation of this name is obviously a fanciful one. Bright rays of light do not come out of the mouths of even the most eloquent preachers of any faith, nor do books, however holy and mouldy, glow with a phosphorescent light. Yet that was what Shōkō is said to have seen issuing from the works of Zendō preserved in the library at the White Horse Monastery.[1] Kaotsung was an enlightened monarch, and if he gave the title of Kōmyōji, it must have been for the quality of the doctrine and not by reason of any doubtful miracle. But it is quite probable that "luminous temple" and *Kōmyōji* may have been used as alternative titles to describe the Faith in One Saviour as taught, both by the Nestorians and the children of Zendō, during the period of collaboration, and that later, when Taitsung ordered the two to keep apart, the name of Kōmyōji was taken by the Buddhist section

[1] See Nanjo, "Short History of the Twelve Buddhist Sects," p. 107.

of the "movement" as their own specific designation, the Mani-chæans distinguishing their temple by the title *Dai-un-kōmyōji*.

This view receives considerable support from Japanese history. Shōtoku Taishi, whom the Shinshu honour as the first of their *Zenchishiki* or Saints, died in 621, shortly after the commence-ment of the Tang Dynasty. Buddhism was, therefore, in full swing in Japan when, in 636, the Nestorian Mission arrived at Singanfu, and Zendō began his preaching, and there were many Japanese students being sent yearly to China for purposes of study.[1] Not only so, but there were many Chinese families residing in Japan and naturalized there (*ayabito*), and it has been noticed that most of Kōtoku Tennō's Taikwa Reforms (A.D. 645-654) were worked out for him by these *ayabito*.[2] The whole of the Nara period was an age in which Japan was peculiarly sensitive to Chinese in-fluences, and especially to the influences of Chinese Buddhism.

This influence seems to have reached its maximum during the reign of Shōmu Tennō (724-748) and his Consort Kōmyō Kōgō (the very name, a posthumous one, is in itself significant). Shōmu Tennō was a very zealous Buddhist. He founded hospitals and charitable institutions, and his Empress distinguished herself by personally undertaking the nursing of lepers [3]—a truly Christian work. Japan was in no position at the time to undertake hospital work unaided. Foreign doctors had to be employed, and the industry of Japanese students has recently shown us the presence in Japan, at the Court, of a Nestorian Christian (the Nestorian Christians were famous all

[1] See Haas, *op. cit.* I am much indebted to this work. I have already shown, in notes on Hiouen Thsang and the Manichees, how quickly Japan, at this particular period, was moved by any new religious movement in the capital of the Tangs.

[2] See "Melanges Japonais," vol. iii. p. 287.

[3] Murakami, *op. cit.*, pp. 145-6. A little point, worthy of remark, is the following. In 639, Olopen, having established his missionaries at Singanfu, goes on to India and visits the court of Siladitya Harsha, at Kanauj. Shortly after this, we read of Harsha's zeal for works of charity, leper hospitals, etc., institutions which Buddhism had scarcely known since the days of As'oka, but which have constantly been a con-spicuous element in all Christian work. In Japan, what I may call the *Kōmyō* doctrines find their way into the country under Jitō and Mommu (687-697). Here also they are followed by a period of enthusiasm for works of charity which continues for a while, until the tares spring up and choke the good seed, and the Tendai, the ancient enemies of Zendō, get the upper hand.

over the East for their skill in medicine).[1] Here, therefore, we have possibly two instances of simultaneous collaboration, Buddhist and Christian uniting in the production of books in China, and in works of charity in Japan.

In 781, the Singanfu monument is erected, and shortly before, or afterwards, the Chinese Emperor finds reason for prohibiting the collaboration. In 782 the Emperor Kwammu comes to the throne of Japan. The Buddhists have been giving themselves airs for some time, and the ambitious priest Dōkyō, intriguing with the Empress Shōtoku (765–769), has assumed the title of Hō Ō, or "religious emperor," a kind of pope! Kwammu determines to put an end to the political intrigues of the Nara clergy, removes his capital to Kyoto, and sends Kōbō and Dengyo to China to investigate religion. They come back, the one with the Shingon, the

[1] The following are the data known about the Nestorian doctor Rimitsu. In the year A.D. 739 there arrived from China a ship-load of distinguished persons. (1) Kibi Mabi, who had been studying in China since 716, and who brought back with him the art of embroidery, the game of go, the biwa, and the Katakana alphabet. (2) Dōsen, the founder in Japan of the Kegon (or Avatamsaka) sect. (3) A Brahman priest, Bodhisena, from India. (4) A musician named Fat Triet (Buttetsu) from Cambodia ; and (5) a Nestorian physician of Persian nationality named Rimitsu. The party were received on behalf of the Government by Gyogi, at Naniwa, and Gyogi was able to display his learning by conversing with the Indian Brahman in Sanskrit. A month later, a member of the Japanese Embassy in China returned to Japan with three Chinese and another Persian. The whole party were taken to court and the Emperor conferred official rank upon them, especial mention being made of Ritōho, a Chinaman, and Rimitsu. In 736 Shōmu was in the midst of his hospital schemes, and Rimitsu was evidently a distinguished physician. The Japanese must have been very different from what they are now if they neglected the opportunity of sucking his brains ! Mr. Tachibana, who has furnished me with the materials for this note, bases his information on an article by Dr. Takakusu in "Shigakuzasshi," vol. iii. No. 7, and on Dr. Kume's "History of the Nara Epoch." That Rimitsu was a Christian was shown some time ago by Mr. Saeki. He could not have been a Manichæan, seeing that the Manichæans discouraged doctors.

Gyogi Bosatsu was the spiritual director of Shōmu and his Empress Kōmyō. He was an advocate of Kōmyō doctrines, very practical, very charitable. He was a syncretist, and first originated the Ryōbu doctrine in Japan, stimulated thereto by the example of the Buddhists and Taoists in China.

other with the Tendai. Again it is significant that these sects, and especially the Tendai, which became practically the State religion of Japan for many centuries, were the very sects which had organized the persecution against Zendō, when he first began to preach his doctrine of Salvation by Faith in Amida.

But the light still shone, in spite of the opposition of the Tendai. Zendō's books came over to Japan, Mr. Tada tells us, at different times between 796 and 858, and several monks, such as Kūya and Eikwan, kept alive the faith in Amida, invoking His Name on Hieizan, or wandering, disguised as travelling priests or horsedealers (*umakata*), from province to province, preaching a simple faith to country peasants.[1] And finally, the great Hōnen (Genkū), breaking with the Tendai, as so many others had done, in order to return to the teaching of Zendō, founds at Kurodani a temple, still known as *Konkai Kōmyōji*, " the Illustrious Temple of the Golden Precept," which is to this day one of the chief seats of the Chinsei sub-division of the Jōdo sect. And it is this Chinsei-ha which preserves Zendō's rule of making the Nembutsu an invocation of the Great Amida alone, to the exclusion of all the rest.

[1] It is said of Zendō that he and his disciples were much given to itinerant preaching. So were the Nestorians. The Greek merchant Cosmas Indicopleustes, who was in India A.D. 535, mentions a Nestorian order of itinerant preachers named Periodeutæ, or wanderers, who were busy in his days evangelizing in N. W. India. Olopen himself may have been one; we find him in China and then in India. It is possible that Kūya and Eikwan may have been itinerant preachers after this type, having learned the value of it from Zendō. So also may have been the mysterious personage who, in 1095, appeared to Ryonin, the founder of the Yūdzūnembutsu, and told him of the "One man that stood for all men, and the one religious act that embraced all others." Ippen (1239–1289), the founder of the Ji Sect, wandered in his allegiance from the Tendai to the Seizanha of the Jōdo, and finally founded a sect of his own. He was a great student of Zendō, both as a teacher and as an artist, and his sect was intended to be a reproduction of Zendō's teachings. His nickname was Yūgyō Shōnin, " the itinerating preacher," and to this day, the head of the Ji sect is supposed to be always travelling about the country preaching.

CHAPTER XX

HEIAN BUDDHISM[1]

IT was in the year A.D. 767, in the first year of the period
known to the Japanese as *Jingo Keiun,* that a child was
born in a village in Ōmi, not far from the shores of Lake
Biwa, who was destined to exercise a great influence on
the Buddhism of his country. The father, a Confucianist
scholar, and yet withal a man of religion and piety, had
often prayed for a son, and, having obtained his desire,
showed his gratitude to Heaven by the care which he
bestowed upon his son's education. Saichō (that was the
name by which the son was later known) grew up a well-
trained lad, with a liking for books and a wisdom a little
(possibly) beyond his years.

His father was a man of religion and piety; it was
small wonder that the son should follow so near an
example. Buddhism was at its flood-tide of popularity
during the eighth century, and the Court, dissolute and
luxurious, and yet, like the Athenians, given to superstition, encouraged a very magnificent system of ritualism
as a make-weight for its moral and ethical deficiencies.
It was very natural that the boy's imagination should be
caught by the outward splendour of the worship he saw
around him, and that his favourite pastime should be

[1] Heian is the old name for Kyoto. Kyoto, which is even now the
sacred city of Japanese Buddhism, was built in 794 by Kwammu
Tennō, as his capital. Its name *Heian* signifies "Peace."

playing at church. His companions nicknamed him the "Little Abbot."

As he grew older his religious sense deepened, and he saw that splendour of ritual was only one side of religion, and by no means the most important. He understood that the outward magnificence of devotion might co-exist with a worldly and unregenerate heart, and the age in which he lived gave him many warning examples. When he was born Japan was ruled over by a woman, the Empress Shōtoku. Shōtoku first came to the throne in the year 749. She was then styled *Kōken,* and succeeded her father, *Shōmu* (823–840), who, after a reign of twenty-five years, had abdicated and retired to a monastery. Shōmu, like his aunt *Gensho* (715–823) who preceded him, had been a liberal patron of agriculture, arts, letters, and religion. The "Nihongi" was published in the reign of Gensho ; under Shōmu were commenced the great temples of Hase-dera and Todaiji, and the celebrated Daibutsu of Nara. Dispensaries and hospitals were opened, bridges built, tiles used for the roofing of houses, and examinations instituted for the selection of candidates for Orders and the public service. Shōmu was the first Emperor of Japan to receive Baptism ; [1] his whole life

---

[1] It is a significant fact that the Buddhist rite of Baptism (*Abhis'ekha,* Jap. *Kwanjō*) comes into prominence just at the period when Buddhism and Nestorianism came into contact. The same may be said of the care devoted by Buddhists at this period to the details of Ordination. Shōmu's reign actually saw the Nestorian Christian—the physician named Rimitsu—at the Nara Court. He evidently honoured, for he was granted official rank along with a Chinaman named Ritsho, who became naturalized and took the name of Kiyomaru (Murdoch). Kiyomaru became the head of the university. It seems probable that Rimitsu was in charge of the hospital in which the Empress Kōmyō is said to have worked as a nurse during the smallpox epidemic. A few years later we find a Nestorian priest, Adam, collaborating with a Buddhist priest, Prajnä, on the translation of a

was devoted to the furtherance of Buddhism and the exaltation of the monks, and in the end he joined the Order, and with his mother, the Empress Dowager, took the vows of the *Bosatsu Kai*.

Kōken, who followed him on the throne, carried her devotion still further. In the great temple of Todaiji 5000 monks recited the daily offices, and an Imperial decree forbade the taking of all life. After a reign of ten years, her minister, Fujiwara Nakamaro, advised her to abdicate in favour of a distant cousin, *Junnin* (759–764), and an unlawful affection which she had conceived for an ambitious and worldly priest, Dōkyō,[1] led her to acquiesce. But the retirement of the Empress was not what Dōkyō desired, and Dōkyō had great influence with the clergy. A civil war ensued. Dōkyō and his followers defeated Fujiwara in a battle fought in the province of Ōmi, after which the victorious monk dethroned Junnin and restored Kōken to power. Junnin was banished to Awaji, where he died the following year. For centuries he was known in history as *Awaji no haitei* (the Imperial Exile of Awaji), and it was not till 1871 that tardy justice was done to his memory by his restoration, under the name of Junnin, to the official list of emperors.

Kōken then reascended the throne as Shōtoku. She had owed her restoration to the fidelity of her paramour,

Persian (胡) or possibly Uigur text of a treatise on the Cardinal Virtues. This can hardly have been a Buddhist book, though the Cardinal Virtues must be much the same in all religions. The treatise known as "Shat parāmitā sūtra" appears in Nanjo's Catalogue as being the work of Prajnā alone. Prajnā was a follower of Zendo's, and there seems very little doubt that Zendoists and Nestorians were supposed to belong to the same ship.

[1] A similar charge was brought against the priest Gembō, who had a temple built to his honour after his death to appease his spirit and prevent it from wreaking vengeance on his murderers.

and he claimed his reward. Dōkyō took the title of *Hō-ō* (the word which the Japanese always use for the Pope), and he claimed a temporal throne as well. But here public opinion stepped in, and the god of the temple of Hachiman [1] at Usa, a god then reverenced by Buddhist and Shintoist alike, pronounced his verdict. Never yet, he said, had a subject dared to raise himself to the Imperial throne. Shōtoku was reluctantly compelled to banish her lover. A very short time after, she died (769).

It was in the midst of these events that Saichō was born. And things did not go much better as time went on. Shōtoku was succeeded by Konin (770–781), but the change of sovereign brought no relief to the country. The Fujiwaras were reinstalled in office, it is true, and the meddling Pope Dōkyō banished to a safe distance, in what was then the remote province of Shimotsuke. But the Nara monks were not pleased to see an end put to their temporal power, and in the next reign, that of Kwammu (782–805), an insurrection of the Ebisu in the north—one of a series of similar outbreaks, and therefore possibly traceable to Dōkyō's sinister influence—gave the authorities a vast amount of trouble. Kwammu resolved that, at whatever cost, the interference of the Buddhist clergy in matters of state must come to an end, and accordingly removed his capital, first to Uda, and eventually to his new city of Kyoto, or Heian.

Now, is it to be wondered at that the lad Saichō, brought up amidst such surroundings, should speedily

---

[1] Hachiman is the god of war. In life, he was the Emperor Ojin, the peaceful son of the warlike Empress *Jingo*, and his transformation into a god of battles has always been a puzzle. Originally a Shinto deity, he was adopted into the Buddhist pantheon (where his position was still more incongruous) by the Ryōbu. It was the ambition of Hideyoshi to be worshipped after death as Shin Hachiman, the *New* god of War.

realize that there is something else in religion besides its outward show ? In the year 786, being then nineteen years of age, he resolved to give himself up to the religious life. But he did not wish to be a monk like those who were bringing the great monasteries of Nara into disgrace. He chose out for himself a solitary spot on the slopes of Mount Hiyei, within the borders of his own province of Ōmi, and there erected a small hut of grass and rushes, which saw the beginnings of his monastic life. Here he lived, prayed, studied, meditated, and contemplated ;[1] in the intervals of these exercises, he tilled a few rods of ground; when he could not do that, he spent his time in carving a statue of Yaku-Ō,[2] which he presently set up in his little chapel.

Saichō's favourite books at this time were those which explained the doctrines of the Chinese sect of *Tien-tai*, a sect which, in China, seemed satisfactorily to have solved the difficult problem of the relations between Church and State. The sect did not then exist in Japan; but there were, here and there, a few men, mainly Chinese, who devoted themselves to the study and exposition of these doctrines. I will mention one name, as it throws a very favourable light on the religious feelings of the time. Ganjin Kwashō, to give his name its Japanese pronunciation, was a Tendai monk in Southern China whose lectures were attended by many students. He was an ardent

[1] By *contemplation*, which must be distinguished from meditation, is meant that quiet sitting, with mind and body perfectly still, which the Japanese know as *zazen*. When the absolute stillness can be attained, and the mind is free from all thought, the Vision of Truth is said to come to it, and the gate leading into the Invisible World is opened.

[2] *Yaku-ō* (Skt. Bhaishajyarāja) is a divinity who plays an important part in the Hokekyō. The Vow which he is said to have taken before attaining to Buddhahood relates almost entirely to physical health and personal beauty.

advocate of Foreign Missions, and often spoke on the subject to his students. At last one day he put the matter very strongly before them, and asked for volunteers. Not a single student answered the call. The next morning he told them after lecture that, no one having volunteered, he should go himself, and the superiority of example over precept was at once shown by the ready response of over twenty men, who had been willing to follow, but did not feel themselves competent to lead.

But it was easier to volunteer than to go. Storms, pirates, shipwreck, a casting away on a distant and inhospitable shore, all combined to delay the journey. Nearly ten years elapsed before Ganjin reached Japan ; when he did so, he had already lost his eyesight through the hardships of his adventures, and it was sheer pluck that pulled him through. But merits like these were not likely to go unnoticed. Ganjin was given an honourable post at one of the Nara temples, where his undoubted sanctity was highly reverenced by many who could lay no claim to a similar virtue themselves. He was put in charge of the *Kaidan*, and thus became the minister of ordination for the monks. He died before Saichō's admission to the Order, but the books he brought with him influenced Saichō's course of life.

Saichō was fortunate (we might almost, I think, add long-headed) in his selection of a site for his monastery. Hiyeizan dominates the plain of Kyoto, and it was only five years after the consecration of the chapel with its image of Yakuō that Kwammu Tennō forsook Nara and established his capital at Heian (794). The following year, Saichō, whose fame for sanctity had spread very widely, was the celebrant at a great *Dai Kuyō-e*, or High Mass, at which the Emperor himself was present, as well as a large number of priests from Nara and the south.

Kwammu remained faithful all his life in his admiration for Saichō. He encouraged him to go from place to place lecturing on the Hokekyō, and one of the last acts of his reign was to commission him to go to China to consult the Tendai authorities at their chief seat, and thus to complete what was lacking in the system which he had been the means of establishing in Japan.

Saichō started in 802[1] as a chaplain (may we call him?) in the suite of Fujiwara Kadomaro, Japanese Ambassador to the Court of the Tangs. Storms delayed the party, and it was not until the following year that he reached China, making straight for the great monastery of Tientai, in the province of Chekiang. Here he prosecuted his inquiries with the energy of a man who knows exactly what he wants and can go straight to the point, and was soon ready to return again to Japan. His studies had touched upon the doctrines of the Zen and Shingon, but his main interest had been the perfecting of his own Tendai system by the acquirement of proper authority under the Vinaya, or Rules of Ecclesiastical Discipline. Here let me digress for a moment to summarize the chief points of the Tendai system.

It will be remembered that the earliest form of Buddhism in China was unsectarian, the early missionaries having been content to call themselves Buddhists without any further sectarian distinctions. From 265 to 589 we get Indian sects, Abhidharma or Kusha, Jōjitsu, Sanron, Jōdo, and Nirvana, some of which have already been summarized. From the beginning of the Sui, who ruled from 589 to 618, we get Chinese sects, the Kegon and Tendai, which gradually drive the others out of the

[1] There is a slight discrepancy in dates in the authorities I have consulted. Some say 804, but Fr. Papinot, in his Dictionary, says 802, and I have thought myself safe in following so good an authority.

field. We have already spoken of Kegon; the Tendai was founded in 538 by Chisha Daishi, who had, however, had predecessors, and who claimed to derive his peculiar tenets from the long-suffering Nāgārjuna, who is claimed as the founder of nearly every heresy or sect in Northern Buddhism.

The fundamental principle of Tendai may be called introspection (*Kwanshin no hōhō*), but it is also a system of harmonization whereby an attempt is made to evolve something like harmony and order out of the bewildering chaos of the Buddhist Scriptures. Its teachings are divided into two great divisions or gates, the gate of teaching (Kyō) and the gate of meditation (Kwan), and it claims that a man can attain to Enlightenment by following either the teachings contained in the Scriptures or the practice of meditation and contemplation. It distinguishes three Vehicles instead of two: the Hīnayāna (or *Shojō*), the Apparent or Quasi-Mahāyāna of the Jōdo and Indian sects (*Gondaijō*), and the true Mahāyāna of the sects which originated in China—Zen, Shingon, Kegon, and itself (*Jitsudaijō*).

It embraced the whole collection of the Mahāyāna books, which it divided into five periods. S'akyamuni, it was said, had begun his ministry by preaching in heaven, to angels and men, the transcendent doctrines of the Kegon. These being too hard for ordinary, sinful men to comprehend, he had descended to Benares with the practical teaching of the Agon Scriptures. As times rolled on the teachings had been "developed" (*vaipulya*) in the Hodo books, as the next class were called. From development to wisdom (*prajñā*) was the next step; from wisdom to the consummated perfection of the Saddharma pundarika Sūtra was the natural conclusion. Thus the doctrines of S'akyamuni were 84,000 in number

beginning with extreme simplicity and ending in the
clouds of mysticism. In the delivery of these many
doctrines Shaka had used many ways of teaching: *ton*, or
suddenness, letting the truth burst with full brilliancy on
the mind of his hearers; *zen*, or gradual advance from
strength to strength; *himitsu*, or esoteric symbolism;
fujō, or parabolic uncertainty. He had adapted his
sermons to all hearers, and had so contrived that in one
and the same sermon the same words had conveyed
Hīnayāna doctrines to some hearers and Mahāyāna to
others who were able to bear it. He had indeed become
"all things to all men."

The Tendai system, which embraced all, comprised
many things which were not Buddhist at all. Its doctrine
of *shō aku no hōmon*, or inherent evil, is dualistic; it
asserts that in *Shinnyo*, which is the pantheistic god,
there is an evil principle as well as a good, that the two
are equal in duration and power. Manichæans [1] and Magi
both held that doctrine, but it was scarcely a Buddhist
principle. It must have been a very difficult task to get
doctrines so mutually antagonistic as those of the Zen and
Jōdo to live side by side in the same religious household.

But the main thing that Saichō wanted was spiritual
and ecclesiastical authority. This the Chinese Tientai
seems to have had little hesitation about granting, and
Saichō was soon back in Japan, with a native episcopate
in his own hands.

When Saichō first went to China he was followed,
within a few months, by another young monk, who went
at his own charges. Kūkai was born at Byōbu-ga-ura
in Sanuki in 774. In 793 he followed Saichō to China,

---

[1] The Manichæan expressions, 二 宗 and 三 際, the "two principles" and the "three moments" are both to be found in the Japanese
Tendai.

and occupied himself with the study of the newly
imported Shingon or Mantra, which had but recently
arrived in China, by way of sea, from South India. He
stayed longer in China than did Saichō. When he reached
his home he found the latter in the midst of carrying out
his plans of Buddhist reform, and engaged in fierce controversy with the monks of Nara and the Nanto.[1] The
controversy was on the subject of the *Kaidan*.

Kaidan is the name given to a platform or *dais*, which
is used for the distribution of certificates and diplomas to
successful candidates for the priesthood. Its existence in
any particular temple implied the right of the authorities
of that temple to confer Orders, and the Buddhist monk
is as jealous of his Apostolic succession as is the highest
High Churchman amongst ourselves.[2] There had been no
ordinations of monks in China before A.D. 250, previously
to which the simple taking of the "threefold Refuge," in
Buddha, the Law, and the Community of Monks had been
deemed sufficient. The first regular ordinations had been
held about 350, the custom having been brought into the
country by an Indian monk of the name of Buddhoganga.
These ordinations had been of the Hīnayāna type (mainly
connected with the old Indian sect of the Dharmaguptas);
they had found their way to Japan, where Kaidan had

---

[1] *Nanto*, "the South," the name given in Kyoto to the district
round Nara.

[2] Thus, when a Buddhist priest is ordained, he receives "letters of
orders" on which are given the principal names of the priests through
whom the succession has come down to him from the Apostles of
S'akyamuni. It seems impossible to trace this practice earlier than
A.D. 250, before which date it was not deemed necessary in China. It
is therefore quite possible that the Buddhists may have learned the
practice from Christian neighbours in Central Asia. The only exception to this rule is the insignificant sect of the *Yūdzūnembutsu*, who
trace their succession, not to S'akyamuni, but to the Vision of Amida
vouchsafed to their Founder in the twelfth century.

been erected, at the Todaiji at Nara, in Chikuzen, and in Shimotsuke. They had also been much discredited by their connection with men like the ambitious and unprincipled Dōkyō.

But a new succession had been inaugurated by the Tientai in China, and Saichō, having received the necessary authorizations, erected, at·his monastery on Hiyeizan, a new Kaidan at which ordinations were to take place according to the Chinese Mahāyāna discipline. Saichō had probably his good reasons for taking so serious a step ; but his action set the whole of the South into a blaze of indignation and excitement. In the midst of it, Kūkai came back to Japan.

Which side would Kūkai take ? He was a Southerner by birth, for he hailed from Sanuki ; by education, for he was at the time attached to one of the great temples at the ancient capital. A feeling of loyalty prevented him from turning against his old friends in the South. At the same time, he was, like Saichō, convinced of the necessity of reform, and he had, moreover, a great friendship for Saichō, who had received Baptism at his hands.

Both sides appealed to him, and he was at a loss how to act. He resolved to steer clear of the controversy altogether, and went off on a series of missionary journeys throughout the land. His first journey was to the Kwanto districts, and right away to Shimotsuke and beyond. He was more than a mere preacher; he planned roads, suggested the making of bridges, encouraged agriculture and education, and simplified the writing of Japanese. The traveller will find his posthumous name of Kōbō Daishi in all parts of the land : he was the Apostle of the North, and the pacification of the troublesome northern tribes was much facilitated by his efforts. When he returned to Kyoto, the Kaidan controversy was still raging. So he went off touring again, and this time perambulated his native island of Shikoku.[1] On his next visit to Kyoto, Saichō, now known as Dengyo Daishi, was dead, and Kōbō felt that he could at last hope to publish his own views of Buddhist doctrine without running counter to those of the friend for whom he had so warm an affection. He retired in the year 816 to his new monastery at Kōya San, in the province of Kii, and there wrote his "Sangō-shiki," "Jūjūshinron," and the other treatises in which he develops his system. He died in 835, a venerable and venerated man. Buddhist Japan scarcely believes him to be dead even now. He is said to be sitting in his tomb in Mount Koya, waiting for Maitreya to come and convert the world. Then he will go forth from his place of waiting and join in the glory of victory.

In the first of the two works that I have just mentioned, the "Sangōshiki," Kōbō Daishi works out a comparison of the three great religions of the East, as he understood them—Confucianism, Taoism, and Buddhism. All three were to be found in the Japan of his day. Confucianism (of the ancient, unreformed variety) had been there longer than Buddhism, and the Confucian literati had joined hands with the Kami worshippers in opposing Buddhism, just as they had done with Taoism, in opposition to the same religion in China. The Shinto of Japan Kōbō seems to have treated as almost identical with the Taoism of China (etymologically, the two words are the same), and with very good reason. The inter-

---

[1] In the *Tsuzoku Bukkyo Shimbun* there appeared, from the beginning of December, 1908, a series of articles describing the journey which Kūkai took on this occasion. It is a favourite route for pilgrims, and might still.be followed by the adventurous foreigner. I have drawn my information as to Kūkai's attitude on the Kaidan question from an article which appeared in the same paper in September, 1908.

course between Japan and China had been going on
for over three centuries, during which period much had
come into Japan besides Buddhism and Confucianism.
The original Kami-worship had been raised, as it were,
into a system by the very fact of its early controversies
with Buddhism, and Dr. De Visser[1] has recently shown
us how much of Taoism there lurks in the Shintoistic
folklore of Japan. Confucianism, Buddhism, Taoism,
formed in Kōbō's mind the three legs of a tripod on
which the cauldron of the State might securely rest.
Only the Buddhism which he taught was not quite
the same as that with which we have been hitherto
dealing.

During the Tang Period, in the first half of the eighth
century, there arrived in China a certain number of men,
mostly from Southern India, and travelling by the sea
route,[2] who brought with them a new and evidently very
late form of Buddhism, which had practically captured
Thibet, then a leading kingdom of Asia, and which, from
its very newness, was likely to captivate the imagination
of the novelty-loving Japanese. This system Kōbō
developed in his " Jūjūshinron," or " Treatise of the Ten
Grades of Existence."

All sentient beings, said the Shingon doctors, may be
divided into ten classes. The lowest were the *sanakudō*,
or three bad classes—the brutes, the demons, and the
hungry spirits ; next came man, and next above him the

[1] In papers read before the Asiatic Society of Japan on Japanese
Folklore.

[2] See, for instance, what Dr. Nanjo says about Vajrabodhi, Subha-
karainha, Amoghavajra, and Bodhiruci (" Catalogue Trip.," App. ii.,
Nos. 150, 153, 154, 155). The Shingon of Japan is very similar to the
Buddhism of Thibet. Yet it is not identical, and the three books on
which the Japanese Shingonists mainly rely are not to be found in the
Thibetan canon. The Japanese Shingon came from South India.

denizens of heaven. These three grades belonged to the natural world.[1] The spiritual world consisted of those who were called out from the natural world to follow after the truth. Its lowest grade was the S'ra-mana, who strove after, and the Engaku or Pratyeka-buddha, who realized, the salvation of his own soul. That included the whole range of Buddhist believers, but there was an election within the election—the doctrines of Hossō, of Tendai, of Kegon, offered three successive steps, each higher than the last, for their respective devotees, and at the top of all stood the Shingon.

My readers will perhaps remember that in my earlier chapters I spoke of Vairoc'ana, the supreme Buddha—a reflection, as it were, of Osiris, whom we found in the Alexandrian Gnosis. Vairoc'ana is honoured as supreme by the Hossō, Tendai, and Kegon, and the order in which Kōbō places these sects seems to depend on the amount of honour which they were disposed to give to Vairoc'ana.[2]

---

[1] It must be remembered that Buddhism never looks upon heaven as a place of moral or spiritual excellence. It is a world peopled by spiritual existences, but very much like our own, with good and bad in it. The least in the kingdom of Buddha is higher than the Buddhist heaven.

[2] Both Hōnen Shōnin and Nichiren criticize Kōbō's arrangement of the order of precedence assigned to the sects—the latter with considerable asperity, as is his wont. It was from Nichiren that I got the allusion to S'akyamuni not being, in Kōbō's opinion, fit to be the cowherd of Vairoc'ana. Nichiren aptly says that if Vairoc'ana is a personage of so great importance, his existence should be proved as S'akyamuni's has been, and he roundly charges Kōbō with being a liar (dai-mōgo) for trying to palm off fictitious Buddhas on his countrymen.

A distinction is sometimes made between the Roshana of the Hossō, Kegon, and Tendai, and the Vairoc'ana (Beroshana) of the Shingon. It is of this latter that Nichiren seeks to have proofs. The fact seems to be that there are, as it were, two strains of cryptic teaching respecting Vairoc'ana. The one (Roshana) came overland, or from North-Western India, and is probably connected with Syrian Gnosticism. The second (Beroshana) came from Southern India, and has Alexandrine affinities.

I fear I must repeat myself here a little to make things clear.

There are two Buddhisms : one is of a plain, simple sort, quite good enough for the practical purposes of this world ; that is the Buddhism taught by S'akyamuni, whether in the Hīnayāna or the Mahāyāna. The true spiritual Buddhism is that proclaimed by Vairoc'ana, a Being so high that S'akyamuni (with a pun on his family name) " was not worthy to be his cowherd." This secret teaching had been delivered to Nāgārjuna by one who had received it from Vairoc'ana himself, had been secretly handed down during the ages, and had finally been published in the fulness of the times.

Like the gods of the Manichæans and Gnostics, Vairo-c'ana is fivefold, and is represented by the five great statues of the Five Dhyāni Buddhas. To the mystic five correspond the five elements, the five senses, the five colours, the five planets, and many other groups of five. But they are really six, for just as Vairoc'ana, besides occupying his seat of honour in the midst of the Five, overshadows and embraces all his colleagues, so there is a sixth sense, a sixth element, etc., which overshadows and embraces everything (*alaya shiki*). The five are repre-sented by five Chinese characters, representing the sounds A-ba-ra-ka-ki, and to these is added a sixth syllable,

The Japanese Tendai has its *mantra* or magic formulæ (Jap. *darani*), as well as the Shingon. But it has no *mudra*, or manual gestures. These are peculiar to the Shingonism brought in by Kūkai, or Kōbō. Neither does the Tendai accept the secret books said to have been found by Nāgārjuna at the Iron Tower in Southern India. It gets its mantra and dharani from the Dragon Palace books, and from Maitreya's lectures in Asangha's lecture hall.

There were always certain differences between Syrian and Alexan-drine Gnosticism. It is interesting to find them cropping up in Japan. They throw a flood of light on the obscure Book of Iao.

un, A-ba-ra-ka-ki-un means " Glory to Abraxas," and
Abraxas is the name found engraved on Egyptian rings
and charms. It was the name used for " God " by
Basilides and other Gnostics of the first century.[1]

As with the Manichæans and Gnostics, the world is
twofold. There is the " Diamond world " (*Kongo-kai,
Vajradhātu*), in which all is at rest and eternal, without
change, without decay. It is the world of ideas, the
world of gods. The other, equally ancient, is the " Womb
World " (*Taizō-kai, Garbhadhātu*), the world of change,
decay, birth, death. The one world is good, the other
evil, and thus—as with the Manichæans—evil and good
are co-equal with one another and co-eternal.

In the Womb World there is a constant struggle ;
from the Diamond World, where dwell the Everlasting
Powers, whose sum-total represents the Mandala or
Pleroma of God, there issue forth countless rays of various
light, incarnated or manifested in many shapes and forms
of angels and gods, to aid man in his struggles. No
lasting value need be attached to these forms. They are
but the transient appearances of Vairoc'ana the Invisible,
who is alone unchangeable and everlasting.

Heaven helps man by the enlightenment of his mind.
In the Shingon system, as with the Manichæans, it is
supposed to do so much more efficaciously by revealing to
him certain magic formulæ and gestures, the performance

---

[1] *Un* is, of course, the *hum* of *Om mani padme hum*. The Shingonists say that *Abarakakiun* may be contracted into *Om*, which represents the first and last syllables of the sacred word. In the *goma*
ceremony the god of Fire, *RA*, is worshipped with a ritual, which has
been described in the publications of the Musée Guimet. The Shingonists still practise *Kwanjō*, as do also the Tendai, and I have in
my possession a tract, emanating from the Temple of Daishi at Kawa-
saki, in which the believer is urged not to delay coming to Baptism,
and to come oft.

of which enables him to put the enemy to flight and com-
pel Heaven to take his part. These formulæ are known
as the secrets of the body, mouth, and heart. They are
found in Manichæism; they also exist in the magical
systems of Hinduism. The *goma* ceremony, which is the
offering of pure fire, seems to connect the system with
Hinduism, and yet the syllable *ra*, used as the name for
" Fire," points to Egypt.

The Manichæans divided their followers into
" Hearers " and " Perfect." So does Shingon. It introduced into Japan the term *sokushin jōbutsu*, which means
that a man may, whilst still living, become a Perfect
Buddha, higher than the gods of the trees and mountains,
and, like S'akyamuni, equal to the Most High.

I will leave it to my readers to imagine what must
have been the effect of a teaching which made the enlightenment of the mind a secondary matter, which laid its
principal stress on magic formulæ and incantations, and
which encouraged its believers to expect, during this life,
a position equal to that of the Almighty.

And yet Kōbō Daishi was very far from being a bad
man. We can look upon him with admiration, we can
read most of his books with reverence, only, alas! we
cannot help being reminded, as we read, of a Being
who is sometimes " transformed into an Angel of Light."
And when we look at the degradation of Japan during the
Heian period, at the worldliness of the Buddhist clergy, at
the trained fighting men of the Hieizan monastery, at the
powerlessness of the sovereigns, at the robber bands which
infested the capital at the very time when the artistic
luxury of the court was at its height, at the Imperial
palace burnt to the ground four times in the course of
one short reign, at the sale of governorships, etc., for the
purpose of raising money for Buddhist temples, at the

R

miseries of the people, and at the piteous spectacle of the *Odorinembutsu* [1] as a remedy for those miseries, we shall be inclined to think that, in Japan also, we have come across some of his traces.

[1] The "*dancing nembutsu*" was the name given to a priest, Kūya, in the fifteenth century, who went round the country repeating the *nembutsu* and dancing. He hoped by this means to convert the people to religious ways. The pathetic part of the phenomenon is that Kūya was an Imperial prince, and that he seems to show us the powerlessness of the Imperial House, kept in subjection by the dominant Fujiwaras, anxious to help the people, and yet too ill-instructed to be able to do it. There are forms of superstition which are absolutely well-intentioned, and such was Kūya's. Such also was the superstition of the man who, in the next century, made it a rule to repeat the formula *Namu-amida-butsu* 60,000 times a day. In the miseries of that age Japan could have been described in Tennyson's words—

> "An infant crying in the night,
> An infant crying for the light,
> And with no language but a cry."

CHAPTER XXI

"NAMUDAISHI"

THE title of this chapter is the title of a Japanese poem on the Life of the great Kōbō Daishi: "Glory to the Great Teacher."

Kōbō Daishi's life, as it has lived in the religious traditions of Japan, is full of wonders. It is true that the present generation scoffs at the wonders, and tries to construct lives of the distinguished monk with all the miracles left out. The rationalized biographies do not suit the popular fancy. It is as the wonder-working Apostle of a new form of faith that Kōbō Daishi lives in popular fancy, and the religious historian cannot afford to leave out the miracles which adorn or disfigure his life. The miracles are part and parcel of the religious history of the country.

The poem "Namudaishi" is a religious ballad, written in the ordinary 7.5.7.5 metre of the Japanese *wasan*. It is not a great poem; but it gives a good summary of Kōbō's life as it appears to the ordinary Buddhist believer in Japan. And it has never yet been presented to the English-speaking public.[1]

1. On the fifth day of the middle decade of the sixth

[1] There is an English translation published in 1909, in a volume on Kōbō Daishi entitled "Namudaishi." But it was made by some Japanese who knew but little English, and had no English friend to correct his translation. It requires some knowledge of "English as she is spoke" to understand it.

month in the fifth year of Hoki,[1] in the Baron's Hall on the shore of Byōbu, in the land of Sanuki, a bright light shone. It was the birth of our great sage.

2. When the lad was but five years old he would sit constantly among the lotuses, and there hold converse with the Buddhas. But what he spoke of he never told, not even to his mother.

3. In his heart there arose the desire to save mankind from all their sorrows and pains, and he sought on Mount Shashin [2] to accomplish this desire by the sacrifice of his own life. Then angels came and saved him from death.

4. Whilst at play he built himself a pagoda of clay. The Four Heavenly Kings [3] at once came and stood guard over it. The Imperial Messenger passing by saw the prodigy and was amazed. "This," said he, "is a divine prodigy."

5. In the fifteenth year of his age, in spring-time, he left his native village and went to Kyōto, where he diligently studied all the doctrines of Confucianism. But he found that they contained no wisdom wherein he might put his trust.

6. In his search after truth he learned all Buddhist doctrines. Of all the Buddhas he learned to trust especially in Hōjō,[4] whom he made his special deity.

7. But [his mind was so nimble] that though he learned but one thing or two, he could thence deduce

---

[1] *I.e.* June 15, A.D. 774.

[2] Mount Shashin is in the Island of Shikoku. The word means "throwing away the body"; and the place "the Mountain of Self-oblation." The idea of religious suicide or self-immolation is one of the saddest features of mediæval Buddhism. It always gives me the idea of a diabolical perversion of Rom. xii. 1.

[3] *I.e.* the Shi Tennō. Originally Hindu deities, they have been pressed by the Mahāyāna into the service of Buddhism.

[4] Akas'agarba, a well-known Bodhisattva.

a thousand. "Many are the ways," he said in his *Sangoshiki;* "but Buddhism is the best of all."

8. At Muroto in Tosa he was performing his devotions. A bright star fell from Heaven, and entered his mouth. At midnight an evil dragon came forth against him; but he spat upon it, and with his saliva he killed it.

9. It was in the nineteenth year of his age that, looking up to Gonzō as his religious guide,[1] he took upon himself the vows of the Bodhisattva, and became a homeless S'ramana, striving after enlightenment, and wearing the black silk robes of the Buddhist priest.

10. At Shusenji in the province of Idzu, and in other places besides, he discovered the hot springs bubbling out of the earth. And it was he that demonstrated to the world the use of coal.[2]

11. Inside the tower of the Temple of Kumadera in Yamato there was revealed to him the doctrine which is above all others.[3] But as there was none whom he could question thereon, he received permission from the Emperor to go to China for study.

12. In company with the ambassadors[4] that were sent

---

[1] *Gonzō* must have been a monk of the Vinaya sect. See above chapter on Dharmagupta. To have a religious teacher seems to be a necessity in Buddhism. I have seen it stated that without a teacher one cannot be saved, because the Way is the effect, the teacher is the Cause, and therefore, however much of the Way a man has acquired, if it is done without a teacher it is an effect without a cause, *i.e.* nothing.

[2] Notice how quaintly the practical Japanese mind mixes up the material with the spiritual.

[3] The legend is that in answer to earnest prayers for guidance he was told in a dream to look for a certain book in the Temple of Kumadera. He looked, and the book which he found was the "Vairo-c'ana Sūtra," brought to China from Southern India by way of the sea, and containing that Shingon doctrine which has such marvellous resemblances to the Egyptian speculations.

[4] The ambassador on this occasion was Fujiwara no Ason. The embassy took tribute to China.

to the Court of the Tangs in China, he arrived at a certain port of China. But the party was not allowed to land, because they had not come to the usual port of debarkation.

13. Then did our sage write a letter in the name of the ambassadors, in the which he described all the pains and perils of the voyage over the sea, with its storms and billows. And then were they allowed to land.

14. Keikwa the Ac'ārya[1] was delighted to welcome him, and having purified the Mandara[2] for him, committed to him the whole of the great law of the Ryōbu[3] in its entirety, to its lowest depths.

15. Keikwa the Ac'ārya told him that the secret treasure of the Shingon law lay hidden within the sacred books, and that it would be well for him to make use of the help of pictures.[4]

16. [From Keikwa] Kōbō received over a hundred books explaining the Ryōbu Mandara as contained in the

[1] Ac'ārya is an Indian word unknown to the earliest periods of the Mahāyāna. Its use denotes a long association of Brahmans and Buddhists.

[2] The Mandara is in one sense the *pleroma*, *i.e.* the sum-total of the divine personalities that go to make up the Godhead. The word is also used (and here, according to the Japanese commentary) to denote a magic ring or circle, used in sorcery. We must never forget the great part that sorcery plays in the Shingon, just as it did in the Egyptian Gnosticism, and its kindred Cabbala.

[3] The Ryōbu doctrine is that there are two worlds, of which one, the world of ideas, is fixed and eternal. The material world corresponds to the world of ideas, with this difference, that the one Idea in the Ideal World may have many material counterparts in the world of matter. Thus the gods of India may be taken as the corporeal counterparts of the incorporeal Truths which the Eternal Buddhas stand for. The same, however, holds good for the gods of China and Japan. And things which are equal to the same thing are equal to one another.

[4] Shingonism has undoubtedly always been a most potent stimulant of art.

doctrine of the Vajrayāna.[1] Also he received many sacred vessels and implements that had been handed down from the days of Amogha,[2] the doctor of the Tripitaka.

17. The boy[3] whom he met wrote the character for "dragon" upon the water. But our Sage, seeing that one small stroke had been omitted, took up his pen and supplied that which was wanting. Then the dragon revealed himself in his true form and flew away to the sky.

18. Under Prajnā,[4] the monk of Nālanda in Central India, and under Munis'ri, the Master of the Tripitaka, he studied Sanskrit, and was by them presented with many books of the Scriptures in Sanskrit.

19. With a pen in his mouth, one in each hand, and one in each foot, he wrote five lines of a poem simultaneously. The Tang Emperor was astonished at what he saw, and gave him the title of the "Five-Pen-Priest."

20. But when Keikwa his teacher died, he wrote his

[1] *Vajrayāna, i.e.* the Shingon, which explains the world by reference to the Diamond World, or World of Ideas (Vajradhātu). The use of this word seems to show that the Shingon is distinct from the other streams of the Mahāyāna.

[2] Amogha (Jap. Fukū) reached China from Southern India during the seventh century. He was a most prolific writer.

[3] This boy is said to have been a manifestation of Manjuśri, the Bodhisattva who represents Wisdom, and who is specially connected with China. We can see that Manjuśri, whose "true form" is that of a dragon, or Nāga, has a special connection with the Avatamsaka (Kegon) doctrine, which I have described in the chapter on Nāgārjuna. His worship in China must at this time have been very popular, for Prajnā went to China especially to make inquiries about him.

[4] Prajnā brings us into close touch with Christianity, for it was he that collaborated with a Nestorian priest in the translation of a book out of the Hu language (Persian?) into Chinese. The book is said to have been a Buddhist Sūtra, but this is doubtful. I have been able to find out nothing about Munis'ri; but it is said that there was a Brahman also in their company—another indication pointing to the Hindu affinities of the Shingon.

memorial on a monument, moistening his inkslab with his tears, and erected it at Ryūgen.

21. Now, when he was about to return to his own land, standing on the sea-beach he threw his vajra[1] towards Japan. Strange to say, the vajra flew straight across, and was found hanging on the branch of a pine-tree at Takano.[2]

22. The secret doctrines which he had learned in the land of the Tang, together with many precious and rare objects for the protection of the land, all these, together with the catalogue, he offered in the Imperial Palace.

23. When, to return thanks for the divine protection afforded to him during his travels, he offered incantations before the treeless temple-ground (of the god of Kasui), straightway green leaves and bright flowers came forth in abundance on what had till then been the "Naked Mountain."[3]

24. Our land had once possessed the tea-plant,[4] but the use of tea had been quite forgotten. Our Sage brought with him a millstone and some seeds of the tea-

---

[1] The vajra is a little instrument of incantation, made of copper or some other metal, and looking somewhat like a thunderbolt, when held in the hand of the celebrant. It plays a large part in the Shingon ritual, and is an element in the names of many Shingon books and Shingon priests.

[2] *I.e.* Kōya.

[3] The story is that, when Kōbō started, he made a prayer at the Shrine of Usa Hachiman, commending himself to the protection of the gods. In answer to this prayer the god of Kasui (whose name is not given) promised to accompany Kōbō on his journey and to protect him wherever he went. In return for this Kōbō produced the trees and flowers. It is clear from this that Kōbō's object in going to China was to find a *moyen de vivre* for Buddhism and Shinto.

[4] The same claim is made in the twelfth century for Eisai, the founder of the Sōtō sect. It would seem that in the long period of civil war the art of tea-growing was again lost.

plant, and taught our people how to prepare tea and drink it.

[I omit verses 25–28, the only one of any importance being the one in which Shōtoku Taishi is said to have appeared to him to teach him the Shōman-gyō, a Sūtra which concerns itself mainly with the duties of lay women. V. 29 is important.]

29. In the second month of the second year of Kōnin (Feb., 811 A.D.), along with the Emperor Saga, he received the Kwanjō of the gods [1] from the hands of Ōnakatomi, the famous ritualist.

30. Then, beginning with Dengyō Daishi, he admitted into his Church the head priests of all the Nara sects who had faith in his doctrines, and administered to them the

---

[1] This was evidently the formal inauguration of the Ryōbu Shinto. The Emperor, Saga Tenno, and Kōbō were baptized (Kwanjō) into the Shinto community by the chief ritualist of that faith. And the Shintoists in their turn were baptized into Buddhism by Kōbō. The bargain was struck on the assumption that the Buddhas and Bodhisattvas were essentially the same beings as the Shinto gods, and that the two religions meant the same thing, though they said it in different language. It does not matter, says the Shingon commentator, in praising the Scripture of the Lotus of the Good Law, whether one says in Sanskrit, *Saddharmapundarika sūtram*, or in Chinese, *Myō Hō Renge Kyō*, or in Japanese, *Tayenaru nori no hachisu no hana no minori*. The meaning and the effect are identical in each case.

Of the Emperor Saga, Murdoch says (" History of Japan," vol. i. p. 227) that he was "undoubtedly a highly accomplished man of brilliant parts . . . deeply versed in Chinese literature; that he did everything to encourage its study, and exerted himself to complete the Sinicization of the country." It was, however, more the splendour and magnificence of the Chinese Court than its solid virtues that appealed to him. Luxury and ostentation crept in, the nobles found it hard to meet the expenses of the Court life, and relief had to be granted them by exempting their domains from Imperial taxes. This impoverished the Court, created great semi-independent baronies, and brought about precisely that state of affairs which Kwammu had been at such pains to avert when he tried to break the power of the great Nara monasteries.

Baptism which admitted them into the priesthood of the Secret Doctrine.

31. At a religious discussion in the Palace of the Seiryōden his body suddenly assumed the appearance of Vairoc'ana. The Divine Light (Kōmyō) streamed out from him, and the whole company, overawed and trembling, fell to the ground and worshipped him.

32. That he might pray for the prosperity of the Fujiwara House,[1] he set up an altar in the Nannendō (at Nara), and there offered worship to Kenjaku Son.[2] Thereupon the god (of Kasuga) made his appearance and chanted a song of praise.

33. From China he brought to Japan the soil upon which the eight pagodas,[3] had stood. This soil he divided amongst eighty-eight places (in Sanuki), so that they who suffer from illness, as the result of Karma either in the past life or present, might go round them on pilgrimage and so be cleansed from their sins.

34. He prayed where the water was brackish, where it was foul, where there was no water at all. Everywhere, to the great joy of mankind, wells of pure water sprang up.

35. In the mountainous districts of the province of Kii, two dogs, one white and one black, and a hunter,[4]

---

[1] The Fujiwara family were coming into prominence at this time. For many years the head of this family was the practical director of the Emperor's councils; and the custom subsists to this day that the Empress of Japan is always a Fujiwara. The god of Kasuga, Ama no Koyane, is the deified progenitor of the Fujiwaras.

[2] Kenjaku Son is a name given to the Bodhisattva Amoghapasa, often identified with Kwannon.

[3] The eight pagodas are the eight stupas in India built over the relics of S'akyamuni, whose ashes were divided amongst eight tribes.

[4] Kōbō Daishi knew better than to forbid hunting. The experiment had been tried during the Nara period, with the result that the nobles and warriors, after a brave attempt to comply with the Buddhist law,

came to show him the way, and brought him to a place where there had once been the shrine of an ancient Buddha.[1] The god was the guardian deity of that hunting-place.

36. Then Nyuzu appeared, the god of that place (Kōya), and offered him that place until the coming of Maitreya,[2] in order that the land might be blessed by him (Kōbō).

37. When first he began to open up Mount Kōya, after he had found on a pine tree the vajra he had thrown, and after the sword[3] had come out from the earth, then indeed he knew that the place was the seat of ancient Buddhist worship.

38. Not only did he make the pool of Tōchi in Sanuki, but in other places also he made pools. In addition to bridges and piers, he repaired a great number of bridges.

had given up in despair and gone back to their hunting ways. My friend, Mr. Yanagita, of Ushigome, Tokyo, was kind enough to send me a few weeks ago a little pamphlet about some peculiar hunting customs in a little village on the slopes of the volcano of Mount Aso. Amongst other practices, it is customary in that village to hold a funeral service over the dead body of the wild boar. The form of service, which is called *indō*, and is very ancient, was drawn up for the villages by Kōbō Daishi.

[1] Said to be Kaśyapa Buddha, S'akyamuni's immediate predecessor.

[2] Kōbō constantly taught that Maitreya, the disciple of S'akyamuni, who has reached to Bodhisattvaship, and is now in the Tushita heaven, from whence he came once to lecture for Asangha (see above, Chapter XVI. p. 163), will come again at the end of the age to restore all things by the confuting of heretics. This is not a universal belief among Japanese Buddhists; but it is very strongly held by the Japanese Shingon.

[3] In India ruling families belonging to the so-called Sun Dynast make a great deal of the Sword. Kōbō Daishi, who was a Sanskritist, probably knew this, and it may have been he that pointed out the importance to the Imperial Family of Japan (also a Sun Dynasty) of the Sacred Sword. We find the same idea with Attila and the Huns, and also perhaps in King Arthur's sword Excalibur.

39. In order to save men from the plague[1] he preached the inner meaning of the Heart-Sūtra. The roads were filled with men that had been raised from the dead; the whole land enjoyed the blessings of peace.

40. He founded the temple upon Mount Bandai and placed there as his successor the priest Furuichi from Tsukuba. He subdued the wilderness of Mount Futāra and called the place Nikkō.

41. He was anxious that the flowers of literature should flourish among our men of the Land of the Day-spring, and composed in the letters of our country a poem on the four verses of the Tathāgata.

42. The doctrines of S'akyamuni are eighty-four thousand in all, the last[2] being the teaching on Nirvana which Buddha himself gave. The most important of these have been thus interpreted.

"Life's naught, Death's naught," said Shaka.   " E'en
    to-day,"
Said Kōbō, "have we crossed the mountain-pass
Of true existence."
                    Shaka : " Now with joy
Nirvana's peace we enter."
                          " Life's a dream,"
Said Kōbō, " Death, the waking of the Soul
From some poor drunkard's nightmare misery."

---

[1] This outbreak of plague is assigned in the Commentary to the year 820. Murdoch does not mention it. The Commentary passes over without a word the clause concerning the men raised from the dead. The Heart-Sūtra is the *Prajnā Parāmitā Hridaya Sūtra*, a very short Sūtra, which will be found in S. B. E.

[2] The Sects are not in agreement as to which is to be considered the last Sūtra that Buddha preached. Some say the Nirvana teachings came last, but others give that place to the " Saddharmapundarika " or the Amida books.

43. "All things are full of change," said Shaka's self.
   "The flowers, that fragrant bloom, will change
   and droop,"
   Said our Sage Kōbō. "Life is but death" became,
   To Kōbō, "Who can hope to live for aye?"

44. Thus any man who can write the *Kana* characters
of the *Iroha*,[1] whether he understand their meaning or
not, becomes the disciple of our great Sage, and receives
the happiness that comes from the Law.

45. This syllabary he founded on the Sanskrit alphabet,
which we venerate as sacred, and arranged according to
the principles of Nirvana,[2] handing it down to us in a
word-picture of fifty syllables. Thus he provided for the
education of future generations.

46. Basing his action on the expressed wish of the
Emperor Saga, he founded in the Tōji Temple at Kyoto a
shrine for the worship of Hachiman,[3] where he worshipped
the god and laid upon him the duty of protecting the
Imperial House.

[1] The word *Iroha*, like our English word "alphabet," represents
the first three characters of the Japanese syllabary, as arranged by
Kōbō Daishi.

[2] This is a reference to the well-known text, of which the *Iroha*
poem is but a paraphrase—

> Shogyō mujō,
> Zeshō meppō
> Shō metsu metsu i
> Jaku metsu i raku.

"All phenomena are impermanent,
   Because they are subject to the law of origination and perishing:
   When this law of origination and perishing comes to an end
   Calm will be found to be the true happiness."

[3] *Hachiman*, a deification of the Japanese Empress Ōjin. Had Kōbō
been contented with identifying Japanese deities with Buddhas he
would have satisfied many minds. But his introduction of unnecessary
Indian deities was much resented. Nichiren, for instance, accepts
Amaterasu as Dainichi, and Ōjin as Hachiman, but attacks the other
identifications most severely.

47. The god of Inari[1] appeared on Mount Fushimi
and received from Kōbō's hand the sacrifice he offered.
"Together, you and I," he swore, "we will protect this
people."

48. When there was a drought, he received an order
from the Emperor, and made supplication for rain in the
Imperial Garden of Shinsen-yen. Then the Holy Maidens
and the Nāga Princes[2] appeared, and there was a gentle
rain over all the land.

49. To Kenne,[3] who had been his companion on his
visit to China, he entrusted the sacred globe as an object of
worship. "This," said he, "has been consecrated by many
mystic enchantments."

50. He mastered all the five branches of knowledge;[4]
he studied the whole of the ten Pitakas. He was proficient
in painting and in sculpture, and in order to promote the

[1] Inari is the farmers' god, the god of rice. Kōbō had already won
the favour of the Imperial House, of the warriors, of the Fujiwaras, by
his skilful identifications of deified heroes with Buddhas and Bodhisattvas. Now he claims the allegiance of the farmers. We can admire
his great ingenuity; all the same, it was a terrible prostitution of the
truth, and we are not astonished that the manly samurai should always
have had the utmost contempt for him as an ingenious and not over-
scrupulous miracle-monger.

[2] Nothing is said in the English translation of " Namudaishi " (to
which I have already alluded) about the Nāgas and maidens. But they
are mentioned in the Japanese original.

[3] Kenne is otherwise unknown. The "sacred globe" (Jap. *hōshū*)
is a crystal ball.

[4] The five branches of knowledge are the same as the five " branches
of learning " which we used sometimes to hear of as children. The
expression "*ten* pitakas," or ten Collections of Scriptures, seems to
point to a conclusion that I have long since come to, though I have
never had the opportunity of working it out, that the Chinese Buddhist
Canon represents a collection of the Holy Books of ever so many distinct religious bodies, each of which requires quite independent treatment.

intellectual welfare of his countrymen he founded the *Shugei-shuchi-in*.[1]

51. During the second week of the first month in every year, there is held in the Imperial Palace a Festival of Prayer for the reigning Emperor. This was instituted by him; it was a most magnificent festival, and was maintained for a thousand years, even to the days of Meiji.[2]

52. On one day after the twentieth of the third month of the second year of Jōwa (A.D. 835) he foretold that he should die, and leaving behind him a hundred esteemed and valuable instructions, departed this life.

53. For those whose affectionate desire should draw their minds to the Sage in after years, the prince painted a portrait of him. The prince[3] did indeed paint the face, but the eyes were painted in by the Sage himself.

54. When he died it was as though a bright light had gone out in the midst of a black night. Thousands of his followers, lay and priestly, followed him weeping to the graveyard of Okunoin in Kōya.

55. And what have the Emperor Saga and the Sage between them? There had been some compact between them, for, lo! when the Emperor died, his coffin was mysteriously borne through the air to Kōya, and Kōbō himself, coming forth from his grave, performed the funeral obsequies.

56. Then did the Emperor Uda himself, wisely following in his father's footsteps, receive from the Sage's hand the sacred Baptism, and thus set a good example for succeeding ages.

---

[1] A sort of College. There were many of these founded during the reigns of the learned emperors. See Murdoch's "History of Japan,' vol. i. p. 229.

[2] This custom has now been given up.

[3] The prince was Shinnyo, the third son of the Emperor Heijo.

57. Eighty years after his decease, an Imperial Messenger opened the gate of his sepulchre. His hair, they found, had grown long upon his head; they shaved it off and gave him a change of garments.[1]

58. The Emperor that reigned in the days of Engi[2] (*i.e.* Daigo) was deeply impressed by the lessons of his life, and honoured him with the title of Kōbō Daishi.[3]

59. When Shunnyū, the Imperial Messenger to the Temple in which our great Sage is worshipped, was unable to see the face of the Sage, the Sage himself guided the worshipper's hand to touch his knee. Never, as long as he lived, did the messenger forget that feeling.[4]

60. The Emperors Kwampyō and Shirakawa, the retired Emperor, Go-Uda, and several others of our rulers had such faith in the Sage's merits that they made pilgrimages to Kōya to worship at his sanctuary.

61. Verily the teaching of the Tathāgata of the Dharma Kaya[5] (the Spiritual Body) has been handed down without change and without break; through the long chain of our patriarchs the lamp of light has been handed down to us.[6]

---

[1] In the minds of his followers, the Sage is still uncorrupted in his tomb, awaiting the coming of Maitreya. The Baptism of the Emperor Uda (if by Kōbō) must have been miraculous, for he did not come to the throne until 887.

[2] The year-period Engi was from 908–922 A.D.

[3] Kōbō's original name was Kūkai, and ultra-imperialist Confucianists always speak of him as such. Kōbō Daishi means "The Great Teacher who spread the Law."

[4] This story is to be found in Satow and Hawes' "Handbook to Japan," p. 416 (2nd edition).

[5] *I.e.* Vairoc'ana, whose body is a spiritual body, and therefore unchangeable and everlasting, without beginning or end.

[6] The patriarchs of the Shingon are well known. They are reckoned as eight: (1) Vairoc'ana, (2) Vajrasattva, (3) Nāgārjuna, (4) Nāgabodhi. These were in India. Then in China there were: (5) Vajrabodhi, (6)

Amoghavajra (Fukū), (7) Hui-Kuō (Jap. Keikwa). Then the doctrine comes to Japan with Kōbō.

There is a second enumeration. Vairoc'ana and Vajrasattva, they say, must not count, as very little is known of them. The eight patriarchs must be reckoned as : (1) Nāgārjuna, (2) Nāgabodhi, (3) Vajrabodhi, (4) Subhakarasiṇha (Jap. Zenmui), (5) Amoghavajra, (6) Keikwa, (7) Ichigyō, (8) Kōbō.

It must be noticed—

(i) that Nāgārjuna gets his information from Vajrasattva, who gets it from Vairoc' ana. It does not, therefore, represent a very old teaching. Nāgārjuna is reckoned as the *thirteenth* Patriarch of the Zen sect; he is at most only the *third* Patriarch of the Shingon. And if we assume Nāgārjuna to have lived about the middle of the second century, the inference is almost irresistible that Vajrasattva and Vairoc'ana cannot date from much before the middle of the first.

(ii) The Shingon Patriarchs, Vajrabodhi, Amoghavajra, etc., reached China, *viâ* the sea-route, during the sixth and seventh centuries. They came from South India and Ceylon, in both of which places there were Egyptian colonies.

(iii) I have already in a previous chapter given many instances showing the close connection between Egyptian Gnosticism and the Shingon. I will now give another.

In the commentary to the last verse of Namu Daishi, the writer says that the Shingon is different from other forms of Buddhism. It has had no great changes, no violent reformations, no developments. Its doctrine has been handed down from generation to generation of the faithful by the transmission of what is called the " Seal of Vairoc'ana." The " Seal of Vairoc'ana is said to be the secret meaning of the letter A in the Sanskrit alphabet. *A-ji*, as it is called, is a very sacred thing to a Shingonist. " The paths which must be trodden in visiting the buildings of Kōya San," say Satow and Hawes (*l.c.*), " together form the Sanskrit letter *A*, which is regarded as the symbol of the Taizōkai " (*i.e.* the Diamond World, or World of Ideas, of which Vairoc'ana is the centre and the life). In " Pistis Sophia " (Schmidt's edition, p. 81) there is a note given by a later hand. According to this, the Seal of the Undying One (ἀθάνατος, in Shingon, Amida is always *amrita*) is *aaa*. He that sitteth on the throne (*i.e.* Christ the " First Mystery ") is *aaa*; the interpretation of the whole Name of God is *aaaa, aaaa, aaaa*. Ὁ μὲν πρῶτος οὐρανὸς φθέγγεται τὸ A, says Irenæus of the Gnostic Marcus (Iren., lib. i. cap. xiv. 7). The Gnostics, it is well known, stole the Christ of the Christians. The Shingon, possibly without knowing it, have been for centuries the receivers of stolen goods.

Dr. C. U. Pope, in a paper on the " Study of South Indian

S

Vernaculars," in *J.R.A.S.* for April, 1885, quotes a distich from Tiru-valluvar, the pariah weaver, which runs thus—

> " A as its first of letters every speech maintains ;
> The *Primal Deity* is first through all the world's domains."

Tiruvallavar came from Mailapûr in South India, where stands the Mani-chæan shrine of St. Thomas. It was from South India that Kôbô's Shingon came with its stress on *A-ji*. The Tamil poet's date is between A.D. 1000 and 1200. Dr. Pope speaks of it as the "Oriental book which more than any other in the wide range of Eastern literature seems to reflect the moral teaching of the Great Master whom all the Western world reveres."

CHAPTER XXII

The Buddhism of the Gempei Period [1]

It is very difficult to describe in a short paragraph, or even in one long chapter, the complicated period of Japanese history which has for its central point of interest the fierce wars waged with such relentless bitterness between the rival families of the Taira and Minamoto and their respective factions. It would be beyond the scope of the present work to try to do so. We must content ourselves with a brief mention of some of the leading features of the period, so far as they are concerned with the history of Japanese religion.

During the ninth and tenth centuries the supreme power in Japan lay practically in the hands of the great family of the Fujiwaras, who, under one title or another, monopolized all the great offices of State, and kept the emperors, always their creatures, and very often connected with them by ties of marriage and affinity, in a state of absolute subjection. Occasional attempts were made to destroy the Fujiwara monopoly. Sugawara Michizane,[2]

---

[1] *Gempei* is the name given to the period of the great Civil Wars between the families of Minamoto (in Sinico-Japanese *Gen*) and Taira (*Hei*). In this chapter I mean the term to include, roughly, the period between the outbreak of the so-called Hōgen war (1156) and the establishment of the Hōjō Regents at Kamakura about 1200. But the term must be treated as very elastic.

[2] *Sugawara Michizane* (845–903), the son of an obscure but talented family, exercised a very great influence over the Emperor Uda (889–897), and laboured with great diligence to break the power of the

now worshipped as Tenjin, and famous alike for book-learning, political science, archery, and loyal devotion, made such an attempt in the reigns of Uda Tennō (887–897) and his successor Daigo (898–930). A few years later (933), Taira Masakado, aided by one of the Sumitomo branch of the Fujiwara themselves, tried to break through the tyranny of the regent, and raised a rebellion which it took some time and energy to quell, and which has a special significance from the fact that its leader aimed at the Imperial Crown for himself. But such attempts always proved abortive, and, during the whole of the period in question, the ship which bore the fortunes of the Fujiwaras rode triumphantly over all waves and came through all storms.

The nominal captain of the Fujiwara vessel was always the Emperor. But it was never forgotten in practice that his command was merely nominal. The real power lay in the hands of the first lieutenant, and for fear the captain should seek to assert his authority, or in any way interfere with the working of the ship, it was necessary to keep him happy and amused in many harmless

Fujiwaras and raise the prestige of the Imperial Family. He persuaded his master to abdicate in favour of his son, Daigo (898–930), under whose reign he continued his political designs, being much aided therein by the ex-Emperor, who had abdicated on purpose to be able to work with more freedom for the attainment of his aims. The Fujiwara, however, contrived, in 901, to poison the Emperor Daigo's mind by false charges against Michizane, who was banished to Izu in spite of all the efforts made on his behalf by the ex-Emperor. He died two years later, constant in his faithfulness to the master who had treated him so ungratefully. He has since been deified, and is worshipped in various localities as *Kan Shōjō*, *Tenjin*, *Temmangū*, etc. He was a celebrated archer. Her Majesty the Empress has a very pretty poem which tells how he rose straight from his writing-table, took a bow, and hit a difficult mark to show that, book-worm though he was accused of being, he was still able to do manly service for his master.

and innocent ways. The luxury which the Fujiwaras encouraged was no mere wanton display, no simple seeking after pleasure. It was adopted with a view to a practical end, and besides succeeding in its immediate purpose, led to other and far-reaching results. The Fujiwaras became the liberal patrons of arts and letters. The pictures for which Japan is so justly famous; her music, poetry, and dramatic art, those creations which are held so vividly to portray the character of the sentimental yet strangely matter-of-fact Japanese people;—all owe their development mainly to the artistic instincts of this gifted and powerful family, and for these things, at least, Japan owes them a lasting debt of gratitude.[1]

It is to be noted here that the arts and letters of early mediæval Japan are all Buddhist, or, at least, are so thoroughly impregnated and saturated with the spirit of that religion that it is impossible to understand their inner beauties without some knowledge of the Faith which inspired the artists. The Emperor Kwammu had moved his capital from Nara to Kyōto to be free from the intervention of the meddling priesthood in matters of State, and Dengyō had founded his monastery upon Hieizan in the hopes of finding a quiet spot where he might be free from "earth's many voices." The event was quite the opposite of what either of these men expected.[2] The Tendai reforms turned Japanese Buddhism into a wide-spreading organization with far-reaching ramifications. The Fujiwaras knew how to use that organization for their own ends, and the Buddhist

---

[1] Articles in the *Hansei Zasshi*, vol. xii., on the luxury of the Fujiwara period.

[2] Nichiren, however, represented the almost simultaneous foundations of Kyōto and Hieizan as having been the result of a conspiracy between Dengyō and the Emperor for bringing the Buddhist Church into political dependence upon the Crown.

priesthood in their hands became a political machine. The monks were the votaries of art and science; they composed the songs, painted the pictures, laid out the gardens, and designed the palaces in which the luxuriously trained court found its pleasures and forgot its feebleness, and when the captain of the ship, as sometimes happened, began to know too much, and to stir about on his soft cushions, some monastery would furnish a convenient desert island upon which the restless skipper might be marooned.[1]

Sometimes a skipper, more long-headed than the rest, did not wait to be marooned, but shut himself up voluntarily in his own cabin, as it were, and continued to direct the ship of State, from the safe shelter of some monastery, through the person of some infant son or grandson, whom he put on the throne instead of himself, and for whom he acted as guardian or regent. Such was the course adopted, e.g., by the Emperors Shirakawa and Toba,[2] and it seemed quite natural in a country like Japan, where the "power behind the throne" has always been so potent a reality. An ex-Emperor, living in a monastery, and from thence directing the affairs of State in the name of his immature son or grandson, would seem to be an ideal state of things from the point of view of an ambitious priesthood. But the Fujiwaras understood the principle of divide et impera. The Nara

---

[1] The list of Japanese emperors during this period shows a majority of names of sovereigns who came to the throne as infants in succession to deposed predecessors, and who were forced in their turn to abdicate as soon as they reached manhood or wanted to exert their powers.

[2] Shirakawa reigned A.D. 1078 to 1086; Toba, 1108 to 1123. Shirakawa did not, however, die until 1129, and Toba lived until 1156. There was a time when three ex-Emperors were all alive at the same time, eating out their hearts in early retirement, whilst one of their number helped to pull the wires for their baby kinsman on the throne.

monasteries were jealous of the new-fangled growths on the slopes of Mount Hiei; the Hieizan household was encouraged to go in for domestic feuds. The appointment of a *Zashū*, or Archbishop, of the Tendai community, chosen not from the monks of the Mother House of Hieizan, but from the inmates of the daughter institution at Ōtsu—the Onjōji, or Miidera—gave the signal for a strange civil war within the fold of the Tendai itself. Hieizan and Miidera became the headquarters of two warring armies, with a military organization of *tera-samurai*, or temple knights, and train bands of fighting men. The other large temples followed suit, and the lay people of Japan had the undesirable privilege, several times during these centuries, of beholding armies of "religious" persons engaging in fratricidal strife, killing, burning, and laying waste.

In the mean time there was growing up in Japan an upper middle class, closely connected with the aristocracy, and yet independent of them, and corresponding very nearly to our English gentry.

It had been the practice, both of the Fujiwara and also, from time to time, of the Emperors themselves, to raise money for political or religious purposes by the sale of certain patents (not unlike the baronetcies of King James I.), known as *shō-en*, which conferred upon their holders the privilege of possessing their estates free from Imperial taxation and exempt from the jurisdiction of the provincial governors. Some of the Emperors, *e.g.* Go-sanjo (1069), had set their faces against this practice; but needy and religious-minded rulers, such as Shirakawa (1073) and Toba (1108), had been very lavish in the granting of these patents, and the holders of these privileges became an important element in the State. They formed the main support of the rival factions of Taira and

Minamoto, and even after Yoritomo's formal and success-ful organization of their scattered members, continued to be, as *samurai*, down to our own times, the true backbone of the Japanese nation.[1]

Independent, freedom-loving, fairly educated, addicted to martial exercises and the outdoor sports which have been the pastime of the country gentleman in all ages and climes, these men had absolutely nothing but contempt for the sickly sentimentalism of the fashionable priests, with their legends and repetitions, and their somewhat hypocritical prohibitions against hunting and fighting. That they were not devoid of religious feeling we shall see in another chapter. For the present let us note merely that they were coming into prominence as a social and religious element, qualified to exercise a determining in-fluence on the destinies of their country.

I have already, in a previous chapter, referred to the social miseries of the country during the period of which many writers speak as though it had been the golden age of Japanese history. With equal justice might we speak of the reign of King Stephen, or the long-protracted miseries of the Wars of the Roses, as having been the golden age of our English history. The miseries of the people, naturally passed over by chroniclers whose eyes were concentrated upon the precincts of the Imperial Palace, were truly great. They cannot have been anything else.

I have also spoken, in my last chapter, of the pathetic figure of the *Odori-nembutsu*, the poor, half-witted, princely priest, dancing his way through the country, with the monotonous *nembutsu* constantly upon his lips, in the hope

[1] Minamoto Yoritomo, the first of the Minamoto Shoguns (1147–1199), organized the Kamakura Bakufu, round which he gathered the military elements of the country, away from the influence of the Court and priesthood. He is often spoken of as *Kamakura dono*. See next chapter.

of thus awakening in the hearts of the people that sense of belief in a Power higher than ourselves, which is man's strongest rock of confidence in the hour of misery and sorrow. This is the place for me to stop my narration, and to give my readers a digression (I fear it may be a long one) on the subject of the *nembutsu*.

Nembutsu means "thinking of Buddha"; the Nembutsu to which I refer is the popular Japanese contraction for the phrase *Namu-Amida-butsu*, which is half Sanskrit and half Chinese, and means "Glory to the Buddha Amitābha," the Buddha to whom I have already so often referred in the course of this present work.

Amitābha, "the Buddha of Infinite Light," or Amitayus, "the Buddha of Infinite Life" (the two are identical in Japan, though, I believe, treated as distinct personages in Thibet), is preached in certain Sūtras [1] of

---

[1] These Sūtras are known in Sanskrit as the greater and Lesser *Sukhāvati Vyūha*, and the *Amitāyur-dhyāni Sūtra*, the two former extant both in Sanskrit and Chinese, the last in Chinese only. All three claim to be Sūtras spoken by the Buddha himself, but no trace of them can be found prior to A.D. 147, when Anshikao and his associates took one of them to China—not from India, but from Central Asia —nor is there any written evidence of a belief in Amida before the times of As'vaghosha and Nāgārjuna, say about the latter end of the first century A.D. Shortly after commencing this chapter I had an interview with a Buddhist priest, now deceased, whose conversation on this subject was extremely interesting. According to him, no Buddhist Sūtras, whether Mahāyāna or Hīnayāna, were reduced to writing for the first five centuries after Buddha's death. (There is some support for this view in Singhalese tradition, though it does not quite agree with the evidence of As'oka's inscriptions.) From the beginning of the sixth Buddhist century began the writing down of the various Sūtras, which had till then been traditional only. Oral tradition is, however, extremely liable to corruption and change, and thus there had arisen discrepancies, between North and South in general, and between different parts of the North in particular. In this way, he said, had been framed the two Vehicles; but it could not be affirmed that either of them was older than the other. The literary forms in which both Vehicles are enshrined are coeval, and both are late, as late as the

the Mahāyāna, to which I have already had occasion
to refer, as the Supreme Being of a certain section of
Buddhists. Amida is without beginning and without end,
all love, wisdom, benevolence, and power. He is the
Father[1] of all the world and of all sentient beings. In

Christian era. No Christian controversialist could ask for more generous concessions than these.

It may be of interest to some of my readers to know that since the
end of 1910, I have been engaged, together with some Buddhist friends
in Tokyo, on a work of translation of early Buddhist documents which
may lead to some interesting developments. Our present immediate ob-
jective is to work out a translation into some European language of all
the Indian books translated into Chinese during the Han period, *i.e.* A.D.
147 and A.D. 220. When these have been translated (it will take several
years to accomplish), we hope that we shall be able to give to the world
a tolerably complete picture of what Buddhism was like when first
introduced into China. We also hope that we may be able to throw some
light on Gnosticism and the developments of Christian heresy during
the second and third centuries.

But more interesting matter for translation will probably be found
in the works of Japanese theologians of the eleventh, twelfth, and
thirteenth centuries, a field as yet untouched by European research.
We are learning to-day to see that Christ's work was far larger than
anything that our forefathers of even a century ago ever dreamt of,
and to comprehend that each nation will contribute and is contributing
its quota to the Perfect Temple of the Future, and that no Spiritual
Building can be expected to be final which does not make adequate
allowance for the glory and honour of all nations to be brought in.

[1] Mr. Tada Kanae, in his excellent volume of "Lectures on the
Shōshinge" (pp. 54, 56), says that Amida may also be called the Creator,
inasmuch as he established the Law of Cause and Effect through which
the Universe came into existence. Some Buddhists, however, are not
willing to grant this. They say that the law came into action auto-
matically from the very nature of Shinnyo, and that in no case are we
justified in considering Amida as a Creator. That he is the Father is
freely admitted by all *Shinshuists*. A Japanese theologian (I think I
may give Dr. Anezaki that title, though he is a Buddhist) pointed out
to me a short time ago that the first draft of the Nicene Creed ran,
πιστεύω εἰς ἕνα Θεὸν Πατέρα παντοκράτορα πάντων ὁρατῶν τε καὶ ἀοράτων : "I
believe in one God, the Father, Almighty Ruler of all things visible and
invisible," and, according to Rufinus, there was a similar omission of

ages incalculably remote he appeared in various forms among men, all his incarnations being to bring salvation to mankind. In his last incarnation he appeared as the Bhikshu Hōzo (Dharmakāra), and as such registered a vow that should the Perfect Consummation of the Buddhahood ever be in his power, he would not accept deliverance unless such deliverance should also mean the salvation of suffering mankind. In fulfilment of that vow he endured much suffering and many agonies, but he triumphed in the end, and the fruit of his labours has been the opening of a Paradise in a Pure Land, into which all may enter who call upon his name with Faith.[1] Other Buddhas also have spoken of Paradise;[2] Amida alone can speak of it as *my* Paradise.

Amida is *Ichi-butsu*, the One Buddha, and besides Him there is none, for all the other Buddhas and Bodhisattvas and gods, in whom men trust, are but temporary and partial manifestations of the Great Father, whose Vow (a Christian might call it his *Will*) is that all mankind should be saved—saved from the miseries of existence, from all those universals of misery which S'akyamuni disclosed to a suffering world, and placed in that Paradise where there is nothing to hinder or to hurt the soul on its upward path to that Perfection which comes from the Beatific Vision of Amida Himself.[3]

an expression of belief in a Creator in the Creed of the Church of Aquileia ("Lib. post-Nicene Fathers," vol. iii. p. 541).

[1] See "S.B.E.," vol. xlix., and my "Praises of Amida," Introd., pp. 1, 2.

[2] *E.g.* Yakushi (Bhaishajyarāja).

[3] According to the Pure Land books, there is a nine-graded Vision of Amida vouchsafed to the soul in Paradise, and the Vision itself, as it grows in intensity, has a purifying effect on the soul. I may point out that the eighty-one previous Buddhas in the Sukhāvati Vyūha are but an amplification of this ninefold Amida, which again is an amplification of a Trinity.

Amida is One and Indivisible, but He has several names, and two of the names by which He is known amongst men have become personified with a quasi-separate existence as His Sons, and sit, the one on His right, the other on His left, in His Kingdom.   The right represents His Wisdom, the left His Mercy ; the latter is occupied by His Son Avalokites'vara, or Kwannon, "the Lord that looked down," incarnate again and again for man and his salvation ; the former, personified as Mahāsthāmaprāpta, or Seishi, whose gift to man is, significantly, not salvation, but life.[1]

To grasp this salvation, wrought out for man by Amida, and brought to him by Kwannon and Seishi, nothing is needed but Faith—no works of the Law, no austerities, penances, or devotions, no resolutions of amendment, no futile strivings, no repentance—nothing but Faith.   It sounds an immoral doctrine, a kind of antinomianism, yet it is not exactly immoral as expounded, at least by its latest preachers, the school of Shinran and his disciples.   For faith brings salvation, the realization of salvation arouses the gratitude of the heart, and the grateful heart, knowing what it is by nature and what it has become by grace, becomes so filled with the expansive power of a deep love that it turns the good deeds, the austerities, the devotions, from being fruitless attempts at obtaining a salvation which is practically beyond man's attainment into the joyful formulæ through which the new life imparted to the soul finds its expression.

Shinran Shōnin (A.D. 1174 to 1268), the founder of the

---

[1] I learned this in conversation with a Buddhist priest. I can but repeat here what I have said elsewhere, that the Ophite Gnostics who appeared in the same localities and at the same time as the original Amida Buddhists, held identical language about Christ.

Shinshu sect, who claimed for his teachings the authority of a Vision of Avalokites'vara himself,[1] has left behind him, amongst other works, a poem entitled the "Shōshinge," which is even now in common use in the family devotions of pious Shinshu households. A writer to whom I am very much indebted for the insight which he has given me into the thoughts and aspirations of the band of Buddhist reformers who owe their inspiration to the life and teachings of the late Mr. Kyōzawa,[2] has written a commentary on the poem, which, while being up to date, as coming from a modern scholar, yet represents the very thoughts of Shinran, the last great patriarch of mediæval Amidaism in Japan.

Mr. Tada's book, following the lines of Shinran's poem, gives us, first, a series of chapters on the Doctrine of Amida; on the connection between Amida and S'akyamuni, on the history, authenticity, and genuineness of the Sūtras on which the Amidaists build their Faith (he considers them genuine records of S'akyamuni's teachings secretly and unofficially handed down in South India during the five centuries of silence which followed S'akyamuni's death, but brings no proof for his statements), and then proceeds to treat, in several chapters, of the Invocation of Amida's Sacred Name and of the New Life of courage, enthusiasm, and hope which comes to us through prayer and adoration.

[1] It is said that two points in the Buddhist discipline caused Shinran a great deal of anxious reflection—celibacy, and the abstinence from flesh. He claimed that Avalokites'vara had appeared to him in a vision, and had taught him that these points were not of the Essence of religion. Shinshu believers all eat meat, and the Shinshu clergy are free to marry.

[2] Kyōzawa, a Shinshu priest, who died but a few years ago, may be said to have given Shinshuism a new impetus, in a direction almost Christian. His memory is still venerated by a group of very earnest Shinshu priests. I give a translation of the *Shōshinge* in my "Shinran and His Work."

He then devotes another series of chapters to the consideration of seven great names which Shinran had selected as embracing the whole history of Amidaism from its first inception to Shinran's time, and, having thus surveyed the whole of the ground covered by the *Shōshinge*, proceeds to base thereon a concluding exhortation to his readers on present duties and prospects.

The names are selected from India, China, and Japan. The Indian patriarchs are Nāgārjuna and Vasubandhu; those from China, Donran, Dōshaku, and Zendō; those from Japan, Genshin and Genkū. Each name has two chapters devoted to it, one biographical and one doctrinal, and the author has cleverly constructed his doctrinal chapters in such a way as to show that there has been a regular and consistent development all the way from Nāgārjuna to Shinran, who brought the system to its perfection.[1]

Thus in Nāgārjuna the doctrine is vague: no mention is made of the Sūtras which tell of Amida, but Nāgārjuna dies with his face set to the Western Paradise, and there are passages in his works which foreshadow the doctrine. In Vasubandhu, we get a step further: the mystic teacher knows of the book which contains the description of Paradise, and, whilst not giving himself up wholly, to the exclusion of every other cult, to the worship of Amitābha, still puts Amitābha at the top of the Buddhist pantheon. In the chapters on the Chinese Patriarchs we are shown how one of them was attracted to Amidaism by its simplicity. The multiplicity of the doctrines in the other books had confused his mind; here was something easy and intelligible and within his reach. The other had been long seeking for the Elixir of Life, had dabbled in

[1] Mr. Tada gives the dates of the seven as follows; (1) Nāgārjuna, about A.D. 150; (2) Vasubandhu, *circ.* A.D. 440; (3) Donran, *circ.* A.D. 356; (4) Dōshaku, A.D. 553; (5) Zendō, A.D. 614; (6) Genshin, A.D. 943; and finally Genkū (Hōnen), A.D. 1130–1213.

medicine and in magic, and had several times imagined himself to be on the point of discovering the formula wherewith to cheat death, yet his search had been in vain. In a moment of despondency arising from one of his numerous failures he came across Bodhiruci, a Buddhist priest of fame. " What ? " said Bodhiruci, " you are seeking for eternal life ? I will give you the secret." And handing him the books which contained the descriptions of Amida's Paradise and of salvation through faith in His Name, he bade him read and believe. The man did so, and in due course became one of the most successful of the Apostles of Amida in China.

In Japan, the Shinshuist notes with pride that the first image sent over by the King of Kudara in the sixth century was one of Amida, with his satellites, Kwannon and Seishi. The first Japanese patriarch on Shinran's list, Genshin,[1] was attracted, as had been one of his Chinese predecessors, by the simplicity of the doctrine and its adaptability to the needs of simple persons. Ere Genshin died the troubles of Japan had begun, and in the midst of those troubles the sound of Nembutsu from many a troubled heart was a cry of pathetic and half-despairing faith. Such was the cry of the Odori-nembutsu, to whom we have already alluded, and that of Ryonen Shōnin,[2] to whom Amida appeared in a vision

[1] *Genshin* (942–1017), born in Yamato, of the Urabe family, became a member of the Hieizan community, being a disciple of Ryōgen, from whom he learned something about Amitābha, which he afterwards made into the principle of his life and teaching.

[2] *Ryonen Shōnin* (1072–1132), founder of the so-called *Yūdzū-nembutsu* sect, which is still in existence. He was a monk of Hieizan ; was warned by a stranger, whom he took to be Amida, to flee from the "den of thieves" in which he was living, and to turn the Nembutsu into an intercessory prayer. *Ichinin, issainin, issainin, ichinin, ichigyō, issaigyō ; issaigyō, ichigyō,* "One man for all men, all men summarized in *One ;* one devotion for all, all devotions summed up in one."

and bade him leave the Hieizan monastery, as being a den of thieves. Ryonen and the Odori-nembutsu[1] both became founders of small sects, which, however, never succeeded in winning a very large amount of popularity. It is the merit of Genkū, better known as Hōnen Shōnin, to have successfully established a definite sect of the Pure Land in Japan; of Shinran, his greater disciple, to have brought the system to its perfection.

Genkū was converted by a death-scene. It was in the time of the Civil Wars; and Genkū's father was attacked by bandits in his house, and after a brave defence, mortally wounded. The mother and her child escaped to a place of safety, and when the bandits had cleared off, returned to the house, where they found the father dying. "You must forgive your enemies, my son," said the dying man; "there is no end to vengeance and vendetta, for wrath begets wrath, and only forgiveness can heal it." The lesson sank into the boy's mind; he became a monk, and might have risen to high honour in the wealthy and purse-proud Tendai sect, had he not preferred the simplicity of his Amida faith to the noisy worldliness of Hieizan.[2] He suffered for his convictions, yet succeeded in establishing a sect known as the Jōdo,[3]

[1] *Kūya*, the Odori-nembutsu, is looked upon as the founder of the small sect of Ji, which is, however, more generally identified with the name of Ippen-Oshō (1239–1289). Ippen, like Kūya, was an itinerant preacher, and to this day the head of the Ji sect, which has its chief temple at Fujisawa on the Tokaido, is supposed to spend all his time in itineracy. Cf. the Nestorian institution of the *periodeutes*, or itinerant preacher.

[2] For a sympathetic account of the "Buddhist St. Francis," as Hōnen has been called, see Prof. Anezaki's paper in the *Transactions of the International Congress of the History of Religions* (Oxford : 1908). When Hōnen was first sent to Hieizan, his parish priest wrote of him to the Abbot of the monastery, "I am sending you a miniature of Manjuśri."

[3] His chosen place of retirement was Kurodani, near Kyoto.

which still reveres him as its founder. The memory of his father's death seems to have remained with him all his life, for the Amidaism which he taught was *ars moriendi* rather than *ars vivendi*. " At the hour of death, . . . good Lord deliver us " is practically the cry of the Jōdo believer, and if at that solemn hour his faith in Amida is pure and clear, and the Nembutsu rises to his lips, he believes that Amida will come to save him,[1] no matter what may have been the character of his previous life. In the meanwhile, the Jōdoist, if he is sincere and earnest, does not neglect the spiritual duties of his religion. They cannot save him (no more can any good works), but they help to create and keep alive in him that faith in Amida which is of such prime importance to him at the psychological moment. But after all, when the hour of death comes, the centurion Cornelius would be no better off than the dying thief, in Genkū's teaching.

Shinran, on the contrary, saw that the dying thief was an exception to the rule of salvation. Like his master, Genkū, he made Faith in Amida's Vow the absolute and only essential to salvation, but the Faith requisite is not of the death-bed variety. It must be the Faith of a lifetime, and where that Faith exists nothing more is necessary.[2] Penances, austerities, abstinence from flesh

[1] In Jōdo circles, when a believer lies dying, a picture of Amida is hung up on the wall in some conspicuous place where the patient can easily see it. From the picture a cord is taken to the bed and fastened to the dying man's wrist, so that when the supreme agony comes he may take fast hold of Amida and not let go till he stands in safety on the other side. The practice is quite analogous to that of holding the crucifix before the eyes of the dying.

[2] There is a well-known scene in the life of Shinran. Whilst still one of Hōnen's disciples, there was a dispute as to Salvation. Shinran maintained that Faith was necessary as well as the Invocation of the Name; the others maintained that Invocation alone sufficed. All sided against Shinran except one layman. During the discussion Hōnen entered the room, and at once declared himself on the side of Shinran.

T

or marriage, works of piety and charity—none of these things will save a man, but the man who has realized the truth of his salvation through the mercies of Amida, will, out of joy and gratefulness, do more than he would ever have done merely as a means to gaining salvation for himself. To this doctrine of salvation by Faith the Shin-shu sect has remained constantly faithful. I have often been told that Shinran was acquainted with Christian doctrines when he framed the system of Jōdo Shinshū. From what I have been able to put before my readers in the course of this history, I think we may say that the probabilities are that he was.[1]

[1] We have seen how close was the contact between Amidaism and Christianity in the China of the Tang period, when Zendō and Olopen worked side by side in Singanfu, and again later, when Prajñā and the Deacon Adam were collaborators in the translations of religious works. We can hardly say of Zendō and Prâjnā that they were ignorant of Christianity. Neither can we say it of the Nara Court at the time when the Nestorian physician Rimitsu came over and was honoured with official rank. Nor again can we say it of Kōbō Daishi, or of Dengyo, the Japanese founders of the Shingon and Tendai. The former was at Singanfu and was a friend of Prajñā the collaborator; the latter had been at Singanfu, where he must have seen the celebrated Singanfu monument. The greater part of his time in China he spent on Mount Tendai as a student of religion, and the Chinese Tendai had been amongst the great instigators of the persecution against Zendō and the Nestorians. Zendō's books came over to Japan more than once between 796 and 858, and Zendō's books contain some very striking Pauline echoes. And what are we to say of Kūya's answer, when questioned of the glory of the life to come, "What I shall be I know not now: I shall know hereafter"? Or of Genshin's metal mirror, "in which he could see his face darkly"? Or of Kakuhan's definition of Butsu (佛), "He is higher than the territorial prince, higher than the Emperor, higher than the Brahma, and He is a Trinity"? Or of Myōe's refusal of an offer of wealth, "I have food and raiment; I am content"? The Spirit of Christianity breathes in these men; there was spiritual affinity if even there was no physical contact. The whole of Shinran's system, his permission of clerical marriage, his hereditary episcopates, savours strongly of Nestorianism.

CHAPTER XXIII

The Buddhism of Kamakura

KAMAKURA is connected with Yoritomo and the Regents of the Hōjō family. Yoritomo, the first of the Minamoto Shōguns (1147–1199), was the son of that Yoshitomo who, after leaguing himself with the Taira against his own clan, and bearing arms against his own father, ended by breaking with the Taira for their want of gratitude, and perished miserably at the hands of one of his own retainers, who hoped to earn the favour of Kiyomori by sending him the head of his misguided master.

His wife, Tokiwa Gozen, who had once been a consort of the Emperor Konoe, and had escaped with her three children from the massacre in which her husband had perished, sacrificed her own person to the vindictive Kiyomori, in order thereby to save the three children whom she had borne to Yoshitomo. One of these children was Yoritomo; the other was Yoshitsune, the favourite hero of Japanese history and romance.

Yoritomo was about thirteen years old when his father died. His mother's self-sacrifice induced Kiyomori to spare him; but he was banished to Izu, where he did not behave very well; though he managed to secure the affections of his guardian's daughter, the beautiful and capable Masa-ko, who ran away from home to join her lover on the outbreak of his war against the Taira, and who may be said to have laid the foundations of the Hōjō family, by procuring for her father the nomination to the office of Regent (Shikken). Yoritomo's arms were successful; he and his associates defeated the Taira partisans at Ichi-no-tani (1184), at Yashima (1184), and finally at Dan-no-ura (1185), after which he found himself practically master of Japan, being invested in 1192 with the title of *Sei-i-tai Shōgun*, a title which for seven successive centuries continued to designate the personage in whose hands nominally lay the practical administrative and military power in Japan.

But long before that, in the early part of his campaigns, after his defeat at Ishibashiyama in 1181, he had (under Hōjō Tokimasa's advice) made Kamakura his headquarters, and had there organized the *samurai* who rallied round the Minamoto standard into a compact military body, which assured to him the victory over his rivals throughout Japan. The Kamakura Bakufu—a state within a state—organized by the genius of Hōjō Tokimasa—was to the rest of Japan in those days what Prussia was to the rest of Germany in 1866, better organized, better drilled, better disciplined, and it was thanks to the Hōjō genius that the Minamoto secured the hegemony of the Empire.

When Yoritomo died, in 1199, his widow, Masako, who knew the impetuous stormy character of the Minamoto family, took precautions to preserve from destruction the system which her father at Kamakura had elaborated with so much care and forethought. Yoritomo's son, Yoriie, was indeed put in his father's place, and in 1202 invested with the title of Sei-i-tai-shōgun; but he was restricted in his liberty by a Council of State, appointed to assist him in his functions, and the chairman of that Council was Hōjō Tokimasa, who now received the title of Shikken, or Regent. The Shōgunate soon passed out of the feeble hands of Yoritomo's descendants; but the Hōjō Regents still continued to exercise their power in the name of the puppet-Shōguns, whom they themselves nominated. Japan thus beheld the spectacle of an Emperor the whole of whose administrative powers had devolved upon a Shōgun, who, again, was but a puppet, with all his functions usurped by a Regent who ruled in the Shōgun's name. Theoretically, nothing could be conceived more hopeless than this extremely anomalous arrangement of the government. Practically, the system worked with fair smoothness for over a century, from A.D. 1200 to 1333. The Hōjō Regents were on the whole men of ability, power, and uprightness (as uprightness was reckoned in those difficult days), and brought the ship of State to a safe haven through some most dangerous storms. But they had nothing to recommend them except their own personal qualities. Takatoki, the ninth and last of the Regents, was weak and dissolute, and his enemies promptly seized the opportunity to overthrow the Hōjō house. The Emperor Godaigo was a strong man, and powerfully supported by the Tendai monks from Hieizan. For a brief space the Imperial House became the ruling power; the Regency was abolished, the puppet-Shōguns disappeared, and a new succession of actual Shōguns (of the Ashikaga House) was inaugurated in 1338, residing once more in Kyōto. The day of Kamakura was over.

The Hōjō Regents were by no means indifferent to the claims of religion. But theirs was a military organization, supported by all that was best and most practical among the military classes of Japan, and neither Tendai, Shingon, nor Jōdo was robust enough to attract the spirit of a true soldier (for the term "soldier" could scarcely be applied to the fighting men who fattened on the revenues of the Hieizan and similar temples, and fought the battles

of the worldly priests).   The Hōjō found in the Zen sects
the particular form of Buddhism that suited them best.

The Zen sects (there are three in Japan) derive their
separate existence from a celebrated Indian priest, Bodhidharma, who arrived in China in the year 526 A.D., just
two years before the foundation of the Benedictine Order
in Europe.

It was in India a period of religious strife and confusion.   The Hindus were protesting, vigorously and
successfully, against Mahāyāna and Hīnayāna alike, and
were gradually absorbing into their own systems all that
was good in the Buddhist religion.[1]   A great opposition
(we might better call it a persecution[2]) was being raised
against the "sons of S'akyamuni," and many Buddhist
priests found it convenient to leave India and seek refuge
abroad.   Many of them found their way to China, which
was then divided into two rival kingdoms, of the north
under the *Wei*, of the south under the *Sung*, with
several minor principalities.   Both dynasties favoured
the Buddhist religion, partly, it may be presumed, for
political reasons, and many embassies came from India
and Central Asia to ask for the assistance of China,
the leading Buddhist power in Asia.   The prince of the
Wei, like Shōtoku Taishi, lectured publicly on Buddhism,
but his Confucianist subjects observed that his Buddhist
principles did not prevent him from waging an active
war against the neighbouring principality of the Liang.
In the early years of the sixth century it was estimated

---

[1] It was this absorption into Hinduism of Buddhistic elements
which enabled it to overcome the Faith of S'akyamuni.   To the
present day a great deal of Buddhism may be found lurking in the
popular cults of India, and the Japanese Buddhist finds himself more
in sympathy with the Hindu than he does with his brother Buddhist
in Ceylon.

[2] *E.g.* the one instituted by Mihirakula.

that there were over three thousand refugee Indian missionaries at work in China. It was observed with concern that there was a tremendous multiplication of Mahāyāna books, many of them evidently spurious, and the rapid spread of magical arts among the Buddhists was very rightly viewed as a matter of very ill omen. The early "harmonists" (as they may be called) were trying to bring order out of the chaos by constructing schemes of S'akyamuni's life and ministry which might embrace the whole of this wide cycle of doctrines and scriptures. The predecessors of Chisha Daishi, the founder of the Chinese Tendai, were already hard at work in framing their philosophy of religion. But the temporal authorities of the time had other and more drastic measures. In A.D. 515 the rulers of the Wei put to death a number of Chinese Buddhist priests for practising magical arts; in 518 the Wei Government dispatched two commissioners to India to report on religion and bring back authentic books; and in 526 Bodhidharma arrived to put things in order.

Bodhidharma was no ordinary priest. He was esteemed amongst the Buddhists as the twenty-eighth Patriarch of their Church, as the legitimate successor of the first Apostles of S'akyamuni, the rightful occupant of the chair in which Mahākaśyapa had sat in the first Council immediately after the Master's death. Troubles in India had undoubtedly something to do with Bodhidharma's visit to China; but, apart from that, he had undoubtedly also come to fulfil a mission of reform. His visit to China had very much the same significance as would have that of an Archbishop of Canterbury who should undertake a "mission of help" to the Anglican Missions in Japan.

He was a man of strong will and character. He did

not stoop to flatter kings. When he first met the Emperor Wu of the Sung Dynasty, the Emperor began to speak of the good works that he had done. "I have built many temples," he said, "and endowed thousands of priests. What merit have I acquired?"[1] "None at all," was the priest's blunt reply. The man who would thus address an Emperor was not likely to spare his own religious household. He sat in the Chair once occupied by As'vaghosha, Nāgārjuna, Vasubandhu, and the great Doctors whose names have come before us so often in the course of this history, but he would not recognize as genuine the many works that claimed to come from their pens.[2] "You cannot get Buddhism from books," was his contention. "If you want Enlightenment you must get it as S'akyamuni did, as the great Kaśyapa did, as Nāgārjuna and Vasubandhu did—by meditation. Books will only tell you about it—meditation and contemplation will *procure* it for you." And he established a discipline of contemplation which may be compared with the spiritual exercises of St. Ignatius Loyola.

[1] "Tsūzoku Bukkyo gimon Kaitoshu," vol. iii. p. 254. It is a book containing a vast amount of information, from which I hope in some subsequent volume to give many illustrative extracts. I have never seen but one copy of it, and I have only succeeded in getting vols. i. and iii. It was published in fairly simple Japanese some twenty years ago.

[2] It is evident that this action on the part of Bodhidharma materially strengthens the view constantly brought forward in this work, viz. that the Mahāyāna books of China must be considered as of late origin, none of them being much earlier (if at all) than the first century of the Christian era.

Bodhidharma evidently held that many of the books were not in any sense Buddhist. Some of them possibly may have been, but it was impossible to distinguish the spurious from the genuine, and therefore during all the nine years of his stay in China he is said never once to have made a discourse based on a Sūtra.

My authority is a long article on " Kenshō-jōbutsu, by Maruyama, in vol. iii. of " Tsūzoku Bukkyo gimon Kaitōshū," p. 498.

Zazen, as the Japanese call it, is a very difficult course
of contemplations, with suggestions from the spiritual
director which furnish topics and hints, but no more.
When the postulant has got through the course, he may
have obtained Enlightenment, or he may not; he has,
at any rate, gone through a course of mental discipline
which has given him to some extent the mind of a soldier.

Such was the Buddhism which the Hōjō Regents
called to their aid when they were engaged in making
Kamakura the military centre of a reformed Japan. The
Contemplative Teaching had, it is true, been for some
time in the country, under the name of the Busshinshū, or
Sect of Buddha's Heart, but it had been too Puritanic to
find favour with the courtiers of Nara or Kyōto. In the
year 1201, when Yoriie, the son of Yoritomo, was Shōgun,
with his widowed mother Masako as the power behind
the throne, and her father Hōjō Masamune as Regent and
Head of the Kamakura Bakufu, Eisai Zenshi, the founder
of the Rinzai Sect of the Zen, was invited to establish
himself, first in Kyōto at the Kenninji, and afterwards at
Kenkōji in Kamakura. A few years later, between 1222
and 1232, Shōyō Daishi, or Dōgen, as he was known to his
contemporaries, founded the sister sect of the Sōtō which
has its headquarters in the province of Echizen.[1]

The *Rinzai* and the *Sōtō*, both of which came to Japan
from the south of China, differ in this, that the former
depends wholly and entirely on contemplation as the sole
means of obtaining saving Enlightenment, while the latter
adds the use of books as subsidiary aids. A translation of
the chief manual used by the Zen will be found in the
published transactions of the Oxford Congress of the

[1] There is in Japan a third Zen sect, known as the *Obaku,* which
was founded by refugees from China in 1659. It will be mentioned in
its proper place (Chapter XXIX.).

History of Religions (1908); when, some twenty-five years ago, I asked a Sōtō priest to give me instruction, he began his lectures by a course of expositions of the Hannya Shingyō, or *Parāmita Hridaya Sūtra*. Nearly all the Sōtō priests whom I have known have been learned men; I think I may say the same of all the Rinzai priests with whom I have become acquainted. It is difficult to talk with them on purely spiritual issues, because they hold that Truth is not communicated orally from mouth to ear, but, without the intermediary of words, by a kind of wireless telegraphy from heart to heart. *Zen wa zeni nashi, Monto mono wo shiradzu.* "The Zen priests have no money," says the proverb, "the Monto (Shinshu) priests no understanding."

The Zen sects have always been more or less influenced by Confucianism. Indeed, I have heard them described as being more Confucianist than Buddhist—an obvious exaggeration of facts. But the Zen monks sat loose to the teachings of the Sūtras, which their first Founder had taught them to look on with suspicion, and in their office as teachers they required some mental food to take the place of the discredited books.[1] Confucianism had never been looked upon in Japan as being antagonistic to Buddhism, and Kōbō Daishi (even if it was not Shotoku) had spoken of Buddhism, Taoism (Shinto), and Confucianism as the three legs of the tripod on which rested the

---

[1] The relations between the Zen sects and the other bodies of Japanese Buddhists is well illustrated by a phrase which I have often heard Zen priests use when speaking of other sects. They call them *hōben no shūha*, "The sects which employ *hōben*." *Hōben* is sometimes translated as a "fraud," sometimes as a "pious device." Both phrases are a little too strong. *Hōben* is an "accommodation of truth to the intelligence of the hearer," and the Zenshuists declare that the anthropomorphism of *e.g.* the Amida or Vairoc'ana sects is such an "accommodation of Truth." They profess not to use such accommodations themselves, but they do not blame those that do.

religious and temporary welfare of Japan. Confucianism had from the earliest times in historical Japan been looked upon as the religious philosophy of the man-at-arms or the man of affairs, and the bid which, under the patronage of the Hōjō Regents, the Zenshu teachers made for the suffrages of the samurai was likely to be all the more acceptable if it came strongly seasoned with a Confucianist flavour. The establishment of the Zen corresponded with the entry into China of the improved and refined Confucianism of the Chinese reformer Chūhi, or Shushi (to give him his Japanese name), and the two systems may be said to have made common cause in their attempts to influence the religious thought of the military and governing classes.

Perhaps the most picturesque figure in the Zen world is that of Hōjō Tokiyori, the fifth of the Kamakura Regents, who held office from 1246 to 1256, and then retired into a monastery, being henceforth known as Saimyōji Nyūdō. But his retirement was not in the least like those of the poor Emperors and Shoguns at Kyōtō, who were dropped from the ship for fear they should want to take part in the management of the vessel of State. Tokiyori knew that, as Regent, it was very difficult for him to learn the true state of the country. He could only make State progresses along roads carefully swept and cleaned for his reception, to see just what the local authorities wanted him to see. And the times made it imperative for the men at the helm of State to have accurate and trustworthy knowledge. Tokiyori accordingly resigned his Regency in favour of his young son Tokimune, whom he left in the care of trustworthy ministers,[1] donned

---

[1] *Hōjō Nagatoki* had been the governor of the northern portion (*rokuhara*) of Kyōtō, but came to Kamakura to assist his young cousin.

the priestly habit, and started off on an unofficial tour of inspection. He learned a very great deal, and, returning to Kamakura, placed the information he had gained at the disposal of his son and successor. The information was most valuable, for Japan was about to pass through one of the most severe crises in her national history—a crisis of which I shall speak in a subsequent chapter.

The Zen system touches the philosophic thought of India very closely. It has also many points of contact with Confucianism. It recognizes a supreme Being; but absolutely refuses to personify Him. To personify God, says the Zenshuist, whether as Vairoc'ana, as Amida, as S'akyamuni, or as Jehovah, is to limit Him. He cannot be tied up to any form; He transcends the widest, highest, deepest conceptions of the human mind. Yet the Zen does not blame those who thus personify God and by personifying limit Him. It recognizes that for certain minds personification is a necessity. The Infinite mind must become Finite, in order that the Finite mind may grasp it. But a personified God is nothing but a *hōben*, an adaptation of the Truth to the weakness of the human intellect. Such personification, it has been observed, always serves to narrow the mind and make it intolerant. The Jew, the Mahometan, the Christian, the worshipper of Amida, of S'akyamuni, of Vairoc'ana—all in turn have become dogmatic, intolerant, uncharitable, and all for the same reason. They start from a personal, and therefore an imperfect, conception of God.

In the same way, the Zen possesses no Canon of Scripture. The Christian has his Bible, the Mahometan his Koran, every sect of Buddhism has formed its own little Canon of Holy Books out of the unwieldy mass of the Tripitaka. The formation of a canon leads to loss of charity. Certain books are taken as representing a divine revelation; all other books of religion are judged by this arbitrary standard, and whatever does not agree with it is rejected. The letter of Scripture has always proved to be a fruitful mother of controversy and dissension. The Zen has no special list of Sacred Books. It does not reject any Sūtras or Abhidharmas; it reads and values them for all the truths they contain, but it sets up no books as being infallible or beyond criticism. It criticizes freely all the Sacred Books of Buddhism; and it accepts, with equal freedom and reverence, the good books of all countries.

It has been said already that Zen, whilst rejecting a personal God, accepts with reverence a Something Beyond Knowledge, which lies at the back of phenomenal existence. We can never know that Being in its entirety, but we can reach to Him in three ways—"feeling after Him, and, haply, finding Him." We may look into our own hearts, by introspection and meditation, and there we shall find Him. We may look into the hearts of others by means of the Word, spoken or written, and there we shall find Him. We may look at Nature, in all its manifestations, romantic or commonplace, and there we shall find Him. For my heart is Buddha; and the heart of my brother whose books I read, is Buddha; and Nature in its entirety, the Infinitely Great, the Infinitely Small, every star or comet, every mountain range or ocean, every insect, every leaf, is Buddha.

Such is the faith of the Zenshuist. For his daily conduct he accepts no infallible guide but his own enlightened conscience, which is one with the enlightened conscience of the universe. For the details, however, of his behaviour he will follow Confucius, S'akyamuni, Epictetus, anything that will help him to lead his daily life in a manner worthy of a religious philosopher.

The Zen, as taught by its Japanese founders, Eisai and Dōgen, and as fostered by the wise counsels of the Hōjō regents, was quite a different religion from the miracle-mongering, worldly, intriguing parody of religion which the Hossō, Kegon, Tendai, and Shingon had been palming off on the country to the obvious disgust of the warrior and the man of action. It was very different, again, from the pietistic solifidianism of Honen and Shinran, with its contempt for this world and its fixed gaze upon the joys of the Western Paradise. The Zen fired the imagination of the warrior, the statesman, the man of letters, and if Japanese art drew its inspiration from the wild fancies of Kegon and Shingon Buddhology, Japanese poetry drew it from the solid quietude of the Zen monasteries, where it was taught to look "within," into the heart and into the innermost shrine of Nature, and there to be comforted by the One, Omnipresent, Heart of Buddha, whom man can feel but not know.[1]

[1] I have drawn the thoughts contained in this description of the Zen from a treatise on *Zengaku*, "The Zen Philosophy," by Mr. K. Nukariya.

CHAPTER XXIV

NICHIREN AND THE EARLIER SECTS

In the year 1257 Japan was visited by a very terrible earthquake. After the earthquake, in 1258, came a destructive hurricane which overthrew much that the earthquake had left standing. In 1259 there was, as a natural result of the two calamities already mentioned, a famine throughout Japan, with the pestilence which always seems to follow in famine's train. The distress was so great, says Nichiren, in one of his letters, that men prayed to die rather than remain alive in the midst of the universal misery. The Government was at its wits' end to know what to do to relieve the general suffering : supplications and prayers were ordered to be offered up in all temples throughout the land. But months passed by without any signs of alleviation or abatement. At last, in 1260, Nichiren took to preaching in the public streets of Kamakura, after having handed in to the Regent and his retired father his newly written treatise entitled "Rissho Ankoku-ron." In the same year, Kublai Khan, the grandson of Jingis Khan, established his capital at Pekin, or Khambalik, where he received a visit from the Italian traveller, Marco Polo. These few facts will serve, I trust, as a sufficient introduction to this chapter.

Nichiren was born in 1222, in a remote village on the coast of Awa. He was in the habit of describing his father as an outcast, from whence some have inferred that he was of low descent. This was not so, however ; his father had been the retainer of a high noble at the Court of Kyōtō, and had been banished, according to the custom of the time, for some fault which had displeased his master. What the fault was is not mentioned ; if the father was at all like the son, we may infer that it was that outspoken plainness which men of high position do not always like. The family, which consisted of father, mother, and the one child born to them in exile, lived alone and apart in the fishing village, shunned by the natives because they were in disgrace, and holding little intercourse with their neighbours. The child, sensitive, tender - hearted, high - spirited, and fearless, grew up solitary and alone, the butt of the fisher lads, but devoted to animals, especially to the injured and maimed.

In 1234, being about twelve years, he was taken by his parents to the Temple of Kyosumidera, not far from his native village, and there placed under the care of an old Shingon priest, who was the incumbent. It has always been, in Japan, the course pursued in dedicating a child to the priesthood, to take him to some worthy priest to be trained and educated, and to let him serve as acolyte and personal attendant on his master until such time as he is ready to take upon himself the Vows of the Order.

Nichiren took his life seriously. One of his first acts after entering the Kiyozumi Temple [1] as a student was

<hr />

[1] I take my materials for Nichiren's life from the following sources : (1) Principally from the " Seigoroku," a collection of extracts from his writings, which is a veritable mine of information ; (2) from two Japanese lives of the Saint, which appeared, one in 1893 and one in 1909 ; (3) from a play entitled *Nichirengi*, which was brought out in 1894 ; and (4) from the chapters on Nichiren in vol. v. of " Bukkyō-Kakushū Kōyō" (1885).

to slip away by himself into the Temple Oratory, and there, before the image of Kokūzō Bosatsu, to offer a prayer that he might grow up to be a good priest worthy of the name; and as he went on with his studies in the quiet seclusion of that country monastery, he felt the premonitory symptoms of his great vocation. He realized that the Buddhism of the Kamakura period had departed very widely from the primitive Buddhism of its Indian Founder; he saw that it was hopelessly divided by sects, schisms, and varieties of contradictory doctrines, and that, being so, it was necessarily incapable of doing the good in the world which its Founder had meant it to accomplish. The condition of Japan was miserable; the Buddhist sects, whether of Kyōtō, Nara, or Kamakura, were powerless to resist the growing evils: a Buddhism purified, vivified, united, might and would save Japan from dangers external and internal. He determined to be the man who should accomplish this great design.

Those who know the precociousness of youthful Japanese will not be surprised at Nichiren's forming this plan before he was twenty years of age. The idea seems to have been suggested to him by the reading of that very remarkable book, the "Saddharmapundarika Sutra."[1]

---

[1] I have already, in my book "The Wheat among the Tares," written at some length on the "Saddharmapundarika." I wish here to add that the book falls into two portions, viz. (1) *Shakumon*, as it is called in Japanese, which comprises chaps. i.–xiv., and consists of a connected series of what may be termed "Visions;" and (2) *Hommon*, which consists of a series of miscellaneous chapters, on Spells, on Avalokites'vara, Samantabhadra, and other Bodhisattvas, etc., which are but loosely connected with the main action of the main part of the book.

It is often held by Japanese Buddhists that the *Hommon* is a series of later additions to the original book, dating not much earlier than Kumarajiva's time (A.D. 350–400), and the Tendai sect, which, like the

U

Having read it and interpreted it to himself, he became quite confident of his mission, and with characteristic energy set himself to work to prepare for executing it. He left the quiet Temple of Kyosumidera, and for several years set himself to work to travel throughout Japan and make a study of every existing form of Buddhism. When he had thus finished his survey of the whole field, he felt himself in a position to formulate his own views on religion and national life. Nichiren has often been described, by those who knew him only superficially, as a mere dreamer and fanatic. A more careful study reveals him as a man of very decided opinions, and extremely outspoken. But he was always able to give a reason for his conclusions, and those reasons were sane and cogent; and in putting his views into practice he constantly showed that if he dared to upbraid error in severe tones, his courage came from reflection and not from mere impulse.

For more than twenty years Nichiren devoted himself with great diligence to the study of Japanese Buddhism. He has told us in one of his letters that from twelve to thirty-two he gave himself up to the comparative study of all Buddhist sects in his country—Kusha, Jojitsu, Ritsu (Vinaya), Hossō, Sanron, Kegon, Shingon, and the Tendai-Hokke, which was the official designation of the sect founded by Dengyo Daishi at Hieizan. To these he

Nichiren, professes to base all its teaching on this Sūtra, confines itself mainly to the *Shakumon* section.

It was Nichiren's claim that to him had been revealed the true meaning of the *Hommon*, which had been concealed from former ages, and been kept for revelation in the last "millennium" of the "Destruction of the Law." The *Shakumon*, according to him, must be interpreted in the light of the *Hommon*, which is the really important part. The gist of the whole is to be found in the syllables *myō-hō-ren-ge-kyō*, which form at once the object of adoration, the protective charm, and the *Kaidan*, or Ordination Vow of the sect. One sub-sect considers only two chapters of the *Hommon* to be really genuine and authentic.

had added the more recent foundations of the Jōdo and
Zen, having pursued his studies at Kamakura and Kyōtō,
at Hieizan and Onjōji, at Kōbo's great shrine on Kōyasan,
and Shotoku's temple of Tennōji at Osaka.[1] At the conclusion of his studies he had some very bitter things to
say about the older sects into which Buddhism, "which
should be one," had crumbled.

My readers will have noticed, in the previous chapters
of this book, that Buddhism, whether in India, in China,
or in Japan, has always shown an inveterate tendency to
shield itself under Government favour and patronage.
Kings were its nursing-fathers in India, where, under
As'oka, Kanishka, and like-minded rulers, it had flourished
and become a mighty tree. When royal patronage was
withdrawn, and Hinduism asserted itself once more, the
zeal of the Indian Buddhist lost its ardour, and the Faith
maintained itself only in those lands where the rulers
were Buddhists. We see the same phenomenon in
China, where the personal creed of the ruling house had
very much to do with the ups and downs of the religion
of S'akyamuni.

In Japan, Buddhism failed to take root at all until

---

[1] I give Nichiren's exact words from a modern Japanese edition of
extracts from Nichiren's writings, which has made this great Buddhist
leader's mind accessible to me. The book is entitled "Seigōroku,"
and was published in 1907.

"Hitotsu no negai wo okosu. Nihonkoku ni waretaru tokoro no
Bukkyō narabi ni Bosatsu no ron to ninshi no shaku wo narai-mi
sōrawabaya, mata Kusha, Jōjitsu, Ritsu, Hossō, Sanron, Kegon, Shingon,
Hokke-Tendai, to mōsu Shu tomo amata ari to kiku ue ni Zenshū,
Jōdo shū to mōsu shū mo sōrō nari. Korera no shūjū shiyō made
komaka ni narawadzu to mo shosen kanyō wo shiru mi to naraba
ya to omoishi yue ni, zuibun ni hashiri-mawari jū-ni jū-roku no toshi
yori sanjū-ni ni itaru made nijū yo nen no aida Kamakura to, Kyō to,
Hieizan to, Onjō to, Kōya to, Tennōji tō no kuniguni tera-dera ara-ara
narai mi-mawari sōraishi," etc. ("Seigōroku," p. 764).

it came as a personal gift from the King of Kudara to
the Emperor of Japan, and it put forth no leaves or buds
until watered by the Imperial hand of the Crown Prince,
Shōtoku Taishi. The Nara priests were nearly all
courtiers, who, though they might intrigue at times
against the Government, still intrigued only as courtiers,
in the interests of one faction against another. The Heian
clergy, followers of Dengyō and Kōbō, had become the
subservient courtiers of the dominant Fujiwara family;
the pietists of the Gempei period had been the favoured
ones of Emperors like Toba and Shirakawa in their resistance to the gloved hand of the Fujiwara; the Zen had
become political tools in the powerful grasp of the Hōgō
Regents. Nichiren could see no hope of social or political
amelioration from the sectwise Buddhism of his time.
Religious and political Japan were, in Nichiren's eyes,
alike suffering from a dangerous disease.

" Awake, men, awake! " he cried in one of his earliest
sermons; " awake, and look around you. No man is
born with two fathers or two mothers. Look at the
heavens above you: there are no two suns in the sky.
Look at the earth at your feet: no two kings can rule a
country." [1]

And yet that was precisely what Japan was trying
to do. Politically, she was giving her allegiance to
Emperor, Shōgun, Regent; spiritually, to Amida, Vairo-
c'ana, S'akyamuni. Politically, the rightful sovereign had
been pushed aside to make way for ambitious subjects;
spiritually, the rightful Lord of the Buddhist heritage had
been thrown " to the moles and bats " to make room for

---

[1] " Same yo hitobito, ma no atari sono mi wo futari no chichi naku,
futari no haha nakute umaretaru hitobito, aogi miyo, Ten ni ni-jitsu
naku, fushite miyo, chi ni ni-Ō nashi " (" Nichiren," by Murakumo.
Tokyo: Minyūsha. 1909).

the ambitious upstarts, Amida and Dainichi, whose claim to spiritual homage rested on no sound rock of Buddhist doctrine.

He therefore constantly condemned the already existing sects of Buddhism. He denounced them in his first sermon ; he continued his denunciations to the very end. *Nembutsu wa mugen no gō.*[1] The Nembutsu was consistently deprecated as a practice which leads men to the lowest of the hells. Nichiren never treated Amida as being in any sense a Buddhist divinity. He looked on him, in the garb which the Shinshu made him wear, as an unauthorized importation from somewhere outside of Buddhism, and his Paradise as a pure fancy. At the very best he held him to be but a partial manifestation of S'akyamuni, the One and Eternal. It was not likely that the peculiar Jōdo tenet of salvation by faith alone, without repentance or works, would commend itself to Nichiren's mind.

Zenshū wa tenma ha-jun no setsu. "The Zen," he continued, " is a doctrine of demons and fiends." We are familiar with the illustration of the man whose house, "empty, swept, and garnished," stood open for the return of a company of evil spirits larger than the one that had been cast out. The Zen house was just in that position. Bodhidharma had cast out of his Buddhism all the superstitious books and doctrines with which the miracle-mongering Mahyānism of Central Asia and China had overlaid the original simplicity of S'akyamuni's teaching. He had put nothing in its place, and had bidden his followers look within to see what form they should see, and to listen for what voice they should hear, coming to them from the empty chambers of their own minds. The practice of Zazen leads to spiritual pride, a

[1] "Seigōroku," p. 774.

failing not rare amongst *bushi* and *samurai,* in spite of their other great virtues, and the many things that Nichiren had to suffer at the hands of Zenshū priests and laymen will perhaps account for the extreme bitterness of this sentence.

Daishō no Kairitsu wa seken ōwaku no hō (or, as it is to be found in a shorter recension, *Ritsu Kokuzoku*). "The Vinaya sects, whether of the Small Vehicle (*i.e.* connected with the *Kaidan* at Nara), or of the Great Vehicle (*i.e.* those connected with the *Kaidan* at Hieizan), are brigands that disturb the peace of the country." We have seen how ambitious priests, in the Nara period, interfered with the Imperial succession in the case, *e.g.,* of the Empress Shotoku, and the Emperor Junnin, and how, after Kwammu had moved his capital to Kyōto, to be free from sacerdotal meddling, the Tendai priesthood had still managed to become the allies of the Fujiwara in their manipulation of Emperors to suit their own policy. We have also seen how the *Kaidan* question, which was mainly one of discipline, and which, therefore, deeply concerned the Ritsu sects, had caused a schism between Hieizan and Nara, and, later, a schism and civil war between Hieizan and her daughter temple of Miidera. When we think of the Fighting Temples, with their train-bands and men-at-arms, we can see some reason for Nichiren's denunciation of the brigand sects that "throw the world into confusion."

Shingon he described as *bōkoku,* "traitors to their country," probably with reference to their adoption of a lord other than S'akyamuni, the rightful lord in spiritual matters in Japan, and their constant reference to India as the seat of authority in matters of religion. His language as to Vairoc'ana, or Dainichi, was more contemptuous even than that which he had used as to Amida.

He maintained that for Vairoc'ana's existence there was no evidence at all that could be brought forward, as in the case of S'akyamuni; that the story of the finding of the Shingon books by Nāgārjuna, in the Iron Tower, in South India, was a pure fabrication; and that Kōbō Daishi was the " prize liar of Japan " (*Nihon no dai mōgo*).

As for the images of Amida, Kwannon, and the rest, he was charged with recommending that they should be cast into the fire or the sea. They had, in his judgment, wrought enough mischief in Japan.[1]

Nichiren first enunciated these views in a sermon preached in the neighbourhood of his native village, which he visited again at the end of his period of study, in 1254. He then took up his abode near Kamakura, where he built a little hermitage for himself in the hamlet of Nagoye; for there was no temple in the capital of the Hōjō Regents which would receive him as an inmate.

[1] " Nembutsu wa mugen no gō: Zenshū wa Tenma, hajun no setsu: Dai-shō no Kairitsu wa seken ōwaku no hō: Toshigoro no Honzon, Mida Kwannon tō no zō wo hi ni ire midzu ni nagasu " (" Seigōroku," p. 774).

It is interesting to observe that there is no idol on the main altar in a Nichiren temple, though the side altars are frequently so adorned. In, *e.g.*, the Temple of Myōhōji at Kamakura, the oldest of all Nichirenist shrines, there is an absolute *stūpa* or tabernacle, such as was found in the ancient *chaityas* in India, and symbolical of the *stūpa* which descended from heaven in chap. xiv. of the " Saddharma pundarika." In front of this tabernacle is the usual " table of prothesis " which is to be found in all Buddhist temples in Japan, and in front of that, again, what may be called the Choir, with the desks for the monks. Over this part, which comes about the middle of the building, is a baldacchino, or umbrella, from which hang strings of flowers in thin brass, the whole being intended to symbolize the " Pentecostal " shower of celestial flowers with which the action of the " Saddharma pundarika " commences. Curiously enough, S'akyamuni is distinguished from the glorified but Invisible Buddha, who is supposed to be within the tabernacle. For the historical S'akyamuni there is a distinct building in another part of the grounds. This is, I believe, the universal practice.

Neither was there any pulpit for him to occupy, except that which has always been open to the agitator and the reformer, the street corner. He became an outdoor preacher, and his sermons, plain, simple, and full of conviction, soon attracted a great deal of attention. The earthquake, the famine, the pestilence, the fruitless prayers offered in the temples, the shadow of the terrible Mongol power creeping closer to Japan, all served to give point to his oratory. He was rapidly gaining the popular favour; the priests of the official sects were conscious that power was slipping from them; the Regent had reason to be annoyed at the boldness with which the hermit of Nagoye addressed him in his semi-political, semi-religious pamphlet on the "Reformation of Religion and the Pacification of the Country." Nichiren's enemies combined to bring against him a formal accusation of fomenting rebellion and promulgating heresy. He was arrested, brought before the Regent's Court, found guilty, and banished to Ito in the peninsula of Idzu. This was in 1261; in 1264 he was once more in Kamakura, more outspoken than ever. Another great calamity was impending—a long-continued drought hung over the land, and threatened a failure of the rice-crops. The official priesthood were praying for rain, but there was none to answer. Nichiren laughed at their vain efforts. At last he took his turn at prayer: Heaven answered, and the people were convinced that he was a prophet.

But he had, in the excitement of his preaching, allowed himself to use unseemly expressions. He had told the people that the late Regent, the well-meaning and devoted Saimyoji, was in hell, suffering torments, and that the present Regent, Tokimune, was preparing to follow him. The words were seized, twisted, and exaggerated. His enemies procured his arrest and haled him before the

Regent's Court, where, after an eventful trial which his followers to-day read with something of the reverence with which we listen to the recital of the familiar story of our Lord's Passion, he was condemned to death, and led out for execution on the sands of Tatsu no Kuchi,[1] halfway between Kamakura and Enoshima.

But the Regent must have felt that Nichiren was in the right. His conscience troubled him after he had passed the sentence of death, and he sent a messenger post haste after the executioner's cavalcade to revoke the condemnation, and changed the sentence to one of banishment to the distant island of Sado. The messenger arrived only just in time. The mats were already spread for the prisoner to kneel on while waiting for the fatal stroke, the prisoner was already kneeling on the mat, and his faithful disciples held, and have ever since held, that their master was given back to them from the dead. Legend has been busy with the embellishment of the story. The executioner, it was said, had already lifted his sword, when a flash of lightning from a cloudless sky rendered the blow innocuous. Before he had recovered for a second stroke, the messenger from the Regent had arrived and the danger was past.

The exile in Sado was not of long duration. Nichiren returned in 1272, busily warning the nation about the danger of the Mongol invasion. When asked by the officers of the *Kingo*, or body-guard, what reasons he had for his predictions of evil, he replied that he had general Scriptural authority for what he said, and that he had come to his particular conclusions as to time, etc., through

---

[1] To the prosaic foreign resident of Tokyo and Yokohama the place is known as "Poker Flat." "What is Nichiren to him, or he to Nichiren?"

"discerning the face of the heavens." [1] He now bore a
charmed life, and was quite secure in the affection of his
followers. His later years were devoted to Minobu and
Ikegami, the two monasteries especially connected with
the memories of his personality, and at the latter he
passed to his rest, in the year 1282. His had been an
eventful life. He still has, among his countrymen, many
friends and many detractors. To the outsider, who
studies him impartially, he will always appear as a
fearless man who had the courage of his convictions.

Now let us turn to the theological remedy which
Nichiren proposed for the ills both of Church and State.

It was his great idea to restore S'akyamuni (not in his
temporal manifestation in fleshly form, but as the Eternal
and Infinite) to his proper place in the Buddhist Heavens.
False brethren, calling themselves Buddhists, had given
to S'akyamuni a place of inferiority. They had spoken
of him as only a temporary manifestation of a part of the
glories of some other Buddha, Amitābha or Vairoc'ana,
greater than himself, and the simpler Sūtras of the
Hīnayāna they had despised as containing a simplified
Gospel watered down to suit the intelligence of the ill-
instructed. Nichiren reversed the position. He had
been much shocked on one of his journeys to find some
children playing with an idol of S'akyamuni which had
been discarded from the temple to make room for a new-
fangled image of Amida, and he was resolved to make
reparation for the insult which had thus been offered to
the lawful Lord of Buddhism. "S'akyamuni," he said,

[1] "Kyōmon ni wa bunmyō in toshi-tsuki wo sashitaru koto wa
nakeredomo, Ten no on-keshiki wo haikenshitatematsuru ni," etc.
("Seigoroku," p. 807). Yet it is quite possible that Nichiren, as a priest,
had means of obtaining information about foreign countries, which were
not accessible to the statesmen of Kamakura. It was still the practice
for Buddhist priests to go over to China for purposes of study.

in one of his voluminous writings,[1] " is the lord of this Saba-world, for three reasons—firstly, because he is the World-honoured One for all sentient Beings ; secondly, because he is both Father and Mother of all sentient Beings in this Saba-world ; and thirdly, because he is the Original and First Teacher of all sentient Beings in this Saba-world." Everything that the Jōdoist said about Amida, Nichiren said about S'akyamuni. S'akyamuni was uncreated, without beginning, without end, unlimited in every aspect. S'akyamuni was the Light of the World, had always been so, would always remain so. Whatever teaching there was in the world, whatever hope there was for man of ultimate perfection, all came to him from S'akyamuni, whose mercies were over all the world, but more especially over the fortunate inhabitants of the *ichi-embudai*[2]—India, China, and Japan—which had embraced his Faith.

S'akyamuni's teachings are summed up, said Nichiren (following herein the teachings of the Japanese Tendai), in the Hokekyō or Saddharmapundarika Sūtra, spoken on the Vulture's Peak during the last few years of his earthly life.[3] But this Sūtra he interpreted in a new manner, with great ingenuity.

[1] " Kono Shaka Nyorai wa mitsu no yue mashimashite, ta-Butsu ni kawarase tamaite, Shabo sekai no issai shūjō u-en no Hotoke to nari tamau : ichiniwa, Kono Shabo-sekai no issai shūjō no seson nite o washimasu ; . . . nii ni wa, . . . Shabo-sekai issai shūjo no fu-mo nari : . . . san ni wa, . . . issai shūjō no honshi nari " (" Seigōroku," p. 131).

[2] The term *ichi embudai* is used in Nichiren's writings to embrace all the countries which had adopted the Buddhist Faith. It is, therefore, strictly analogous to our word " Christendom," used to denote the sum-total of Christian countries.

[3] Nichiren was, however, fully aware of the chronological difficulties connected with the acceptance of the Hokekyō as a genuine Sūtra actually preached ;by S'akyamuni himself. In a passage quoted in

The Hokekyō, in Nichiren's interpretation, was an Apocalypse containing a forecast of the things which should come to pass in Buddhism after the death of its founder. It deals with the "Millenniums" of Buddhism—the three periods, one of five hundred, and two of one thousand years each, which should cover what might be called the present dispensation—a conception which is quite a familiar one to the whole family of Japanese Buddhism.

In the Hokekyō itself the scene is laid on the Vulture's Peak, the favourite haunt of S'akyamuni in his later years. The Master, now an old man, is weary with teaching and has fallen into a trance. " His body was motionless, and his mind had reached perfect tranquillity. And as soon as the Lord had entered upon his meditation there fell a great rain of divine flowers, covering the Lord and the four classes of hearers, . . . and at that moment there issued a ray from within the circle of hair between the eyebrows of the Lord. It extended over eighteen thousand Buddha fields in the Eastern quarter." The trance Nichiren took as denoting the Parinirvana of S'akyamuni. Then comes a period of silence, that period which we have already noticed in our historical review of the Buddhist Church—a period much longer to the Northern Buddhist who knows nothing of As'oka, and passes straight from the Vaiśali Council to that held under Kaniskha. At the

"Seigōroku" (p. 645), after enumerating the early patriarchs of the Northern Buddhism, he adds that during their terms of office there is not to be found even the name of a single Mahāyāna Sūtra (*sho-Daijo Kyo wa myoji mo nashi*), and on the following page there is another passage in which he describes the astonishment and perplexity of the Hīnāyāna doctors when As'vaghosha and Nāgārjuna began to propound their Mahāyāna doctrines. Nichiren's thought was that the Hokekyō, as a kind of Apocalypse, was far too advanced for the immediate disciples of S'akyamuni, and that for this reason it lay fallow for several centuries, gradually winning recognition for itself as the spiritual intelligence of the Buddhist communities increased.

close of that period there comes the "great rain of divine flowers," and the ray of light travels from S'akya-muni eastward. The first "Millennium," [1] the period of the Upright Law (*Sho Hō*), was over, the activities of As'vaghosha and Nāgārjuna represent a kind of Pentecostal shower of Buddhist revival, and Buddhism travels to China. When the Lord awakes from his trance, he explains the meaning of the shower and ray. The wheel of the Law is to receive a fresh turn, a higher form of Buddhism is to be preached, and the idea of the twofold Vehicle of Salvation is enforced by many parables. [2] The early Apostles of Buddhism, Kaśyapa, Ananda, Rahula, etc., whose labours had kept Buddhism alive during the first Millennium of its existence, are praised and thanked, and the reward prepared for them is announced. A number of discontented monks leave the assembly in anger on hearing of the impending changes in Buddhist doctrine (Nichiren explains this as referring to the discontented Hīnayānists who opposed the Mahāyāna at its first inception), but eighty thousand remain faithful, and S'akyamuni turns to Bhaishajyarāja (Jap. Yaku-Ō) as the representative of the new order of preachers. The period of Image Law (*zō hō*) [3] has begun ; a *stupa*, or

---

[1] We must remember that Nichiren, in common with all northern Buddhists until quite recent times, placed S'akyamuni's birth B.C. 1027, and his death, consequently, about B.C. 947. The true date places the end of the first age in the first Christian century, and squares very well with what we know of the beginnings of Gnosticism, as well as of the Mahāyāna. Nichiren speaks of the pre-Mahāyāna Sūtras as *ni zen* ("before the rain "), an expression which somehow seems to be an echo, as it were, of phrases like "Pentecostal showers."

[2] See " S.B.E.," vol. xxi., and my "Wheat among the Tares " (Mac-millan, 1908).

[3] It is significant that this period of the Image Law should coincide so strangely with the testimony of the Buddhist Stupas in India. See Dahlmann's "Indische Fahrten," vol. ii. capp. 22–27.

tabernacle, descending out of Heaven, reveals to the
worshipping multitude the image of S'akyamuni fusing
itself into that of his predecessor, whom the Japanese
know as Tahō Butsu; and crowds of smaller Buddhas,
partial manifestations (*bunshin*) of S'akyamuni the One
and Eternal, sit on lotus-thrones around the throne. The
great preachers of the New Law are the Bodhisattvas,
Manjuśri, Avalokites'vara, Yakuō, etc., whom Nichiren
treats as having been historical personages,[1] and the work
before them is to prepare for the third Millennium, the
Period of the Destruction of the Law [2] (*Mappō*);
which Nichiren places about the middle of the eleventh
century A.D. Thanks to Chisha Daishi, Dengyō, and
other labourers in the field of the Mahāyāna, the true
meaning of S'akyamuni's teaching was gradually being
brought out during the whole of this second period.
The author of the Hokekyō had spoken of it as the period
of the " Destruction of the Upright Law;" with the
Mongol terror lying thick and gloomy over two continents,
the phrase must have been a significant one.

But Nichiren had a word of comfort for this period of
gloom.[3] In chap. xiv. of the " Saddharma pundarika "

---

[1] Similarly, the Thibetan history of Buddhism published by Sarat
Chandra Das (Calcutta, 1908) speaks of the conversion of India as
due to S'akyamuni; of Udyāna, to Vajrapani; Bactria, to the frightful
manifestations of the Bodhisattva; of China, to Monjughosha; of Thibet,
to Avalokites'vara; ("Pag. Sam. Jon. Zang," part ii., Table of Contents,
chap. i.) See also "Une Bibliothêque Médievale retrouvée à Kansou,"
in *Bulletin École Franç. de l'Extreme Orient*, viii. 3, 4 (Hanoi, 1908).

[2] See, for instance, "Sacred Books of the East," vol. xxi. p. 273.

[3] Nichiren divided the "Saddharma pundarika" into two parts. The
first thirteen chapters he calls the *Shakumon*, or Preliminary part.
This part was understood by the Tendai doctors. The second part,
Hommon, or the Real Section, was not understood until its meaning
was revealed to and through Nichiren. See chapter on Nichiren in
"Bukkyō Kakuha Kōyō," vol. v.

there is a scene which reminds the reader of the " multitude which no man could number " in the Book of the Revelation. An innumerable host of Bodhisattvas (" Saints," we might call them in Christian language) is seen issuing from the gaps in the earth and standing before the stupa throne of S'akyamuni. At the head of them are four Great Saints (Bodhisattvas Mahāsattvas) who lead in the worship of the Eternal S'akyamuni and receive his commission. " The very first of those afore-mentioned Bodhisattvas Mahāsattvas " (" S.B.E.," vol. xxi. p. 364) was named *Visishta-c'aritra*, which in Sinico-Japanese is Jōgyō-Bosatsu. Nichiren proclaimed that he himself was Jōgyō-Bosatsu, the minister of S'akyamuni, predestined by his Master to preach the Faith in the dark period of the Destruction of the Upright Law. Thus had the Master provided for each Millennium in the duration of his Community, and for each of the three great countries comprised in the *ichi-embudai*—for India, which had been the centre of teaching during the first Millennium ; for China, which had received it during the second, and for Japan, from which had now come forth the Apostle and Teacher of the third.

And the saving doctrine which Nichiren felt himself moved to proclaim in the third dark Age was that contained in the Daimoku or Title of the Book which he revered with all his soul—*Myō-hō-ren-ge-kyō*, " the scripture of the Lotus of the Good Law," the name carved on stone or painted on wood, which is found all over Japan as the honoured symbol of the Nichirenist worship, the name which is constantly on the lips of the Nichirenist believer. The title signifies the doctrine contained in the whole book, and that doctrine is one of Unity.[1] There

---

[1] Some years ago I had a pupil who always spoke of himself as a Unitarian, who afterwards went to America, and there again posed as a Unitarian. When he returned from America he turned out to

are many saints, many Bodhisattvas, many Buddhas. And yet there is but One Buddha—Eternal, Unlimited, in Past, Present, Future, and that Buddha is He whom men know as S'akyamuni, of whom the rest are but partial manifestations or, in some cases, spurious counterfeits. The teachings of that One Buddha are absolutely true and conformable to Reason and Nature; for the Oneness is more than a mere Unity of Person. The One Eternal Buddha is one with all Reason, and one with all Nature. There are not two; there is only One.[1]

be a Nichiren priest. He had no intention to deceive. The term " Unitarian," to his mind, exactly described what he was.

[1] I think it is best to let Nichiren speak for himself here. He says as follows :—

" Our merciful Father, the Tathāgata, manifested himself in Central India in historical times (lit. since man's life has been limited to one hundred years), and expounded, for the benefit of all sentient creatures, the whole of the Holy Teachings of his lifetime. The sentient creatures of the times when the Tathāgata was in the world, being closely bound to him by the merits of good actions acquired in the past, entered upon the way of Truth (and were saved). ' But what,' he lamented, ' shall happen to the Sentient Beings who shall come after my Nirvana ? ' So he caused the whole eighty thousand of his Holy Teachings to be committed to writing, and out of these entrusted to Kaśyapa the monk (sonja) all the writings of the Lesser Vehicle, whilst those of the Greater Vehicle, together with the Saddharma pundarika and the Nirvana Sūtras, etc., he entrusted to the care of the Bodhisattva Manjuśri. But the kernel of all the eighty thousand Teachings, the five syllables Myō-hō-ren-ge-kyō, which contain the gist (or main section) of the Saddharma pundarika Sūtra, he entrusted neither to Kaśyapa and Ananda, nor yet to Manjuśri, Samantabhadra, Avalokites'vara, Maitreya, Kshitigarbha, Nāgārjuna, or any of the Great Bodhisattvas, though they desired him to do so; but summoning, from the depths of the earth, the old man Visishta-c'aritra, he did there, in the presence of the Buddha Prabhūtaratna and all the Buddhas of the Ten Quarters, from the centre of the Stūpa of S'akyamuni made of Seven Precious Substances, deliver to Visishta-c'aritra the Five Syllables of the Myō-hō-ren-ge-kyō. Hence, after his Nirvana he considered all Sentient Beings as his sons, to be treated with absolute equality of consideration. But, just as it is the wont

It is not difficult for a modern critic to pick holes in Nichiren's argument. We know, thanks to modern research, that S'akyamuni's birth must be put no earlier than the fifth century B.C., and that therefore what Nichiren calls the first period cannot have ended earlier than the first century A.D. We feel sure that if Manjuśri, Yaku-ō, and the other Bodhisattvas are meant to be true historical personages, the prophecies announcing their future destinies must be put on a par with, *e.g.*, the prophecy in the Lankāvatāra Sūtra,[1] which mentions the coming of Nāgārjuna, or that which announced the coming of King Kanishka,[2] prophecies made up after the event. What is really of interest is the connection traceable between the millennarian teachings of the Hokekyō and the similar teachings which were so rife among some of the Gnostics and some of the early Fathers. Still more curious is the similarity of thought between Nichiren and

---

of physicians to give medicines according to the disease, so during five hundred years he bade Kaśyapa and Ananda to administer the medicine of the Small Vehicle Doctrines to all beings, and during the next five hundred years he gave to Manjuśri, Maitreya, Nāgārjuna, and Vasubandhu, etc., the medicines of the Avatamsaka, Vairoc'ana, Prajnaparāmita, and other Sūtras. A thousand years after his death, in the period of the Image Law, he bade Yaku-Ō, Kwannon, and the other Bodhisattvas, impart to all Sentient Beings all the other doctrines, with the exception of the Real Section of the Hokekyō. ' When the period of the Failure of the Law shall commence,' said he, ' the Scriptures which I give to Kaśyapa, Ananda, etc., to Manjuśri, Maitreya, etc., to Yaku-Ō, Kwannon, etc.—the Scriptures of the Great and Small Vehicles—shall remain in the letter, but shall no more serve as medicines, for the sickness shall be grievous, but the medicine light. At that time shall Visishtac'aritra be manifested, and shall give the medicine of the Five Syllables of the *Myō-hō-ren-ge-kyō* to the Sentient Beings within Buddhadom.' "

[1] Mr. Tada Kanae quotes this prophecy in his chapters on Nāgārjuna in " Shōshinge Wasan " (p. 224).

[2] See Kern's " Buddhismus " (German Trans.), vol. ii. p. 187 (150).

Abbot Joachim[1] of the Franciscan Order, who was almost his contemporary. The Christian Friar, who had travelled in the East, and was the protégé of three successive Popes, also postulated three millenniums or periods of 1000 years, connected respectively with the names of the Three Persons of the Trinity. His calculations did not quite coincide with those which Nichiren based on the Hokekyō, but he significantly gave the year 1260 as the date for the inauguration of the third millennium, that of the Holy Ghost. And 1260 brings him very close to Nichiren.[2] Possibly our next chapters may throw some light on the subject.

---

[1] Abbot Joachim was born 1145, and was Abbot of Corace (1178) and of Floris (1196).

[2] Nichiren, however, writing about 1254, speaks of himself as 220 years after the commencement of the Last Period, which must therefore have begun about 1034. The student will perhaps remember the peculiar wave of excitement which swept over Europe as the year A.D. 1000 approached.

CHAPTER XXV

"RISSHŌ ANKOKU RON"

THE "Risshō Ankoku ron" is the title of Nichiren's essay which, being presented to the Kamakura Regent, brought down upon its author all manner of persecutions and troubles. It was Nichiren's warning against the evil courses which were bringing his country to decay. It has by no means ceased to have its prophetic value in the present day. I have, during the last few months, met with two new editions in Japanese of this essay, which, so the Nichirenists tell us, is as applicable to the Japan of to-day as it was to the Japan of Nichiren's time. The essay has, to the best of my belief, never been translated into any European language up to the present.

It is in the form of a dialogue. The reader must imagine the master of a house, who must be Nichiren himself, seated before his books in his study. The house is probably the hermitage which Nichiren built for himself among the sandhills behind Kamakura, where he gathered round him his earliest disciples, and where he actually composed this historic treatise. To him comes in a visitor, who at once plunges into the subject that lies nearest to his heart.

The Visitor. We have seen many signs in heaven and in earth :—a famine, a plague ; the whole country is filled with misery. Horses and cows are dying on the road-sides, and so are men, and there is no one to bury them.

One half of the population is stricken, and there is no house that has escaped scot-free.[1]

Hence many minds are turning to religion. " A sharp sword is the Name of Mida," [2] say some, and turn in prayer to the Lord of the Western land, whilst others take up the magic charms and formulæ against disease, which belong to the Lord of the Eastern Quarter.[3] Others, again, comfort themselves with the thought that disease is but a short-lived phenomenon, that old age and death are but phantasies, and stay themselves with the comfortable doctrines of the Hokke Truth.[4] Others, again, say that " the seven troubles come merely as a matter of rotation, soon to be succeeded by the seven forms of prosperity," [5] and with this thought they set themselves to the details of countless services and litanies. Others, again, in accordance with the doctrines of the Secret Shingon,[6] use copious sprinklings of Holy Water from the

[1] A chronological study (if possible) would show that this statement is no exaggeration. During the whole thirteenth century Japan was visited, as were other countries, with the black plague.

[2] This is a quotation from a book called the "Hanshūsan." It reminds one of the " two-edged sword " of the New Testament.

[3] The Lord of the Eastern Quarter is Akshobya. The Sūtras connected with him are mostly incantations, very different from the Amida Sūtras. The Chinese are much given to magic and sorcery, even Confucius having written a book on the subject. This may have been one of the reasons why one of the Han translators took with him some of the Akshobya Sūtras. Those men, with a strange inconsistency, discouraged astrology whilst advocating the use of magic formulæ.

[4] *Hokke Shinjitsu*, " the Truth of the Hokke." I believe this to be the name of some interpretation of the " Saddharma pundarika," possibly a commentary. It is interesting to find the tenets of " Christian Science " thus anticipated in Japan.

[5] As the seven fat kine in Pharaoh's dream were succeeded by the seven lean ones.

[6] According to the Secret Rules of the Shingon ritual, the Holy Water, which is used both for baptismal purposes and also for lustrations, is not absolutely pure. It is mixed with Five Treasures

five vases. Then, again, some enter into ecstatic meditation, and calmly contemplate the truth free from all
care.[1] Some write the names of the Seven gods of luck [2]
on pieces of paper, and affix them by the hundreds to the
doorposts of their houses, whilst others do the same with
the pictures of the Five Dairiki [3] and the various (Shinto)
gods of Heaven and Earth.

In other parts of the country the lords are in fear.
They remit taxes and govern their people with benevolence.
But let men do what they will, the famine and the plague
still rage, there are beggars on every hand, and the
unburied corpses line the roads.

Now, Sir, when we see Sun, Moon, and Stars go on in
their courses, when the Three Treasures (of Religion)
continue to be respected, and when kings rule peaceably,
we know that the world is not going to come to an end.
But look around at the misery of the age, at the decay of
Buddhism. What can be, think you, the cause of all
this ?

The Master. That is just what I have been moaning

(I do not know what they are), Five Cereals, Five Drugs, and Five
Species of Incense. When mixed, the water is placed in five jars or
vessels on the altar, and used for lustrations.

[1] The practice of Zen, or meditation, is still in constant use, and
it is always more popular in times of stress and anxiety.

[2] The Seven gods of luck are to be seen constantly as charms on the
doorposts of Buddhist houses. So are many of the Shinto deities.

[3] I have never yet come across the *Dairiki* (the Five Powerful
Ones) in actual use. Their names are Kongōku, Ryūōku, Muibōku,
Raidenku, Muryōrikiku. They are probably Chinese, and may have
come into Japan through the Kegon sect, which, though based on the
Avatamsaka Scriptures, was actually organized in China. There is a
fable about the demons having once invaded a certain country
(Midaikoku), and having been driven out thence by the Dairiki invoked
by means of amulets and charms. There are so many thousands of
different amulets in use in Japan that it would be impossible to say
that the Dairiki have now gone out of fashion.

about to myself. I see that our thoughts are running in the same channels. Pray forgive me if I enlarge on this topic.

When a man embraces the Buddhist religion he expects that his religion will be a means of obtaining Buddhaship; but, at the present day, neither does the power of the gods manifest itself, nor are there any signs to be seen of men attaining Buddhaship. When I look around me, my foolishness fills me with doubts about the future, when I look up to the sky I am filled with resentment, when I contemplate the earth I see matter for earnest thought. But when I come to examine things more closely [1] in the light of the Scriptures, I find that the whole world is in rebellion against what is right, and that men have universally become the slaves of evil; further, that on account of this not only have the good deities left the country, but even the saints abandon the place and refuse to come back to it. Evil spirits and demons have come to take their places, and calamities and sorrows have befallen us. These are matters that we cannot help speaking of, and that we can but fear.

The Visitor. I know that I am not the only one that bewails the sorrows of the Empire [2] and the miseries of my country. But I have never before heard the suggestion made that the gods and the saints were forsaking the country, and that demons and evil spirits were taking their places. Please tell me what Scriptural proof have you for your statement ?

The Master. The proofs are many and most varied. For instance, it is said in the "Konkōmyōkyō," [3] "Although this

---

[1] Lit. "Looking through a hollow reed."

[2] *Ten ka,* "under Heaven."

[3] *I.e.* Suvarnaprabhāsa sūtra, "the Sūtra of the Golden Light" (see Nanjo's "Cat. Trip."). It is a late Sūtra, certainly much posterior to S'akyamuni's time. But it was much read in Japan in the early Buddhist centuries.

Sūtra exists in the land, it has no proper power or influence, for the people are backsliders at heart. They do not wish to hear it read, they do not offer it worship, nor respect, nor reverence. Neither are they able to pay proper respect and homage to the men of the Four sections when they see them. For this reason both we [1] and our families and all the hosts of heaven have lost our proper dignity and power; for men close their ears to the deep mysteries of the Sūtra; they turn with aversion from the sweet dew (of religion), and get out of the current of the stream of true Buddhism.

" These men cherish the causes of evil, they do despite to men and angels, they fall into the river of life and death, and wander from the road of Nirvana. Therefore, O world-honoured One, we, the Four Kings, and all our followers, with the Yashas and others, seeing these things taking place, shall forsake that country and cease to act as its protectors. And not only shall we forsake the king, but all the good deities whatsoever, that are the guardians of the land, will depart from it. When this forsaking shall have been accomplished then shall many calamities befall this land, so that it shall entirely lose its dignity and self-respect. Its people shall lose their virtuous minds and become criminals and malefactors, they shall rage against one another, they shall slander one another, and even wag their tongues against the innocent. There shall be plagues and comets; two suns shall appear simultaneously in the sky, with disturbed courses; [2] two-coloured rainbows, black and white, shall be seen with distressful omens; there shall be falling stars and earthquakes, and

---

[1] The speaker is one of the Four Guardian Kings whom Buddhism has adopted from the Hindus. They stand " at the four corners of the earth."

[2] I am quite uncertain of the translation.

voices shall come forth from wells. Storms and hurricanes shall come out of their due seasons ; there shall be constant famines, and the rice shall perish even in its tender shoots. Brigands shall invade the country from foreign lands, and plunder it. The inhabitants shall suffer all manner of evils, and peace and comfort shall not be found there."

[Similar prophecies relating to the condition of the world in the days when Buddhism shall have perished are given from various Sūtras of the Mahāyāna. They differ from the one I have reproduced only in minor details. I therefore omit them here, and pass on to the conclusion of the Master's speech.]

These Sūtras put the case very clearly, and there can be no doubt as to their meaning. But men's ears are deaf and their eyes blinded : they believe in the corrupt teaching because they want to believe it, and they have lost the power to distinguish between truth and falsehood. In short, the whole world has departed from Buddha and the Holy Scriptures, and there is no desire to protect them. Can you wonder that the good deities and the saints should forsake the land, and that evil spirits and heretics [1] should bring about calamities and distress ?

The Visitor (changing colour). The Emperor Ming-ti of the Later Han Dynasty understood the meaning of the vision of the Golden Man, and accepted the teaching that was brought to him on the White Horse, and our own Venerable Crown Prince,[2] when he had defeated the rebel Moriya, built temples and pagodas in our land. Ever since that time every one, from the Emperor down to the lowest of the people, has reverenced Buddhism and paid respect to the Scriptures. The great temples, Enryakuji, Kōfu-

---

[1] *Gedō*, " outside of the way." It is a common word for all non-Buddhist religions—Confucianism, Manichæism, Christianity.

[2] *I.e.* Shōtoku Taishi.

kuji, Onjōji, Tōji, and others, erected in all parts of the land, bear witness to the continuity of the Faith; copies of the Scriptures are as plentiful as the stars in the firmament, and the overhanging roofs of the temples are like a protecting cloud over the land. The sons of S'ari-putra [1] still set their faces to the Vulture's Peak; the disciples of Kakuroku still preserve the holy garments and vessels of S'akyamuni. How can you say that the traces of the Three Precious Things have disappeared, and despise the teaching of the present day? If you have any proof for your assertion, please show it me.

The Master. Quite true. Temples are very plentiful, and there is an abundance of sacred books. Buddhism has never lost its outward succession of preachers and adherents. But the priesthood is so corrupt that they lead men away from the paths of virtue, and the rulers are so ignorant that they cannot distinguish good from evil. Hear what is said in the Sūtra of the Merciful King (Ninnōkyō): "Evil monks, whose thoughts are on their own aggrandizement and wealth, preach doctrines which are destructive of religion and social order; princes and rulers, whose minds are ignorant and who cannot tell right from wrong, issue decrees and ordinances which are not after the Law. When these things come to pass, religion perishes and the country is brought to confusion." Again, it is written in the Sūtra of the Great Decease: "The Bodhisattva need not fear the rutting elephant: but evil knowledge is a thing to be dreaded. The rutting

---

[1] If this translation is the right one, I believe it refers to sects, such as the Kegon, who accepted as genuine the collection of Sūtras said to have been made independently by S'ariputra and Maudgalyāyana. The scene of all these Sūtras is laid on the Vulture's Peak near Benares. I have not been able to identify Kakuroku; but there have always been sects that have laid much stress on the possession of personal relics of S'akyamuni.

elephant can kill the body, but the soul may be saved :
the evil knowledge which comes through bad friends will
cast a man's soul into hell." [1] The same thing is said in
the Saddharma pundarika Sūtra,[2] and there is a passage
in the Sūtra of the Great Decease which tells us that when,
at the end of the Period of the Upright Law, all the saints
shall have entered into Nirvana, there will be monks, in
the period of Image Law, who shall recite the Sūtras only
as a means of gaining a livelihood ; who, although wearing
the monkish *Kesa*,[3] shall be like hunters in search of prey,
like cats watching for mice. Pretending to be wise and
righteous, they will be full of jealousy and covetousness.
Through them will the way of Buddhism be evil spoken of.

Now, sir, when I look round me at the world, that is
exactly what I see. How can I help speaking my mind
about the wickedness of the monks ?

The Visitor (angrily). I assure you you are wrong.
Wise kings rule over their countries according to the
eternal rules of Heaven and Earth ; holy men bear rule
by showing them the differences between right and wrong.
By virtue of his being a holy man, it is the office of a priest
to exercise influence in the State, and none but a good man

---

[1] Cf. St. Luke xii. 5.

[2] I have omitted the quotation from the Saddharma pundarika and
abbreviated the one from the Sūtra of the Great Decease. I will here
merely call attention to a parallelism between Christian and Buddhist
history. About A.D. 70 or a little later all Christ's disciples have passed
to their rest, and a new era begins. About this time in Buddhism
comes the era of the Image Law. About A.D. 1000 commences a new
era of ignorance with the Crusades, followed by a very imperfect
Reformation. It is the period of *Mappō*, during which in both religions
the doctrines of Faith are preached. This second Millennium is not yet
finished, but one can see the dawn of better things beginning shortly
after Clive's victory at Plassey—in the simultaneous and gradual
religious awakening of both East and West.

[3] The monk's stole.

ever gets the respect and reverence of ruler and people, however great may be his merits in other respects. But we see in our country a continued succession of wise men and saints who have been venerated by the people, and we may infer that the fact that they have been so venerated shows that they were deserving of reverence. Why, then, do you speak evil of dignities, and say that they were bad monks ?

The Master. In the reign of Gotoba (A.D. 1184–1196) there was a monk of the name of Hōnen, who wrote a book called the "Senchakushū," in which he abused the holy teachings of the age, and misled men by the thousands. Now this man, basing his arguments (*again I abbreviate*) on a mistaken interpretation of Nāgārjuna's writings, in which he follows Dōshaku, Donran, and Zendō,[1] his predecessors in heresy, divides Buddhism into two gates, the gate of Holy Practices, and the gate of Faith in the Pure Land, and advises all men, in this age of decay, to embrace the latter. As to the other forms of Buddhism, and as to the other Sūtras, including even the Saddharma pundarika and the Sūtras of the Shingon tradition, he uses four words to describe what should be our attitude towards them. "Give them up," he says, "close the books, lay them aside, fling them away."[2] By means of this doctrine he has misled thousands of his followers, both lay and clerical.

[1] I must refer my reader to what I have said concerning these Patriarchs of the Pure Land Sects in my little book, "Shinran and his Work" (Tokyo: Kyōbunkwan). I would also refer him to Dr. Haas' very excellent treatise, "Amida unsere Zuflucht," in the "Religions-urkunden der Völker" (Leipzig: Dietrich). Dr. Haas has made a very useful collection of the writings of leading Amidaists, and I am very thankful to have had the opportunity of consulting his work before sending these pages to the printer.

[2] The words in Japanese are *sha* (捨), *hei* (閉), kaku (閣), bō (抛).

Now, this teaching is in direct contradiction to one of Amida's Vows,[1] as contained in the three Pure Land Sūtras in which alone he puts his trust. I mean the Vow that Amida takes to " clear away the five obstacles to the truth, and to remove the abuses of true Buddhism." It is in contradiction, likewise, to the teachings of the " whole life according to the five periods." [2] It can lead its author nowhere but to the lowest hell. We live in an age when saints are few ; there are not many that can discern the dangerous nature of these teachings. Woe unto them ! They do not smite the offender. Woe, woe ! they acquiesce in the propagation of a false faith. From the princes and barons down to the common people, every one is now saying, that there are no Scriptures but the Three of the Pure Land, and no Buddha but the Triune Amida.[3] But in ancient days it was not so. The teachings which famous priests,[4] such as Dengyō, Gishin, Jikaku, and Chisho, brought with them from over the seas were revered by all the people. Mountains, rivers, and valleys were consecrated by the erection of sacred images of the Buddhas, and pilgrims flocked from all parts to worship at these holy places. S'akyamuni and

[1] This charge is perfectly true. As a matter of fact, the believers of the Pure Land sects never talk of any except the eighteenth Vow, leaving the other forty-seven strictly on one side. But then it is quite clear (see my " Shinran and his Work ") that there is a non-Buddhistic strain in their doctrines, which is almost Pauline.

[2] According to the Tendai, who accept the whole of the Mahāyāna Canon, Shaka's ministerial life fell into five distinct periods, according to which the whole body of the Scriptures ought to be arranged.

[3] *Amida sanzon*, referring to the Three Bodies of Amida—a striking parallel to our conception of the Trinity.

[4] All these priests belong to the Tendai sect, which was marvellously comprehensive in its attempts to arrange all the Sūtras according to one system.

Yakushi Nyorai,[1] Kokūzō and Jizō, duly reverenced, bestowed peace after death upon their worshippers. Princes and nobles were generous in finding endowments for temples, and the services were frequent and reverent. And then came Hōnen, who turned away from his master, rejected his disciples, and bade men worship none but the Buddha of the Western land.

Hōnen pushed aside the Nyorai of the Eastern Quarter,[2] he exalted only the four volumes containing the Three Books of the Pure Land, and threw away the whole sacred Canon of the "Whole Life in Five Periods." As a consequence of his preaching, men refused to make contributions to temples that were not dedicated to Amida, and forgot to pay their tithes to priests who were not of the Nembutsu. Thus temples and halls have fallen into ruin, so that for a long time they have been uninhabitable, and many cloisters have fallen into disrepair, and are covered with rank vegetation on which the dew lies thick and undisturbed. But none heeded the ruin of the temples, none would repair or give support ; and therefore the priests who lived there, and the deities who protected the people, have left the temples and refuse to return. For all this who is to blame but Hōnen and his Senchaku ?

Woe, woe ! During the last thirty or forty years, thousands of people have been enchanted and led astray, so that they wander in Buddhism as men without a guide. Is it not to be expected that the good deities should be angry when men depart from the truth ? Is it not natural that evil spirits should make the most of their

---

[1] Yakushi Nyorai, the Master of Medicines, had twelve disciples, and went about healing sickness.

[2] *I.e.* Akshobya, whose special virtues were magic and a supposed gift of long life.

opportunities, when they see men forsake justice and love unrighteous deeds? It is better far to exert ourselves to stay an impending calamity than to repeat the vain Nembutsu.

The Visitor (changing colour). Since the time when our true teacher S'akyamuni preached the Three Sūtras of the Pure Land,[1] we have had a succession of teachers elaborating this theme. Donran Hōshi preached much on the Four S'āstras [2] and devoted himself solely to the subject of the Pure Land; Doshaku ceased to think about the great work of the Nirvana, and gave himself wholly to the service of the Western Direction; Zendō laid aside all miscellaneous devotions to concentrate himself upon this special worship; Genshin organized (within the Tendai) a society of Nembutsu worshippers whose faith rested on many Sūtras. All these men worshipped Amida. Were not their labours blessed to the salvation of many? (*Ojō nō hito sore ikubaku zo ya?*)

Again, you must remember that Hōnen Shōnin, as a young man, went up Mount Tendai (*i.e.* Hieizan), where he read through sixty volumes [3] of Sūtras, though he was but a young man, and mastered the principal doctrines of all the eight sects. He read the Sūtras through, seven times in all, and no commentaries or biographies escaped his attention. His knowledge was as bright as the sun,

---

[1] We must remember that it is the constant teaching of Japanese Buddhism that these Sūtras were actually spoken by Buddha. The Visitor evidently belongs to the Tendai, but the Tendai opened its wide heart to Amida worship as well as to other forms.

[2] The sect of the Four S'āstras is one which never reached Japan; it was purely Chinese.

[3] Fasciculus, though rather a pedantic word, would be a better translation for the word *Kwan*. *Kwan* is really a bundle of six or eight volumes, enclosed in a case. Sixty kwan would therefore be 360 volumes at least.

and his virtue was higher than that of any of his predecessors. Yet he lost his way in Buddhism, and could not
lay hold of Nirvana. Then he studied more diligently
and meditated more profoundly than he had ever done
before, and at last, throwing aside the Sūtras, he devoted
himself to the invocation of Amida's Name. This he did
by revelation,[1] having been commanded to hand down to
posterity the practice of the Nembutsu.

Men spoke of him as an incarnation of Seishi, or that
he was Zendō come to life again, and crowds of all ranks
and of both sexes flocked to his sermons. His doctrines
have now stood the test of many years, and yet you
presume to set yourself up against the authority of
S'akyamuni, and to deride the faith in Amida.

Why do you lay on the august administration the blame
for the misfortunes of recent years ? And how do you
dare to abuse the teachers and saints of the preceding
ages ? You are blowing hair to find a wound ; you are
cutting the skin to make the blood flow.[2] I have been
astonished at the violence of your language, and I advise
you to be cautious and to fear, lest trouble befall you.
Even now it is risky to be seen speaking to you.

(Rises from his seat, takes his cane, and prepares to
leave the house.)

The Master (detaining his visitor, and smiling). A

---

[1] This was in A.D. 1206 or 1207. Hōnen (otherwise known as
Genkū) acted upon it, left Hieizan, built himself a cabin at Kurodani,
near Kyōto, and there commenced his preaching of salvation by faith,
thus being the founder of the older Jōdo. It is noteworthy that
Nichiren never attacks his contemporary Shinran, who went much
further than Hōnen in his preaching of Faith. This is, I think, due
to the fact that Shinran's activities were at that time confined to
remote districts.

[2] Proverbial expressions for needlessly scratching old sores or raking
up forgotten controversies.

bitter taste and a bad smell are nothing when we are used to them. But when you are not used to a thing you are apt to be troubled by it. When you hear truth for the first time you think it is falsehood ; you mistake a rogue at a first glance for a saint, and a true teacher for a false prophet. But let me explain the whole matter to you. When our master Shaka was preaching the Sūtras of his whole life arranged according to the Five Periods, he preached his doctrines in a consecutive series so that he might the more easily distinguish the apparent Truth from the Absolute.[1] Donran, Dōshaku, and Zendō, however, seized hold of an Apparent Truth, and forgot the Absolute Truth that was yet to come. They did not understand the whole Truth of Buddhism. Hōnen was worse than they, for instead of merely following, he went beyond them, and advocated the giving up, closing, laying aside, and flinging away of all the many thousand works of the Mahāyāna Scriptures, as well as of all the innumerable Buddhas, Bodhisattvas, and gods. And it was by such preaching that he deceived the people.[2]

---

[1] According to the " Five Periods," Shaka preached (i) the *Kegon*, which was *absolute Truth*, but which was too strong for mortal ears. The Kegon was delivered in the Heavenly Regions ; (ii) *Agon*, the elementary truth of the Agamas for ordinary mortals ; (iii) *Hannya ;* and (iv) *Hōdō*, periods of apparent Truth, *i.e.* absolute Truth adapted to the circumstances and capabilities of the hearers—" accommodations ; (v) *Hokke-Nehan*, " absolute Truth." Between Amidaists and others the controversy is, which Sūtras most truly represent this period, the Saddharma pundarîka, or the Amida books? It is very difficult to decide ; it is also very difficult to fit the three Amida Sūtras into any place in the Canon.

[2] One difficulty which Amidaists have to face is that their doctrine of the Sole Supremacy of Amida is not quite borne out by the teaching of the three books themselves, in which there are many other Buddhas mentioned, though undoubtedly in inferior positions to Amida. But of the joy with which the common people heard this simplified doctrine (from whatever source it was taken) there can be no doubt.

But in all this he was preaching, not Buddhism, but his own private opinions. He was a deceiver (*mōgo*) and blasphemer (*akku*) such as we have but seldom seen hitherto, though now there are many of them, and it is a great pity that so many people should be captivated by his preaching and admire his Senchaku. The Books are now neglected, for no one reads anything but the three Sūtras of the Pure Land; it is all the Buddha of the Western Paradise now, and the other Buddhas and Saints may go hang! A man like Hōnen can only be termed the pronounced enemy of the Buddhas, of the Scriptures, of the Saints, and of the common people. It is a terrible calamity that this heresy should have spread so widely.

You found fault with me just now for laying the blame of our recent calamities on the shoulders of the present administration. I have been afraid of the consequences myself, but allow me to give you a few historical examples to prove my assertion. [The historical examples are taken from China, and are intended to prove that when a Government neglects to promote the interests of true religion the country always has to suffer for it. The most striking instance is that of the troubles from invasions by barbarians which followed the Tang Emperor Wutsung's attacks on Buddhism in the seventh century A.D.] Hōnen himself lived during the administration of Gotoba; [1]

---

[1] The Emperor Gotoba reigned from A.D. 1184–1198. Then he abdicated in favour of his son Tsuchimikado, and became a monk. But as a monk (Gotoba-*in*) he continued to direct affairs in the name of his two sons, Tsuchimikado and Juntoku. When, in 1219, the real power passed into the hands of the Hōjō family, Gotoba tried to recover the lost prestige of the Crown, but was utterly defeated. The Hōjō used their victory without mercy. Gotoba, Tsuchimikado, Juntoku, were all banished, and Juntoku's baby son, Chūkyō, deposed after a reign of only seventy days. And yet the stupid hyper-loyalists of

we cannot find, even in the history of the Tang, a more striking instance than that. Please do not doubt or wonder at what I say. It is our duty to turn from wickedness and to follow after justice ; to check wickedness at its source, and cut evil at the root.

The Visitor. I catch your drift, though I do not fully understand your meaning. I would, however, suggest that Buddhism is a wide topic, and that there are many ways of looking at it. By the way, have you ever yet presented a memorial to the authorities on this matter ? Until you have done so, you, a man of the middle classes, have no right to speak as you do.

The Master. It is quite true. I am an insignificant person. Still, I have some knowledge of the Mahāyāna, and I know that a fly can ride a thousand miles on the tail of a racehorse, and that ivy can climb a thousand feet with the help of a pine tree. I am the servant of the Buddhas, and owe them fealty. How can I help being grieved when I hear the ruin of my Faith ? It is said, in the Sūtra of the Great Decease, that if a monk sees a man injuring Buddhism and fails to reprove him, he is a worthless brother ; but that if he speaks up and reproves him, he is a true brother. I am scarcely worthy to be called a monk, yet I am trying to do my duty.

Are you aware that during the year of Gennin (1224–5) the monks of the Enryakuji and Kōfukuji [1] memorialized

Japan try to make out that the Japanese loyalty to the sovereign has always been a far superior article to anything produced elsewhere ! Gotoba was a steadfast patron of Hōnen Shōnin. Hence Nichiren's criticism.

[1] These two temples, the one at Hieizan, the other at Nara, represent practically the old Indian sects and the newly established Japonicized establishment. It is as though we should say "Canterbury and Westminster," to denote Anglicans and Roman Catholics in England.

the throne on the subject of the punishment of Hōnen; and that, in consequence, the plates from which the Senchaku was printed were forfeited, and publicly burned as a thankoffering for the mercies of the Buddhas of the Three Worlds? Did you know that Inujin-nin of the Kanjin-in [1] was ordered to destroy the tomb of Hōnen? Or that Hōnen's disciples, Ryūkwan, Shōkō, Jogaku, and Sassho,[2] were sent into exile and have not yet been pardoned? I don't think you can say that the authorities have not been memorialized on the subject.

The Visitor (somewhat mollified). I quite agree with you that Hōnen did advise his disciples to have nothing to do with the Sūtras, or with the other Buddhas and Bodhisattvas. What he always impressed upon his disciples was that they ought constantly to pray to Amida, and if men would always pray, the country would be at peace. The peace of the country is what we all desire. I cannot see how it can be the duty of the Government to put these people down.

The Master. I am not speaking from my own wisdom. I can but repeat that which I find in the Sūtras. And there I find the doctrine laid down most clearly. I cannot quote all the instances; I will give a few. [Here follow various instances from Sūtras in which the doctrine is laid down that the extirpation of heretics with the sword is the duty of every right-minded Government. S'akyamuni is brought in in one case as relating that in a previous existence, when he was the king of a country in Southern India, he had once slain a Brahman for speaking evil of Buddhism. But he had not suffered for his crime

[1] I have not been able to find the particulars about this incident.

[2] It is noteworthy that Shinran is never mentioned by Nichiren. Still, though Shinran's main activities lay in districts far remote from the places where Nichiren laboured, he was also exiled.

in hell, because the Brahman was a heretic, and the killing of a heretic is no murder.[1]] Thus Buddha provided for the preservation of his doctrines. But these men, the slanderers of Buddhism, have departed from the true ways. They have made graven images of Hōnen himself, and have carried his impious opinions from one end of the Empire to another. They have mutilated the images of Shaka, and placed Amida in his stead. They have removed Akshobya from his seat, and placed thereon the Lord of the Western Paradise. They have ceased to copy out and reverence the Scriptures, and their zeal is only for the Three Books of the Pure Land. They refuse to hear the lectures of Tendai Daishi,[2] and have ears only for those of Zendō. Woe be to this people. They disregard the warnings of S'akyamuni, and listen to the foolish words of the false prophets. If a man wish to secure the peace of the country, let him first begin by bridling the slanderers of Buddhism.

The Visitor. But is it necessary to punish with death such transgressions against religion ? Do the Sūtras you quote bear you out in this ? Is not such a punishment in reality a murder, and is not murder a sin ? I find it written in the *Mahāsampāta Sūtra,* that " when a man shaves his head and assumes the monk's cowl, whether he keep the commandments or not, he is one whom angels and men should reverence, for he is a son of Mine. To

---

[1] It would be amusing, if it were not so inexpressibly sad, to remember that this treatise was written in 1258. In 1229 the Council of Toulouse revised the measures of Innocent III. for " the detection and punishment of heretics," and in 1232 the Inquisition in several countries was put into the hands of the Dominicans. Three centuries later, the Dominicans and Nichirenists meet face to face in Japan ! The parallel is very striking; it is one of the bitterest sarcasms of history.

[2] Not Dengyō, but the original founder of the Tendai in China.

thrash him is to thrash a son of Mine, to revile him is to
revile Me." Now, is it right for me to grieve the heart of
our Great Father by injuring his sons? The man who
attacked Maudgalyāyana fell into the lowest hell, and
Devadatta, for the murder of an ecclesiastic, suffered long
and continued torments. I cannot accept your doctrine,
I cannot agree with your views. You may perhaps be
able to prevent men from slandering the law of Buddha,
but you will only do so by violating the Precepts.

The Master. After all that you have heard, after all
my quotations from the Scriptures, do you still hold this
position? Can you not perceive the truth of my arguments? I am talking about the hatred we should have
for the slanderers of Buddhism : I am putting no limitations on the sons of Buddha. Beheading was the punishment assigned by the law of Buddhism before Shaka's
times ; the principle of the Sūtras since Nōnin has been
only so accommodate the principles of the primitive faith
to the prejudices of later ages.[1] If only all classes of
people everywhere in the country would unite in abjuring
error and following that which is righteous and true, what
trouble or misfortune could happen?

The Visitor (composedly). Buddhism is a very wide
subject. It embraces a very wide range of opinions, some
of which are very obscure, so that it is hard to discover
the exact meanings. Hōnen's Senchaku is still in circulation, despite its condemnation, and the entire rejection
of the Scriptures, of the Buddhas and Bodhisattvas, is
still being preached. You have given me Scriptural
authority for your assertion that, under such circumstances,

---

[1] I must confess myself to be utterly at sea as to the interpretation
of this sentence. I do not know where to look for a description of
Buddhism before Buddha, and the Buddhist dictionary (*Bukkyō Iroha
Jiten*) which I have consulted throws no light on Nōnin (能 仁).

saints and good deities will forsake the land, and I am more
than half convinced by your arguments. And it is my
sincere desire that the country henceforth may be peaceful
and happy, from the sovereign on the throne to the lowest
classes of the people. If we cease paying reverence to
a single heretic, and, instead, reverence the mass of the
priesthood, we can, I think, calm the white waves on the
sea of Buddhism and clear its mountain-sides of scrub,
so that our land will compare with the happiest periods
of Chinese history, and men shall rightly appreciate the
good points of Buddhism by noting its depths and its
shallows.

The Master (highly gratified). Ah ! A dove transformed
into an eagle, a sparrow into a clam ! This is delightful.
You have come here and have been enlightened. It is
true : if men will consider our misfortunes in this light,
and will believe the words of Scripture, then the storms
will abate, and the billows settle down, and the harvest be
plenteous. But, unfortunately, men's minds change with
their circumstances, like the reflection of the moon on
waters, smooth and rough, like the aspect of an army with
its swords sheathed, and with them drawn and brandished.
You believe me now, but what guarantee have I that you
will not speedily forget your good resolutions ? But
mark my words, if you wish the country to be peaceful
and blest, you must consider well, and punish the wrong.

Five misfortunes out of the seven mentioned in the
Yakushi Kyō have befallen us. Two still remain—a
foreign invasion and a rebellion.[1]

Two of the three mentioned in the *Mahāsampāta Sūtra*
have been fulfilled, the one remaining is a foreign war.

---

[1] The invasion came in 1280; the rebellions were really going on all
the while.

Of all the misfortunes mentioned in the *Suvarnaprabhāsa*
and in the *Ninnōkyō*, but one remains that we have
not yet experienced, the misfortune of foreign invasion.
When a country is badly governed, the first result is
that the deities are disturbed : when the deities are
disturbed, the minds of the people are thrown into
confusion. When I consider these Scriptural prophecies
and then look at the world around me, I am bound to
confess that both the gods and the minds of the people
are confused. You see the fulfilment of the prophecy
in the past : dare we say that the remaining prophecies
will fail of their fulfilment ? And if, by reason of the
bad state of our religion, these remaining calamities
should come upon us, in what condition are we to bear
them ?

An Emperor can rule, because he is the Lord of his
country ; a Prince can rule, because he is the owner of
his barony. But if a foreign invasion should come, or if
rebellion should raise its head amongst us, what then ?
If country and home be lost, whither shall we turn ?
Is it not right to pray for one's country, if one desires its
welfare ?

But now men are anxious about their happiness in
the world to come. So, forgetting present duties, they
listen to the words of this heresy, and reverence the
blasphemer of the Buddhas. They do it in ignorance :
they have no desire to turn from the right way, and yet
they have not the courage to follow the true Buddhism.
In their hearts they are faithful—why, then, do they give
ear to this heresy ? They will die in their stubborn
ignorance, and their souls will not return to the earth,
but will sink to the bottomless pit of Hell (*mugen no
jigoku*).

It is said in the *Mahāsampāta Sūtra*, that though a

king be respectful towards the clergy, though he obey the precepts of morality, though he have wisdom to discern the right from the wrong, yet if he fail to protect Buddhism from the attacks that are made against it, his rule will only serve to bring unhappiness to his land, sickness and misery to himself, his queen, his children, and his courtiers, and in the end he will fall into Hell. The same is the testimony of the Ninnōkyō. As sure as the sound follows the striking of the drum, as sure as the shadow follows the substance, or as characters written in the light remain (though invisible) after the light has been extinguished, so surely is it a fact that a grievous sin brings its own punishment. And what sin more grievous than to blaspheme against the Buddhas?

Woe unto them! They have missed the entrance gate that leads to the true Buddhism, and have fallen into the prison-house of a false sect. They are fettered, entangled, bewildered. Whither will their blind wanderings lead them? Stir up, I pray you, your slight desire for salvation and devote yourself with your whole mind to the unique excellence of the True Vehicle.

If you do this, then shall the Three Worlds become truly Buddha Lands, and the Ten Quarters treasure-houses that cannot be destroyed. If there be no decay and no destruction, the body will be in health, and the mind at rest. And the country will be in peace.

[The rest of the dialogue is unimportant. The visitor professes himself converted to the Master's views, and promises to take part in the active warfare against heresy.]

CHAPTER XXVI

THE MONGOLS

IN the year 1282, Nichiren, reviewing his own life, said that there were three things for which he considered himself deserving of commendation.[1] He had published his treatise of "Risshō Ankoku," and presented a copy to the Regent, at great personal risk to himself, thereby calling the Regent's attention to the evils of the State, and the only apparent remedy for them. He had next, some years later, dared to tell the same exalted personage that the only safety for the State lay in the adoption of the doctrines which he himself so earnestly advocated. This boldness had almost cost him his life. And, lastly, not content with general warnings about the Mongols, he had foretold the exact time when the much-dreaded invasion was going to take place, and events had fully justified his prophecy.

We have spoken of Nichiren's famous writing ; we have also treated of the doctrines which he preached in season and out. It remains for us to speak of the Mongols and their attempted invasion of Japan.

Central and North-Eastern Asia was for centuries the cradle of fierce and barbarous races which started out on a career of conquest, and acquired permanent homes for themselves in the fertile and more favoured districts of Europe. Scythians and Goths, Alans and Huns,

[1] "Seigōroku."

Bulgarians and Cumani, Yuëtchi and Uighurs, were merely
" reshuffles of the same cards," [1] different strata, as it
were, of the same peoples, going forth from their homes in
Central Asia to worry the civilized nations of two continents.

In the twelfth, thirteenth, and fourteenth centuries, it
was the Mongolian power that made itself feared throughout the world.[2] The Mongols and the Tartars were, as it
were, the aristocracy and *plebs* of a large semi-barbarous
tribe of nomad herdsmen, hunters, and warriors, whose
home lay to the north of China proper, around the Gobi
Desert, by the banks of the Amur river, and among the
mountains south of Lake Baikal. Here was born in the
year 1162, in the tent of the tribal chief, a child to whom
was given the name of Temujin, a name afterwards ex-
changed for that of Gengis-Khan, or the Perfect Warrior.[3]
Gengis Khan in due time succeeded to the chieftaincy of
the Mongol and Tartar tribes (1206), and then commenced
a series of victories, campaigns, and conquests, which fairly
throws the exploits of Alexander and Napoleon into the
shade, the Mongol conqueror having this advantage over
his two European rivals, that he was able to transmit his
power and military genius to descendants as remarkable

[1] H. E. Parker.

[2] I have consulted D'Ohsson's "Histoire des Mongols," Karamsin's "History of the Russian Empire" (German trans.), and Black,
"Proselytes of Ishmael."

[3] It has pleased certain Japanese writers to identify Genghis Khan
with Yoshitsune, the popular hero of the Minamoto, who disappears
from Japanese history in the year 1189, at the age of thirty-one. No
proof can be given for the assumption. It is made to rest on the
Sinico-Japanese reading of the name Minnamoto Yoshitsune, which is
Gen Gikyō, a fair approximation to *Genghis Khan*. Yoshitsune certainly had the same adventurous spirit that is to be found in Gengis
Khan and his descendants, and the suggested identification is a very
flattering one to certain Japanese minds.

and as talented as himself. The first conquests of the
Mongols were in Northern China ; their next exploit was
the overthrow of the Chowaresmian Kingdom, which
reached from India to the Caspian Sea, with its capital at
Bokhara. From the Caspian to Russia was but a step ; in
1237 (only thirty years after Gengis Khan's election) his
grandson Batu, at the head of a Mongol army, had subdued
Russia, burnt Moscow and Khiew, and compelled the
Russian princes to do him homage and pay tribute to the
Great Khan, his uncle Octaï, the son of Genghis, who ruled
at Karakorum, somewhere halfway in a straight line
between Pekin and Lake Baikal. Entering Poland and
Silesia, they were met by a German army at Wahlstatt in
1241, and, though victors in the battle, pushed their
advances no further in this direction ; but, devoting themselves to the strengthening of their dominions in South
Russia, pushed their conquests into Hungary, drove the
king of that country to take refuge on an island off the
coast of Dalmatia, and advanced to within two days' march
of Vienna. Their line of march was everywhere marked
by terrible traces of vindictive cruelty. They spared
neither age nor sex, neither town nor country, neither
palace nor church. They had no respect for, and less fear
of, the chivalry of Europe. They knew that Christendom
was a conglomeration of States hostile to each other ; they
knew, also, that the best elements in Christendom were
frittering away their strength in vain attempts to recover
the Holy Sepulchre, and so long as it pleased Western
Europe to keep up the Crusades, they did not trouble
themselves much about attacking the Saracens. Nevertheless, in 1258, their Asiatic armies overthrew the Khali-
fate of Bagdad and destroyed that city, and when,
between 1274 and 1279, Kublaï Khan, the grandson and
fourth successor of Gengis Khan, added the whole of China

to the dominions of the Mongols, their Empire could fairly claim to be the largest that the world had ever seen. It embraced the whole of Asia (except Hindustan, which was afterwards conquered, Burma, Siam, Arabia, and Japan), the whole of European Russia, and the eastern half of Hungary.

When Kublaï Khan was in the midst of his conquests in China, having already overthrown the dynasty of the Kin, and being then meditating the subjugation of the rival dynasty of the Sung, he remembered the Empire of Japan, as having been at one time in the habit of sending presents to the Tang Emperors, which those rulers accepted as tribute. At once, in 1268, he sent an arrogant letter to the Regent, demanding the submission of Japan to the rule of the Mongol Khans, and the transmission of tribute in recognition of that suzerainty. We know what was the tenour of that letter. The Mongols had for several years been sending the most insulting and arrogant epistles to the Russian princes, the Kings of Hungary and France, the Emperor of Germany, and even the Pope, and the letter to the Regent of Japan was couched in no less arrogant language than the other missives. But Hōjō Tokimune was a match for the Tartar Khan (were they not all chips of the same block? and may not Japanese blood have been mixed with that of the Mongol chiefs?), and well understood the art of meeting arrogance with arrogance. The first letter was left without an answer. A second letter, sent with an embassy in 1271, was returned unopened. In 1274 Kublaï sent a fleet of 150 ships, which ravaged Tsushima and Ikishima, and effected a landing at Imatsu in Chikuzen, an expedition which might have been very serious had not the Mongol commander been killed in battle and a large part of the fleet destroyed by a typhoon. Tokimune must have known by this time that he was running tremendous risks in opposing a Power whose rulers openly boasted that they were lords over the whole earth ; yet he never swerved from the line he had taken up of meeting arrogance with pride. In 1276, Kublaï sent an ambassador to Kamakura. Tokimune caused him to be led out to Tatsu no Kuchi (the same spot that had witnessed the attempted execution of Nichiren), and there beheaded him. Two others, who came on the same errand, were beheaded at Hakata in Kyūshū, as soon as ever they landed on Japanese soil. Further hostilities were now unavoidable. In 1279, Tokimune ordered the Daimyōs of Kyūshū and the West to prepare to resist a hostile invasion. In 1281, an Armada, carrying 100,000 Mongols and 10,000 Koreans, appeared off Dazaifu in Kyūshū, having ravaged the island of Iki on the way. The invaders landed at Goryū-san in Hizen, where they met with a strenuous resistance. At the end of a week's fighting, neither army could claim to have gained much advantage. Then came one of those terrible storms that from time to time visit the shores of Japan ; the invaders were obliged to look to the safety of their ships ; they were literally " between the Devil and the deep sea," and, being in that awkward predicament, were practically annihilated. Of all the mediæval nations of Asia and Europe that were obliged to face those terrible conquerors in the heyday of their power, Japan was the only one that scored a complete victory. It was also probably the only one that absolutely refused to be cowed by Tartar bluster.

But we must not forget that our present concern with the Mongol invasion of Japan is its bearing on the religious history of that country.

We mentioned in a previous chapter that Nichiren expounded a system of millenarianism very similar to that which the Franciscan Abbot Joachim advocated in his

Commentaries on the Book of Revelation, between 1170 and 1200, A.D. Abbot Joachim's work enjoyed a very great reputation during those last years of the twelfth century. Is it possible that these two sets of Apocalyptic speculations can in any sense have had a common source or origin ?

First, I would mention the fact that Abbot Joachim travelled in the East as a young man, before commencing his work on the Apocalypse. It is quite possible that he may have there gathered the ideas which he afterwards put into definite literary form in his books.

Secondly, it is a certain fact that the religious world of Europe took a great deal of interest in the Conversion to Christianity of the Great Khan of Tartary, and that several embassies were sent from Europe for that purpose. The matter was brought before the Council of Lyons, in 1245, by Pope Innocent IV., and a resolution arrived at that the Pope should send missionaries to the Mongol Emperor, urging him to abstain from further bloodshed and to turn to the true faith. In consequence of this resolution, Innocent IV. sent two embassies, which left Rome the following year. The first, which consisted of four Dominican monks, was sent to Persia, to plead with the Mongolian generals in that country.[1] The second was taken from the Order of St. Francis, and consisted of Brother Benedict of Poland, Brother Lawrence of Portugal, and John de Plan Carpin, an Italian. This embassy, of which John de Plan Carpin has left a very minute account,[2] made its way right across Central Asia and Siberia to Karakorum, somewhere to the south of Lake Baikal, and was present in that city during the whole of the prolonged ceremonies connected

[1] Cf. D'Ohsson, " Histoire des Mongols," bk. ii. cap. 4, p. 208.

[2] Karamsin, " Geschichte des Russischen Reichs," vol. iv. cap. 1, pp. 33 ff.

with the election and enthronement of Mangu, the fourth of the Great Khans of the Mongols, and the grandson of Genghis Khan. About the same time, Louis IX. (St. Louis) of France sent a similar embassy, which arrived at Karakorum a little before the election of Mangu, and presented its credentials and letters to the widow of the late Khan, Gaiyuck, who was acting as Regent during the vacancy of the throne. Three Dominicans (of whom one was Rubruquis) were charged with this duty, but their embassy was scarcely a successful one, as the Mongols interpreted it as an act of submission on the part of the French monarch. Russian Princes were also compelled, as tributaries to the Mongols, to make periodical journeys to the Court of the Mongol Khans ; amongst them were the sainted hero of the Russians, Alexander Newsky,[1] and another brave man, also canonized, a certain Michael, who preferred martyrdom at the hand of the quick-tempered Mongols rather than bow his head before the symbols of idolatry.

We have thus a very fair amount of information as to the state of the Mongol Court in the days before the accession of Kublaï Khan, and the singularly consistent information thus given is reinforced and confirmed by the testimony of subsequent writers, such as Orpélian, John de Mandeville, Marco Polo, and some Arabs.

All the accounts represent the Mongols as monotheists. There is one God in Heaven, the Ruler and Judge of all, and there is One Sovereign upon Earth, whose privilege it is to rule over the whole earth.[2] " God in Heaven, the Khan upon Earth," was the motto which they engraved

---

[1] *Ibid.*, vol. iv. cap. i. p. 30.

[2] The resemblance to Nichiren's initial and oft-repeated sermon is striking. There is also a general resemblance in the ecclesiastical policies of the Mongols and Japanese which should be kept in mind.

upon their official seals, and to this short creed they expected
and exacted universal obedience. About further religious
details they did not trouble themselves very much. One
of their Khans said that there were as many ways of
serving God as there were fingers upon a man's hands, and
provided that the Universal Sovereignty of the Khan was
acknowledged, they let men serve God in any way they
liked. Nestorian Christians were frequently found at
their courts, in places of high honour, and we sometimes
read, in the pages of D'Ohsson and Karamsin, of women in
Mongol families receiving baptism; indeed, it was even said
of Sartac, son of Batu, who governed in Russia, that he was
a Christian. The Mongols, when they had once established
their rule in Russia, treated the Russian Church with
kindness and consideration, and the Metropolitan Cyril
felt himself justified, says Karamsin, in appointing an
archbishop for those portions of Russia which had come
under direct Mongol rule, and in creating a special province
to be under that prelate's jurisdiction.[1] Constant mention
is made of Christian services held at the Great Khan's
Court, under the direct patronage of the Sovereign and his
family.

This toleration led many in Europe to believe (the more
readily because the wish was, in this case, father to the
thought) that the Khans of Tartary were about to become
Christians.[2] This was, however, very far from the truth.
The Mongols had their own religion (which we have already
explained), with priests or magicians (*Kame*) of their own.
These priests guarded the avenues leading to the palace
with magic rites and ceremonies which all were expected

---

[1] Karamsin, *op. cit.*, iv. 1.

[2] The French Court was on one occasion hoaxed by a pretended
embassy which came professedly from the Khan to ask for Christian
instruction.

to treat with reverence. But they tolerated all faiths alike, and the Buddhist and Mahometan had exactly the same privileges as the Nestorian, or indeed any other species of Christian, if he was not hampered by a belief in a Vice-gerent of Heaven whose claims could clash with those of the Mongol ruler. We are told that on certain occasions Christian, Mahometan, and Buddhist priests would be admitted in quick succession to bless the food of which the Great Khan was about to partake, and that all were treated with absolute impartiality. It is possible (and indeed Carpini expressly affirms it of the Nestorian priests)[1] that there was not much of real religion in any of these Court chaplains of various creeds. Religion was at a low ebb everywhere throughout the Asiatic dominions of the Mongols, otherwise this happy family arrangement could not have continued as it did ; one result, however, must have ensued from this strange fraternization—the various religions must have learned a good deal about one another from their close propinquity at the Court.

Another fact, about which all the writers are agreed who have written about the Mongolian Court under the three or four immediate successors of Genghis Khan, is that, in addition to priests and monks of the various religions, there was a considerable number of lay persons from many countries. We find mention of Frenchmen, Italians, Englishmen, serving the Mongols in various capacities.[2] Koreans were there, and Chinamen. It seems hard to suppose that there were no Japanese. It was still the practice of Japanese in those days to cross to China for purposes of study and research, and the Mongols, living as they did on the northern frontiers of the Celestial Empire, were looked upon as half Chinese, long before Kublaï made

[1] Cf. D'Ohsson, "Hist. des Mongols," vol. ii. chap. 4.
[2] D'Ohsson.

himself Emperor of China on the overthrow of the Sung dynasty. There does not seem to have lurked in the Japanese mind any suspicion as to Mongol designs until Nichiren's writings and preachings forced the authorities to be on their guard against the danger.[1]

If, therefore, we put all these considerations together, we shall see that it is far from impossible that some of Abbot Joachim's speculations may have been derived from the same sources which furnished the religious writers of Japan with the materials for their speculations, though through a different channel. There is a law of action and re-action in the world of ideas as well as in more material spheres.

D'Ohsson (op. cit., vol. ii. p. 265) tells us in a note that the Mongols called the Christians *Arcaoun* or *Arkhaïoun*. I have not been able to identify this word absolutely in the only Mongolian Dictionaries accessible to me; but I venture to conjecture that it is the same word as the Sanskrit *Arhat*, which appears in ordinary Japanese as *Rakan*, but which Nichiren seems consistently to have written as *Arakan*.[2] It is quite probable that the Christianity of the Nestorians may have appeared to the Mongolians as merely a variant form of Buddhism ; for the Buddhism of Central Asia and China embraced in its wide bosom a very varied assortment

[1] Dr. Haas, in his "Chronological Notes on Buddhism in Japan," published in the *Transactions* of the Deutsche Gesellschaft für Natur und Volkerkunde Ostasiens (Tokyo), mentions five or six priests who went over to China during this period, some of whom made very long stays; and there were probably others. Nichiren's information about the doings of the Mongols was so very accurate that he must have had an informant who had seen with his own eyes what he related.

[2] "Seigōroku," p. 208. Nichiren seems to have been almost pedantic in his use of Sanskrit words rather than the popular Sinico-Japanese corruptions. Ḳowalewsky (vol. i. pp. 144, 150) and Schmidt (p. 4, col. a) give a word, connected with the Sanskrit *arhat*, which seems to be pronounced *archaiun*, and which means "the saints."

of heterogeneous elements. Nichiren knew of the *Shat-parāmita* Sūtra,[1] referred to in a former chapter, which was produced by the collaboration of the Nestorian priest Adam with the Indian Buddhist Prajñā, and he rejected it with scorn.[2] Two centuries later, when St. Francis Xavier landed in Kyushu and desired to preach the Faith of Christ, he received from the local Daimyo a written permit authorizing him to preach the doctrines of Buddha.[3] It did not at first occur to the average Japanese mind that the Faith which the Jesuit Fathers had come to preach was anything more than a new variety of the multiplex Mahāyāna.

Kublaï was the first of the Mongol rulers who formally adopted Buddhism as his own personal religion. It is to him that the world owes that peculiar institution, the Dalai Lama, the Supreme Pope of the Thibetan and Mongolian Buddhists. The first Dalai Lama was appointed in 1261, not long after the visit of the Franciscan ambassadors from the Court of Rome. Imitation is very often the sincerest form of flattery. But the Dalai Lama and the Lamaist form of Buddhism has nothing to do with the Japanese Mahāyāna. We may therefore content ourselves with the bare mention of the fact of the institution. Kennyo Shōnin, one of Shinran's successors in the fifteenth

[1] See above, Chapter XII. p. 128.

[2] "Seigōroku," p. 681. He says that the Sūtra was brought from India by Amoghavajra towards the end of the Tang dynasty, that it was unknown in China until then, that none of the teachers in the period of the "three Southern and seven Northern States" knew anything about it, and that it was inconsistent with the Hokekyō.

[3] Murdoch and Yamagata, "History of Japan," p. 67. The licence runs as follows: "This deed witnesseth that I have given permission to the priests (*sō*, a Buddhist term) who have come to this country from the Western regions, in accordance with their request and desire, that they may found and erect a monastery and house, in order to develop the Law of Buddha."

century, is credited with having harboured designs of establishing something very much like it in Japan [1] for his own benefit.

It is of distinct importance for the student to keep in mind the Buddhist conception of the three "millenniums," the last of which is to witness the decay of the Faith taught by S'akyamuni. There is a tendency to shirk the obvious conclusions of the doctrine as at first enunciated, by expanding the third millennium to a period of two or even ten thousand years. It is a tendency caused by fear. Buddhists not unnaturally dread the coming of the time when their faith shall disappear. There is another way of looking at the question. If it should disappear it will do so only to make room for something better, and that " something better " is what the whole world is prepared to welcome. I shall refer to it again in my concluding chapter.[2]

[1] Murdoch and Yamagata, "History of Japan," p. 22.

[2] It is well to observe the way in which persons and nations, dwelling in remote parts of the world, and apparently without any dealings with one another, become, as it were, simultaneously obsessed by the same ideas. We may find illustrations of this in the development of Greek and Indian philosophies, in the reforms of S'akyamuni as contemporaneous with those of the post-exilic prophets and law-givers, in the simultaneous realization both in East and West of the need of a personal Saviour who shall be of kingly race and born out of the common way of men. Simultaneously, both in East and West is proclaimed the doctrine of Salvation by Faith, of the approaching end of the age, of the need of using the temporal sword for the suppression of heresy. We cannot always trace an actual contact; it is perhaps enough to recognize the fact that these thoughts were in the air.

CHAPTER XXVII

The Buddhism of the Muromachi Age

The Hōjō Regents fell in the year 1333. Their fall was due to many causes, and had been in preparation for some time. The immediate and ultimate cause was the conjunction of a real, substantial grievance, which alienated the sympathies of the people, with the fact that the Imperial throne was at the time occupied by an Emperor of exceptional ability—the ill-starred Go-daigo (= Daigo II.).

The grievance was caused by the rapacity of Nagasaki Takasuke, the Minister of Hōjō Takatoki, the last of the Kamakura Regents. Takatoki was a very different personage from the Saimyōji who resigned his high office in order to study the wants of his people, or the Tokimune who organized the forces which beat off the Mongols. He was a weak, vain man, engrossed in intrigues against Shoguns, Barons, and Prelates, who found no time to attend to the details of administration. He left all such disagreeable matters to Nagasaki Tadasuke, and the minister made a profit of the free hand which his master gave him, by selling rice to the people during a period of famine at very high prices. What made this enormity more enormous was that the rice had been stored by the earlier Regents for the purposes of free distribution in time of need.

The consequent unpopularity of the Regent gave

Godaigo an opportunity for restoring the Imperial House to its rightful position in the country. The design was not accomplished at one blow; but Go-daigo had staunch supporters in Kusunoki Masashige, Nitta Yoshisada, Ashikaga Takauji, and other loyalist knights and barons, and with their help Kamakura was destroyed, and the Hōjō Regency overthrown. It had been an unconstitutional usurpation from the very beginning, but it had done good service to the country in the earlier years of its existence.

Unfortunately, however, Go-daigo speedily offended his chief supporters by the grants of land and fiefs, which he made to unworthy parasites and favourites, instead of to the warriors whose arms had placed the reins of administrative power in his hands. The men who had, as it were, made the Emperor, felt, perhaps, that they could also unmake him, and Ashikaga Takauji, seeing an opportunity for turning the discontent against the Emperor to his own advantage, raised the standard of revolt, and proclaimed himself Shōgun in the place of Moriyoshi, the newly appointed Shōgun of the Imperial Blood,[1] whose scandalously luxurious life had speedily shown him to be unfit for his office.

The Civil War which was thus commenced was a terrible one for Japan. It led to the setting up of a Rival Dynasty, intended to supplant the House of Go-daigo,

---

[1] The pre-Tokugawa Shōguns may be distributed as follows : (1) *Three* of the Minamoto family—Yoritimo (1192), Yoriie (1202), Sanetomo (1203) ; then (2) *two* Fujiwaras—Yoritsune (1226), Yoritsugu (1244) ; then (3) *seven* Shōguns of the Imperial Blood—Munetaka (1252), Koreyasu (1266), Hisa-akira (1289), Morikuni (1308), Morinaga (1333), Narinaga (1334), and Moriyoshi (1338). These all resided at Kamakura, with Regents of the Hōjō family to look after them. Then came (4) *fifteen* Ashikaga Shōguns (1338–1573), residing at Kyōto. They were for the most part quite as insignificant as their Kamakura predecessors.

which was declared to have forfeited the throne. For a period of sixty years there were two rival Emperors in Japan—the Southern Line, that of Go-daigo, which was clearly the legitimate one, holding its own in Kyushu and the South; while the Northern line, which was the usurping one, was recognized throughout the North. The strife ended in a compromise, which was, however, clearly to the advantage of the usurping North, for it was Go-Komatsu, of the Northern line, who re-united the two dynasties on the abdication of Go-Kameyama of the South, and after the death of his son Shōkō, the inheritance passed, with Go-Hanazono, Go-Tsuchimikado, etc., to the descendants of Sukō, the third Emperor of the Northern line. Go-Komatsu reigned from 1392–1412 ; but his power was only what the Shōgun Yoshimōchi permitted him to have.

Let us follow the history of the country closely for a few years longer.

The Emperor Shōkō (1413–1428) was raised to the throne by Yoshimochi on the abdication of his father Go-Komatsu. By this act Yoshimochi deliberately broke his faith ; for the understanding between the two dynasties had been that the Emperors should be chosen alternately from the North and the South, and it was now the turn of the South. The appointment was not made without opposition, and many of the supporters of the Southern Dynasty rose in rebellion at the breach of faith ; but the South had allowed the Sacred Treasures [1] to pass into the keeping of the North, and so long as the North held them they felt themselves to be safe. Amongst the supporters

---

[1] The Sacred Treasures are the Sword, the Mirror, and the Magatama, the possession of which constitutes in Japan the right to the Imperial Crown. Even to-day the Japanese are extremely touchy on the subject of the Rival Dynasties and the consequent displacements in the line of Imperial Succession.

of the North there were also dissensions, for the Ashikaga Shōguns had offices of power and emolument to bestow upon their followers, and there were many rivalries and jealousies among the great families who desired to increase their territories and wealth. Yoshimochi was not such a great man as his father Yoshimitsu, who had reduced the country in favour of Go-Komatsu, had built the beautiful *Kinkakuji* at Kyōto, and treated with the Mings, the Chinese successors of the Mongols ; but he had inherited a large amount of authority and influence, which he used without scruple. In 1418 he slew his own brother, whom he suspected of aiming at the Shōgunate. In 1423 he became a monk, but continued to be the power behind the throne until his death five years later.

Shōkō's successor, Go-Hanazono (1429-1465) had a long reign of thirty-six years entirely filled with civil wars. The great families of Hosokawa, Hatakeyama, Yamana, Shiba, etc., were engaged in a constant scramble for territories, power, and wealth. The Shōgun Yoshimasa, who lived in luxury in his palace at Muromachi, added fuel to the fire by a high-handed act which produced a schism in his own family. He had been for a long time childless, and, an heir being imperatively necessary, had adopted his own younger brother Gijin, whom he took from a monastery for the purpose. The next year, however, a son was born to him, and he then proposed to disinherit Gijin and send him back to the monastery. But Gijin, having tasted the sweets of secular life, refused to go, and the distracted state of the country made an appeal to arms seem an obvious remedy. The Civil War which followed is known in Japanese history as the *Ōnin no tairan*. It lasted for over ten years (1467–1477) ; then, after a short interval, broke out afresh at the death of Yoshimasa, after which it raged for an unbroken century. When the

Emperor Go-Hanazono's son, Go-Tsuchimikado, died in
A.D. 1500, his corpse remained unburied for forty days,
because there was not, in the Imperial Palace, the money
with which to bury him. Such was the poverty to which
the Imperial House was reduced.

Go-Kashiwabara reigned from 1501 to 1527. The
fighting was still going on, but a few of the more enterprising
daimyos, the Mori, the Shimazu, the Otomo, the Hōjō of
Odawara, and others, were organizing their territories into
semi-independent states, and a few well-administered
daimyates here and there stood out like oases in the
wilderness of confusion and distress. In the succeeding
reign, that of Go-Nara (1527–1558), the same kind of thing
went on. Some of the great families, the Ouchi and the
Hosokawa, etc., disappeared ; whilst others, such as the
Mōri and the Hōjō, increased in power and wealth. When
the Emperor Go-Nara died, neither he nor the Ashikaga
Shōgun had any actual power. But Nobunaga was
twenty-four years of age, Hideyoshi twenty-one, and
Iyeyasu fifteen, and there was the first dawn of the Hope
of Peace and Order. St. Francis Xavier and his band of
Jesuits were in the country, and Christianity was being
openly preached.

And what, we may ask, did Japanese Buddhism do,
during this period of terrible misery, to alleviate the suffer-
ings of the people and to bring about a better state of
affairs ?

It would seem as though its record throughout the
thousand years of its existence in Japan had been nothing
but a dismal chronicle of broken promises. How often
have we not read, in the pages of this history, of distinguished and saint-like men, Shōtoku, Kōbō, Dengyō,
Hōnen, Shinran, Nichiren, and the fathers of the Zen sects,
who, moved by the afflictions of their times, set their hands

to the work of religious reformation, and devoted themselves to the propagation of doctrines theological and
practical, which gave hopes of something better at hand !
Alas, that in every case these hopes were shattered, and
that, in every case, the disciples of the reformers exhibited in
their lives those very vices which the reformers had sought
to eradicate. When the saddest hour of Japan came,
the Buddhist sects were not only powerless to help their
countrymen, but they had actually become active aiders
and abettors of the very evils of those distressful times.

The Tendai monks of Hieizan and Mi-idera had been
old offenders in the practice of turning their monasteries
into barracks and making religion the bondservant of
political intrigue and oppression. The other sects followed
suit. The disciples of Kōbō had turned the monastery of
Kōya San into a military encampment. They had become
divided into two sects, the leader of the schism (the Shingi-
ha of Shingon, as it was called), had founded a rival temple
at Negoro, in the province of Kii, and this daughter temple,
which could raise an army of 3000 fighting monks, waged
wars on its own account, and ended by being besieged,
taken by assault, and razed to the ground by Hideyoshi in
1585. The Jōdo-Shinshu were the ruling power in Echigo,
Kaga, and other provinces, where they dwelt just as the
Prince-Bishops of Germany, ruling their States as temporal barons or lords. These Hongwanji armies had more
than one pitched battle with their brethren of Hieizan,
and the Monto power counted for very much in the civil
quarrels of the time. The older Jōdo, the followers of
Hōnen, were quieter in their demeanour, but there were
times when even they took to the sword to maintain their
opinions ; [1] the same may be said of the quieter Zen sects,

[1] A tale which redounds to their honour is told of this sect. They
were engaged in a controversy on some theological point with the

who stood very high in the favour of the Ashikaga Shôguns.

The Nichirenists speedily became the greatest offenders of all. They quarrelled amongst themselves, the sectarian differences between the various sub-sects or schisms of Nichirenism being clearly and antagonistically marked. They quarrelled with Monto and Jôdo ; with the Tendai they had a formal private war of their own, which history designates as *Tembun Hôran* (1532), the " Religious War of the Tembun period." [1] They quarrelled with the authorities. They enunciated a principle known as *Fuju fuze*, " not giving and not receiving," which may be translated as " *intransigeant*." The term was adopted as a denominational designation by one of the many Nichirenist sub-sects, and the extremist *Fuju-fuze* sub-sect of Nichirenism was proscribed by the Tokugawa Shôguns at the same time as Christianity. All manner of disreputable characters joined the ranks of the Buddhist clergy to escape from offended Justice (what little there was of her in those sad times) ; [2] wandering *Ko-musô* spread the doctrines of the

Nichirenists, and both sides appealed to Nobunaga, who appointed a day to hear their disputations. The night before the disputation he sent for the Jôdoist leaders. " If the decision should be given in your favour, what punishment do you think should be given to your adversaries ? " " None at all," they replied ; " we only want to have a clear statement of the Truth." Nobunaga then turned to the Nichirenists. " We," they said, not knowing what the Jôdoists had answered, " should demand the death of our obstinate opponents." The verdict was given in favour of the Jôdoists ; the full penalty was exacted from the defeated Nichirenists.

[1] An indication of the miseries of the time may be found in the list of *Nengô* or year periods. It was always customary that these periods must be changed whenever any great calamity occurred. During the whole of the Muromachi period they were changed on an average every three years.

[2] The miseries of this time have been set forth far more forcibly than I can do it in the Introduction to Murdoch and Yamagata's " History of Japan," which I strongly recommend to the student. It was published at Kobe in 1903.

Hokekyō, whilst they brought religion into disrepute ; and one of the favourite themes for dramatic performances was skits on the gross immoralities of the Buddhist clergy.[1]

A few bright names, to be sure, adorned the period. Such was, for instance, that of Rennyo Shōnin (1415–1499), the poet, preacher, and religious writer, eighth Patriarch of the Shinshu, who was driven from the capital by the Hieizan monks, jealously incensed at the influence which he had gained by his sanctity. Shortly afterwards, he was able to return to Kyōto as Patriarch of his sect, but again, and in spite of Imperial protection, the Hieizan monks attacked him, burned the Hongwanji, and drove him into exile. He now went into the provinces of Echizen, Kaga, and Noto, preaching, building temples, and exhorting to a better life, with such vigour and success that his own Shinshu clergy rebelled and set fire to the monastery in which he was living. In spite of all his efforts, a civil war amongst his own people ensued. It is known as *Ikkōtō no ran*, " the civil war in the Ikkō sect," and filled all the earlier years of the sixteenth century, until Nobunaga arose to put it down with a strong hand. It is from Renuyo Shonin's time, and from the schism which these family squabbles engendered, that we get the division of the disciples of Shinran into the two Hongwanji of the East and of the West, which still remains.

When Catholic Christianity reached Japan, Buddhism was morally and spiritually bankrupt.[2] With few excep-

---

[1] See K. Florenz, " Geschichte der Japanischen Literatur," and my notes on the Japanese Drama in *Transactions of Ass. Society of Japan*, vol. xxxv. pt. 2.

[2] Yet in spite of what I have said here, with justifiable reason, it must be remembered that there have always been in the ranks of the Buddhist clergy a certain number of devout and pious men whose lives and precepts have served to keep religion alive and in

tions, all the elements that worked for good came from the purer forms of Confucianism, which were gaining ground everywhere, and from the improved moral discipline which some of the better *daimyōs* were introducing amongst their followers.   In the popular imagination, Buddhism was associated with magnificent services in magnificently decorated temples, performed by men who were extremely punctilious on points of ecclesiastical order, but who enjoyed a bad reputation for worldliness, hypocrisy, and avarice.   The fighting man, who monopolized education outside of the clerical ranks, had seen enough of these things.   He had no desire to make even the acquaintance of any other system which might seem to reproduce the blemishes which he so vigorously blamed and so heartily despised.   He was much strengthened in his opinions by the philosophy of Shushi, the Confucianist reformer of the Middle Ages, whose teachings had recently been introduced into Japan, where they had met with a very hearty welcome amongst thoughtful people.   The Zen priests, especially, had been much drawn towards these views, which very largely coincided with their own.

popular estimation.   But these have mostly been the incumbents of rustic temples whose lives have been spent far from the pressure of contemporary life.

CHAPTER XXVIII

The Period of the Catholic Missions

Had St. Francis Xavier and his associates been acquainted with Nichiren's apocalyptic interpretation of the Hokekyō, it is possible that they might have been tempted to apply to themselves the fulfilment of the prophecy, and to claim that they and theirs constituted the multitude headed by the four great Bodhisattvas who should appear in the middle of the last Buddhist Millennium, for the purposes of preaching salvation to a world that was forgetting the Law.

The Buddhism of Japan, in the course of its long development since the time when the Chinese Emperor Ming-ti had had his epoch-making dream, had on more than one occasion rubbed shoulders with Christianity. But it had either been the Christianity of the Nearer Orient, the vague syncretism of Gnostics and Manichæans ; or the dull apathy of the Nestorians, deprived of vigour in consequence of their estrangement from the main body of their co-religionists. When the Franciscans reached Pekin in A.D. 1300, and when, in 1549, the Jesuits landed at Kagoshima, the Mahāyāna of the Far East found itself confronted for the first time with the militant Christianity of Europe, which had gone half round the globe to challenge it to mortal combat.

It is not my intention to write even a sketch of the history of the Catholic Missions of the sixteenth century.

Others [1] have done this at considerable length and with carefully weighed judgment. My task is somewhat different. It is to trace the movements, if any, that were going on in Buddhism during this period, and the effects, if any, that the Jesuit Missions had on the native faiths of Japan. In doing this, I shall be obliged frequently to mention the Christian propaganda, though without intending to make it the main purpose of this chapter.

Here let me say, by way of introduction, that none of the Histories, not even that of Murdoch, who is no great friend of the Jesuits, can establish anything against the personal uprightness or probity of the Jesuits, who had the lion's share of the Christian evangelization of that time, and who have had to bear more than their proper share of the hatred and ill-will which has, ever since the seventeenth century, clung to the Catholic name in Japan. That they made mistakes is quite evident ; but the best of men may do that. They came to the Far East without having shaken off the traditions and atmosphere of the Far West. They brought with them what I may call the " Walls-of-Jericho " theory of Christian Missions—the theory that they had only to blow the Gospel Trumpet long and loud, and lo ! the walls erected by inveterate error and falsity would fall down in a moment, and leave the way open for the hosts of Light to make a triumphant entrance into the beleaguered city. They were, consequently, in a very great hurry with their

---

[1] For detailed information on this period, the student is referred to papers in the *Transactions of the Asiatic Society of Japan*, by Sir Ernest Satow, Mr. Gubbins, the late Rev. J. Summers, and others. Also to the more recent histories, *e.g.* " Die Entwickelung des Christentums in Japan," by Dr. Haas, the " Christian Daimyos," by Father Steichen, and Murdoch and Yamagata's " History of Japan." Papinot's " Dictionnaire d'Histoire et de Géographie du Japon " gives very useful information.

earlier, if not with their later, Baptisms, and speedily found their strategic operations hampered by a mixed multitude of half-converted disciples, who were a weakness rather than a strength to their cause. Again, they brought with them the traditions and atmosphere of Europe in the sixteenth century, and there was not much there to commend itself to the statesmen of a country like Japan, who were earnestly seeking for ways and means of bringing peace to their distracted country.[1] Neither were they fortunate in the companions they brought with them, for all Europe in those days looked upon slavery as an institution not contrary to the law of Christ, and the Portuguese merchants, besides selling arms to restless daimyos whose activities were hindering the pacification of the country, did a very considerable trade in Japanese slaves.[2] The Jesuits do not seem to have had anything to do with this trade themselves, but their reputation had to suffer for the ill deeds of their associates. In their mission work they neglected to hallow the Japanese language by consecrating it to the uses of Christian worship,[3] and they made the fatal mistake of allowing their young converts to ridicule and denounce the Buddhist clergy, and to urge the people to destroy temples and

[1] We read of the Jesuits sending some of their converts to Europe to show them the glories of the Catholic countries. But it was a dangerous remedy. One man, at least, went as a spy, got himself ordained, and then, returning to Japan, threw off the mask, and became one of the most determined enemies of the Jesuits. And Iyeyasu sent a special envoy of his own, a man named Nishi Sōin (Murdoch, p. 495).

[2] Murdoch, pp. 241, 242. See also what he says of the slur cast, through slave dealing, on the charitable institutions of the Jesuits, p. 76.

[3] Thus, the Christian converts from Buddhism went from the use of one unknown tongue to another. See what I say below about Ingen and the Ōbaku sect.

shrines.[1]   It is true that Nobunaga and others did the same, but things which a native may do with impunity wear a very different aspect when done under the inspiration of a foreigner.

The national rivalries between European nations had also much to do with the ultimate ill success of the Catholic Missions.   It is quite certain that the English and Dutch, though not very friendly towards each other, were united in their enmity against the Jesuits.   But the Catholics themselves were disunited, and the Franciscans and Dominicans, coming under Spanish auspices, did much to thwart the Jesuits, who represented the Portuguese monopoly of trade and missionary effort.[2]

[1] Murdoch, p. 241, etc. Had the Jesuits, instead of constantly aiming at the conversion of the great men, and of then urging them to extirpate "heresy" and paganism within their dominions, been content to work quietly as a leaven amongst the mass of the people, their work might have been far more lasting. The wonderful tenacity of the humble folk of Urakami and Amakusa, who remained faithful through more than two centuries of relentless persecution, shows how strong they were in this kind of work.

[2] The following extract from Murdoch (p. 282) shows that the charges of political aggrandizement schemes ought to be laid at the door of the Shōgunate rather than at that of the Spaniards:—

"Among the converts made by the Jesuits was a certain Harada, who later on had found his way to the Philippines as a trader, and had taken full note of the weakness of the Spaniards in their new possessions. In that weakness he saw his own account, and he made haste to return to Japan, where he struck up an acquaintance with one Hasegawa, a courtier of Hideyoshi. Through Hasegawa, Harada represented to the Regent how easy it would be for him to take possession of the Philippines. Hideyoshi . . . listened to Hasegawa's exposition of Harada's notions readily enough, and in 1591 he penned a very haughty letter to the Governor of the Philippines, calling upon His Excellency to recognize him (Hideyoshi) as his suzerain." Hence, for the Shōgunate to make capital out of the missionaries, by accusing them of conspiring against the political liberties of Japan, was, to say the very least, for the pot to call the kettle black.

2 A

The Jesuits first landed in Kyūshū, their labours in that island forming as it were the first chapter of their activities in Japan. Kyūshū was at the time divided into several small principalities, practically independent kingdoms, which scarcely recognized the authority of Kyōto at all, and which were busily engaged in contests for supremacy within that island. Here, at first, the new-comers were eagerly welcomed, for wherever the priests went the merchants followed, with the guns and implements of war so dear to a warlike people, and the missionaries had their choice of many daimyates for their evangelization. Even the Buddhist bonzes spoke well of them, and received them kindly; for Christianity seemed to them to be but one more sect of the Buddhist faith, and, indeed, it was so described by Ōuchi Yoshitaka, lord of Suwo, when Xavier crossed over the Straits of Shimonoseki into the territories of Yamaguchi. But it was soon found that the new religion was not in the least disposed to accept so humiliating a classification. The Jesuits were as intolerant of other creeds as were the Nichirenists themselves, and the kind sentiments of the Buddhist monks soon changed to feelings of suspicious hostility.

But before these feelings turned into acts of serious opposition, the Jesuit leaders had concluded that if the friendship of local daimyos, such as Ōtomo and Ōuchi, was so advantageous to their cause, very much more might be expected from the favour of the Emperor and Shōgun. They had accordingly made their way to Kyōto for the purpose of winning the ear of those potentates, little knowing that Emperor and Shōgun counted for so little in those days that the reigning Emperor Go-Nara could not have been crowned, as one of his predecessors could not have been buried, had not one of his generous subjects paid the expenses of the coronation. The generous subject in this case was Ōuchi, the Daimyo of Suwō, and the friend of Xavier.

The Jesuits did not succeed so easily in gaining a footing in the Imperial City, though it ultimately became one of the chief seats of their activity. But their sojourns in Kyōto brought them into contact with Nobunaga, and thus ultimately with Hideyoshi, Iyeyasu, and Iyemitsu, and it is around these names that centres the religious as well as the political history of Japan during the eventful century of the Catholic Missions.

Oda Nobunaga (1534–1582) was fifteen years of age when he succeeded his father in the headship of a small daimyate in Owari. He did not at first realize the importance of his position at this critical period of his country's history, when the supreme power in Japan lay waiting for the first bold man to come and take it, and his youthful escapades gained for him the nickname of Bakadono, "the Fool-Lord." He was recalled to a sense of duty by one of his retainers, who wrote and presented to his master a dignified protest against his follies, and then added point to his remonstrances by committing suicide. Nobunaga mended his ways, and, fortunately for himself, found amongst his retainers another faithful adviser—an old man, Tokichirō, who is considered to have been a very great judge of human character.

Acting on Tokichirō's advice, he put down, in 1557, a revolt amongst his own subjects to which his foolish conduct had given occasion, and in which his own brother was a participator. Three years later, his neighbour, Imagawa, lord of Suruga, Totomi, and Mikawa, one of the most powerful of the great princes, started for Kyōto with an army, intending to seize the persons of the Emperor and Shōgun, and thus to legalize his own designs of making himself supreme in Japan. Nobunaga refused permission for Imagawa to pass through his diminutive territories, met the invader at the village of Okehazama, and defeated him utterly. He now found himself the master of four wealthy and populous provinces, and universally looked up to as the " coming man." In 1562, two years after his victory over Imagawa, he received from the Emperor Ōgimachi, the son of Go-Nara, who had succeeded in 1558 to the impoverished [1] Imperial throne, a secret commission authorizing him to take steps for the pacification of the country. Nobunaga accepted the task, and set his hand to the work, being assisted therein by Hideyoshi and Tokugawa Iyeyasu,[2] who had passed into his service as a consequence of the defeat of the Imagawas. By 1568 he had overthrown the Saitō family in Mino, which he annexed, moving his own residence to Gifu, and had further spread his victorious arms into Ise.

But his progress was not rapid enough to satisfy the Emperor, who saw himself harassed on all sides. A second envoy reached Nobunaga, urging him to make his way to the capital, and this message was enforced by an appeal from Ashikaga Yoshiaki, the brother of the last Shōgun, Yoshiteru, who had been assassinated by his ministers, Miyoshi and Matsunaga. The assassins had appointed a puppet Shōgun of their own, and now Yoshiaki appealed to Nobunaga for assistance in the recovery of his rights. Nobunaga, who had in the meantime strength-

[1] Ōgimachi had to wait for his coronation three years, the expenses of the festivities being ultimately defrayed by Mōri Motonari, who had ousted the Ōuchi family from Suwō and Yamaguchi.

[2] The differences in the characters of these three great men has been well summed up by the Japanese wit. "If you don't sing," said Nobunaga to a silent nightingale, "I'll wring your neck." "If you don't sing," said Hideyoshi, "I'll make you sing." "If you don't sing," said Iyeyasu, "I'll wait until you do."

ened himself by family alliances with the Asai, the Takeda, the Tokugawa, and other powerful families, accepted this double invitation, marched straight into the province of Omi, overthrew the Miyoshi and their allies, the Sasaki, or Rokkaku, set Yoshiaki on his Shōgunal throne, and rejoiced the heart of the Emperor by the pacification of the provinces of Settsu, Kawachi, and Omi.

Nobunaga's successes entailed an immense amount of ill-will from rivals and competitors, and especially from those enemies whom he had had the good fortune to vanquish. The mutual jealousies of the great Daimyos of the North, Uesugi, Takeda, and Hōjō of Odawara, together with the faithful watch kept by his trusty henchman, Iyeyasu, kept him secure from armed attack from that quarter; but it needed constant vigilance to control the provinces he had already subdued, and the Shōgun Yoshiaki, who had passed from a monastery to a palace, was of no practical value as an ally. The Miyoshi and others despised him, and he himself bitterly resented the limits which Nobunaga placed upon his extravagance. At last, in 1570, while Nobunaga was absent in Ise, finishing his projects in that province, his enemies revolted. Nobunaga returned, blotted out the families of Asakura, Asai, Miyoshi, and Sasaki, which now disappear from history, deposed Yoshiaki, abolished the Ashikaga dynasty of Shōguns, and received from the Emperor the high-sounding title of *Gon-Dainagon*. The suppression of this rebellion brought him into dealings with the Buddhist monks. About the same time, he came into personal contact with the Jesuits.

It was in 1568 that Nobunaga had the eventful interview with the Jesuit Froez, which led to an informal alliance between the Dictator and the Missionaries. Some years before that time, the criticisms of Father Vilela had led the Nichirenshū priests to depose an abbot for immoral conduct, and the tension between Christian and Buddhist in Kyōto was considerable. The Nichiren sect had given considerable aid to the Miyoshi and Matsunaga at the time of the assassination of Yoshiteru, and Nobunaga, who already saw that the great worldly monasteries would be amongst his bitterest enemies in the pacification of the country, had ordered the demolition of several of the chief houses, using the materials thereof for the construction of the new palace which he was constructing for Yoshiaki. After his interview with Froez, Nobunaga deliberately determined to use the Catholic missionaries as one of his instruments for crushing the Buddhist monasteries. His heart remained absolutely untouched by the Christian verities ; his head saw the advantages which were to be gained from an alliance with the Christian organization.

In 1570, Nobunaga disgraced, and sentenced to death, a Nichiren priest, Nichijō Shōnin, who had taken a prominent position in the opposition to his measures. (It was this Nichijō who, in a heated discussion with Froez about the nature of the human soul, had wanted to cut off the Jesuit's head in Nobunaga's presence, in order that the Dictator might see what the soul looked like as it escaped from the human body.) From that time the Buddhists showed unmistakable signs of hostility. Nobunaga gave them but short shrift. The Hieizan monks had sided with Matsunaga and the Miyoshi in their rebellion against him. With a strong army from Gifu, Nobunaga marched against the monks, stormed the Hieizan heights, and wiped out the monastery. " The final assault," says Murdoch, " delivered September 29th, 1571, ended in the extermination of every occupant of the three thousand monasteries that had studded the faces of the mountain, and its thirteen valleys, a few days before."

Nobunaga next turned against the Monto priests, who, under Kennio Kosa, had established themselves in what is now Ōsaka, in a strategic position of prime importance, which they had fortified elaborately. It took him several years to reduce this priestly fortress, and it was not until 1580 that he made himself master of it. "The slaughter," says Murdoch, "had been immense, and the stench of burning flesh poisoned the air for miles around." A small remnant surrendered and were spared, but the fortress itself was burnt to the ground. Kennio, said Hideyoshi, in his later years, "had given Nobunaga more trouble than all his other enemies combined."

In the meanwhile, a dispute had taken place between the priests of the Jodo and their bitter enemies of the Nichiren sect, and Nobunaga was invited to act as umpire, an office which he accepted on the condition that the defeated controversialists should agree to be decapitated. The Nichiren champions were obliged in the disputation to own themselves defeated. Nobunaga not only enforced the penalty agreed upon, but further laid on the whole sect a money fine so heavy that the Nichiren priests were unable to pay it, and withdrew to remote provinces where Nobunaga's hand had not as yet made itself felt.[1]

Thus Nobunaga became the "scourge of God" to the worldly and carnal-minded priests of the various sects of Buddhism, and the Jesuit Fathers felt that the ground was being cleared for them by the drastic measures of the Dictator. But they were mistaken in their estimate of the situation. Stern measures, such as these were, could

[1] Nobunaga never came into collision with the Shingon priests. It was left for Hideyoshi to destroy their great monastery fortress of Negoro with its four thousand fighting priests.

not be taken without stirring up bad feeling and resentment, and the Jesuits, whom Nobunaga had befriended, were the ones to bear the resentment of the Buddhists, whose feelings Nobunaga had so terribly outraged. The time came when they had to pay most dearly for the sins against humanity of which their ally Nobunaga had been guilty.

For Nobunaga himself it could not be pleaded that he had intended to act *ad majorem Dei gloriam*. Nothing was further from his intentions. He looked upon the Jesuits merely as convenient tools; his own views of religion were sufficiently exposed by the great temple (the Sōchenji) which he built, with a stone image, representing himself, placed higher than all the other idols of gods and *hotoke*, to receive the adoration of the people. A few months later (June 22, 1582) his trusted general, Akechi Mitsuhide, conspired against him, and Nobunaga perished miserably by an assassin's hand.

The successor to Nobunaga's power was his friend and trusted lieutenant, Toyotomi Hideyoshi, the famous Taikōsama. Hideyoshi had first come under Nobunaga's influence after the victory at Okehazama, and had become allied with the Dictator's family by marriage. When the news of Nobunaga's death reached him, he was engaged in the Western provinces, reducing the clansmen of Mōri Terumoto, and the troops with which Akechi Mitsuhide rose against Nobunaga were troops which Hideyoshi had asked for as reinforcements for himself. When the news reached him, he promptly made peace with his enemies and hurried to the Imperial Capital, where, by a series of triumphs, diplomatic as well as military, he shortly succeeded in getting into his own hands all the powers that Nobunaga had wielded, and a great deal more.

Hideyoshi did not wring the neck of the poor nightingale as Nobunaga had done, but he contrived to make it sing to his tune. In establishing himself in Nobunaga's place, and in extending his authority over the rest of the Empire, he used the arts of diplomacy much more than of military compulsion. His aim, as Murdoch says, was " not to kill two birds with one stone, but to use the same missile for the purpose of laming a considerable number of fowls, whom he would then catch and train to lay golden eggs for his own advantage." He did occasionally use the sword, and then with a cruelty which even Nobunaga might have envied. When he slew his nephew and adopted son, Hidetsugu, and hacked his whole family to pieces, he showed how monstrously cruel he was capable of being, should political expediency demand drastic measures. But he always stood ready to temper his cruelty by wise diplomacy. Thus he stormed and de- stroyed the great Shingon Temple-Fortress of Negoro, in Kii, with its four thousand armed bonzes, but he spared the Mother-Temple of Kôya, and practically made the Shignon priests serve him in the capacity of warders of a prison for political offenders. He laid a very heavy hand on the Monto priests, but, having done so, he used Kennio Kosa, who had contrived to escape Nobunaga's massacre of the bonzes at Ōsaka, as a political agent of his own in the territories of the Satsuma Daimyo.[1] When he thought that he had reason to fear the influence of the Jesuits (as before he had seen reason to fear Hidetsugu), he suddenly dropped his mask of friendship and ordered the execution of the twenty-six victims who were crucified on the Martyrs' Mount at Nagasaki on the 5th of February, 1597. Yet, to

[1] The Monto priests made themselves so much hated in Satsuma that, until comparatively recent years, they were not allowed to enter the province, and the Satsuma men have nearly always been hostile to Buddhism.

the end of his life, Hideyoshi understood how to use the Christians and their teachers for his own purposes, and Konishi's Christian Brigade did yeoman service for him in Korea.

It was part of Hideyoshi's plan to impoverish those whom he had reason to fear. He would invite the powerful and wealthy daimyos to come into residence in Kyōto, where they were forced to spend huge sums of money in costly and lavish entertainments. He made one Daimyo bear the expense of building a great castle or palace; others had to entertain envoys from Korea, China, or the Philippines, in a manner worthy of the dignity of a great Empire. For the monks, who still were wealthy, he prepared a heavy burden in the shape of an immense Colossus—a Daibutsu—and many sumptuous temples, in the place of those which Nobunaga had destroyed. The Daimyos and the monks had to bleed their subjects with a sharp lancet of taxation to meet the expenses of these costly undertakings, and the peasants in these districts turned envious eyes towards the happy inhabitants of the provinces under Hideyoshi's direct rule, who were free from the imposts under which they themselves were groaning. There were two religious powers that Hideyoshi dreaded—the Jesuits and the intolerant followers of Nichiren. He placed the Christian Konishi in command of one battalion, composed mainly of Christians, the Nichirenist Katō Kiyomasa in command of another battalion, composed mainly of Buddhists, and sent the two generals to Korea to spy on one another, and, possibly, to get shot.

Hideyoshi was no more a friend of the Buddhists than he was of the Christians. What little religion he had inclined him towards the *Kami* of the native Shinto. Shinto makes little or no demand on the moral nature of man. It does not forbid the taking of life, nor yet the breach of what we Christians call the Seventh Commandment. It also holds out to a distinguished man, such as Hideyoshi undoubtedly was, the prospect—an extremely gratifying one—of deification after death. Hideyoshi suffered from *megalomania*. He dreamed of making himself Ruler of All Japan ; he dreamed of conquests on the mainland of Asia ; he seems in his dreams to have seen himself sitting in Pekin on the throne of the Mings. He certainly saw himself the object of posthumous worship, for he too, like Nobunaga, spent time and money on the erection of a magnificent temple to be dedicated to Shin Hachiman, the new god of war, and Shin Hachiman was his deified self. The temple of Shin Hachiman was in course of erection when Hideyoshi died. The apotheosis of the Taikōsama was celebrated in it, with great pomp, by Iyeyasu, in the days before his final breach with the family of Hideyoshi. After the breach had been accomplished, in 1615, the temple was quietly demolished by the Governor of Kyōto, and no one remonstrated. The new god was not much of a success in his new *rôle*.

We now come to Ieyasu (1542–1616), the founder of the Tokugawa line of Shōguns, the man who had the wisdom as well as the good fortune to be able to wait patiently until the nightingale sang to his tune. He was in a position to do so. Nobunaga and Hideyoshi had laboured at the unification of the Empire. Ieyasu had but one battle to fight : after Sekigahara, he was able to enter into the labours of his illustrious predecessors.[1] His talents were shown in the wonderful administrative

---

[1] A well-known caricature, reproduced by Father Papinot in his Dictionary, represents Nobunaga and Mitsuhide pounding the rice, Hideyoshi kneading the dough, and Ieyasu sitting apart and eating the cake.

machine which he constructed, and the minute care with which he provided for the transmission of the supreme power to his descendants of remote generations.

We need not here speak of his secular administration and reforms. Of his activities in the sphere of religion it may be said that, whilst disapproving of Christianity and mistrusting, nay disliking, the foreign missionary clergy, he never put a single one of them to death during the whole of his tenure of office. It was reserved for Iemitsu, his grandson, the third Shōgun of the Tokugawa line, to become a persecutor, and Iemitsu was a very different person from his grandfather.

With regard to Buddhism, Ieyasu was in a position to make use of it for his own purposes, and he did so with great success. Nobunaga and Hideyoshi had broken for ever the military power of the Buddhist monasteries. There was no fear of a new Hieizan, or Negoro, rising out of the ruins of the temples, and the sects whom the sword had spared, Hideyoshi had managed effectually to impoverish by his heavy imposts. Ieyasu was able to use the broken forces of the clergy for his own purposes. He encouraged the monks, and made of them a kind of religious police. For himself, he claimed to have been converted to the Tendai faith, and his great mausoleum at Nikko was entrusted to Tendai hands, as was also the great temple he erected at Uyeno Park. But the women of his household seem to have divided their attention between the Nichiren and Jōdo, and the Jōdo Temple of Zojoji was likewise of his founding.

But it is evident that his ideas of Buddhism were those of a reformer. The Confucianist school of Shushi, with its enlightened views of statesmanship and statecraft, was much encouraged, and it was Ieyasu's evident endeavour to graft this reformed Confucianism on to a

Buddhist stock, in the hopes of thereby producing a better variety of fruit. Many of the early leaders of this new Confucianism were Buddhist priests, and this was notably the case with Jigendaishi, the Abbot of the Great Temple at Uyeno, and the friend and counsellor of both Ieyasu and Iemitsu.

The Zen, whose record has always been a good one, and whose tenets made the adoption of Confucianist notions comparatively easy, was much favoured by the half-philosophical, half-religious priests whom the policy of the early Tokugawas did so much to encourage. In 1654, a little while after the death of Iemitsu (1651), a celebrated priest was summoned from China to become the founder of a new and enlightened sect of the Zen. His name was Ingen, and the sect he founded is known as the Ōbaku, a small body, but always influential. It shows the practical character of the Buddhism which the Tokugawas tried to propagate that Ingen's sect adopted modern Chinese as the language in which the Buddhist Scriptures and services should be read. The great mass of the Buddhist worship is in a dead language, the Chinese of fifteen centuries ago ; in the Ōbaku worship, the ordinary Sinico-Japanese of the modern literary style has been, as it were, consecrated to the purposes of religion.

One part of Nichiren's contention had been now fulfilled. He had said that but one Sun ruled in the Heavens, but one Lord in the religious world, but one Ruler in the Empire. The Empire had been unified, and there was but one Ruler. It is true that it was not yet the legitimate ruler, but the reign of the usurper seems to have been necessary for the welding together of the whole.

Our sympathies as Christians naturally go out to the heroic martyrs and confessors of that strangely interesting period. They seem to have been only the pawns on the chessboard, played by the hands of Nobunaga, Hideyoshi, and Ieyasu. In our next chapter we shall see how the great men themselves were, after all, but the knights and castles on the same great chessboard of history, and that the Master Hand that played them was one far greater than they deemed Him to be when they set aside the testimony of His servants.

CHAPTER XXIX

The Buddhism of the Tokugawa Period

AFTER Ieyasu's victory at Sekigahara (October 21, 1600) over Ishida Kazushige and the daimyos who supported the claims of the family of Hideyoshi, Japan became, for the first time for many centuries, practically united under one head, and was at last in a position to feel herself a national unit. It is true that the Imperial House still continued, as before, to sit on the throne in Kyōto ; but its position was a shadowy one, and the new Dictator made provision for its remaining such ; for, in readjusting the finances of the country, an annual income of 150,000 *koku* of rice was deemed sufficient to meet all the expenses of the Imperial establishments, and even that modest sum came, not from any special appropriation, but out of the liberal income of four million *koku*,[1] which the Shōgunate appropriated to itself. The Imperial House thus became the pensioner of the Tokugawas, and it is a matter for wonder and admiration how, under most adverse circumstances, the Court at Kyōto contrived to retain for itself even the modicum of power and influence that remained in its hands. Those who believe in a Divine Providence which shapes the destinies of nations, will readily see in

[1] This sum did not, of course, exhaust the resources of the Shōgunate. A very large number of fiefs, some of them of considerable value, was in the hands of members of the Tokugawa family, or of adherents on whose absolute fidelity Ieyasu felt that he could rely.

it a gracious Design watching over the line of the lawful
Sovereigns until the right moment should arrive for the
Imperial House to resume its rightful place as the active
head of the nation.

The *Pax Tokugawica*, which Ieyasu inaugurated, rested
on very solid foundations, for it was supported by all the
best elements of the Japanese social system.

It rested, of course, mainly on the power of the sword.
The Hōjō Regents had demonstrated the potential
importance of a comparatively small principality carefully
administered on strictly military lines.   Nobunaga, Hideyoshi, and Ieyasu trod in the footsteps of the Kamakura
Regents, and, during the early days of the Shōgunate, the
samurai of the Tokugawa clans maintained the superiority
of their military traditions.   "After a victory," said
Ieyasu on the bloody day of Sekigahara, "tighten the
strings of your helmet ; " and the maxim was acted upon
by his descendants.   The new capital at Yedo was the
symbol of the new power, which could here expand itself,
without a rival, as freely as the Hōjō had done at Kamakura.   It was the rallying-point for the Tokugawa clansmen and partisans, who were constantly brought together,
and taught to appreciate the strength that lay in their
unity of obedience and discipline : it was the ruin of the
distant daimyos from Kyūshū and the South, whose
attendance was required for half the year at the Court
of the new Dictator.   It reduced the Imperial Power to
a shadow and a sentiment, for there was no use in raising
the standard of loyalist revolt, or in occupying the city
of Kyoto, so long as the military forces of the country
were centred in and directed from the recently strengthened
Castle of Yedo.[1]

[1] The ancient Castle of Yedo, on the site of the present Imperial
Palace in Tokyo, was built in 1456 by Ōta Dōkwan.

Again, it is certain that Ieyasu had the support of the merchant classes in the administrative reforms which he established. Even the closing of the country to foreign trade by the Government of his grandson Iemitsu was effected without much protest. The truth is that the closing of the Japanese ports to foreign commerce touched no vested Japanese interests. The volume of trade was very small : the millions of Japan had no use for the articles which Europe had to bring them, and the products of the country, after those long years of anarchy and trouble, were not much greater than what the nation needed for its own private consumption. The Southern Daimyos, crushed and crippled, had no longer any need for the guns and military ammunition which the Portuguese had brought a century before, and whatever was needed in this line was made by the Japanese themselves. The closing of the ports to foreign ships injured no one at the moment ; it only prevented the creation of new and artificial wants among the people, and the merchants were quite content to have it so. In the development of the internal commerce, which has always been a great feature in the mercantile life of the country, they could see their profits before them. They wanted peace and a steady market, and Ieyasu's administration assured them both.

And the Buddhists were contented ; for Buddhism has always been a merchants' religion, and in the prosperity of the commercial classes there would always be something to spare for the alms-bowl of the mendicant friar. They had good reason to be quite satisfied. Ieyasu did not treat them as Nobunaga or Hideyoshi had done. He summoned them to his councils ; he invited them to instruct him in the tenets of their religion ; he professed himself a convert to the Tendai sect ; he decorated his

2 B

new capital with magnificent temples [1]; and he gave the Buddhist clergy considerable inquisitorial powers by making them his registrars, charged with the special surveillance of persons suspected of Christianity.[2]

Allied with the Buddhists were the Confucianists and the Shintoists. The former of these had, as we have already had more than one occasion to mention, always cultivated good relationships with the Zen priests. These relationships were much strengthened by Chinese refugees, who came over to Japan after the fall of the Ming dynasty, and more especially by Ingen and the priests of the Chinese Zen sect of Ōbaku, whom I mentioned in my last chapter. Priests of other sects likewise professed themselves followers of the Chinese sages, and many a Confucianist scholar shaved his head and entered a monastery in order that he might thus, in greater quietness, prosecute his favourite studies. But the political wisdom of the Tokugawa Government led to the establishment of schools and colleges, such as the *Shōheikō* in Yedo (inti-

[1] The *Kwan-ei-ji* at Uyeno (burned in 1869 and never restored) was one of the Tokugawa temples. Its abbot was always a Prince of the Blood, who was thus practically a hostage. It was probably for this reason, and for its memories of the degradation of the Imperial House, that the temple was never restored. Other temples of this period were the *Zōjōji* in Shiba Park, the popular *Kwannonji* at Asakusa, and the *Higashi Hongwanji*. They are all imposing structures. Nor must we forget the great mausolea at *Nikkō*.

[2] Popular education was also in the hands of the Buddhist clergy during this period. The so-called *tera koya*, or temple-schools, first established under the Ashikaga, continued their activity until the Meiji Restoration. The education was not of a very high order, but it was the best that was generally accessible. The Tokugawa Government, for its own retainers mainly, founded a certain number of schools, of which the best known was the *Shōheikō* in Yedo, founded in 1630. Hayashi Razan was a professor in this school, the programme of studies becoming in a sense official for the other schools. In most of these, medicine was taught as well as philosophy. But they did not profess to give a popular education.

mately connected with the Temple of Confucius on Yūshi-
madai in Hongō), and from the middle of the seventeenth
century we get a lay-Confucianism which, in process of
time, completely overshadows the priestly Confucianism,
to which it becomes almost hostile.[1]

The Shintoists were but of little account at the
beginning of the Tokugawa age. But Hideyoshi had
patronized them, and Hideyoshi remained for Japan a *beau
ideal* of knightly virtues. Very few samurai ever found
much to content their souls in the life and teachings of
Buddhism ; only here and there was there a studious soldier
to be found to whom the bookish habits of the Confucianist
appealed with anything like the voice of attraction.
Shintoism, with a slight flavour of philosophy, a vague but
deep-seated religiosity, a good deal of common sense,
and a strong appeal to Japanese pride, satisfied most
minds, without demanding from them the adoption of
any denominational designation. It was destined in the

---

[1] Papinot (s.v. *Tokugawa-jidai no Keigakuha*) divides the Tokugawa
School of Confucianism into four : (*a*) The school of men like Fujiwara
Seikwa, Hayashi Razan, etc., who, basing their teaching on the most
ancient works of Confucius, placed the Way of Wisdom in the cultiva-
tion of human nature, intelligence, heart, and instinct. (*b*) Nakae
Tojū, Kumazawa Ryōkai, who preached Mencius rather than Confucius,
and placed the *summum bonum* in the harmonious co-operation of
knowledge and energy. These men were practically independent
of the school of Fujiwara. (*c*) Itō Jinsai, Ogin Sorai, etc., opposed the
School of Fujiwara, which was based, they said, on a false interpretation
of Confucius. For them, wisdom lay in the imitation of the ancients.
(*d*) Inouye Kinga mediated between (*a*) and (*c*). His principles led him
to the *Han* and *Tang* dynasties for a true interpretation of Confucius.
One of the best Japanese expositions of the history and teachings of
Confucianism in Japan will be found in the writings of Professor
Inouye Tetsujirō, of the Imperial University of Tokyo. See Lloyd,
" Development of the Shushi Philosophy in Japan " (*Trans. As. Soc.
of Japan*, xxxiv. 4) ; papers by Dr. Knox and Mr. Haga, which take up
the whole of vol. xx. pt. i. ; and Mr. Dening's very valuable contribution
in vol. xxxv. pt. iii. of the *Transactions* of the same Society.

course of years to become a very potent factor in the development of the country.

Only two factors were excluded from the new national life—the Catholics, and the extreme left wing of the intolerant Nichirenists.   Ieyasu found it necessary in 1610 to inflict a most severe punishment [1] on some Nichiren monks who had been speaking too freely against Christians and the inoffensive Jōdō believers, and Iemitsu felt himself obliged to proscribe the *Fujūfuze* branch of the Nichirenists, exactly as he did the believers in Catholicism.

Every one knows (who has read anything of Japanese history) that the persecutions of Christians were of a most severe and cruel character, and that the Buddhist clergy became the willing instruments of the Shōgunate in the execution of a cruel legislation.   No noblemen or persons of any position survived that ordeal, except through apostasy : a few of them were martyred, the rest saved their lives through a timely return to the religion of their fathers.   It was reserved for the farmers of Kyūshū to set an example of heroism under persecution worthy of the earliest ages of the Christian Church. Without priests, without sacraments, except the Baptism which they kept up amongst themselves, without any of

---

[1] Murdoch, p. 491 : "Iyeyasu gave orders to strip this *bonze* and all his *confrères* of the marks of their dignity. He had them ignominiously promenaded in Yedo and in all the places where the *bonze* had spread his calumnies, and finally he had the ears and most of the nose of the chief *bonze* cut off.   These unfortunates became the talk of the whole people, and were banished from Kyōto, leaving there twenty-one magnificent houses." Murdoch notes that the Nichirenists had almost exterminated Christianity in the former domains of the Catholic daimyo Konishi, beheaded after Sekigahara.

The hostility between Nichiren and Jōdō has always been most marked.   The former frequently maintain that the Pure Land Sects, who worship Amida, should openly declare themselves for what they really are—Christians.

the aids that are used for maintaining the Christian life, and obliged to practise their religion in the strictest secrecy, in daily peril of torture and death, these brave men clung tenaciously to the hope of the Gospel, and when, in 1859, the French missionaries discovered them in the neighbourhood of Nagasaki, they were keeping their Lent with simplicity and reverence.[1]

But all this was not known to the Shōgunal authorities. Christianity had disappeared from the surface of affairs, and had ceased to be a force to be reckoned with by the statesman. And when the noisy left wing of the Nichi-renist extremists had been silenced, the land seemed at peace.

But the peace was only of short duration. The first of the great Confucianists of the Tokugawa age, Fujiwara Seikwa (1561–1619), renounced his Buddhism and left the Temple in which he had been living, on coming across the commentaries of Shushi (Chin. *Chu-hi*) on Confucius. But he was not a controversialist, and seems to have been gentle towards Buddhist and Shintoist alike. His

---

[1] The story is well told by Marnas in " La Réligion de Jésus Christ resuscitée au Japon." See also Wilberforce, " Dominican Martyrs in Japan." One or two attempts were made by the Roman Church to communicate with these isolated Christians, but in vain. See *Trans. As. Soc. of Japan*, vol. ix. pt. 2, and xxiii. pt. 3 ; also *Mitteilungen d. deutschen Gesellschaft für Natur und Völkerkunde Ostasiens* (Tokyo), vol. vi. (54), v (45). Occasional relics of the prosecution are still to be found. The Ven. A. F. King was once shown by a convert an old box which had been in the possession of his family for very many years. It had never been opened, and none of the family knew what it contained; but it had always been the practice for the head of the family to go into the storeroom where it was kept, on certain fixed days, and to spend some time before the box in silent worship. When the box was opened, it was found to contain Christian pictures and other sacred emblems. A few years ago a Catholic priest in Tokyo found the bowl of a chalice said to have belonged to a native Jesuit priest who had been martyred. It still belonged to the family of the martyr.

successor, Hayashi Razan (1583–1673), who exercised a far greater influence than Seikwa on the development of thought under the Tokugawas, hated Buddhism only less than he hated Christianity. Both were to him anti-social forces, because they preached celibacy and retirement from the world. Kaibara Ekiken (1630–1714) renounced Buddhism at an early age ; Tani Jichū (1598–1680) was a life-long foe of the monastic system and of the religion of S'akyamuni. These men were not anti-religious. "What does it mean," asked one of Kinoshita Junnan's (1621–1698) scholars, "when we are told that ʻHeaven is Intelligent, Upright, and One ' ? " "It means," answered Kinoshita, " that Heaven knows what we have in our minds at the very moment our thoughts arise, that It judges with impartiality, that It is always the same." Yamazaki Anzai (1618–1682), who was reproved as a lad by his monastic superiors for laughing in "chapel," excused himself by saying that " that fellow Shaka talks such nonsense ! " And yet that same man, whose doctrines had much to do with the ultimate restoration of the Imperial House, had a great deal in him that was worthy of a Christian. The same may be said of Kaibara Ekiken. In the non-Christian world it would be hard to find a judge more fair and impartial than Arai Hakuseki, or a philosophical guide more trustworthy than Kaibara.

It must be admitted that when the Buddhist clergy got things all their own way, as they did once for some few sad years during the eighteenth century, they gave their allies cause enough for grief. The first four Shōguns, Ieyasu (1603–1605), Hidetada (1605–1622), Iemitsu (1622–1651), and Ietsuna (1651–1680), were men of power and intelligence, and the ministers of the last-mentioned ruler had been trained in the school of Iemitsu according to the traditions of Ieyasu. The Confucianist politicians had therefore a weighty voice in the management of affairs, and extravagances of all sorts were avoided; for even Catholic writers will admit that, with the one notable exception of the Christian persecutions, Japan was well governed, on the whole, during the early Tokugawa administrations.[1] Yet, even under Iemitsu, the Confucianists had been restive in double harness, and the accession of Ietsuna had brought on an abortive revolt against the Shōgunate. It became necessary to forbid absolutely the translation of European books, and the publication of all criticisms on the Shōgunal Government or the morals of Yedo.

But the fifth Shōgun, Tsunayoshi (1680–1709), was a literary pedant with a superstitious mind. He built schools, reformed the calendar, and spent large sums of money on the encouragement of art. On these undertakings he wasted his substance, and by neglecting the sound political precepts of his Confucianist advisers,[2] got his finances into disorder. To remedy these disorders he applied to men with little experience,[3] and on their advice tampered with the coinage and adopted measures which led to an increase in the prices of all articles of food. This did not make him popular with the common people, and even the submissive Court of Kyōto began to be restless when the state of the Shōgunal exchequer would not permit of the payment of the annual allowance of 150,000 koku of rice. Then, as though this were not enough, Tsunayoshi gave himself up to monkish advisers, and embarked on a series of most remarkable enactments.

[1] The esteem in which Iemitsu was held by his immediate retainers is shown by the fact that ten of his samurai committed suicide at his grave. Ietsuna's Government subsequently forbade the practice.

[2] *E.g.* Dazai Junsui. See articles by R. J. Kirby, *Trans. As. Soc. Japan*, xxxii., xxxiv. 4, xxxv. 2.

[3] Yanagisawa Yoshiyasu and Ogiwara Shigehide.

The taking of animal life was absolutely forbidden, kittens and puppies were saved from the water-butt, and the Yedo police had to keep track of all the litters that were born, and make accurate lists of sex, markings, etc. A samurai of Akita, who had the misfortune to kill a swallow, was put to death for the crime, and all his family sent into exile (1686) ; the whole legislation being based on the theory that life is sacred—unless it were human life, which in Japan of the Middle Ages was far from being treated with reverence. The good citizens of Yedo were powerless against their master, but they took their revenge in lampoons on the *Inu-Kubō*, or Dog-Shōgun, as they nicknamed him. Tsunayoshi was murdered by his wife in 1709, and it took the great Arai Hakuseki all his energies and skill, during the next two reigns, to restore the Shōgunate to popular favour. The Tokugawas were nearly always fortunate in the fidelity of their ablest followers.[1]

It was under these circumstances that men's minds began to turn once more to the Imperial House in Kyōto, and to dream of a Restoration of that House to its legitimate place. Strangely enough, the first impetus to this movement came from the Tokugawas themselves. Tokugawa Mitsukuni, a grandson of Ieyasu, succeeded in 1656 to the Daimyate of Mito. He at once, being a studious and enlightened man, commenced the compilation of a vast History of his country, for the carrying out of which he gathered in his fief-city a number of prominent scholars. Eminent amongst these was a Chinese scholar, *Shu Shunsui*, a refugee, who had left his country rather than

---

[1] Among these must be reckoned the celebrated O-oka Tadasuke, the judge under Tokugawa Yoshimune (1716–1745), whose wise though eccentric judgments did much to reconcile the people to the Shōgunate. Yoshimune was very popular. His nickname was " Rice-Shōgun."

bow before the illegitimate Manshu dynasty, and who now, in his Japanese retreat, imbued Mitsukuni's undertaking with a spirit of legitimacy. The whole of this colossal work was not finished until 1908, after a chequered history of one hundred and fifty years. Its volumes, as they appeared, taught the country to appreciate rightly the great wrongs that had been done to the Imperial House by Minamoto, Hōjō, and Ashikaga, to acknowledge the rightful succession of the South at the time of the Rival Dynasties, to feel for Go-daigo, to applaud the loyalty of the brave Masashige. It was but natural for the reader to pass on to the question of the legitimacy of the Tokugawa Dictatorship. One by one, converts were gained for the new Crusade; it was not without danger that such principles were enounced in the face of the hard-handed tyrants of Yedo ; many of the bolder spirits fell as martyrs in the good cause ;[1] when at last, in 1867, the crisis came, and the Emperor claimed his rightful inheritance, the heir of the Mito Tokugawas was to be found fighting for the principles of legitimacy against his kinsman the Shōgun.

With the loyalists must be also reckoned the men who wished to see, not merely the Restoration of the Imperial power, but also that of the old national Shinto. Kado Azumamaro (1668–1736), Kamo Mabuchi (1697–1769), Moto-ori Norinaga (1730–1801), and Hirata Atsutane (1776–1843), are all names of persons well known among their countrymen for their painstaking boldness in the elucidation of the ancient chronicles, the Kojiki and Nihongi, and in the enunciation of loyalistic principles. The well-known story of the Forty-seven Ronin derives

---

[1] We might mention Yamagata Daini and Fujii Umon, executed in 1758, and Takenouchi Shikibu, exiled the same year. See also the "Life of Watanabe Noboru" in Trans, As. Soc. of Japan, vol. xxxii.

its interest to the Japanese from its connection with the
slow struggle between Emperor and Shōgun, with which it
was indirectly connected.

Another group, not to be neglected, was the small
band of Dutch scholars. The policy of the Shōgunate had
left one little loophole, the Dutch factory at Deshima, for
the entrance of Western thought. The books and
scientific instruments, which thus came into the country,
sufficed to keep alive in many hearts the eager desire for
a wider and less restricted intercourse with the wonderful,
because unknown, nations of the West.

All these elements combined against the Shōgunate
and its allies, the Buddhist congregations. In the course
of the two centuries between the accession of Iemitsu and
the arrival of Commodore Perry, the Shōgunal Government had lost its predominant military strength, and the
Buddhists that chastened meekness which had marked
them after Nobunaga, Hideyoshi, and Ieyasu had taken
them well in hand. Neither was as strong as it had
once been, and neither was generally popular. Commodore Perry's arrival was the occasion, but not the cause,
of the successful Restoration of the Imperial Power. It
would have come in any case, for the simple reason that
intelligent Japan was agreed in wanting it.

Shortly after the accomplishment of the Restoration
Buddhism was disestablished and disendowed. The
Buddhist emblems were removed from the Imperial
Palace, the Ryōbu Temples purified by the removal of
Buddhist Idols and the ejection of the Buddhist clergy,
who lost not only most of their special privileges, but a
very large proportion of their revenues. The newly
established Government, while proclaiming its adhesion
to the newly revived Shinto faith, took care to be absolutely
neutral in everything that concerned the religious life of

its subjects. It was the only possible course to adopt : the Government could not favour one religion with the same hand with which it pulled down another. In process of time, the prohibitions against Christianity were allowed to drop ; the promulgation of the Constitution formally guaranteed to every subject of the Empire the free exercise of his religion.

Nichiren, who may be looked upon as the prophet of Buddhism, called the attention of his hearers to the condition of Japan as he saw it, distracted by many Lords and many Faiths. The subsequent religious development of the country has been, as it were, a commentary on that prophecy. The terrible troubles of the sixteenth century, the wars and the bloodshed, were the necessary instruments in the hands of Providence for the working out of the first step in the elevation of the country. Nobunaga and Hideyoshi hammered on the hot iron, and Ieyasu welded it into a consistent whole, able to stand the test of time.

Japan was united into one body, under one Ruler— but the Ruler was an usurper, and the legitimate House of Sovereigns did not seem to be in a position, at the time, to do what the powerful Tokugawa was able to accomplish. In this chapter I have tried to show the attainment of the second step. The Meiji Era has seen Japan still united, and united under its lawful Sovereign. No one can read the moving history of the Imperial House of this country, with its strange vicissitudes and its long-continued afflictions, without feeling that it has had some Divine mission to perform. Nothing but the special protection of God could have preserved that House through all the troubles of so many centuries, and these special gifts of Divine protection generally imply some very special motive in the Giver.

One more step seems to be before Japan. She is now One Nation, united under One Ruler, who has the legitimate right to rule. When she has taken her next step, and has reached the acknowledgment of the One God, who also has the legitimate right to rule, she will have reached the true apex of her moral greatness. In that consummation, the Mahāyāna, which has for so long had our thoughts, will find its proper place and its proper meed of honour and reward, for it also, like Nobunaga, and like the Jesuits, has been but a piece on the chessboard played by the hand of God, and not one such piece

> " shall be destroyed,
> Or cast as rubbish to the Void,
> When God has made the pile complete."

What agencies shall be employed in the future development, or what other pieces shall be moved in the course of this interesting game, is a matter of secondary importance. The real player in the game is God, and we men, the best of us, are but pawns and knights, and here and there a bishop. Only, when the last move takes place, and the game is about to be finished, I will ask for myself ' that I may be there to see."

CHAPTER XXX.

Recapitulation

It shall be my pleasant task in this concluding chapter to recapitulate for my reader all that I have put before him in a long and rather prolix narration.

I would, first, call attention to the remarkable parallels between the history of Christianity and that of the Buddhist Mahāyāna.

Both faiths begin in that marvellous sixth century before Christ, which saw the beginnings of so much that has been for the benefit of mankind. Philosophy began for man in Greece, in India, and in China. S'akyamuni was founding a religion which, if not perfect, is at any rate one that commands our most reverent sympathy and affection, and the later exponents of Judaism, the exilic and post-exilic prophets and psalmists, the teachers of the law, and the great Fathers of the later Faith of Jerusalem, were distinctly raising the faith of Israel to a higher plane in preparation for a great event to come.

The great event came. It came at the right moment for East and West. It was like a stone flung into the midst of a large pool, that falls with a mighty splash and sets up ripples which go forth equally on all sides, and never rest till they break upon the distant margins. We have been accustomed to watch the ripples that have gone out West and North from the splash made in the world's religious history by the Advent of Christ. We have seen those ripples bringing new life to Europe, revivifying philosophy and art, giving men nobler thoughts and aspirations, and laying the foundations of that religion of humanity which is bound up with the name of Christ.

I have tried in this book—tentatively and with the uncertain tread of a pioneer going through untrodden brushwood—to trace the ripples that flowed out eastward from the splash of the stone. Occasionally I have seemed to myself to see the traces of Christ distinct and clear, though few and far between, and not sufficient in number or quantity to allow of anything very elaborate in the way of deduction and inference. But during the whole of the first millennium of the Christian era, a period corresponding very nearly with the millennium of Image Law of which Buddhists speak, I find the same phenomena both East and West—a chaos of heresies, each claiming to be heard as the sole exponent of the Truth, and amidst them all one fact : the proclamation that there is one Being who has given Himself for man, that man through Him might have life. The proclamation in the West, in spite of heresies and in spite of the manifold superstitions of a dark age, is clear and distinct. In the East it is not so distinct ; it is like a lotus-seed, sown deep down in the slime at the bottom of the pool. It is there, and it grows, but it takes some time to reach the surface.

With the end of the first millennium of Christendom comes the period which the Buddhist knows as *Mappō*, the " last days," the period of the " Destruction of the Law." As this period comes on, the Christian, forgetting the spirit he is of, grasps the sword, for the conquest of the Holy Land, for the extirpation of Albigenses and other heretics. So does the Buddhist. It is the age of the great barrack monasteries, and of the wars waged by the monks of Hieizan, Onjōji, Negoro, Hongwanji, for the defence of their supposed rights and the injury of their neighbour. In the midst of this period, disciples of the inquisition-loving Nichiren, who was yet a seer, find themselves brought face to face with the disciples of the inquisition-loving St. Dominic, and the seventeenth and eighteenth centuries see in Japan the establishment of a permanent Inquisition. Yet the same period sees the loud proclamation, so comforting to the outcast and the sinner, of Salvation by Faith alone, through the mercies of One whose compassion has from the first been known, though under different names, to the Mahāyānist and to the Christian. St. Francis and Wiclif (they will forgive me for thus coupling their names) are the Christian counterparts of Hōnen and Shinran. The Schoolmen, too, whose labour it was to reconcile Aristotle and Christ, find their counterparts in the labours of the great Japanese scholars of the middle ages, who worked to reconcile S'akyamuni and Confucius.

The first Christian millennium did not pass away without its warning of impending change. The Moslem peril profoundly moved Christendom, the same peril threatened China under the Tang. In both parts of the world, the meaning of the warning was largely misread, as was, probably, the similar warning of the Mongols, at the commencement of the second millennium.

This second millennium, which is the Buddhist period of the Mappō, is not yet finished ; but may we not say that we have had the warning of an impending change ? A man of the eighteenth century, a man of science, a dreamer, and yet a seer, amused his contemporaries by proclaiming that the year 1757 had seen in " the heavenlies " a spiritual judgment which was to be the precursor of a new Age and of a new Church. He brought no proof for his assertion, except the testimony of one of his own visions, and his testimony was rejected all but unanimously. And yet the year 1757 saw the declaration of the Seven Years' War, which brought in its train the rise of Prussia, the unification of Germany, and all that Germany stands for in the civilization of the world. It saw the accession to power in England of the elder Pitt, and the commencement of those operations against France which led to the conquest of Canada and the ultimate securing of Anglo-Saxon supremacy on the Continent of North America. It witnessed the battle of Plassey, which secured the British supremacy in India, and for the first time in the world's history enabled Eastern thought and Western to meet each other and compare notes. If it had not been for Plassey there would have been no Oriental studies, and possibly but few Christian Missions in India. It saw, in France, those attacks on Christianity, led by Montesquieu, Rousseau, and the Encyclopædists, which led to the French Revolution. It found the Wesleys at the commencement of their labours. Surely it was a year full of pregnant significance.

The significance becomes deeper for us, whose hearts are in Japan, when we remember that it also found Kamo Mabuchi preparing to retire from his active duties in order to devote himself to those historical studies which ultimately led to the restoration of the Imperial House, and the entry of Japan into the world of civilized nations.

The mills of God grind slowly. There is no hurry or haste in the workings of Providence. A long time has passed since the Swedish seer made his announcement, but to-day it needs no prophetic gift to tell us that a new era is at hand, that the old is passing away, that a new day dawns.

One thing never passes away. Heaven and Earth may change, the whole political and social fabric of the world may perish, but God's Word will not do so. Whatever form the new world may take, it will have a religion, and that religion will be based on the Eternal Verities.

The Christian—I will claim nothing for myself but that—finds it to be his duty, his pleasure, and his pride, to commend those Eternal Verities, quietly, soberly, temperately, to the people amongst whom he lives. And he must do it sympathetically, for the most eloquent sermon, if devoid of sympathy, will necessarily fail to touch the heart of the people.

Buddhism is the religion of the great bulk of the Japanese people. The farmers are Buddhists, so are the shopkeepers, so are the rank and file of the people. The ladies of the upper classes are Buddhists, so are most of their husbands, if they will be honest with themselves. Buddhism does not go well with the frock-coat and top hat which are the joy of the Japanese gentleman, and so he affects to lay it aside as a thing past use; but there comes to one and all a time when frock-coat and top hat fail to protect the head and heart against the terrors of a change inevitable and universal, and then I find that the Japanese turns after all to the faith which he has spent his life in professing to neglect. One has but to learn the Japanese language, and study the literature of to-day's daily life, to understand what a hold Buddhism has on the thoughts and affections of the people.

Christianity, if it would win Japanese Buddhism for Christ (and surely that is an inspiring ambition), must take these things into consideration. Buddhism needs its special preachers—men of sympathy and patience; men who, while proud of being Christians, are yet willing for Christ's sake, to be followers of S'akyamuni in all things lawful and honest; men who can say to the Buddhist, "I will walk with you, and together we will go to Him to whom you say S'akyamuni Himself bore witness." It is for such readers, primarily, that I have ventured to write this outline of Mahāyāna History.

2 c

"Charity never faileth; but, whether there be prophecies, they shall fail; whether there be tongues, they shall cease; whether there be knowledge (γνῶσις, *bodhi*), it shall vanish away."

INDEX

PRINTED BY
WILLIAM CLOWES AND SONS, LIMITED,
LONDON AND BECCLES.

27 Buddhism